KEN SARO-WIWA
(a bio-critical study)

by

Femi Ojo-Ade

AFRICANA LEGACY PRESS, INC.

New York
808 Lexington Avenue
Brooklyn, NY 11221
USA

Lagos
P.O. Box 5525
Surulere, Lagos
Nigeria

Phone/Fax: (718)574-9452

Copyright © 1999 by
Ojo-Ade, Femi

ALL RIGHTS RESERVED
No part of this book may be reproduced
without written permission.

Cover Design: Dapo Ojo-Ade

Library of Congress
Catalog Card Number: 99-90114

ISBN 0-9663837-1-0

Printed in United States of America

ACKNOWLEDGEMENTS

Thanks to my loving family and friends, for being there, always.

To that special colleague, for mooting the idea of this painful, but healing project.

To Saro-Wiwa, for living a life of commitment and, indeed, controversy.

To that sweet soul from the sunny side of the street, for the special support (all of thirty-something ways!) in a project addressing the survival of so many oppressed people.

To Jane, for her typing skills, and to Falo-Falo and my *barrio* brother, Israel, for the proof-reading help and other brilliant suggestions.

To Karima, for her generous help in formating the final text.

To Ice, for the adventure in obtaining the books.

To all those who, in various ways, offered me some insight into the enigma of Saro-Wiwa.

Finally, to all those institutions making it possible for African exiles to work and contribute, and, simply to stay alive, while waiting... hopefully, not for death.

for Claude Ake, killed in a plane crash
near Lagos, on November 7, 1996

Here stands the funny little sweet
The Nigerians loved to cheat
So much so that e'en in death
They denied him six feet of earth.
*(Saro-Wiwa's epitaph, a manuscript smuggled out
of his cell a month before his execution in 1995)*

TABLE OF CONTENTS

ACKNOWLEDGMENTS
PREFACE
INTRODUCTION

I. DECIPHERING ENIGMAS, 1
II. *SOZABOY*: DARK SATIRE OF NIGERIA'S CIVIL WAR VICTIMS, 31
III. PRISONERS AND THE PRISON: THE *JEBS* NOVELS, 69
IV. THE *MR. B.* SERIES, IN PRINT AND ON TELEVISION, 113
V. *A FOREST OF FLOWERS*, SHORT STORIES, 133
VI. *SONGS IN A TIME OF WAR*, POETRY, 169
VII. *ON A DARKLING PLAIN*: A PERSONAL CHRONICLE OF A MEANINGLESS WAR, 197
VIII. *SIMILIA*, AN EXAMPLE OF POLITICAL JOURNALISM, 231
IX. THE OGONI TRAGEDY AND SARO-WIWA'S COMMITMENT, 259

CONCLUSION: *AFRICA KILLS HER SUN*, 283
SELECT BIBLIOGRAPHY, 294

PREFACE

I met him but once, at one of those academic get-togethers included on his itinerary as a 1990 distinguished Visiting Fellow of the United States Information Agency. What struck me immediately was that pipe hanging from his thick lips and bulky enough—with a curve making one think of a curvaceous sensuous feminine body—to call attention to his big head. And, yes, he was very short, even by Nigerian standard. Throughout the almost two hours we were together with other Africans, the pipe was not lit; it was just there, as a mouth-piece, or microphone, or, indeed, a loudspeaker beaming forth his booming voice and that effusive laughter emanating from, as it were, the depths of his soul.

Ken Saro-Wiwa loved to laugh, and to make others laugh. Looking at him, I saw, instantly filing before me, Basi and the other characters of the popular television series, *Basi and Co.* That night in a cold, Mid-Western city, windy and naturally reminding one of the tropical warmth left behind in search of greener pastures and a more gratifying period of lives caught in the confusion of neo-colonialism, we were all, as usual, full of intellectual righteousness and boisterousness. We had just left a session on the works of the late Senegalese writer, Mariama Bâ, whose novel, *So Long a Letter,* has been snatched up as the African feminist manifesto by an increasingly vociferous vanguard determined to visit hate and havoc upon anyone daring to advise caution in espousing Western culture and civilization. Saro-Wiwa stood up to the feminist fire in the conference hall. He continued his humorous banter in the hotel room, making everyone laugh, and more importantly, think. About African man and woman, and our past, present, and future.

He playfully, but seriously, wondered aloud why I, who ought to be at the forefront of the struggle of our people at home, by educating the children, had preferred to scurry back to the so-called Civilization. Then he laughed that full-bellied, body-shaking laughter; he was, as I would come to read later in his works, "in stitches." I did feel hurt at that instant. Later, thinking, I felt ashamed, because, far from laughing at me, he was challenging me to stand up and be counted, as he had chosen to do.

I recall that, on that cold, dreary night lit up by Saro-Wiwa's hilarious jokes and words on the necessity of struggle, I patted him on the shoulder and warned him to be very careful. Because my experience in

Nigeria had convinced me that the self-anointed saviors did not care for the people, only for their pockets, and for the power that they had seized through the barrel of a gun. "They'll just kill you for nothing," was my response to his admonition about my exile and to his call for me to return home.

Later, and since that seemingly meaningless exchange has become prophetic, an innocent remark suddenly transformed into a portent of tragedy, there I was responding to another call, from a publisher and friend, to write a book on the *late* Saro-Wiwa. I immediately accepted the offer partly because I was feeling guilty for ever making that statement of warning; partly because, maybe, by writing the book, I might exorcize the feeling of cowardliness and betrayal consequential to Saro-Wiwa's challenge in that hotel room.

So, with the help of friends and family caught in the confusion called Nigeria, I set out to buy as many of his books as I could find. The tales surrounding the purchasing process would be exciting content for some Hollywood thriller, what with the government agents' threats of annihilation against anyone caught with a piece of paper bearing the executed author's name. I read and re-read the books, not with an open mind (objectivity, I daresay, is too often one of the hallmarks of "civilized" hypocrisy, when the subject is humanity), but with the shock and shame of a coward in the face of the senseless slaying of a compatriot and a fellow creative artist, by reckless reactionaries without respect for human life or any interest for the people whose salvation into hell they are determined to dictate, absolutely. Upon reading those books that, interestingly enough, never attracted my attention while Saro-Wiwa was alive, I have come to understand why he laughed so loudly on that cold North American night. Tragically, I have come to know why his killers were so single-minded in their plan to "pacify" his Ogoni people (think of the Europeans' pacification of Africa) by ridding the land of his immensely powerful presence.

Yet, questions remain because, in spite of it all, Saro-Wiwa's books reveal a deep affinity for the Nigerian military. His is symptomatic of the dilemma of the potentially progressive elements within the African intelligentsia, confused in their quest for change by their inexplicable and often fatal attraction to the military, whose ultimate objectives, ever retrogressive, have always been geared towards self-perpetuation in power.

INTRODUCTION

Kenule Beeson Tsaro-Wiwa (best known as Ken Saro-Wiwa)[1] was born in Bori in what is now known as Ogoni in Rivers State, Nigeria, on October 10, 1941. He attended Government College Umuahia, considered among the most prestigious high schools of the pre- and immediately post-Independence period, as a scholarship-holder. He later studied, again as an award-winner, at Nigeria's premier university, Ibadan.

He was a graduate assistant at Ibadan when the political crisis broke out in 1966 and he was compelled to go back East where he took up another assistantship at the University of Nigeria, Nsukka. From his own affirmations, he felt uneasy, indeed, unwelcome among his colleagues, mostly hard-core Ibo nationalists convinced that secession from Nigeria was the only way out of the deepening dilemma. His departure from Nsukka was only a matter of time. As the war erupted in 1967 after the East, under Odumegwu Ojukwu, declared the Republic of Biafra, Saro-Wiwa made his way back to his Ogoni homeland. There, he engaged himself in secondary school teaching and pro-Federal Nigeria activities. He has also become a business man, purchasing a bus for public transportation in 1966 or 1967[2]. He and Maria, his young wife, escaped in September 1967 to Lagos, the then federal capital, where he became a leading participant in the movement to create Rivers State as a member of the state Interior Advisory Council and the Rivers State Study Group. He also became a teaching assistant at the University of Lagos.

Little wonder that at age twenty-six, he was appointed Administrator for Bonny island in November 1967 although, due to the on-going fighting, he could assume office only three months later. His civil-war account, *On a Darkling Plain* (1989), details his activities during those difficult days. He spent "six eventful months in Bonny" (*Plain*: 161), intent upon positively impacting the lives of the people and contributing to the progress of the island. He brought food from Lagos; made sure that it was properly distributed, not hoarded and then sold off at astronomical sums by unscrupulous officials; provided much needed medical care, and had schools re-opened and run by government, without parents having to pay fees. He declares with pride, "I look back now with fair satisfaction to what we were able to do to keep the light of learning burning in those darkest of days" (p. 164)

Simultaneously, the Administrator was learning a lesson that would prove significant in his future, "that government affairs do not move fast" (p. 160), and that the relationship between the military rulers and the civilian population is hardly ever cordial. He left Bonny in September 1968 when the new military Governor of Rivers State arrived in Port Harcourt. While he was at Bonny, federal troops had entered Ogoni and the Biafrans were engaging them in a fierce battle. Port Harcourt, the Rivers major city, was under heavy fire. Saro-Wiwa thus returned to visit a home under siege, being pillaged by both sides of the war, "so much like the peeling of an orange." (*Plain*: 171).

He went back to his job at the University of Lagos and to his wife who was expecting their first child in November. However, before the year ran out, he went back East, appointed Commissioner and member of the Executive Council of Rivers State. "I had not expected my appointment, my relationship with the Secretary to the Government being decidedly sour," he comments. "Nor was I entirely at peace with the Military Governor and his style of governance. What made me accept the offer was the realization that there was an enormous job to be done and that *there were not enough Rivers people around to do it*." (*Plain*: 206; emphasis mine). He remained a Commissioner, holding several portfolios (Works, Land and Transport; Education), until 1973. His disagreements with the Military Governor, Alfred Diette-Spiff, led to his being relieved of his duties.

From then until his death, Saro-Wiwa remained *more or less* in private life; for, his abiding passion for, firstly, the Rivers people and, secondly and particularly, the Ogoni, was to invariably lead him to the political arena with all its filth. His detention diary, *A Month and a Day* (1995), expresses his evolution into an Ogoni nationalist: "My worry about the Ogoni has been an article of faith, conceived of in primary school, nurtured through secondary school, actualized in the Nigerian civil war in 1967-70 and during my tenure as member of the Rivers State Executive Council, 1968-73." He began writing on the Ogoni as an exploited minority in 1968: a pamphlet, *The Ogoni Nationality Today and Tomorrow*, published personally and containing the ideas that were to be crystallized later into a philosophy, indeed, a matter of life and death. He won the local government election in 1976, but declined to become the Council Chairman. He actually tried to directly engage in the federal political game: in 1977, he wanted to become a member of the constituent

Assembly mandated to fashion a new Nigerian constitution in preparation for return to civil rule. Unfortunately, he did not make it, "blocked first by some educated Ogoni people and then by the rulers of Nigeria" (*Diary*: 55). He was decidedly dejected by the new Constitution which established "a stronger central government and left the ethnic minorities totally unprotected in terms of their economic resources and their culture" (ibid.). That political failure increased his desire to be more committed to the Ogoni cause, and to organize the people. For the latter endeavor, funds were of the essence. Not one to sell his soul for a pittance, Saro-Wiwa wanted an honest means of livelihood and of support for the struggle that would later bring him face to face with the gallows. His civil-war capitalist forays into the transport enterprise provided some experience; so also did his grocery and wholesale stores kept during his tenure as commissioner.

Now, even though he claims in his *Diary* (p. 57) that he considered his business career to be over as soon as he had satisfied his mother's yearning that he own a house in Bane, the village where she was living, the belief here is that Saro-Wiwa never ceased to be a business man. Writing and publishing and television production, which became prominent on his list of activities, could definitely not have succeeded without a business acumen, particularly given the cut-throat conditions and circumstances of neo-colonial Nigeria. Longman Nigeria published his children's books in 1973, but were tardy in indicating their intention regarding his first novel, *Sozaboy*. He therefore decided to become a publisher himself. His company, Saros International Publishers, put out *Sozaboy* in 1985. Many other titles, over twenty in all, were to follow, including novels, short stories, plays, poetry, collections of critical essays and articles, as well as texts on the Ogoni cause. By his own account (and I am in total agreement with him), theater was his forte. His play, "Transistor Radio," earned him an international reputation when it was broadcast on the BBC Theater Series in 1972. In his student days at Ibadan, he was President of the Dramatic Society and a performing member of the Traveling Theater.

A friend and director of Programs at Nigerian Television Authority, Victoria Ezeokoli, asked him, as a joke, to become a television producer. He took up the challenge. He "created, wrote, produced, financed and marketed a comedy series [*Basi and Co.*] which ran for five years (October 1985- October 1990) on Nigerian network television, receiving much praise locally and internationally." (*Diary*: 58). The series also translated into several books regaling the reader with satire on the foibles of the bumbling, ambitious hero and his supporting cast of equally inept types caught in the dying dream of cosmopolitan, corrupt Lagosian society. One is not sure of where the artist in Saro-Wiwa metamorphosed into the business man, or where the latter merged his image-driven qualities with the imagination of the creative writer versed in the exchanging imageries of theater and television. In essence, the business man, the artist, and the political activist, are all microcosmic to the totality of the self. One could not have survived or succeeded without the others in that existential complexity.

With regards to the publishing enterprise, the reader may have reason to wonder about aesthetic factors in a large corpus facilitated by the proprietor-status of the writer. As a writer and critic, I personally find in the books quite a bit of avoidable repetitiousness to the point of redundancy, especially where the Ogoni agenda is concerned. Furthermore, there are sometimes cases of rambling, as well as artistic ego-tripping, which might have been expunged were the publisher other than the author. Nonetheless, Saro-Wiwa is to be credited for the courage, the conviction, and the controversy to try, and succeed, where many others would not venture. The quality of his craft as writer is attested to by the awards he has won: *Sozaboy*, an honorable mention at the 1987 Noma Award for Publishing in Africa; the short-story collection, *A Forest of Flowers*, short listed for the Commonwealth Writers Prize; the play, "Transistor Radio," a BBC African Theater Prize (1972).

In the final analysis, what the publishing avocation accorded Saro-Wiwa, is that independence, and that easy access to the public craven but hardly actualized by many a writer. Publishing in Nigeria is particularly problematic, the writer being at the mercy of the publisher who, in turn, is at the mercy of a subtle but menacing censorship and an economy on the brink of collapse. In that out-of-this-world situation, books and their creators are the primary victims of an illiterate leadership sworn to arresting the people's development by holding them in intellectual bondage. No doubt that, if Saro-Wiwa had not been his own publisher, a good number of his writings would never have seen the light of day in Nigeria.

Such is the fate of a committed artist. Saro-Wiwa defines thus his notion of literature: "Literature in a critical situation such as Nigeria's cannot be divorced from politics. Indeed, literature must serve society by steeping itself in politics, by intervention, and writers must not merely write to amuse or to take a bemused, critical look at society. They must play an interventionist role." (*A Month and a Day*: 81) This viewpoint explains why fact and fiction almost always jostle for space in Saro-Wiwa's writings; in fact, his fiction is inescapably realistic, that is, based upon real events and experiences, addressing current socio-political and economic issues, and exploring and exposing real personalities, so that the reader may view this mirror of life and the author's vision as to necessary changes. *Sozaboy* draws from Saro-Wiwa's personal experiences and observations during the civil war. The two novels, *Prisoner of Jebs* and (its sequence) *Pita Dumbrok's Prison*, borrow from the myriad actions and attitudes of contemporary Nigerians and Africans mired in corruption and confusion as they are led towards the abyss by counterfeit, self-sanctified fathers of moribund nations. *Jebs* was, indeed, first serialized in a Nigerian newspaper, *Vanguard*, before becoming a novel. It was in recognition of his writing and leadership skills that Saro-Wiwa became president of the Association of Nigerian Authors.

A Nigerian academic and writer being interviewed by a BBC correspondent was once asked, "Could Saro-Wiwa not have concentrated on his poetry, his prose, his drama?"[3] The response comes out loud and clear in Saro-Wiwa's literary work; for, as a committed writer, his creative work is constantly centered upon, and critical of, the excruciating realities thrust as an unshakable burden upon him and his people. Facts, as is often said, are sometimes stranger than fiction. And perhaps in no place is it truer than in Nigeria. A striking aspect of Saro-Wiwa's non-fictional work (articles, essays, speeches) is their artistry; the satirist, the dramatist, the poet, each is ever present in the now caustic, now comical, always compelling descriptions that leave the reader asking questions, laughing and wondering why things are not the way they ought to be. *On a Darkling Plain* is one of such titles. Its details are mind-boggling, bordering on a maddening maze of complexities that a careless reader could mistake for figments of the author's imagination. On the other hand, the author also reveals his own personality, as one of the players on the scene, as one of the makers of this horrible history called Nigeria, and one of the victims of its insanity. Concerning his personal attitude, Saro-Wiwa can easily be accused of pomposity. At times, he appears to feel that he is better than all others, that he knows it all, while they, his compatriots—all of them!—are stupid. He does not hide his disdain for the Biafran leader,

Ojukwu, for whom he hardly has a positive thought in *Plain*. The same negativity fills the pages of *Jebs* and *Prison*.

The present study seeks to carefully examine Saro-Wiwa's *Ojukwuphobia*. It will also analyze the texts to assess the writer-activist's art and ideas; the characters of each text, both male and female; the Nigerian question, and the contributions of the military and the politicians, within the context of the still-born nation and the boon named oil with which the Creator, or Nature, blessed the minority areas, paradoxically to their detriment; most significantly, we shall carefully assess Saro-Wiwa's Ogoni activism, his "judicial murder" (the words of John Major, the British Prime Minister) and what the future holds for the cause for which he sacrificed his life.

Saro-Wiwa held one more government post before he died: in September 1987, he was chosen by the Babangida administration as Executive Director of the directorate of Mass Mobilization for Self reliance, Social Justice and Economic Recovery (MAMSER). Not a few people wondered why he would smear his image by working with a government long on promises and paper-work, but pathetically short on performance and progress, not to mention its proclivity for creating organs used by unarmed robbers to siphon money from the cash-strapped treasury. Saro-Wiwa did that job for one year, taking responsibility for research in the directorate. He was simultaneously continuing his campaign on behalf of the Ogoni. He used his *Sunday Times* newspaper column, "Similia", to promote his philosophy critical of the majority ethnic groups' exploitation of the oil-producing areas. He was mobilizing the Ogoni people. As president of the Ogoni Central Union, he organized seminars. Under the auspices of the Union, an *Ogoni Bill of Rights*, written by him, was signed at Bori in 1990 by representatives of five of the six kingdoms, with the exception of Eleme. The Bill of Rights is published in both *Genocide in Nigeria* (p. 93ff) and *Diary* (p. 67ff). "As I expected," he states in *Diary* (p. 71), "we only got acknowledgment from the bureaucrats in the residency (Babangida being the only unelected President, perhaps, in the whole world). But the die had been cast." The Bill was launched in the six Ogoni kingdoms, using the local languages to educate the masses on its contents.

Henceforth, Saro-Wiwa would devote practically his whole time to the Ogoni struggle. At every forum, he pressed the case against Shell, the main oil-exploiting company in Ogoni, and the Nigerian government.

He preached non-violence in a violence ridden environment. He led the move to create MOSOP (Movement for the Survival of the Ogoni People) in early 1991. MOSOP was to become the galvanizing force of the Ogoni agenda to reclaim the people's economic rights and to protect the environment against oil-exploration devastation.

Now attaining international fame in a world where the degradation of the ecosystem was considered sacrilegious, Saro-Wiwa was invited to various places in Europe and America. He used each occasion to hone his organizational skills and to expand his network of supporters, particularly the Non-Government Organizations. In the process, he was fast becoming a *persona non grata* and a pariah to the thin-skinned Nigerian rulership. The Ogoni political elite, whose inability to play partisan politics (banned by the military regime) had facilitated their cooperation with him in the nationalist struggle, later showed their true colors of reaction and retrogression; government either bought them over or threw carrots of political office at them by lifting the ban on politics in 1992. Notwithstanding the internal frictions and fractions, Saro-Wiwa pushed ahead with extraordinary vigor. He formed a youth wing of MOSOP, partially as a result of his growing despondency over the Ogoni elite and elders' unreliability, partially because the youths represent the future that need be solidified by conscientizing its makers.

Life was becoming more and more difficult for Saro-Wiwa. Between being prevented to give speeches within Nigeria or to travel abroad, he was organizing the 500,000 odd Ogoni to come together to celebrate Ogoni Day, an event of unprecedented success that took place on January 4, 1993, with music and dance and a rally in each of the Ogoni kingdoms. Even at that period, if not earlier, the danger of violent outbursts within the ranks, was very rife. Some Ogoni personalities had advised against the Ogoni Day, in response to the appeal by the Rivers State governor, Ada-George. Others, including Saro-Wiwa and the younger elements, had insisted on going ahead with the demonstration, deemed a peaceful celebration of Ogoni culture and a demand of their human rights. His *Diary* addresses at length the events leading to his arrest and detention for "a month and a day," from June 21 to July 22, 1993. Before his arrest, Shell had been forced (March, 1993) by the people's protest to abandon operations.

That first detention was not the one for which Saro-Wiwa was eliminated. It was just a kind of warning, like the Mafia giving their quarry a thorough beating and a broken nose, so that he may desist from actions deserving of death. The detention described in *Diary* was consequential to Saro-Wiwa's successful organization of an Ogoni boycott of the June 12, 1993 presidential elections.[4] According to an "unpatriotic" (read, anti- government) magazine, *Tell* "Abacha's Revenge," (November 13, 1995: 10- 16), the current "owner of the land," that is, Nigeria, Abacha, invited Saro-Wiwa, after his release to the capital, Abuja, in late 1993. The big boss pretended to be sympathetic to the Ogoni cause, and to be outraged at the activist's "uncivilized and unintelligent" detention. He pointedly asked Saro-Wiwa what precisely he and his people wanted. The latter outlined the Ogoni Bill of Rights and mentioned political autonomy within the context of a federation of Nigeria. Out of the blue, the almighty Father of the Non-Nation asked whether the Ogoni man would mind being a federal minister in the new cabinet. The man rejected the indirect offer. End of the meeting of unlike minds.

By April 1994, it was evident that military operatives in Ogoni were on a "pacification" mission, as witnessed the leaked secret document, Operation Order 4/94, titled, *Restoration of Law and Order in Ogoniland*, placed under the command of Okuntimo. Ogoni became a conquered territory, with all arms of the military pummeling the people into submission. Shell was invited back, but it demurred, and then decided not to. The oil company's intransigence probably touched the cord of savagery in the masters on Ogoni land. At a press conference in Port Harcourt, Okuntimo boasted of perfecting two hundred and twenty-one (221) ways of destroying or destabilizing Ogoni. Additional forces were detailed to the area in April 1994 for "ruthless operating [and] wasting operations during MOSOP and other gatherings." Of course, *wasting*, in any parlance, mens killing, death, destruction.

On May 21, 1994, a meeting was being held by the Ogoni leadership at Giokoo, to plan a reception for two Ogoni sons recently appointed into the Rivers State government. One of them was Barinem Kiobel; he was absent from that meeting. So also was Saro-Wiwa, away in a neighboring town where he was accosted and turned away by the police for illegally campaigning for the upcoming constitutional conference elections. Tragedy at Giokoo: four of the elders were murdered by an irate mob. The authorities claimed Saro-Wiwa had incited youths to murder, that he had, by his earlier pronouncements threatened elimination of anyone ("vulture") opposed to the Ogoni revolution. Even before Saro-Wiwa was arrested, the Military Administration held a press conference to condemn him and MOSOP for the murders for which he and eight associates, including Kiobel, would be hanged.

Saro-Wiwa was arrested on May 22, 1994, tried months after being held incommunicado in what he himself called "a kangaroo court," a special tribunal created in his honor, condemned to death by hanging on October 21, 1995, and, without enjoying what was supposed to be a thirty-day right to appeal (even if it was to the very military bosses that had decreed his and his comrades' death through their faithful servants in the tribunal), unceremoniously hanged until he died in a shallow pit twenty minutes after, on November 10, 1995.

As has become the fashion in this civilized, post-modern world, medicine came after death. True that world powers expressed outrage at the tribunal's verdict. True that some threatened to impose sanctions if Nigeria's military junta dared ratify the death-sentence. All too true, too, that human interest is minimal in the overall concerns of the imperialist masters. Nigeria's death-minting machine had earlier humored them by commuting the death-sentence of alleged coupists to life or fifteen-year imprisonment. They should have been intelligent enough to realize that the beast does not bend down twice before the master owing it his daily bread. Nigeria's monster murdered Saro-Wiwa, right in the middle of the annual, meaningless meeting of the commonwealth leaders in Auckland, New-Zealand. It dared them to do their civilized worst: nothing!

The United States, Britain and other European countries, even South Africa symbolized by the universally revered Nelson Mandela, they were all *reacting*, instead of *acting*. The worst we have heard to date is the Americans' withdrawal of some innocuous military aid to Nigeria, Britain's similar decision, and both countries' suspension of visas to military personnel, their families and those working for government. Hard upon the heels of the dastardly hanging, ambassadors were recalled for consultation, and, naturally, the Giant of Africa retaliated by recalling its own representatives which, indeed, was a great opportunity to put to pasture some of them, overtime residents at posting where they had become probably tired of fabricating tall tales to save the face of a criminal rulership. And Mandela, the same Mandela who spearheaded the African National Congress and helped create its armed wing, "the Spear of the Nation," was there, before Saro-Wiwa's death, insisting upon "constructive [quiet] persuasive diplomacy" with inhuman individuals whose definition of diplomacy reeks of deceit and duplicity. Mandela's deputy vice-President, Mbeki, had gone to Nigeria; the now retired Archbishop Tutu, too. Both discussed the general anomie of a land of riches ransacked by rascals pitiless of the fate of millions cowered into hiding or silence or collusion with the forces of armed robbers. Those visits were before Saro-Wiwa's death-sentence. The dribbling tactics of their hosts ought to have taught Mandela and his men a basic lesson about today's Nigeria: do not trust them. Such a lesson would have helped Mandela to avoid the major mistake of "quiet diplomacy" just before Saro-Wiwa's death.

After the fact, South Africa withdrew its invitation to Nigeria to participate in a soccer tournament, as well as in the Miss World competition. Mandela led the move to suspend Nigeria from the Commonwealth. As if Saro-Wiwa knew something of the farcical dimensions of his own death; Nigerians love to play games, especially football (soccer). In *Prisoner of Jebs*, the Prison Director visits Britain in search of support for his prison- republic. The Iron Lady, Margaret Thatcher, the one whose real-life policy was to encourage the apartheid government to "waste" worthless Blacks, advises him: "If I were you, I'd return home, keep my citizens busy playing football to stop them from thinking..." (p. 150). Perhaps Mandela was convinced that, by disallowing Nigerians from playing football, he would compel them to think. His only, big mistake: those supposed to think but who never do, are the very important spectators, too fat to keep their uniform-shirts properly tucked into their pants, too pumped up by power to pay attention to minor details of human rights and lives. Nigeria's absence from the Miss "Meat Market" competition was equally inconsequential; it meant one less black body to parade before an audience looking to market white meat. And, finally, it is an open secret that the commonwealth Club of the Ex-Colonial Masters and their Faithful Servants, has no real power to punish any rascally member. Suspension may cause some embarrassment, but it does no harm to the transgressor in terms of economics.

That, indeed, is the determinant of power; all those games couched in mysterious language and acronyms can only deceive fools. Mandela once mooted the idea of oil sanctions against Nigeria. The United States also made that noise, from time to time. In order to con its critics out of their accusatory stance, it blamed Britain and its European Union stable-mates for not cooperating because, in America's mind, only well coordinated sanctions could be meaningful. Not to be outplayed in this civilized game of hypocrisy, Britain and its allies complaining that the world's Police enforcer, America, is not leading the way. Two facts: one, the United States would rather have Nigeria razed to the ground than lose that cheap, high-quality oil it is buying and saving for rainy days. Two, Britain would rather re-colonize Nigeria than lose all those billions in business deals, and more billions deposited in its banks by Nigerian money-mining monsters. So, those calling for oil sanctions and freezing of assets are just whistling in the wind. Which is to be expected; for the same Britain stood firm against sanctioning South Africa, and the same U.S. of A. pleaded for "constructive engagement" while Mandela was spending twenty-seven years in jail.

Meanwhile, those ambassadors have all completed their consultations and duly returned to their Nigerian beat, doing business as usual. Saro-Wiwa is almost forgotten by the big bosses. His name crops up here and there, mental organizations engaged in an uphill battle against leeches of the environment and of human beings. A report says that Saro-Wiwa was nominated for the 1995 Nobel Peace Prize. He won the Right Livelihood Award, an alternate Nobel.

For those of us engaged in the dissemination of knowledge and the search for truth and the victory of justice, and humanity over bestiality, Saro-Wiwa's work remains a viable consolation, as it makes us *think*. Questions. Did the satirist lose sight of the seriousness of the Nigerian situation while eliciting laughter from his audience? Did he take adequate cognizance of the facts of Nigeria's history in his political struggle? How did he resolve the class issue—the gulf separating the writer (privileged, intellectual, bourgeois) from the people (underprivileged, illiterate) with whom he sought community? And, his opponents, within and without the Ogoni "kingdom," are they correct in claiming that he was "a habitual liar; a person (...) prepared to engineer the elimination of his elders" (*Tell*, Nov. 13, 1995: 15)? Why did Saro-Wiwa not escape into exile, as did others like the Nobel Laureate Soyinka, whose character is central to the philosophy espoused in Saro-Wiwa's *Jebs*?

This book addresses these questions and others, not with the ambition of finding answers, but with the humble intention of arousing a discussion among those interested in Nigeria, "that unhappy country" (*Jebs*: 118). While ministers and others in officialdom are lying and pretending that there are no problems, no political prisoners in Nigeria, the list is growing of those exiled, detained or dealt the hand of death by gamesters and gangsters at the helm of power. Ken Saro-Wiwa is on that list. The hope is that it will not continue to grow, unabated. An incontrovertible fact: individuals die, but invaluable ideas live forever.

NOTES TO INTRODUCTION

1. The vast majority of his books bear "Ken Saro-Wiwa." One, *Tambari in Dukana*, bears "K.B. Tsaro-Wiwa." His father is know as *Pa* Bison Wiwa (i.e. Papa, Father, title used for aged, respected men).

2. Here is an example of some confusing details in Saro-Wiwa's life and work. In his civil-war account [he also calls it a "diary"], *On a Darkling Plain*, he first refers to his investment "in passenger transport in 1966" (p.115). Recounting a 1968 visit to Ogoni from Bonny where he was Administrator, he mentions seeing, at the Okrika waterfront, "the bus I had purchased early in 1967" (p.200).

3. Taiwo Oloruntoba-Oju, "Comets for General Wiwa," *TheNews*, Jan. 8, 1996: 10. The Lagos-based magazine, one of the publications of the so-called South-West press--considered unpatriotic for standing up to the end-of-century enslavers running Nigeria like their family farm--, chose Ken Saro-Wiwa as man of the year for 1995 and this article is one of those written in his honor.

4. Saro-Wiwa called for a boycott because he was convinced that the elections in no way symbolized anything positive for his people. Maybe if he had known that Nigeria's self-styled evil genius, the anointed Maradona of the Military, President Babangida, was going to annul what was recognized at home and abroad as the freest and fairest balloting ever, the beleaguered activist would not have bothered to muster his anti-election forces. Which is not to say that "the final solution," Saro-Wiwa's death, could have been avoided by that single non-act.

1. DECIPHERING ENIGMAS

-Struggle is a pain, to be the symbol of a struggle is to suffer. It is a sacrifice which must be made. I know it, I accept it. (Saro-Wiwa's final statement to murder tribunal)
-If Saro-Wiwa was selfish, he would not have stuck out his neck. (Ibani woman, unpublished interview, Feb. 1995)
-In Nigeria, you can be put to death for placing humble human well-being as a value even equal to, let alone above, the value of oil profits. (Nadine Gordimer)
-In Nigeria, there is no permanent friendship. (Rivers State associate of Wiwa, unpublished interview, April 1998)

SHORT MAN, TALL AMBITIONS AND A PLETHORA OF TALES

Since Ken Saro-Wiwa's hanging by the Nigerian military junta on November 10, 1995, controversy has continued to swirl over the man's personality and political purposes. The debate is not only among his compatriots, but also in the international community. In researching the present book, I decided to interview individuals close to Saro-Wiwa, while also examining statements by others who claim genuine knowledge of his life and activities. These efforts have, to some extent, led to clarification of a few contentious issues; they have also raised more questions than answers. What remains incontrovertible is the impact of Saro-Wiwa on the world: Nobody interested in Nigeria, and Africa, can avoid an opinion on the life of this man who, through his advocacy for freedom and rights of his Ogoni people, has become a beacon of popular struggle against ethnic and economic oppression.

Saro-Wiwa was small in physical stature, just as is his ethnic group numbering only about half a million. That diminutive condition has been used by some critics to ridicule him, based upon the mythical, gigantic ambitions of men of gnomic proportions. "Short man devil," some would say, reeling off names such as, Napoleon of France, Franco of Spain, Marcos of the Phillipines, Bokassa of the Central African

Republic, Selassie of Ethiopia, Pol Pot of Cambodia, Mao of China. One fellow Nigerian told me the story of Saro-Wiwa, ever dictatorial, ever aspiring to be in control, never satisfied with being like other common people, jumping up on a table at an intellectual gathering and shouting at the top of his remarkably assertive voice, to insist on his viewpoint, and to impose that opinion on others. One might ask, however: Do tall people, as a rule, display more self-control and equanimity? Are they more at peace with themselves? Are they more acceptable human beings? Should a short man accept oppression and any kind of imposition, so as not to be fingered for a passport to the madhouse? Besides, there are giants as dictatorial, as fearsome, as self-possessed as those short men on the world's honor-roll of symbols of opprobrium: Amin of Uganda, Mobutu of Zaire, Mussolini of Italy, Stalin of Russia, and (the relatively tall) Hitler of Germany.

Saro-Wiwa had a knack for laughing at everybody and everything, including himself. He regularly joked about his physical size. To a critic who, angered at the then columnist's satire on the Yoruba, accused him of parochialism and myopia as diseases resulting from his small stature, Saro-Wiwa responded: "He was as impressed as I am with my shortness of stature. Unfortunately, he is ignorant of my tall parts." (*Similia*: 159) A lewd remark to male anatomy, some would quickly note, but it is an appropriate rebuttal to a commentator unwilling to take cognizance of the writer's many activities, and popular activism.

In the light of such remarks, it is also pertinent to note how critics react to Saro-Wiwa's private life. I was tempted to delve into the matter and draw conclusions. However, I have decided to refrain from doing so, for the simple reason that, much would be based on hearsay which could draw attention away from the serious issues of the man's public life and work. I am in agreement with that Rivers State intellectual and Saro-Wiwa associate[1], who opined that any meaningful assessment of his private life can come only from his wife, Maria. As time goes on, there will hopefully be opportunities to interview not only Maria but other women close to him, including Hauwa Madugu, whom Saro-Wiwa calls "my young friend" (*A Month and a Day*: 29, 119), and Mina, "my friend" (196), who used to take food to him in detention. It cannot be overemphasized that my own main interest in Saro-Wiwa is not his private life. History is replete with stories of revered geniuses whose idiosyncrasies would hardly stand up to the microscopic scrutiny of what may be termed morality. In the case of Saro-Wiwa, the idea here is not to give room for distraction, not to allow his detractors to use any ploy about his private foibles, to further denigrate his achievements.

Those who have talked to me about him fall into two categories: of admiration, or condemnation. Some hail him; others hate him. Some have honored him in life and death, while his country's rulers hounded and, finally, hanged him. Interestingly, with regards to his private life, one observer's remark started me on what I consider an important thought. The Wiwa associate reminded me that Saro-Wiwa went about his public activities alone, never in the company of any woman. He noted a similar habit in Saro-Wiwa's now deceased friend, the eminent political scientist, Claude Ake. Ake, like his friend, was a very private man. Depending on whom one talks to, various stories may be heard about both men's marital lives.

On the contrary, one is struck by a phenomenon of recent vintage in present-day Nigeria: the very public presence of the country's First Ladies. Starting with Maryam Babangida, architect of the much debated program, Better Life for Rural Women (1985-1993), and her successor, Miriam Abacha (1993-98), mother of the similarly controversial and money -guzzling Family Support Program, these women have shared center stage with their husbands. Both programs have done everything to enrich a few individuals, but hardly anything to better Nigerian women's lives, or to enhance the quality of of life of Nigerian families. One may ask: What is the reason for this development in Nigeria's militarized polity? Could it be another avenue for siphoning more public funds into private pockets? Could it be an attempt to enlist the support of Nigerian women, given the history of their political activism? Or, to appear to be "politically correct" in the eyes of Western observers?

With regard to commitment, Saro-Wiwa is the object of two diametrically opposed opinions. There are dichotomies galore, between hero and villain:

Courage and commitment, versus grandstanding and self-aggrandizement. Selflessness, or selfishness. Patriotism, or parochialism. Populism, marked by earthiness, symbolized in the small-framed figure clad in his favorite, simply sewn Yoruba top, working among the Ogoni grassroots, versus the capitalism of a patronizing materialist amassing wealth by exploiting the people and collaborating with the military oppressors. The professionalism and integrity of the poet and dramatist, versus the slyness of a businessman -politician impossible to trust.

In order to decipher this enigmatic figure, one cannot but strive at the same time to understand that other enigma, Nigeria,[2] the peculiarities of which are habitually used by its leaders to support their stranglehold on power.

The monster named Nigeria help to create the myth of Saro-Wiwa, and the martyr. It would make sense to say that, without Nigeria's peculiar character and its rulership's inhumanity, Saro-Wiwa might have survived and, perhaps, he would have lived an ordinary life. Perhaps he would have used his immense qualities to help build a nation out of that country blessed with limitless human and natural resources. However, a sensitive, conscious, intelligent, and stubborn person, such as he, could not be silent in the face of Nigeria's evolution towards feudal enslavement, particularly with regards to his people, the Ogoni. The country's history, which the young Saro-Wiwa avidly studied, shows that conditions for conflict, and conflagration, were present from the very day the British decided to "protect" the vast land mass that they ultimately called Nigeria. Characteristics of the country have included, lack of commitment, that is, absence of the essentials for creating a nation; deceit, introduced by the colonial master in his divide-and-rule system, used initially to maintain his power and, later, as the sun set on his almighty empire, to retain his outrageous economic interests in the neo-colony; and cultural and economic enslavement to the ever-superior West. This last characteristic, we must affirm, has benefitted both the former master and the latter-day imperialists, as well as the new, local rulers. These so-called national leaders have been able to twist the foreign powers between their fingers, due to their unholy and dubious economic alliance.

In a country fabricated by colonialists and maintained by a complicated process of collaboration and deceit and, currently, by death-decrees, one can imagine how lies and rumors would prevail, and the abnormal would be the norm. Nigeria must be one of the few countries in the world where nobody is sure of the national origins of their leader; where accountability is used as a weapon to punish those attempting to reveal horrible secrets of high-level philanderers and pillagers passing for patriots; where budgets and policies, not to forget the constitution, are mere rumors. This state of decadence is heightened by the military's dominance of governance: Since independence in 1960, Nigeria has been ruled by military dictators for almost thirty years. Interestingly, the military, in a perverted and paradoxical fashion, has categorically claimed to promote *democracy*, perhaps because civilian politicians have always been willing and able to collaborate and collude in performing what is called *service to the nation*. Paramount among the duties reeled off by every successful *coupist* (an excellent Nigerian coinage), is that of maintaining *one Nigeria*.

Saro-Wiwa himself bought into that propaganda when he sided with the federal government during the Nigerian civil war (1967-1971). He later found that it was largely a lie, but it was too late. In addition, one still wonders whether he fully understood the contents of that lie. Yet, it would be difficult to condemn him for believing in Nigeria; for, even in these dark days of the late century, some people still have faith. In order to understand the man and his times, one has to be aware of his commitment, far beyond personal aggrandizement. His detractors -and it is no surprise that they are often on the pay-roll of his killers- tend to ask questions which immediately revel their bias, or their belief in stories fabricated to support the government's act of elimination. Concerning the 1995 trial, Saro-Wiwa's death-sentence ought not to have been based upon his denunciation by prosecution witnesses as an advocate of violence, a non-pacifist, and a non-respecter of his elders[3] who, out of a desire for absolute power, urged his young followers to kill those whom he condemned as *vultures*. The pertinent question is, to know whether or not Saro-Wiwa and his comrades were given a fair trial.

ISSUES OF EDUCATION, CLASS, AND CULTURE

One of the oft repeated comments on Saro-Wiwa is his sophisticated, or pompous outlook. Ironically, that aspect is also linked to his easy accessibility to common people to whom he was proud to have brought "education and hope." (*Month*: 51) He never hid the fact that he was from a middle-class family. He was one of the few Ogoni children of his generation privileged to attend school. He later went to Government College, Umuahia, from where he moved to the University of Ibadan.

Now, anyone cognizant of Nigerian education system would understand the way governments colleges, precisely during the period of the 50s to the 60s, molded young men and women after the British model

(Eaton), and students of Ibadan, Nigeria's first university, after those of Cambridge and Oxford. Saro-Wiwa was proud of his elitist alma maters, especially Umuahia, the products of which he constantly mentions in his writings as being of superior quality. The Old Boys' network might have prompted his friendship with men of the military, but that should not justify his strange fascination with the military.

The clear elitism of that education must not blind the observer to another fact, that those colleges did inculcate in the young men and women passing through their gates, a sense of dignity and integrity that could be useful to the whole society. Unfortunately, more often than not, those kept on the outside of the privileged colonial training had a tendency to mock both the government college and missionary school products as spoilt brats and self-opinionated, and bad imitation of the British elite.

As for Saro-Wiwa's military friends, one must remark that, in his youth, many, if not most, of the recruits were among the worst achievers, academically. That, therefore, could make one criticize the pride displayed by Saro-Wiwa about the quality of his military friends. Which is neither to say that the military is full of men of brawn and little brain, nor that the artist-activist did not place premium on the intellect. For example, his friendship with Olusegun Obasanjo, then commander of the federal forces based in Port Harcourt during the civil war (1969) and later Head of State (1975-79), arose out of the latter's "enlightened comments" on Saro-Wiwa's published poems (see Onukaba Ojo, *Olusegun Obasanjo*: 142) Briefly, one can see here a combination of interest in the power wielded by the military, and the power of the intellect. Would that constitute a contradiction?

A similar observation may be made about Saro-Wiwa's use of language. For a degree-holder in English and a stickler for correct usage "putting the right word in the right place" (*Month*: 20), it might appear strange that he chose to use "rotten English" in his first novel, *Sozaboy*, and to use similar tongue in some of his poetry. During the final, activist period of his life, he used to address his Ogoni audience in his native Gokana. This probably represents a positive evolution in the character of the man: Originally, he embraced Western education as an essential formation for anyone desirous of operating within a world led by the West; at the same time, he saw the necessity for the well educated to reach down to those without that training to uplift them, in the sense of obtaining their rights in society. Later on, he appeared to have woken up to the alienation inherent in that education and to the necessity to relate better to his culture and his people. He thus resolved to place himself fully in the service of his people. He became their voice, their spokesman, their messenger, and ultimately their leader.

In the latter part of his life, Saro-Wiwa came to the realization that acquiring Western education should not alienate him, or anyone for that matter, from their own culture. Some critics could think otherwise. For example, from the literary point of view, one might ask why the writer never wrote anything in his mother tongue. Such language debate has long been going on over the authenticity of foreign-language African literature. While we are not attempting to defend Saro-Wiwa, it need be said that the themes of his works are deeply rooted in Ogoni culture, and the Spirit of Ogoni remains a driving force behind many of the stories told in his collections. Of course, his extra-literary work is engaged in the popular cause. Whatever criticism may be leveled at his elitist background, we cannot deny that engagement, and the people's overwhelming appreciation and support of Saro-Wiwa. Besides, what may be called "the Ogoni phase" of his life, the three years leading to his arrest in May 1994, clearly show that he was less interested in matters of individual and intellectual excellence, and much more in dedicating himself to the cause for which he would be killed. I fully appreciate the opinion of the Ibani woman according to whom Saro-Wiwa's choice of language serves as a means of promoting his vision and grassroots philosophy. Thus, he succeeded in building "a bridge between his poetics and political life."

SARO-WIWA, THE ELITE, AND THE OGONI CAUSE

Saro-Wiwa's singular skills at organization, his perseverance, and commitment resulted not only in the success of MOSOP (Movement for the Survival of Ogoni People) against all odds, but in the international attention ultimately accorded the Ogoni cause. Once again, his role in the Movement has become clouded by controversy amidst all sorts of allegations. All those allegations have, nonetheless, done nothing to reduce the force of his personality, and his achievements.

He was the brain behind the Ogoni Bill of Rights, a document unique in Nigerian annals, with its straightforward demands for autonomy, and economic, political, and human rights of the producers of oil,

Nigeria's main source of economic survival. Were he to be an outright egomaniac or a power-hungry, selfish man, Saro-Wiwa would have, could have, sought and won the post of MOSOP President from its inception. On the contrary, one is impressed by his careful efforts to bring together into the fold all the Ogoni elite, most importantly, those older and more experienced in politics than he was.

It is in that light that one could best understand the whole scenario of the murder accusation and conviction that sent him to the gallows. One of the victims of the May 21, 1994 murders, Edward Kobani, was Saro-Wiwa's mentor, friend, and fellow Ibadan alumnus. As a student, Saro-Wiwa used to spend his vacation at Kobani's flat in Port Harcourt. Both men were at the 1966 meeting of the Rivers Leaders of Thought were the idea of statehood was mooted for the Rivers people. They later worked together in MOSOP.

Although he was not as close to the other very important figure in Ogoni affairs, Garrick Leton, Saro-Wiwa respected him and worked hard to have him elected as first President of MOSOP. Both Kobani and Leton were at various times federal ministers and holders of other political posts. There appeared to be no reason for the cleavage that erupted and caused havoc within the Movement, and led to Saro-Wiwa's demise. Appearances, as they say, are often deceitful; for, deep down, there was mutual mistrust, and Saro-Wiwa later expressed his personal misgivings and other people's warnings regarding the character and actions of Kobani and Leton.

The episodes recounted in *Month* make one wonder why Saro-Wiwa did not sever relationships with Leton, Kobani, and others in the MOSOP leadership earlier than he did. We learn, for instance, that both Leton and Kobani were pro-Biafran during the civil war. They were employed in propaganda. Saro-Wiwa helped to rehabilitate them after the war. He saw them nurture their political ambitions and achieve their dreams as cabinet members in various regimes, from Obasanjo's (1975-79), to Shagari's (1979-83), as well as their collaboration with subsequent rulers of the land. It was Kobani who stymied Saro-Wiwa's own ambition to participate in the Obasanjo-arranged Constituent Assembly, charged with crafting a new constitution ushering in the civilian regime of 1979 (*Month*: 204).

Saro-Wiwa was warned about Kobani's shady character and cowardliness, by Uche Chukwumerije, a journalist who later became a major player as information officer in the military regime of Babangida.[4] Earlier on, in 1969, he had been warned by a fellow Rivers State intellectual and cabinet member, Obi Wali, that the educated Ogoni would jeopardize his work among the grassroots. Saro-Wiwa lamented: "The great unanimity I had achieved among the Ogoni, as I set their sights on a greater dawn, would be disputed and brought to a standstill, if I weren't careful. How right he proved to be!" (*Month*: 52) He continued: "Uniting the Ogoni masses proved an easier task than associating a handful of graduates with my vision for the Ogoni."

According to Saro-Wiwa, he did not act earlier against the likes of Kobani and Leton, because he deemed it necessary "to take everyone on board, particularly the spoilers among the Ogoni elite." (204) The success of MOSOP would support that viewpoint. Kobani's son designed the Movement's flag. (205) Kobani himself coined the term, *vulture* (161) as epithet for government sycophants and Ogoni traitors. Both of these facts are significant since, at the trial, Saro-Wiwa was accused of leading a secessionist cause because of the Ogoni flag, and the use of the much dreaded terminology to designate those marked out for murder.

It is, of course, true that Saro-Wiwa himself was a politician of sorts. Witness his cabinet post, at age twenty-six, in the first Rivers State government under the governorship of navy commander Diette-Spiff; his foiled candidacy at the 1977 Constituent Assembly election; and his overall savvy in organizing MOSOP and other Ogoni bodies. By the same token, one cannot overlook the distinct quality of that brand of politics. Unlike his Ogoni colleagues, and the generality of Nigerian politicians. Saro-Wiwa showed a high sense of integrity. In *Month* (203), he discusses his being "given the boot unceremoniously in March of 1973," because of his constant disagreement with "the inefficiency, the dictatorial nature of decision-making, the corruption, the tribalism" of the government. He was, by any standard, a rich man. In the course of his life, he managed to amass considerable wealth which he ultimately used in the crusade on behalf of his people. This opinion is shared by many of his supporters. "If Saro-Wiwa was selfish," affirmed the Ibani woman whom I interviewed, "he would not have stuck out his neck. With his connections, and his wealth, he could have simply sat back and enjoyed his success."

For his part, Saro-Wiwa's aforementioned Rivers associate gave some insight into the workings of MOSOP, and the inevitable falling out between Saro-Wiwa and his youthful associates on one hand, and Kobani, Leton, and the elders, on the other. He mentioned the membership of the Southern Minority Movement, formed in 1991, including many riverain ethnic groups, specifically to create solidarity for the struggle against oppression and exploitation. Leton, Kobani and others were members; but not Saro-Wiwa. As early as that period, the friction was patent. The two elders insisted that the younger Saro-Wiwa must not be admitted. He himself actually refused to join. His books on his role in the Ogoni cause makes the reader think of the lack of a broad base, that is, beyond the confines of Ogoni, to include other minorities in similar situations.

In the contest for power as Ogoni spokesman, he and the other leaders ended up doing a disservice to their people, although all indications point to Saro-Wiwa's superior commitment. While Kobani and others were involved in seeking, at the center, political power which would enhance their financial profits, Saro-Wiwa was engaged at the grassroots. He became a local hero or, in his enemies' opinion, a dictator. He looked down at the jealous Ogoni elite as despicable gerontocrats easily bought over by the people's oppressors. "The mentality of the educated Ogoni," he wrote, "was always to keep close to the government of the day in order to pick up crumbs from the master's table." (*Month*: 51) In a culture emphasizing respect for elders, one can imagine how such pronouncements would engender envy, mistrust, and a desire to do away with an overwhelming presence such as Saro-Wiwa's.

Perhaps he was too harsh on those lacking his kind of commitment, or was too impatient with his fellow Ogoni elite who had more modest objectives than his. Maybe he was too possessed by the dreams of the Ogoni cause to realize that a tree could not a forest make. Perhaps, finally, he was a man too progressive for his mediocre times, a period far too mired in the mud of corruption and selfishness to accept and understand the deep meanings of freedom, equality, and national development.

Posterity will be the arbiter of the murder of the four chiefs for which Saro-Wiwa was hanged. One fact is clear, however: The cards were stacked high against the accused by a regime that reached a conclusion without knowing, or wishing to know, the facts. The very qualities that propelled the man to the top as his people's leader, were used as reason to condemn him to death. The youth wing of MOSOP, NYCOP (National

Youth Council of Ogoni People), founded in 1993 by Saro-Wiwa to bring urgency to the organization's activism, was viewed by the government and its allies as "a private army that, in time, ran vigilante squads, kangaroo courts and even executions." (Chris McGreal, in *Weekly Mail & Guardian*, April 4, 1996). Saro-Wiwa also organized women, teachers, religious leaders, and professionals. Leton, erstwhile MOSOP President, expressed his personal disgust and disappointment: "Everybody who was a chairman or president of those organisations was controlled by [Saro-Wiwa]. This is where the trouble started, with these parallel organisations. He was doing things all on his own. He didn't want us elders any longer." (Ibid.) Thus, one may suspect Leton of being jealous of Saro-Wiwa's superior organizational capabilities and his charisma as Ogoni leader, or he may have been genuinely opposed to the often noted dictatorial tendencies in Saro-Wiwa.

One of my interview subjects stated that NYCOP "did the dirty work, from what the government tells us." The Ibani woman categorically declared that any claim of Saro-Wiwa's lust for power, is "an outrageous attempt to deny the facts of oppression and bigotry existing then and now in Ogoni. To be called *Ogoni* means to be bad, stupid, *nothing!*" Discussing the murders of the four chiefs, she reminded me that, generally, chiefs are an epitome of corruption, that they are ready to dine with the all-powerful devil, as long as they will make money. Furthermore, she rejected the notion that Saro-Wiwa was violent: "Knowing him, I don't think he would ever order anyone to kill. He didn't believe in violence; that's one thing he held against the military." Her following remark on activism gave me food for thought: "It's quite a jump from activism to violent activism." My own response: In an atmosphere as charged as the Ogoniland's, it would be difficult, if not impossible, to maintain discipline. As the armed security details up the ante -and Nigeria's military has been known to be truly reckless and brutish[5]- and turn unarmed protesters into mere targets for shooting practice, it is predictable that quite a number of the youths would decide to retaliate, primarily against those conspirators aiding and abetting the people's destruction. The Ibani woman is correct to also point out that activism implies extremism. In the Ogoni example, Saro-Wiwa's followers were a mixed group. If they were eager to follow him, it would be inconceivable to believe that he would find it easy to control them. "I have the support of at least 98 per cent of the Ogoni people in the struggle for Ogoni survival," (*Month*: 16) he proudly wrote in his detention diary. Such popularity could not but arouse government's ire. Saro-Wiwa's speeches and activities, at home and, more importantly, abroad, probably culminated in the decision to silence him. If government were sure of the facts of the murders in question, then Saro-Wiwa should have been given a proper trial, before a legally constituted court, and in public. As it was, the simmering intra-Ogoni wrangling were used to advantage. Anti-Wiwa elements were encouraged to condemn the one person perhaps most committed to the Ogoni cause, thus hoping to reduce to a minimum the possibilities for success, and retaining the mass of the people in a state of enslavement.

It is also significant that, when he was finally elected as President of MOSOP in June 1993, Saro-Wiwa was absent. Leton and his reactionary colleagues had resigned in anger, and the youths had taken over; the other six executive members were younger than he. During those months preceding his May 1994 arrest, he had many reasons to fear for his life. He underwent a spate of detentions, and harassments. He was disallowed from traveling abroad on a couple of occasions. He was courted by the authorities in an attempt to make him a collaborator. When those efforts failed, he was threatened by "Babangida's bloodhounds." (*Month*: 153) He still refused to back down, not even when a special task force was planted in Ogoni, and a special decree was enacted to ensnare him. "Detention," he wrote, "only makes writers stronger." He added: "In the quest for justice for my people, neither prison nor threat of death, nor death itself, could ever deter me." (171)

When his son died in Eton College in March 1993, Saro-Wiwa traveled to Britain for the burial and returned in time to fulfill a lecture engagement with Itsekiri students in Warri, only to find himself "deported" by policemen ordered to prevent him from entering the town. Other examples attest to his courage. Added to his leadership qualities, one would imagine why Nigeria's oppressors, afraid and angry, would be so single-mindedly desirous of his demise. One of my Rivers interview subjects stated that Saro-Wiwa was actually given access, by his military guards, to escape from prison, but he refused because, to his mind, that would constitute a betrayal of his comrades, and his people who remained imprisoned by Nigeria. According to that commentator, Saro-Wiwa's final statement before the tribunal was consequential to his earlier exchanges with the guards urging him to flee from prison.

SARO-WIWA AND NIGERIA

Now, commitment to the Ogoni cause is generally acknowledged as Saro-Wiwa's most significant contribution. This assessment seems inevitable. Resistance to domination, and the desire to give voice to the people's cause, are very striking in Saro-Wiwa's works. Given Nigerian realities, the definition of *his people* became more and more particular, and personal. In the opinion of my Ibani interview subject, this was due to the overwhelming domination of Eastern minorities by the Igbo (a word that Saro-Wiwa insisted on giving the old, colonial spelling, *Ibo*). Oppression of the Ogoni dates back to many years. For no reason at all, they were regarded as inferior to others, and their condition was much worse than that of other minorities.

In subsequent chapters, we shall take a close look at Saro-Wiwa's writings on the civil war, in which he chose to work with the federal forces against secessionist Biafra and its leader, Ojukwu. At this juncture, it suffices to note that what is called Saro-Wiwa's *Ojukwuphobia*, or *Igbophobia*, was rooted in Ogoni history of oppression, exploitation, and alienation by the Igbo. Saro-Wiwa's civil war text, *On a Darkling Plain*, is roundly condemned by the Igbo.[6] He has also been accused of playing a major role in the thorny issue of Igbo abandoned property in Port Harcourt: It is alleged that he, in particular, illegally acquired Igbo property and refused to surrender the buildings to the rightful owners after the civil war. It should be noted that, in Nigeria, legal ownership of landed property hinges on one document, the Certificate of Occupancy (C. of O.), given to whoever buys a piece of land. Without this title, the owner of the biggest building on earth has no legal right to the property; it would be analogous to constructing a building in the air! It has been affirmed by Rivers indigenes that, when the Igbo converged on the State years ago in search of land that they lacked in their own area, they did not go through due process of law. Indeed, they were considered by many indigenes as colonizers who quickly became overlords and landlords. At the outbreak of the civil war, they heeded the call by Ojukwu to return home. Thus, they left behind their landed property, which was taken over by the original owners of the land. Saro-Wiwa himself is alleged to have acquired much of this property, and there is no proof that he did so in a strictly legal and fair manner. It was Obasanjo who raised the issue on behalf of the Igbo, because "he did not fight the war to reduce the Igbos to serfs in Nigeria." (Ojo: 154) Saro-Wiwa asked his good friend to define "abandoned property." The latter firmly believed that those who had built on the land and spent years there, owned the land. That was one aspect of Obasanjo's love for the Igbos, "his genuinely aggrieved brothers and sisters who had been led into war by a recalcitrant, selfish leadership." (Ojo: 142)

The friendly disagreement between Saro-Wiwa and Obasanjo reveals both men's biased assessment of the Nigerian situation. Obasanjo was wrong in failing to understand Saro-Wiwa's genuine commitment to the Ogoni who were preyed upon by the Igbo; for his part, Saro-Wiwa was wrong in not taking full cognizance of Obasanjo's desire to foster brotherhood in a Nigerian nation. Having said that, one realizes that Obasanjo, a member of the military hegemony, should have better appraised the facts of the Nigerian mess. Concerning the Igbo abandoned property, Obasanjo failed to follow the law to its full extent. Ironically, Saro-Wiwa's property in Port Harcourt, which he acquired legally, is now sealed off, and his business, destroyed (even as he was being tried).

Obasanjo stated only half-truths about the civil war itself, conveniently forgetting that the Igbo did not simply follow the Ojukwu leadership like foolish sheep. We shall see, in analyzing *Plain*, that Saro-Wiwa, too, deliberately downplayed the genocide committed against the Igbo during the period preceding the war, while sensationalizing Ojukwu's power madness. The writer-activist seemed to have become more forthright, as he wrote in *Month:* "Many of the issues raised by Ojukwu and which led to war are as valid today as they were then." Yet, certain misconceptions remain in the new text. For example, it is said that "Ojukwu scuttled" Head of State Gowon's Ad-hoc Conference of 1966 "when the discussions did not appear to be going in the direction [Ojukwu] wanted." (86)

In reality, Ojukwu's overt ambitions and defiance of Gowon notwithstanding, the conference was scuttled, not by Ojukwu, but by Gowon himself. Press reports, quoting speeches and comments of that watershed in Nigeria's tragic history, prove this point. Any interested observer would enjoy reading the five Regions' (East, Lagos, Mid-West, North, and West) proposals for Nigeria's future. The unanimous choice was for a confederation, or a sort of commonwealth of Nigeria. In its paper, the North declares: "The colonial master who ruled Nigeria introduced a system of unitary government not for the present or future unity or well-being of all the indigenes of the country, but for his own administrative convenience (...) The new Nigeria shall comprise a number of autonomous states. [The President and Head of State is] to be provided by States in rotation. His term of office shall be four years." (*Daily Times,* Lagos, Dec.1, 1996:11) As if all five Regions had worked in concert, their proposals were very similar. All the regions agreed that "Nigeria is a multilingual and multinational country *par excellence*." (The West's proposal, in *Daily Times*, Nov.30, 1966:9) A correct, realistic assessment of the country's situation, and an honest, practical vision for its future existence, one would say.

Suddenly, Gowon suspended the proceedings. On November 30, 1966, he made a public broadcast, affirming that confederation was "unworkable... This is not the future to which our children are entitled and we have no moral right to commit future generations of Nigeria to this disastrous course." (*Daily Times*, Dec.1, 1966:1) His viewpoint was clear enough: "In a confederation, there will be no effective central authority." (2) In essence, Gowon and his group were interested in forced unity, which they were prepared to ram down everyone's throat. Meanwhile, the six-page "White Paper" reviewing the Nigerian crisis (*Times*, Oct.21`, 1966), referred to Ojukwu's Eastern government as a small group of dissenters and trouble-makers. That Paper was mainly a defense, and an exoneration, of the North in the evolving mess, as well as a blanket accusation of Southerners.

Why did Saro-Wiwa persist in his condemnation of Ojukwu, and the Igbo? We have already noted that the minority cause was Saro-Wiwa's main interest. He was hopeful that, once the Eastern minorities were saved from the Igbo, everything would work smoothly in Nigeria. Certain individuals have mentioned to me that, towards the end of his life, Saro-Wiwa was actually prepared to make peace with the Igbo. On the contrary, other observers have declared that he stood his ground to the bitter end, because the Ogoni condition grew worse and, in spite of their sacrifice during and after the war, Ogoni were not given any relief, whereas the Igbo, perpetrators of indescribable crimes against the Ogoni, were welcomed back to the fold. Ojukwu's "triumphant" return to Nigeria after his shameless flight to Ivory Coast at the end of the war, never ceased to annoy Saro-Wiwa. The already quoted Rivers State intellectual said: "Ken had no remorse; he never wanted peace with the Igbo."

The Igbo anti-Saro-Wiwa position may not be unconnected with their animosity towards Obafemi Awolowo, recognized as Yoruba leader during the civil war and therefore considered the one figure that had the power to take definitive decisions on behalf of his ethnic group. The Igbo have accused Awolowo of betraying them, for having reneged on his word, that the Yoruba would follow, if the Igbo seceded from the Nigerian federation. Awolowo it was, too, who single-handedly swung the pendulum of the war in favor of the federal government by having the currency changed, an abrupt action that sent the self-proclaimed nation of Biafra into immediate bankruptcy, because the Nigerian money they had became absolutely worthless. Later in this study, we shall see how much Saro-Wiwa revered Awolowo who was the very first to highlight the plight of the minorities. His position aided the creation of the Mid-West and the Rivers States. The Igbo never forgave Awolowo and the Yoruba, just as they never supported Saro-Wiwa.

One more word on Obasanjo. Continuing to witness Nigeria's headlong sprint towards the political abyss, the former Head of State came to re-assess his civil war stance, to recognize the validity of the Ogoni struggle. By February 1994, Abacha, the new "landlord" who had replaced the colorless contraption of a government headed by a figurehead named Ernest Shonekan, was showing his plans for perpetual power, as well as his readiness to snuff out any opposition. Obasanjo had begun to criticize him. On Ogoni, Obasanjo wrote: "Ogoni is symbolic of most minorities' plight and thinking all over the country. There are many Ogonis, our dispensation must allow for the right of minorities including the enjoyment of part of the God-given resources in their area. We must respond warmly and imaginatively to their special demands." (*TELL*, Feb.14, 1994: 16) When Obasanjo wrote this apparently perspicacious piece, he was long out of power, far off the center of power, but not free of ambitions. Himself a Nigerian enigma, he loved to be regarded as an "eminent personality," which was his designation as a member of that group of international statesmen that brokered Nelson Mandela's release and the dismantling of the apartheid machine; but he also elicited rumors about some mad ambition for state headship. Analysts of Nigerian history will have a big task, to explain the saga of the man who fell from the highest point to the depths, where he has been despatched for an alleged coup against the dictator who used to be one of the underlings following his every command, and the same dictator that sanctioned Saro-Wiwa's hanging.

SARO-WIWA AND THE NIGERIAN MILITARY

That task would include the understanding of a military established by the colonial master, the internal power-play, and parochialism (the aptly colonial term, *tribalism*, may be best suited here, for a country where ethnic affiliation seems to loom ever too large to allow for the creation and cultivation of a true nation). Regarding Obasanjo's disgrace, any surprise would be lessened by a statement made by one of those with whom I discussed Saro-Wiwa: "In Nigeria, there is no permanent friendship. No condition is permanent... Your friendship is permanent when you have a friend that's there [in power] now." It would appear that Abacha's predecessor, Babangida, respected Obasanjo as a superior and an elder statesman; hence, the latter freely condemned the dictator's attempt at self-succession and the annulment of the June 1993 presidential elections. One recall also that the Babangida regime used millions of dollars to campaign for Obasanjo's candidacy as Secretary-General of the United Nations. Abacha, on the contrary, would not accept his superior's scolding sitting down.[7] A few days before his arrest in Nigeria, Obasanjo was reportedly advised in Geneva, or some place abroad, by American intelligence operatives, not to return home. He waved them off with the swagger of a man in absolute control of his destiny.

A similarity could be identified in Saro-Wiwa's fate. Given his vast array of friends in the military, it might be surprising that he was so summarily eliminated, like a stray dog on the route of out-riders paving the way for another stern-looking coup-winner heading to the venue of his speech to an elated nation. Needless to say that Saro-Wiwa wielded significant influence during the civil war period, when he became Obasanjo's and other officers' friend. He was in charge of Head of State Gowon's reception to Rivers State. According to one of my sources, he was once the ears of the military governor, to whom he recommended Kiobel as commissioner, the same Kiobel later convicted and killed with Saro-Wiwa. And, later, we shall examine Saro-Wiwa's work as a Babangida appointee. All this would imply that Saro-Wiwa generally was on good terms with the military. He fell out of favor when it came to the particular issue of the Ogoni. Further work on this relationship should throw more light on Saro-Wiwa's personality and life. For now, certain questions may be asked, about his cooperation with that one empowered group which has laid waste much of the good components of the country; his silence over atrocities outside of his home base; his failure to see through the absolutist ambitions of Babangida; and, perhaps most significantly, his refusal to understand the fact of Hausa-Fulani hegemonic ambitions. To the very end, Saro-Wiwa insisted that the minorities were victims of the majority groups. He refused to make distinctions. Maybe it was a way of simplifying the problem, and thus finding a straightforward solution, as per the civil war encounter between federal and Biafran forces. Maybe he considered it progressive not to engage in fragmenting a nation in which he expressed faith. But the very struggle for Ogoni autonomy is predicated upon a preparedness to fragment what was, and is, a superficial unity. One would have liked to as Saro-Wiwa today, how he reads the post-1993 events, whether he still believes in a devilish collusion among the so-called majorities.

If Saro-Wiwa had contemplated the entity called Nigeria with the same care that he gave the Ogoni condition, he would have realized that, at least from the first coups of 1966, Nigerian leadership embarked upon, at first subtle, then bold-faced, *nothernization* in which the Hausa-Fulani gradually entrenched themselves in power.[8]

Within that configuration, the evolution of the military is of particular interest; for, each coup witnessed a change of personnel, elimination of individuals and groups, and the building of new power-bases. We repeat that in its thirty-eight years of independence, Nigeria has been ruled by the military for almost thirty years. All but two of the military Heads of State have been Hausa-Fulani. In the civilian interregnum, the only Prime Minister and the only executive President that Nigeria ever had were both from the same ethnic group. It would be useful to examine statistics on members of the officer-corps. The strong feeling here is, that there has been a deliberate attempt to reduce the number of non-Hausa-Fulani either through forced retirement, or physical elimination.

Saro-Wiwa was one of those that cooperated (cynics would say, collaborated, or conspired) with military dictators. The usual reason proffered for such action is, that it is necessary to the process of democratization and development. On several occasions in 1993, Saro-Wiwa met with members of the military regime. He seemed to still have some faith in them (see *Month*: 172). He still enjoyed small but significant privileges, such as having an overseas trip facilitated by a National Security Adviser friend of his, who retrieved his impounded passport (174).

As the 1990-1992 President of the Association of Nigerian Authors (ANA), Saro-Wiwa showed that it was possible to work in a sensitive post, in a country ruled by a military dictatorship, and maintain a high level of integrity. The renowned Nigerian poet, Niyi Osundare, attests to Saro-Wiwa's strong desire to become the association's president, and his readiness to perform his duties to the best of his ability. Saro-Wiwa was instrumental in obtaining for ANA the highest literary award, the Nigerian Newsprint Corporation Prize, worth 25,000 naira. Thus, the Association benefited from Saro-Wiwa's position as a board-member of the corporation. Osundare also recalls that a most memorable donation by the same corporation, was a used bus which went a long way in facilitating ANA's activities. Saro-Wiwa also mooted the idea of a journal for the association.

I brought to Osundare's attention, a 1993 argument between a member of ANA and Saro-Wiwa's successor as President, Odia Ofeimum, over the member's allegation that ANA was anti-government, and therefore involved in politics when it should be apolitical. I wondered whether such allegations were ever made about Saro-Wiwa. In Osundare's view, ANA's relationship with the government was normal during Saro-Wiwa's tenure. "He was never accused of selling out, or being too radical." Osundare added: "Odia wasn't against government either; he was against bad governance. We should also remember that both Ken and Odia served ANA during two different (?) military dictatorships... Ken was not the fire-eating radical. Even in the Ogoni case, it was not radicalism that drove him. It was communal commitment to people's plight. He was not a Marxist. Not pro- or anti-government." These comments would appear to run counter to that of another Nigerian who, comparing Saro-Wiwa and Obasanjo, believes "Saro-Wiwa was a revolutionary and often argued strongly in favor of a radical overhaul of the entire Nigerian polity, while Obasanjo favored an evolutionary process." (Ojo: 142) Whether one considers him a moderate or a radical, one continues to perceive a certain ambiguity in the combination of activities in which Saro-Wiwa engaged, as well as the personalities to whom he related.

Ironically, the very political act which Saro-Wiwa condemned as undemocratic and irrelevant to Ogoni interests, has led to the current stasis and a linkage between the Ogoni plight and that of other Nigerians held in bondage by dictatorship. When Saro-Wiwa led his people to a successful boycott of the 1993 presidential elections,[9] he did not know that the results would not be released specifically because a non-Hausa-Fulani (a Yoruba) was the winner. He continued on his Ogoni path, paying no attention to the unfolding larger problems. Had he lived, he probably would have happily come together with others in a struggle which his people's aspirations have, in a way, galvanized. Soyinka describes Saro-Wiwa as "a feisty and passionate writer," as metaphor, and the Ogoni as "the first Nigerian experimentation with 'ethnic cleansing'." The Nobel laureate continues: "Ogoniland is, alas, only the model space for the actualization of a long- dreamt totalitarian onslaught on the more liberated, more politically sophisticated sections of the Nigerian polity, which have dared expose and confront the power obsession of a minuscule but obdurate military-civilian hegemony." (*The Open Sore*: 6) So, the *Ogonization* of Nigeria, the decidedly brutish domination of the people by a power-hungry clique ready to mow down any dissident, poses a problem that includes and, indeed, goes beyond, the particularity of Ogoni. And, in every debate, in every assessment, the shadow of the military stands taller than the rest.

This is a military that has no qualms claiming to be democratic. It must be special, this Nigerian illogicality. Hardly do these patriotic leaders talk of hierarchy, authority, lack of initiative, orders that must be followed to the letter, and the law of the gun, all patent facts and factors of their rulership. Rather, they mouth a desire to establish, and to nurture, a "home-grown democracy."

THE WEST AND NIGERIA

No surprise, because *democracy* is the word the Western powers love to hear. Witness the articles in American newspapers, for instance. "After 35 years, Nigerians still stumbling along road to Democracy," laments Stephen Buckley (*The Washington Post*, Oct. 1, 1995: A1/A28). Nigerian dictators play the word-game to the hilt. After seizing power, the present one imitated his predecessor and announced a "transition to democracy." Even as he has continued to manipulate people and his phantom policies to suit his purpose -to remain in power-, Western rulers and their powerful media insist that he be given a chance to democratize. The most astonishing comment of recent times came from no less a master than the American President, Bill Clinton, during a visit to Africa. He and his host, President Mandela, held a press conference in Cape Town, South

Africa, at which a question was asked about American support of authoritarian regimes, particularly the Nigerian regime which sells to the United States about 50% of its oil. Clinton responded by affirming Nigeria's major role in regional security, that is, in Liberia and Sierra Leone.[10] He stated: "My policy is *to do all that we can to persuade General Abacha to move toward general democracy* and respect for human rights... *If he stands for election, we hope he will stand as a civilian.* There are many military leaders who have taken over chaotic situations in African countries, but have moved toward democracy. And that can happen in Nigeria."[11] Those remarks may be disconcerting, but only to those hoodwinked by American rhetoric. For, the United States must know that the so-called democratizing process in Nigeria has lacked every basic element making for real democracy. The process has been overtly manipulated with impunity. It seems always set up to fail. In Nigeria, they call it rigging, that is, reaching the conclusion before beginning the process. The five political parties sanctioned for the ongoing exercise in futility, have proven to be what is now popularly known as "five fingers of the same leprous hand."[12] Playing the role of obedient servants, they recently announced that Abacha is their one choice as presidential candidate. In response, the regime has said that, instead of elections, a referendum will be held. Clinton's words of encouragement were most welcome by the government; they have taken the President's statement as a sign of American support for Abacha to remain as Nigeria's savior. It will be interesting to see how the Nigerian version of the theater of the absurd unfolds.

One may do well to define democracy and, no doubt, the result of such an exercise would reveal the West's shallow, or lack of, interest in freedom, justice, and national development in Africa. In democracy, at least the following elements must be present: political competition for office, and in policy-making; the people's freedom to participate in the process, through partisan politics, allowing them to choose their representatives in governance; accountability of rulers to the ruled through a system of representation and a free press, and an independent judiciary upholding the rule of law and all citizens' equality. Freedom is a watchword of democracy. To express one's views without fear of retribution. To associate with others as one sees fit. To seek any public office of one's choice. Freedom goes with rights, and with responsibility, not only of the led but, most importantly, of the leaders who must realize that they are not above the law; that they are in the people's service; that they are not privileged masters, but equal to everyone else. Above all, to the common person, democracy is subsumed in the right to live, and thrive, in a country that one calls one's home.

Of course, there can be no one, single definition acceptable to everyone or every group. Which, however, does not mean that every and any animal can decide to throw out all reason and concoct some illegality and madness in the name of democracy. That, unfortunately, is exactly what has been happening in Nigeria. The rulers have seized upon the controversy and flexibility of the term. They emphasize its Western origin, so as to reject it as an instrument of imperialism unacceptable to the free daughters and sons of Africa. Such hypocrites would claim not to know that democracy as a concept is not new to even pre-colonial Africa. Meanwhile, Africa's self-chosen democrats craft crazy policies and patterns purporting to prepare the way for some so-called Nigerian democracy which, according to them, is based upon the spirit of cooperation, and rejecting the idea of winner-takes-all. Each new ruler, upon ascending to the seat of power, loudly announces a new beginning, of another journey to the paradise of Democracy. The most annoying part of the whole fraud is the ease with which the West, the self-appointed police of global democratization, buys such a lie. But, then, should one be surprised?

It does not take much intellectual effort to realize that the military, in any setting, cannot symbolize, cannot choreograph, cannot construct, democracy. Therefore, all the time-consuming, money-squandering programs to nowhere called transition, should have been shown up for what they are, from the instant the new arrival climbs the stairs to the podium to make the usual speech about salvaging (savaging!) the stillborn nation. Nigeria's history of coups ought to have instructed the international community that the military has been about spilling blood, killing perceived opponents, cowering the population into silence, with one goal, to keep power, absolutely. The foreign keepers of democracy, themselves hypocrites and selfish imperialists, pretend not to know, not to see. The Nigerian dictators, always getting wiser, would now mouth democracy, for a while. They would announce the release of a few prisoners. They would even announce a date for handing over to "a democratically elected government."[13] Foreign powers, elated by this sign of what they call progress and, blinded by Nigeria's crude, would applaud in unison. One or two of them would threaten to impose sanctions if the dictator fails to keep his word. Then, it is business as usual: Oil, Nigeria's "Bonny light," among the best in the world, incessantly flows out, on its merry way to the civilized storage in America while, in Nigeria, there has been fuel scarcity for some five years.

Since we are here concerned with the Saro-Wiwa example, a few questions come to mind. Can chronic coup-makers claim the right to condemn fellow travelers on the armored train, because the latter's coach stalled on the tracks before reaching the destination where power resides? Can those whose very breath reeks of blood seriously bring to book a group forced to use counter-violence to defend their right to life and survival? And, in the Ogoni saga, we are not going as far as to note the lack of firepower of the besieged oil-owners as against the sophisticated weaponry of the bloodhounds backed by officialdom. Oil, one daresay, is more valuable than human life! The South African Nobel laureate in literature, Nadine Gordimer, notes:"In Nigeria, you can be put to death for placing humble human well-being as a value even equal to, let alone above, the value of oil profits." (In *The Guardian*, Lagos, June 2, 1997: 35)

In the infamous trial, Nigerian government tried to play the innocent: The humanitarian, peace-loving, progressive regime determined to protect its citizens against any aggressors, arrested Saro-Wiwa and his cohort of killers. Whereas, in truth, the regime itself was built on violence, injustice, and lawlessness. Did the United States and other powers not know that the government of Nigeria was at once accuser, judge, jury, and executioner, in the case? Were they unaware that the special tribunal has been one of the all too common creations urged to work towards a guilty verdict against anyone accused by the government?

While the United States has tried to hide behind one finger, as it were, several analysts have revealed its policy of self-interest in the Saro-Wiwa case, as well as others. "There can be no illusion over the importance of the oil industry to Nigeria," declares Gordimer. That importance goes for the United States, too. Firstly, Shell, Chevron, and other exploiters, have never bothered to establish any meaningful safety standards in Nigeria, whereas, in Euro-America, they are compelled to respect human lives and ecology. When the *Exxon Valdez* spilled oil into the seas, the company had to pay $5 billion damages. Taxes to Euro-American governments are also high, and regular. In Nigeria, the story is often told that only the oil companies know exactly how much oil they pump out of the land; whoever among the Nigerian employees tries to find such information, runs the risk of being sent to eternal rest in the seabed or in the belly of a big fish. Secondly, the United States may talk till doomsday about democracy. That, in fact, is secondary to its economic interests. African authoritarian regimes are able to survive with American support, because it derives something concrete from them. The late Mobutu of Zaire is but one example.[14] Nigeria's precious oil brand is coveted by any and every oil buyer, and it comes relatively cheap to America which, in the dark days of the Middle -East crisis of the 60s, turned from the Arabs to Nigeria. And Nigeria is also a big market for other kinds of trade, due to its vast riches and population. Now, one can, in all cynicism, understand why the United States is refusing to concretize the contents of its own constitution based on human rights, freedom, equality, and democracy.

Saro-Wiwa's death elicited from all and sundry, at home and abroad, pleas for clemency. The Nigerian dictatorship's decision to dispatch the condemned men to their death, during the meeting of Commonwealth leaders in Auckland, shocked many people. However, those aware of the personality of the regime's leader, did expect him to dare anyone to do their worst, because he knew well enough that they would bark, but not bite. They could scratch, but not scorch, their invaluable economic ally.[15] Since that late 1995 relatively difficult period, the Nigerian government has learnt useful lessons in the art of lobbying, which must be essential to democracy!

Lobbying demands money, and Nigeria has it to burn; hence, the ease with which the governments carries out its shameless propaganda overseas. The United States claims to uphold the rights of the most criminally-minded. It is therefore normal to find Nigeria's extensive advertising supplements in expensive publications, such as *The Wall Street Journal* (April 21, 1997: D1-D16). An "Open Letter to President Clinton," was published in *The New York Times* (Oct. 25, 1994: A10-11) by "Committee of Concerned Delegates of the National Constitutional Conference," begging Clinton for compassion and support for the government. As usual, the group claimed to be "committed to democratic civil rule." Lobbying requires the expertise of that mercenary group of *lobbyists* capable of strutting in the corridors of power, to open doors, and to pressurize decision-makers to exercise patience with despots trying to democratize.

Lucy Komisar, a correspondent of *The American Reporter* (no.250, March 22, 1996), provides some eye-opening facts on "American lobbyists feeding on repressive Nigeria." They include present and past congressmen and women, and State Department officials. Among them are Democrats and Republicans; usually, the former are African Americans, the latter, whites. Adwoa Dunn-Mouton, ex-staff director of the Senate Africa Subcommittee, and Leonard Robinson, former State Department deputy assistant secretary for Africa, are working in the firm of Washington and Christian. Robert Washington, once chief counsel to Rep. Charles Diggs of Michigan, is quoted as stating that there is no viable alternative to Abacha. On the case of Saro-Wiwa, he said: "There was a trial. We have African Americans put in jail every day and having capital punishment... I can't be responsible for everything my client does."

Usually respectable African Americans have been targeted by the Nigerian regime. As a matter of atavism, or materialism, quite a number have responded positively. Jesse Jackson, President Clinton's special envoy to Africa, is an advocate of moderation. Louis Farrakhan, leader of the Nation of Islam, has traveled to Nigeria on several occasions to express support for a fellow Moslem nation.[16] To simultaneously reward Farrakhan and shame his country, the Nigerian regime changed the name of the street where the American embassy is located in Lagos, to Louis Farrakhan Avenue.[17] There is the Baptist leader, Rev. Lyons, who, while battling against charges of embezzlement and adultery at home, found solace and stardom in Nigeria's capital as the government attempts to show its extra- Moslem popularity. In addition, Senator Moseley-Braun, the only African American in her country's senior house, is a well known friend of the military junta. Finally, and perhaps the most convincing example of the power of almighty dollar, Rep. Jefferson of Louisiana, Abiola's one-time friend and the very first anti-Nigerian regime campaigner in congress, is now so devoted to the junta that he would leave whatever he is doing, to answer their call and do their bidding. True that some African Americans have withstood the onslaught of the buying-and-selling political hawkers. Among them: Randall Robinson of TransAfrica; Rep. Maxine Waters, chairperson of the Black Caucus; and former United States ambassador to Nigeria, Walter Carrington.[18] Unfortunately, such voices of honor in support of justice, civil rights, freedom, and true progress, remain but a whisper in the cacophony of vociferous yells on behalf of those dealing away whatever is left of Nigeria's destiny.

Saro-Wiwa's death, his companions', and subsequent events moving Nigeria more closely to the abyss, reveal what Soyinka calls "the comatose nature of global conscience" (*The Open Sore*: 152). They also challenge Nigerians, in particular, to ruminate on Saro-Wiwa's poignant question as the hangmen were trying desperately to make the rusty, rickety scaffold squeeze life out of the human ram: "What sort of a nation is this?" Saro-Wiwa's activism and the government's reaction serve the purpose of showing how fragmented have been the forces of progress. I recall Osundare's words, "One of the reasons tyranny succeeds is the tyrant's ability to sow discord within the oppressed." The Ogoni elite, the elders, who saw in Saro-Wiwa a threat and an enemy to be eliminated, must not have understood that they were mere instruments to be used and thrown away like dirty rags. Nor were they aware that it could be their turn to twist to their death from the master's order. Or, did they know, and simply could care less? Those fellow Nigerians trudging along in misery, or wallowing in their ill-gotten wealth, and thinking only of self-survival, must not be aware that the Ogoni example might be the first step towards the subjugation of everyone by that hegemony convinced that the Almighty created them to be rulers. Or, are they, and resigned to God's will as they congregate in prayers to prepare for life hereafter? Indeed, prayer seems to have become the daily bread of many a Nigerian. Strange bedfellows, all those growing numbers seeking peace in various churches and mosques. They include former and current dictators and conspirators, such as the civil war hero, Gowon. The personalities involved lend weight to the belief that Nigeria is truly a big fraud.

In his final speech before the special tribunal (*Tempo*, Oct.12, 1995: 15), Ken Saro-Wiwa appraised the country's condition, thus: "The presence of oil and gas does not mean automatic wealth. If it were so, Nigeria should be rich and not a debt-ridden country with educational, health and other services in a parlous state, its people hungry and malnourished. The only beneficiaries of oil wealth are the multinational oil companies and their shareholders." No doubt that his judges were angered at such defiance and straightforward condemnation of a country blessed with everything but mired in corruption, deceit, and thoughtlessness. Saro-Wiwa's works, which we shall study closely in the following chapters, offer a detailed assessment of that sad country. They also show how, due to his refusal to succumb to threats and overtures by internal colonizers, he simply had to die. Talking of Nigeria itself, Saro-Wiwa's life and works may be reason enough to fear that the worst is yet to come.

NOTES TO CHAPTER 1

1. This exiled Nigerian is one of several who kindly agreed to talk to me, but on condition of anonymity. Their fear of reprisal from Nigeria's repressive regime underscores the seriousness of the current situation in that country.

2. Nigeria's enigma is embedded in a system, and a society, built on rumors, half-truths, and lies. Take, for instance, the civil war. No reliable records exist. Those in charge were either not interested, or they doctored or destroyed, documents. Another point: no one is certain of the population figures; yet a great deal of policies depend on those imaginary numbers, e.g., budget allocation to states.

3. For example, see Chris McGreal, "Ken Saro-Wiwa: Not entirely innocent?" in *Weekly Mail & Guardian*, April 4, 1996.

4. One has ample reason to question the quality of Chukwumerije himself. As information minister, he was known for peddling dis- and mis-information, a pattern espoused by his successors in office, such as Ofonagoro.

5. The late Panafricanist musician, Fela Anikulapo-Kuti (died Aug. 1997), had an appropriate description for military operatives: *Kill and go*, that is, morons made to follow orders to maim and murder, carrying them out absolutely, then moving on to the next assignment, without looking back, without any sense of remorse or guilt.

6. It is true that not every Igbo finds Saro-Wiwa's murder justifiable. Nonetheless, many, if not most, no doubt believe that he deserved what he got.

7. Some see Nigeria's continuing change for the worse in terms of the personalities of Babangida, a smart dictator for whom power was "an intellectual challenge," and Abacha, a mole "incapable of the faculty of defining the intensive light" of an oncoming vehicle, and a man with "no idea of Nigeria." (Soyinka, *The Open Sore of a Continent*: 14) Soyinka is currently living in exile, and he and others have been charged *in absentia* for treason.

8. It would be advisable to go back further, to the attainment of independence in 1960, when the Northern Region refused decolonization and had to be coaxed into it with assurances of political power at the center. A most astounding development, when it was others who had struggled, made sacrifices, and prepared themselves for post-colonial life through a period of self-government.

9. Since the annulment of those elections, Nigeria has been in turmoil.
See Gani Fawehinmi's comments in *TheNews*, March 23, 1998: 19; and Soyinka, *The Open Sore*: 34-44.

10. Another first for Nigeria: It must be the only country in the world that simultaneously insists on killing democracy at home while spending billions of dollars and sacrificing precious human lives to restore same in another country. The West is very impressed with that great performance, no doubt.

11. The White House Office of the Press Secretary (Cape Town, South Africa), "Press Conference by President Clinton and President Mandela," March 27, 1998. Emphasis mine.

12. Phrase coined by erstwhile civilian governor of Oyo State, Bola Ige, and often used by observers critical of the political process.
For example, see *TELL*, Feb.23, 1998: 20; interview given by Abubakar Umah, retired colonel and a northern "blue blood" who, since the 1993 annulment, has been calling on the military regime to declare the results and let the winner, Abiola, form a national government as a prelude to a conference that would determine the country's future.

13. One awaits, with baited breath, a serious study of the destruction of democratic process in Nigeria. An excellent document to use for establishing the deep-rooted deceit, lies, and arrant callousness symbolized by the rulers, would be the series of take-over declarations, and the inaugural speeches of newly arrived Heads of State or, in the case of Babangida, military executive President.

14. After President Clinton's 1998 visit to Africa, the American Congress has been debating "the Africa Bill," meant to strengthen economic ties with the continent. Essential to this process is, naturally, what America will gain from it.
See The Washington Post editorial, "Wrong About Africa," Jan. 13, 1995: A22. "A growing, politically open and prosperous Africa promotes our long-term economic and political interests," states the writer.

15. The scenario of pleas for clemency after a death-conviction, is fast becoming another Nigerian trademark, a source of boredom, and a shameful joke. Before Saro-Wiwa, there was the Vatsa group, shot by the Babangida-Abacha regime while everyone was scampering to the presidential palace to beg for mercy. After Saro-Wiwa, there were Obasanjo and others, whose death and life convictions were commuted, in a political act. Now, in mid-1998, Abacha's deputy, Diya, is awaiting death, and governments, organizations, and private individuals, are on their bended knees before a man who must be enjoying the power to decide who will live, and who will die.
See Wafula B. James, "Good Abacha; hang Oladipo [Diya]," commentary, The Monitor (in Africa on line, May 7, 1998). James wonders why "no one has taken time to examine whether, in the first place, General Diya was guilty of the offence."

16. By its Constitution, Nigeria is a secular state. Nonetheless, from the Babangida reign until now, the government has been islamizing the country. It has been participating in the affairs of the Organization of Islamic Conference (OIC). First, it was claimed that the country enjoyed only an observer status. In May 1998, the Sultan of Sokoto, president of the Nigerian Supreme Council of Islamic Affairs, announced that the country has changed its status to a full member. The usual, contentious debate has ensued.
See Post Express, May 8, 1998.

17. The name-change was a direct reaction to the New York City Council's decision to name a Manhattan street corner in memory of Kudirat Abiola, the assassinated wife of the jailed Nigerian presidential election winner. It is widely believed that the Nigerian authorities spent a great deal of money to fight that act of honor. A notable African American, Roy Innis, is Nigeria's pointsman in New York.

18. Carrington worked assiduously as ambassador (1993-97), to make Nigeria change for the better. He was harassed by officialdom. The send-off party organized in his honor by his friends, was stormed by military and police. Carrington, who is married to a Nigerian, recently made a statement to Maryland State House during debate of a bill to sanction Nigeria (Africa Policy Information Center, April 7, 1998).
Several private businesses and individuals opposed the bill. The State Department also sent word discouraging the State from taking unilateral action that could jeopardize government policy, and American economic interests in Nigeria.

II. *SOZABOY*: A DARK SATIRE OF NIGERIA'S CIVIL WAR VICTIMS

—"I do not know why we are fighting the war."[1]
—"Even sef I don't want to think.
What they talk we must do. Myself, if they say fight, I fight.
If they say no fight, I cannot fight. Finish."[2]

INTRODUCTION: A NOVEL IN "ROTTEN ENGLISH"

Ken Saro-Wiwa immediately makes himself controversial in the "Author's Note" to this, his first novel with a descriptive/restrictive title. But first, let us present the plot; it is the first-person narrative of a naive young primary-school leaver, Mene, of the village of Dukana in Eastern Nigeria. It is the civil-war period and the fighting is approaching Dukana. Mene's ambition is rather pedestrian, to obtain his driver's license, make money, buy his own lorry, thus become "a big man"...Until he meets a girl who fled from Lagos, Agnes. It is Agnes, who says her husband must be a soldier, so as to defend her, and Zaza, a world war veteran bragging of his exploits, and constantly harassing Mene, not to mention the lure of the respected uniform, that initially press the young man to enlist. Soon after he pays his way to join the army (he is first rejected as being too short), his village is bombed and deserted, and evacuated. His unit is also bombed; he is captured, escapes, and all the while determined to return home to find his mother and wife, Agnes who, in the meantime, died during an earlier raid. He finally returns home only to learn of the tragic news and to find that his people, informed of his death, now consider him a ghost killing people. To save his skin, he is forced to flee the village forever. Let us quote the author's words on the artistic result of his "fascination with the adaptability of the English language" and of his close observation of the speech and writing of "a certain segment of Nigerian society":

> "Sozaboy's language is what I call 'rotten English', a mixture of Nigerian pidgin English, broken English and occasional flashes of good, even idiomatic English. This language is disordered and disorderly. Born of a mediocre education and severely limited opportunities, it borrows words, patterns and images freely from the mother-tongue and finds expression in a very limited English

vocabulary. To its speakers, it has the advantage of having no rules and no syntax. It thrives on *lawlessness*."

Critics have been greatly impressed by this statement, so much so that the vast majority of them have limited their views to this linguistic aspect of the novel (see, for example, Charles Nnolim, ed., *Critical Essays of Ken Saro- Wiwa's Sozaboy*, 1992). It is easy to fall into such a trap, because the eponymous hero is the narrator of the story, thereby supposedly the creator, the maker of his history, enjoying an independence unknown to others enslaved to the whims of the omniscient narrator. In other words, Mene, Sozaboy, has the will to manipulate the English language in his "disorderly" manner, borrowing freely from his "mother-tongue." Yet, it remains a basic fact that the novelist can never be absent from his novel, and that, no matter how hard he tries, he cannot, as we say, hide behind one finger. Reading *Sozaboy*, I agree with critics that it "throbs vibrantly enough and communicates effectively" (author's notes). On the other hand, I do not see those mother-tongue patterns and images referred to by the author (whose/which mother-tongue?), nor do I perceive any particular "rottenness" in the language as distinct from other bastardized, any Africanized, forms of English practiced everyday in the former British colonies.

For the benefit of those interested in the language debate, let us refer to a few critical perspectives on *Sozaboy*. According to Augustine Okere, "the language of *Sozaboy* is the product of two impulses: the impulse to rebel against the norms of English set by the elite oppressors and the impulse to amalgamate the narrator's very limited knowledge of English with the resources of his mother-tongue in order to communicate to an audience larger than the usual novel-reading elite." (*Critical Essays*: 10) Such an outlandish statement is debunked by the fact that Sozaboy at no time "rebels" against the elite's language because, indeed, the elite (Saro-Wiwa?) Themselves do not set any norms—it is not their language! Furthermore, the larger audience does not, cannot, read this story. The quoted comment somehow raises an important question, that of Saro-Wiwa' s audience.[3] With the long glossary of words and expressions at the end of the novel, it would appear that the novelist is seeking an international audience. Which, nevertheless should not mean that his primary audience is not local, Nigerian, and therefore informed and engaged in the use of rotten English.

Helen Chukuma states that "this quaint and robust language must be confronted and overcome as one overcomes the first splashes of cold water during a bath on a biting cold harmattan morning." (*Critical Essays*: 39). The critic would appear to have forgotten that the majority of the people are used to harmattan and cannot even afford a hot-water bath. Hence, they are at home with the robust language from which they derive a great deal of *humor*. We agree with Asomwan Adagboyin: "Humor is the effect much of the language used achieves in *Sozaboy*." (*Critical Essays*: 37).

To my mind, by far the most cogent criticism of the novel is that of the editor of *Critical Essays*, Nnolim, who points out that what Saro-Wiwa dubs "rotten English" is "natural" and "not unexpected considering the narrator's background and the context. "And no reader will deny that Sozaboy's unconventional usage of English is fresh, with its own vibrancy, its internal dynamics, its own piquant moments, its felicities, its unforced consistency, its own registers, and is a mighty vehicle of the humour, the irony and the tragedy of the novel." (76). This English "of the half-literate, poorly-educated, English-speaking Nigerian," must therefore be viewed as a matter of normalcy, and symptomatic of, and consequential to, a certain psychological conflict, between the hero's occasional use of idiomatic English and the usual "jargon" (note: an elitist standpoint) into which he relapses. It all reveals the confusion in the hero and his society, the futility which the novel dramatizes, indeed, the inferiority complex of a people enslaved by the standard of an imported language (and culture), and living in limbo in a situation where they "have not [their] being."

Saro-Wiwa's text allows a deep analysis of this psychological problem, specifically in the context of a meaningless civil war, if one is not misled by the statement in his "Author's Note." And the problem, it need be emphasized, does not exclude the author himself. The very first sentence of the novel introduces us to the world of dislocation, disarray, disorder. "Although everybody in Dukana was happy at first." (*Sozaboy*: 1). Normally, a conjunction implies another clause, another reality, a fact, to be considered and compared to the first reality presented. Sequence and Consequence. Cause and Effect. Harmony and Disharmony due to the presence of two forces. In Mene's world, no such topic exists. And that is a state that runs through the novel. It is also noteworthy that it is *not only* Mene that uses "rotten English"; everyone does, and certain words and mannerisms (e.g. *props* = perhaps; *porson* = person) are fashionable in everyone's diction. Also interesting is the rare use of the mother-tongue, Kana.: when the soldiers arrive to harass the villagers of Dukana into providing them with food, the Chief, Birabee, calls Mene and speaks to him in Kana. The "thick man who preaches in church and tells the young man to join the army, sings in Kana. For his sermon, Mene wonders, "Will he speak English and use terpita [interpreter] or will he speak Kana?" The man speaks English, choosing a parable from the Bible. Mene is impressed, and confused: "Abi, dis man think that we are in University? Am I not common motor apprentice?" (42). That, no doubt, is the main problem posed by the language dislocation; the idiomatic English symbolizes a condition, a state a position of privilege, a world to which the vast majority are not committed; yet they are expected to, they want to operate there, because it represents a heaven away from the hell to which they are used.

Thus, Mene is effusive in his love for the English language. In his work as apprentice driver, he always speaks English to passengers and other drivers and apprentices. He buys books at the motor park, to "improve [his] English. So I was getting money and learning plenty things." (12). Talking of his new girl-friend, "Agnes na good name. Na English name. I like am." (18). In one of his bad dreams, he sees a man talking to the villagers to join the army:

"The man h fine shirt stood up. And begin to talk in English. Fine fine English. Big big words. Grammar. 'Fantastic. Overwhelming. Generally. In particular and in general'. Haba, God no go vex. But he did not stop there. The big grammar continued. 'Odious. Destruction. Fighting'... Long long grammar. 'Ten heads. Vandals. Enemy.' Everybody was silent... Then they begin to interpret all that long grammar plus big big words in Kana. In short what the man is saying is that all those who can fight will join army." (46-47).

Anyone who speaks "fine fine English" never ceases to make an impression on him; so also does anyone, such as his army friend Bullet, who "have read plenty book." (91).

Now, due to his lack of understanding (internalized inferiority complex), Mene is not always happy with those speaking that "fine fine English," and he complains of his ignorance. Of Bullet: "I don't like how he used to talk big big grammar sometimes." (12). Rather than reject the incomprehensible language, he, however, strives to improve himself, to be worthy of the language. He continues to learn, until "even the big big grammar that used to confuse me proper proper before no dey confuse me too much again. Even, I can speak some big big grammar sometimes myself... And I will say it carefully with my mouth and with style so that if you hear me talking by that time, *you will even think that I am oyibo man*. Even Bullet come give me one book and every time when I get small chance I will try to read the book." (93, emphasis mine). The implication is very clear, that *oyibo* man is superior, and it is a point that we need to bear in mind in reading all of Saro-Wiwa's work.[4] Mene's assessment of people and situations depends as much on his vaunted *naivete* as on this basic inferiority complex. And it is all part of the humor, the satire of this tragic novel. As a hospitalized prisoner of war, the hero meets the man who is his nemesis, Manmuswak, who, on this occasion appears to be his friend and brother. The man tells Mene that, in a period of hallucination, the sick Mene was "talking mambo-jambo like stupid idiot goat. Mambo-jambo. I like that word. Mambo-jambo. And that is what I was talking." And when he hears others, he says they are all talking "mambo-jambo." (119)

MENE, THE "NAIVE" HERO

Our "mambo-jambo" man is of simple background. He introduces himself to us as "free-born of Dukana" (full citizen, not a slave),[5] having lost his father but still with a mother that sends him through primary school which he finishes with distinction. Due to dearth of funds, he is forced to give up further education and thus loses the opportunity to become "big man like lawyer or doctor riding car and talking big big English" (11). He mentions his pain at this loss of opportunity, particularly since English was one of his best subjects at school. His consolation: when he becomes a licensed driver (the profession he is now learning), he can become "big man like any lawyer or doctor."

However, unknown to him the setting o f his story, the outbreak of the civil war, the birth of "the new government of soza and police" and the death of "the old, bad government" (1), are to change his life, forever. The irony—and Saro-Wiwa's novel is full of it—is that Mene and his fellow villagers are singing and dancing to welcome the death of their dreams. In that wise, and that at the very beginning of the novel, the hero's naivete is not singular, but communal; and, in reality, those knowledgeable of the Nigerian civil war would admit that such crazy celebration is common spectacle (not to forget the people's reaction to another *coup d'etat* announcing the continuing incarceration of the people's soul). We must at the same time note that this naive Mene is not so simple or so gullible after all: he asks questions, he expresses his *confusion*[6] regarding the whole, sudden change to "better" government, particularly given the similar suddenness of the return (did any change actually occur?) of "bad." Talking of personal ambitions, the irony is, that Mene's do not change even while he is engaged in the war. When the village Pastor, Barika, predicts that, with the advent of "trouble" (war), the world will soon come to an end, the outraged Mene reacts thus: "I no like that one at all. How will the world end and I never get my licence? (...) And I never marry self?" (5). That is his reason for calling the Pastor useless. A similar reaction occurs when the chief, Birabee, announces levies to support the war effort. "What will happen? I never marry. My mama go vex with me because I never marry yet and the world don begin to end." (9) Paradoxically, the seemingly simple opinion on the lack of godliness and of integrity on the part of those two "VIPs" [very important personalities] is later borne out by their vicious acts during the war.

  With personal ambitions come selfishness, exploitation of others, and failure/refusal to see reason and to face facts. Like his master, the driver of the lorry, "Progres," Mene is happy that there is "trouble," so that they can "make plenty money" (5) from the masses of the people running away; they charge passengers "as lawyers used to charge people who get case. Heavy." (3) Because he travels outside of the village, making the Dukana-Pitakwa run, Mene considers himself superior to others; for, another town is "another world." He even has some delusion of grandeur and wisdom from his two-year experience: "If not to say I am very old man in Pitakwa self I should have confused completely." (52) he basks in this sunlight of "civilizatoin": "they will begin to ask me of how the world is." (38) His narcissistic cloak makes him call everyone in Dukana stupid and ignorant. "All those people do not know anything." (4) "These simple people" [fishermen and farmers] are to be looked down upon, and even pitied. In reacting to the people's celebration of the new moon, he says: "True, true, these people no get sense at all. How can they be dancing, singing and joking when there is trouble for the country? If they no take time something will happen for this town and when that thing will happen it is because they cannot *think* as other people are thinking." (36)

there is that key word that Saro-Wiwa will accord particular significance in his work. If Dukanans had thought about the war and escaped before the battle reached their village, maybe the devastation would have been avoided...But, more importantly, if all of Nigeria, particularly the leaders, had thought about the consequences of war, maybe the tragedy could have been avoided. At this juncture, it is patent that Mene's naivete is not as all-pervasive as some critics would have us believe. His personality, by the same token, proves to be quite complex.

Mene's superiority complex does not annul his pride at being a Dukanan. "It is my own very village." (18) He is also proud to love Agnes, "a Dukana girl" (17). All the Dukanan girls tell him he is "very fine boy" (21), so he has no "surprisation" that Agnes, too, loves him. He has enough elegance to dress well after work, using powder, But-el-Sudan scent...And, he is proud of his profession: "Driver work is good work and drivers must preserve their persy all the time. Otherwise someone can start to mess up with their senior commando." (13) Which does not preclude his being a subordinate to his master, or being a messenger to Chief Birabee.

In fact, more than the naivete highlighted in several studies, what drives Mene's character, is a well embedded tradition of respect for elders and a newly superimposed (modernizing?) artificiality—superficiality coupled with a belief in anything extraordinary or out of this world (new), as well as a desire for acceptance by others which is marked by that superiority complex. We have already addressed the influence of English. Fine clothes, too; for example, the man who comes to talk about the war to Dukanans "is wearing better cloth, so you can see at once that he is a very important person." (46) Therefore he must be believed. Duzia the cripple, the voice of Dukana, "knows everything. Everything. About Dukana. About the world." (7) This is an implicit acceptance of Mene's own ignorance, which makes him very angry at being called stupid by anyone. It is noteworthy that he regularly tells us about his anger at so many situations and events, without however putting this thought to action. "That is what I was saying to myself," (83), never what led him to act. Another facet of this non-action is his fear. While he wishes to exhibit his courage, both at the beginning and after he has joined the army, "fear begin catch [him] small small" (3) until, in the face of death, he takes to his heels.

The decision to join the army dramatizes very well the complex evolution of Mene, what may variously be called his quest for knowledge, his self-search, his growth from adolescence into adulthood, his process of conscientization before the society's corruption and immorality, and—perhaps the most valid judgment of all-his triumph over the dilemma of war. For each of these, however, the very presence of irony and satire makes their negation a strong possibility. The questions are, does the young boy[7] that joins the army grow into a man at the end? Does the naive Mene transform into the experienced, reasonable, perspicacious Sozaboy? Is he any wiser for the tragic experience? Does he become a more likeable character to the reader, or to his creator, the novelist? Is he, as one critic claims, an anti-hero, with "the converse of most of the traditional attributes of the HERO" (Tony Afejudu in *Critical Essays*: 113)?

As the war approaches his village, Mene shows a certain human characteristic by changing his mind on several occasions: He fears the "trouble;" he does not and is ready to go; he is not sure of what to do; then he is sure. This combination of courage and cowardice is overridden by his gullibility as regards tall tales, specifically those recounted by one of the village clowns, the veteran Zaza who strings together incredible stories of Hitler, and Zaza's lies: "Sometimes he is better than Hitla sef. At least he can fight better." (76) Sozaboy's wild whims become so strong that he thinks that, maybe, he and his fellow recruits are going to Burma. Then, he is convinced that they are, only to be brought down to earth when the army lorry screeches to a halt in the war-front. Zaza's Burma fabrications constitute the extreme point of a *culture of rumors* embedded in the society where no one ever knows the truth. This is a result of the villagers' superstitiousness and the larger society's lack of education, a neo-colonial condition used by the rulers as a weapon of oppression and suppression. "People will gather round to talk about what they have heard. And everybody was saying what entered his mind whether it is true or it is not true." (4) In Saro-Wiwa's later works, the impact of rumor-mongering is highlighted. That Mene falls prey to it is not unexpected; the whole of real-life Nigeria was built upon, and lives by, rumors.

Mene's final decision to enlist in the army is precipitated by his girl-friend Agnes whom he wants to marry. When he meets her for the first time, they engage in a discussion on the stories of "trouble" circulating from Lagos to Dukana. "Trouble no dey ring bell," he says, indirectly expressing his fear and uncertainty of the meaning of it all. Agnes's comment: "When trouble come, I like strong brave man who can fight and defend me." (19) There and then, his head full of alcohol and his heart filled with love written in bold figures of the "proper two J.J.C. breasts" bulging "like calabash", "standing like hill" (13) before his mesmerized eyes, Mene begins to think of doing whatever Agnes wants to make her his wife. Although his mother objects-"this Soza business is foolish nonsense" (56)- he does not relent, he cannot relent, because he is a victim of circumstances, not the controller of his destiny. Once again, however, we cannot be absolute in that assertion. Mene exhibits cleverness in trying to please both his mother and Agnes. He will marry Agnes to please the former (all she wants him to do is to marry, have children, take good care of her, and buy her property), and make the latter happy by asking his mother to allow him to go join the army afterwards. After the marriage, there is a lull for a while; life is going on as if there were no "trouble." It is left to Agnes to bring back the idea: "I think you have to go to soza soon. All this fighting...strong man like you cannot stay in the house. And everybody in Dukana is saying that you cannot fight again because you don marry. I do not like that kain talk." (65) After that reminder, nothing happens again for many days until, finally, Mene himself tells the mother; Agnes' tears convince her. Mother: "When husband and wife 'gree on one thing, that is all." (67) From this episode, it is clear that Mene does play a role in the decision to enlist in the army. He proves to the Dukanans that he is not just "woman rapper proper" (that is, attached to his wife like her loin-cloth) but a man, brave and ready to defend her and his people. In his own way, he can claim to be a responsible husband.

Mene's views on the army are expectedly ignorant. Like other villagers, all he knows are Zaza's tall tales, rumors from various sources, the forays of hunger and angry soldiers into their land in search of supplies, the grandiloquent speeches of military officers and their civilian cronies. On the eve of his departure, he enjoys the whole village's support; in the almost solemn atmosphere, there is a unique unity in the air; Mene is a hero, the son of the soil going away to bring back victory, and Dukana is transformed from the backwoods that it is to the road leading to heaven. Mene, "prouding," tells everyone "that I will fight *the Enemy* to nonsense. That I will bring plenty things back to Dukana after-words...I begin to like this Dukana more than [because everyone thinks he is wonderful.] All those houses begin to fine for my eye..."(69) Duzia, Boni and the other clowns go to his house to offer sacrifice to the gods for his safety. For the first and only time, those talkative gossips drink in absolute silence. When Mene leaves in the morning, Agnes and his mother shed hot tears; it is as if this is a keen for a dead man, a premonition of what will occur later in the novel. The solemn departure also resembles a farewell to innocence by Mene.

The *new* sozaboy (another satirical point succinctly made by Saro-Wiwa throughout his work, that Nigerians love anything new), ironically, is not all that new in the sense of change, or transmutation or metamorphosis into a persona with a distinct original character. The traits already witnessed in Mene are still very evident. One, his ambitions are still as personal as ever: "I am proud to be soza with gun. I think that one day I will be like that soza with spectacle, tall and fine speaking with brass band voice, enjoying myself inside fine car and fine house, giving command to small boys who are just entering new soza life." (77) "Power pass power;" therefore, this short man with extraordinary expectations is dreaming of growing tall, and becoming the tallest and the most decorated of officers, "fine fine tall men in fine fine uniform." Two, he is dreaming of returning home a hero, and, three, when the fighting is becoming too fierce for his liking, he is desperate to get back there to save his wife and mother. The consuming irony is, that a short man is convinced that he can increase his height.

The paroxysm of stupidity, too. Sozaboy knows about the military. He does not know that a white handkerchief hoisted by an enemy soldier is a sign of surrender, or truce (92). That trenches (which he calls pits) are dug as safety-pits for sleeping and watching the enemy; for him, they are "like burial ground." (84) The opinion here is, that he is no different from many a recruit pressed into battle by an ill-established, ill-prepared army. Besides, his ignorance is engaging. There is that side of him that has a foreboding of danger and death. Manmuswak, the soldier holding up the white handkerchief, happens to be a spy who, after surveying the location of Sozaboy's unit, facilitates a bomb attack that takes the life of Bullet, Sozaboy's unit leader and best friend. When the unit is bombed out, the trenches do become their burial ground. Such simple smartness is also documented elsewhere, by Sozaboy's seemingly innocent comments or reaction to events. Upon arrival with his mates as replacement for troops moving elsewhere, he observes; "Those who are going away are laughing. Those who are coming in, some are crying. Is this a good thing at all?" (83) "Sozaboy's" narrative has almost lost the laughter that fills the pages of the pre-war narration by "Mene." References to fear have also become rampant in this second section; instead of fearing "small small," he now fears "plenty."

That fear must not be misconstrued as a sign of cowardice. Sozaboy recounts several occasions when his mates burst into tears, while he remains calm. At no time does he fail to carry out his duties, or to obey orders. To all intents and purposes, he has continued to learn, from such people as Tan Papa, his first trainer, and his friend and "san major", Bullet. "War is war," says the first. "War will finish when everybody don die finish," jokes the second. (87) The most evident lesson, remarkably enough, is that war, after all, may not be the heroic exploits fabricated by old Zaza, or the patriotic performances painted by the Chief Commander that visited Dukana. That lesson is the humanization of Sozaboy. He begins to distinguish between himself- "innocent people like myself" (169)- a victim, and those vultures like Manmuswak, using war to suck the blood out of the people. If we say that Sozaboy has bidden farewell to innocence, it is to affirm that he is no longer a naive boy dreaming of wearing a uniform that gives him the image of a powerful hero, without facing, and even succumbing to death. It is the very face of death that ultimately drives home the lesson. Fear thus becomes a constant companion. Afraid that the enemy captain is going to order him shot, he cries and begs" "I will do anything they ask me to do. I will even carry shit. I will be his houseboy and slave anything, but I do not want to die. Because I am young. I do not mind to go the war front sef." (123) But, on another occasion, when the torture in the prison becomes unbearable, he prays for death: "I think it is better to die than to stay alive and suffer as I was suffering that day." (124) Finally, the thought of seeing his wife and mother again gives him the will to live, to run in search of them and his village. This fluctuation between life and death is best understood within the context of Sozaboy's education about war.

He asks the question: "Why are we fighting?" (90) when he begins to understand that fact is different from fiction. The urgency and relevance of his question are made more so by the bomb-raid that kills his mates. Added to that are the experiences of people like Bullet, forced to drink urine because he gave to the recruits cigarettes and drinks hidden by the Major. His conclusion: "War is very bad thing. War is to drink urine, to die and all that uniform that they are giving us to wear is just to deceive us. And anybody who think that uniform is fine thing is stupid man who does not know what is good or bad or not good at all or very bad at all (...) All that one that Zaza is talking about is not true at all. Zaza have not gone to any Burma to fight any Hitla (...) I just carry gun, fight, (...) Everything they tell me, I must do, no question." (113-114)

Yet, and this is one of the overriding and riveting factors of Saro-Wiwa's novel, Sozaboy does ask questions. If he obeys, it is because he is afraid, because he is ignorant, because he has no choice before the power of the gun and the goons commanding him. When he asks, upon reaching the stinking refugee camp, "Which one I dey? Which one be my own?" (157), he is speaking for millions of poor people mesmerized by the military myth. And, as he grown is wisdom, as he begins to see his options and recognize his (albeit skewed) responsibilities, he gradually weans himself of the milk of beastliness offered by the military. He who has been "prouding" like a peacock because of his sozaboy status, reaches a point where he tells the enemy captain, "I am not a soza...I am apprentice driver." (122) During his flight towards freedom, he runs into Zaza, the wily Burma veteran whose high-wise tales of his anti-Hitler exploits contributed to Mene's desire to transform into Sozaboy; the self-proclaimed near-hero instructs him to throw away his gun, the very symbol of military might, the very instrument of survival and supremacy. One irremediable aspect of Mene's character is that superiority complex present in him from the beginning of the story, thrust to the front by his enlistment in the army, and exacerbated and transformed into alienation by the war experience. Saro-Wiwa has convincingly painted the portrait of a *human* protagonist whom we cannot categorize or pigeon-hole, in spite of certain traits shared in common with individuals in his condition and circumstance. Hence, the matter of Mene's *stupidity* remains contentious. Remarkably, it is he, deemed stupid by many a critic, that is quick to call others that: Chief Birabee is "a fool" (45); his fellow Dukanans are "useless people" (46). On the contrary, Mene hates to be called stupid (30); he hates to look stupid, particularly before the girl that he has chosen as wife, Agnes. (16)

THE FEMALE FACTOR

Perhaps the high (or would it be low?) point of Mene's nugatory perspective of his metamorphosis into sozaboy, is the role of the girl Agnes.

> "As I am walking to see Agnes, I begin to glad. I think if is good thing to fight after all. If porson will marry beter woman after the fight. Oh yes, it must be good thing to fight. And I not just fight with hand and leg oh, but better fight with gun. And not just for

Dukana but for Burma. By the time I get to the house of Agnes him mama, my brain don begin to clear small small. I was glad by now. Even, when I think that I will see Agnes again I begin to glad more then. My man begin to stand up like snake wey no get house." (35)

Stupid, or insane, or simply facetious, this young man reaching sexual paroxysm just at the sight of his Lagos-trained beauty? Would it be a matter of chivalry, or chicanery, this idea of going to war in order to be able to protect one's wife from unknown attackers? It would be simplistic to condemn Mene to any category. In truth, he is inextricably and inevitably attached to Agnes; for, the girl is beautiful, experienced, indeed, *civilized* in a sense that only the truly conscious African would condemn. Agnes is a city-girl, having recently returned from Lagos, and therefore considered by everyone to be superior to others. Once this superiority is established, one would understand how quickly she conquers the impressionable Mene.Between the two love birds, it is all a question of physique. He ogles her insatiably, refers incessantly to her "calabash breasts" which she unashamedly bares to him in an instant of audacity and frivolity (14). She is "slender like palm tree" (17); "Beautiful like full moon in Dukana" (57); her "teeth [are] white like paper and her mouth small with black gum" (63). Mene, become sozaboy, and even during his most difficult days, never forgets this his "young wife Agnes with J.J.C." (cf. 119, 122, 126, 129).

For her part, Agnes is impressed by Mene's chest-hair, his smile, his dancing capability, and his "thing wey dey stand like snake wey not get house" (59). At the bar where she is a waitress, she plays for him the record entitled, "Ashewo" (prostitute) and asks him if he is "hungry" because his penis is rising, and she jokingly asks him "make you tell your snake make 'e no too stand like say 'e dey hungry." (14). Agnes's aggressiveness and shameless sensuousness, rather than put off Mene, arrests his attention, forever. A critic of Saro-Wiwa's novel, Helen Chukwuma, correctly talks of the novelist's "ambivalence on women portraiture" (*Critical Essays*: 44). The pertinent question would be whether the portraiture is realistic, is negative in regards to the female character, is chauvinistic...Note that, as Mene himself is from Lagos, and there is definitely a real-life distinction between Lagosian women and those living in the village. Besides, Agnes, a bar-girl, reminds one of such girls serving not only food and drinks but also serving as "service" (13) to satiate the sexual needs of male customers (of the record, "Ashewo"). When Agnes calls Mene "a small boy" (16), she strikes that cord of city superiority that arouses in the villager a feeling of shame and anger, and a determination to elevate himself to the civilized heights. Conceived from this angle, Mene's enrollment in the army becomes a matter of necessity; and the female factor, decisive, absolutely.

"Everybody [in Dukana] say she [Agnes] is clever girl" (20). Mene, naturally agrees: "very clever. She knows so many things. And she is beautiful. Everyone was saying she will make good wife...and she can take good care of me as she used to take good care of her master in Lagos." (22) Here, one sees an element of chauvinism that would *apparently* contradict the forge of the female factor noted above. Let us emphasize the quality of the physical in female-male relationship, not just between Agnes and Mene but in all of the Dukana community. And sleeping with a woman is the daily delight of the men who "carry their prick like bamboo waiting for woman that they will chook." (63); "fuckers [always thinking of] beating woman *toto* like drum" (64). Whenever the village cripple and clown sees Agnes he thinks: "If better man puts his prick into that bottom, he will see Jesus Christ."[8] He and his friends think that it is unadvisable for Mene to marry, (join the army) and leave wife ("fine dish") behind for other people. Coupled with the sexual "beating" is the actual brutality visited on women: "If you love a girl in Dukana then you must beat her small small. That will show that you love her. *But I don't htink that Agnes is just like those stupid Dukana girls*. Even, she can discuss anything you like. She is a clever girl...I must marry her. (37) So, Agnes is special, different, and Mene treats her that way. It is this particularity (superiority) that leads to Mene's enlistment and flirtation with death. In other words, while he shares in the general chauvinism of his community, he sets himself and his woman apart through his own brand of love.

Returning to the theme of male chauvinism, other aspects include, women's silence: "Women do not talk in Dukana meeting. Anything the men talk, the women must do. Dukana people say women does not get mouth. And it is true." (8) Yet, once again, Mene's behavior breaks the rule: Agnes is the determinant of his destiny; after she has spoken, his fate is sealed, forever. Which does not mean that Mene's vaunted manhood is destroyed. Saro-Wiwa is more attached to reality than that. Complementary to Agnes' influence is Mene's forces submission to what he considers a disgraceful search at a road-block by women of the "Simple Defence" (Civil Defense). "I begin to vex because it is not good for my persy to have woman giving me orders." (54) His mother has stood firm against his enlistment, concerned as she is for his safety and survival so that he may marry, have children, take care of her in her old age, and give her proper burial when she dies. After the "Simple Defence" encounter, he asks contemptuously, "So does my mother want me to be woman-man?" (56) In his view, courage, not cowardice, is expected of a man. Therefore by joining the army, he will escape the condition of the victim, the women-man subjugated by the women road-corps; he will be seen as a brave man by his people; and Agnes will be proud of him as her man, her defender, her savior in time of trouble. "No woman whether Simple Defence or no S.D. cannot begin to give me order on the road like say I no sabe anything. And I will wear uniform." (54)

The scope of Saro-Wiwa's satire must always be borne in mind; for, he does not want us to take his characters, or the situation, too seriously. One of the many funny moments of the novel is, when Mene proposes marriage to Agnes. She tells him that he is foolish, that while his mates are joining the army he is desirous of staying home and of marrying "with that your thing standing like snake wey not get house" (38). Funny, but critical. Laughter is not far removed from tears. Mene is serious about marriage and he will do anything necessary to have his woman. Agnes, too, is not just joking. If on the one hand she behaves like a wayward, street-wise and worldly woman fixated upon her personal desires and pleasures, she comes across, on the other hand, as a realistic, down-to-earth woman interested in pushing her man to improve himself within the accepted norms of the society. She calls Mene foolish also for not staying to school. Thus, she recognizes the importance of education. Her opinion complements that of Mene's mother who single-handedly sees him through primary school and laments his inability to attend secondary school. Faced with the fact of Mene's life, Agnes consoles herself with his natural qualities as a good man. "Anyway, she does not mind that driver work because, after all said and done, the most important is for man to like his wife, take very good care of her, help her every time and to know what woman like." (20) From the time of Agnes's arrival at Dukana until Mene's departure for the war-front, we witness a relationship marked by mutual respect and care. Agnes evolves into a quiet, responsible wife (65) still influential in her husband's life. She tells his mother what she, the wife, wants him to do. In the final analysis, the army is meant to serve as a means to an end, that is, to prepare Mene to be a good husband, and a respectable member of the community. When Mene's mother changes her mind and helps him to buy his way into the army (67), she, too, comes to be a part of that process of realizing manhood and, in a sense, humanity.

The two women, Agnes and Mene's mother, remain the most compelling figures of his existence to the very end. As wife and mother, they constitue the driving forces for his desire to survive, the sole reasons for his efforts to return to the village, the only remaining dream in his nightmarish war-experience. If it is true that, out of a chauvinistic superiority complex, Mene-sozaboy flaunts his courage in a battle as opposed to other cowardly soldiers, it is no less true that he is doing it all in order to be a worthy husband and son. Mene's departure for the army ushers in a moment of quiet before the storm, an indication of future turmoil, and the hero's quest for self through the protracted struggle to return home. The picture of both mother and wife, "standing in front of the house, holding each other (...)crying plenty" (70, is indicative of that whole life of struggle for survival; of the search for happiness liable to culminate in failure; of the loss of life and the finality of separation, all precipitated by a tragedy, war, the meaning of which is contained in one word, *confusion*.

THE ARMY AND WAR, OR VARIATIONS ON THE NIGERIAN CONFUSION

The confusion is not just the sozaboy's but that of his village, and of the unnamed country, Nigeria. We witness Mene's vacillation between staying home and enlisting in the army. We hear the pronouncements of local jesters, such as Duzia and the veteran, Zaza, the educated class and the military masters, calling on young men to be patriotic; yet, what stands out is the selfishness and nonsense of the whole event. Besides confusion, *trouble* is the other key-word in the narration. The story begins at the point where old, civilian government is ousted by the new government "of soza and police" (2). Everybody is elated, believing that bribery and corruption have been wiped out forever. Their dream is immediately dashed. Corruption becomes institutionalized in the uniform. Contrary to people's hopes, the sun does not shine better; there is no more medicine than before in hospitals; people are still dying and, with the war, are dying more. In short, new does not mean good, nor does military mean better. Mene mentions the case of the policeman Okonkwo, who, as sargent, used to be a heavy collector of bibes from drivers; promoted to inspector and therefore removed from the center of action, the man bursts into tears. "Dis promotion, na demotion." (2) And, soon enough, the people come to know that the new government is not made up of sozas and police; that the former are the true masters, and the latter, marginal collaborators in the subjugation of the people.

As Mene narrates the story -and he, of course owes this dexterity to his creator, Saro-Wiwa- it is easy to conclude that here is a society run by a set of irresponsible individuals, without a culture of commitment and accountability, without direction, without purpose or principles. The people of Dukana simply wake up one day to hear of the new government, and they begin to jump for joy. The rumor continues in the tales of trouble, unfounded, unconfirmed, but spreading like wildfire and with ever increasing outrageous ramifications. Of course, the notion of newness and betterness immediately invalidated by actions of the empowered, but, given the psychology of an underdeveloped people, no one asks questions, no one dares disobey orders. The new government means power over others, and it is this aspect to which everyone clings, consciously or subconsciously.

A battalion visits Dukana for provisions. Everybody runs for cover. Everyone is cowered by the Uniform and the Gun, starting from the village chief, Birabee, "sweating, shaking like *shage,* smiling like idiot fool, his mouth shaking." (39) When the soldiers leave, Birabee assumes the position of power, ordering everyone around, threatening them in the name of a faceless government. All the while, the voice of "trouble" rises on the radio, with increasing propaganda. "Radio begin dey hala as 'e never hala before. Big big grammar. Long long words. Every time. Before before, the grammar was not plenty and everybody was happy. But now grammar begin to plenty and people were not happy. As grammar plenty, na so trouble plenty. And as trouble plenty, na so plenty people were dying." (3) This "big, big grammar," who is supposed to understand it? The illiterate mases to whom nobody has ever explained anything? "Plenty trouble, plenty money." (3) Mene's master, the lorry-driver, and the soon-to-be-sozaboy himself, "are prouding," eager to exploit the situation to the detriment of the rattled population returning home from their outside habitations. The village chief collects money and food, for the army and for himself, too. But Mene, perspicacious in his disarmingly simple manner, wonders: "if the trouble become fight, then wetin go happen?"⁹ The prople are ordered to stop all dancing and beating of drums. The town-crier announces meetings of the villagers with the visiting government representatives.

Then comes the call to enlist in the army. Before that call, Mene witnesses the conversation of two strangers in the bar where he meets his future wife, Agnes. Their words are ominous, confusing, "a sign of bad omen" (to use the man's language). They repeat Chief Birabee's prophesy, that the world will soon end, and the necessity to fight, without explaining why.

"'Well, the only trouble is that there is trouble. And we must fight... Everyday they hala about it. Many people have dead. Therefore some more people must to die again.'

'And you think it is good thing?' the short man was asking.

'Well, I don't think it is good thing or bad thing. Even sef I don't want to think. What they talk, we must do. Myself, if they say fight, I fight. If they say no fight, I cannot fight. Finish.'

....

'Well, as for myself, anything that will disturb me and stop enjoyment, I cannot like it.'" (17)

Certain questions remain: "Why dem they kill now?" (15), and "is it good thing to fight?" The tall man of the Pitakwa bar-conversation reappers later in the story as Manmuswak, the double agent fighting on both sides of the war.

We have already discussed Mene's avowed reasons for joining the army. What it means is, that there are as many reasons as there are individuals, each imbued with their own selfish ends, thus underscoring the confusion engulfing the society. Even the most respected among the characters have little commitment to a higher cause. Witness the position of Mene's friend, Bullet: "He knows that when the war don finish all those who have fight the war well will become big man." (91) Mene learns his lesson well: he begins to dream of becoming officer "with rope" and, "when the war ends, I will be very big man. Somtetimes they can even make me the chief of Dukana instead of that stupid man, Chief Birabee." (99) Thus, his humble dream of pleasing and defending his Agnes, becomes enlarged by his meeting with others (a process of growth, or descent into decadence?). It is to his, and Saro-Wiwa's credit that Mene ends up denouncing war and its attendant death and destruction, even though the basic confusion remains.

The main culprits in the unraveling tragedy are no doubt, the leaders of the people. In Mene's passing out parade at the end of his preparation for battle, is the Chief Commander General, resplendent in his uniform. *"I do not think he was seeing us at all,"* comments sozaboy. In his speech, the man uses "big big words that I cannot understand. But every time he will be calling that Enemy. I begin to fear this Mr. Enemy you know... Alle these things were wondering me as the Chief Commander General was speaking. 'You boys have got excellent training. You must be brave and proud of your country.' Fine fine grammar. 'We shall overcome. The Enemy will be vanquished. *God is on our side.'"* (78; emphasis mine). Mene's crude naivete is in full flight. He is as funny a ever. Nonetheless, the low-down humor shows the ridiculous extent to which war-mongers would go, to throw their unwary young men into battle. Mene notices the Chief Hawk's demeanor, his total lack of interest in the boys being sent to their death. For him, they are already an Absence, that is, already dead. They are of no importance; he, the VIP, the master, the savior, in order to prove his supremacy, must put on an air, to impress the soon-to-be-slaughtered recruits. He is fully aware that their training is far from being excellent; that the country of which he is extolling them to be proud is but a geographical entity; that in all likelihood, they shall be overcome; that he does not even know God and, most significantly, that he himself is part of the Enemy.

Proof abounds of the inadequate training undergone by Mene and his fellow recruits. He has no idea of the war-front until the truck carrying the group arrives at a point where they are ordered to get down and replace a departing bunch of worn out, teary-eyed soldiers. "Praps na Burma we dey go, oh. No. Bullet no fit call Burma front. Na one place dem dey call FRONT we dey go. Wetin we dey go do dere? God alone sabi. Especially as Mr. Enemy don die finish and we no go shoot am again. And we do not hold gun sef. Ha!" (80) And the web of lies begun by the rumor-bearers at Dukana and supported by the army officers, including Mr. Commander, is woven so intricately that it finally ensnares Mene. Tan Papa (a nickname coined from one of the recurring commands during Mene's training, *Stand Proper*), the training officer, and one of the trainers in lies, confuses the boy further when he asks whether Agnes would still love him if he were to lose a hand or a leg in the war. When Mene expresses his lack of understanding of the question, Tan Papa claims not to imply that Mene may become maimed or killed, just to inform him that "war is war." (75) Mene buys the lie, believing that death is foreign to war. He is proud of his relationship with Tan Papa who uses him as errand-boy and he does everything to prove his courage. When other recruits are shedding tears, out of cowardice, Tan Papa explains to Mene that it is tears of joy, that they are overwhelmed by the news of the Enemy's acceptance of defeat. "Therefore all that training we are getting cannot be used at all. We cannot get nobody to shoot and kill. So I was not very happy to hear that. I think I have to join the boys to cry." (79) Mene, sozaboy, has assumed the psyche of a killer undergoing a pang of depression due to unsatiated thirst for blood.

The army discourages people from thinking.[10] Mene's low level of education and the yawning crevice separating officialdom from the populace encourage the policy. Obedience and discipline. In a scene filled with satire and hilarious humor, Mene and other recruits are drilled into reacting to commands that they understand only by recognizing repeated sounds rather than the meaning of words. And sozaby loves the training. And he and his mates stand at attention, even though they are being whipped by the wicked "San Major." And he is impressed, "prouding because of this uniform! Look how it is strong and can stand by itself." (72) When at night the gun is taken away from him, sozaboy is exceedingly disappointed; for, he would have preferred "to sleep with it and love it like wife," just as Tan papa has taught them. Ironically, Mene never has a chance to shoot a gun throughout the war. A consolation, however: his first assignment is in a canoe, good for him as a riverine inhabitant, but bad for most of the other recruits who have never seen water before. Another consolatoin: the uniform and the gun in hand give the soldiers a feeling of power. "Everybody seem bigger than before(...)I am proud of the gun when I remember that with that gun Chief Birabee go fall down for ground when he see me call me 'sah,' 'Oga' and 'massa' and all those fine fine names." (88)

Obedience, that word is a constant in Mene's war narrative. "Because as you know in the army you cannot say what you like. You must obey and do what they ask you to do." (73; see also, 74, 80, 84, 88, 89) "You know this soza life. You cannot talk or do as you like. Every time you must follow your leader like goat. [And] it is not everything that your eye see that your mouth will talk." (108) obedience and discipline would be acceptable in an army led by disciplined, responsible officers. On the contrary, Sozaboy's superiors are beasts and robbers that should actually be disciplined. One of such, a captain, is used as an example by

Bullet, Sozaboy's best friend and unit leader. The captain has been sleeping with young girls and keeping his troops' ration of drinks and cigarettes for himself. An enemy soldier sneaking into the camp informs them of the captain's picadillos. Bullet therefore enters the absent captains' cabin, takes out all the ration and gives it to his men who become drunk and sleep off. They wake up in detention. The captain makes Bullet drink urine, demotes and sends him on a dangerous surveillance trip on the river. Bullet, now a changed man determined to avenge himself, lures the captain onto the patrol boat and shoots him. (108) Sozaboy and others are pleased with the discipline of death meted out to the captain.

The character that reveals the captain's sins is Manmuswak, the same tall man expressing his willingness to go to war, at the Pitakwa bar on the day Mene meets his Agnes. *Manmuswak* (Man must wak + Man must eat, survive, by all means necessary and possible, unscrupulously, by hook or crook), is the Enemy incarnate, and a cross between man and monster. His identity is nothing, and everything; no one, and everyone. The opinion here is, that the critic, N.V.Inyama, misreads this compellingly iniquitous Wiwan character by describing him as "difficult to understand" (*African Literature Today*, 10, 1996: 44). Indeed, the man is easy to understand, as a symbol of the Nigerian confusion, opportunism, and exploitation. Manmuswak, the man who tells Mene 'that his work is war" (120), helps us to understand Saro-Wiwa's interpretation of the civil war as a meaningless effort at the socio-political level. It is undertandable only as a means of realizing individuals' personal, dastardly dreams. Mene's failure to place Manmuswak can be shared by everyone, particularly those without knowledge of Nigeria's history. Saro-Wiwa dexterously fashions that cornucopia of confusion by refusing to define and describe with clarity the two sides of the war. Critics with facts of the conflict have affirmed that Mene is enlisted on the Biafran side (since he "paid Okpara" after having been rejected as being too short for the army). However, when Mene-Sozaboy is captured, hospitalized, and escapes with Manmuswak engaged in all these experiences, there is no certainty as to which side is the enemy. Mene is engaged on both sides; it is during his stint on the other side that he becomes a driver and uses the jeep to go on a clandestine visit to Dukana. Manmuswak's attitude and behavior towards Sozaboy are fraught with similar confusion: how courteous and considerate, he is loved by the boy as a brother; now cynical and surly, with an all-too-apparent murderous mien, he is abhorred by Sozaboy like the plague. Manmuswak is two-faced like the friend-fiend.

We have already quoted the Chief Commander's tireade against the Enemy; Sozaboy is not able to distinguish his identity from that of his friends, until the end of the novel. Before joining the army, he hears rumors about "one porson called Enemy that plenty people will go to kill. Plenty people including the girls. This Enemy na strong man." (54) Assigned to Iwoama where he is captured, he and his mates are ordered "to stop" the enemy from coming into that town. Because "he will tief everything inside the town. Then he will take away all the women and begin to use them [and] he will not stop at Iwoama(...) Then they will carry away my mama plus Agnes and then begin to use Agnes. I beg, God no gree bad thing. Instead of that, we go fight sotey the world broke into two. No worry , soza captain, the enemy no go fit enter Iwoama. At all." (87) the enemy enters, captures Iwoama, and Sozaboy. The enemy? He himself is never sure; for, as he later learns upon returning to Dukana on a quick visit, both sides perpetrate the same havoc on the people. Duzia tells him: "All you sozas are the same thing." (134) the village wag continues: "Everybody is enemy in this our war. There is nobod to trust. Your friend today can be your enemy tomorrow." (137) And Sozaboy, learns his lesson: "I call of anybody tell me that this is enemy... They are all doing the same thing." (139) Rape, forced labor by the people, beatings, mental torture, shootings, bombing-raids, such are the joys of war recounted by Duzia when Sozaboy visits his deserted village. And the forced evacuation of the people maeans that they are actually moved to where fighting will later occur. "[Bombing] was small compare to what happened the day after that and the dy after that and the day after that and the day after that." (133)

As the war is drawing to an end, Sozaboy goes looking for his wife and mother in refugee-camps. There again, he finds it impossible to define the Enemy. Dukanans, evacuated from their village, are kept in a camp with homebased compatriots as their hosts. The latter treat them as strangers, or foreigners. Zaza, the Burma veteran, laments that these hosts "are our worst enemy. They are worst than prison... Here we are among friends and they are hunting us like animals (...) Kwashiokor show us pepper for one eye; our friends show us pepper for the other eye; God too far away to hear Dukana people"[11] Zaza is only partially right, because there are also Dukanans in the camp acting as their own people's enemy. Prominent among them are Chief Birabee and Pastor Barika. The narrator-protagonist has always resented these two characters; the chief, because of his cowardly and wormy demeanor before government representatives, contrasted with his insensitive, dictatorial behavior towards his people; the pastor, for his panicky, doomsday predictions. Birabee is "very coward man" and Barika "is uselsess man inside useless church(...)talking nonsense." (4) Both characters are depicted as thoughtless and reactionary, accepting their conditions as fixed, absolute. Meanwhile, they exploit the societal situation to suit their selfish objectives. Barika inadvertently serves as agent of official fraud by spreading rumors about the war and then, instead of facing facts of the approaching fighting, he and other church-leaders arrange open-air prayer meetings "begging God to take smell of war from Dukana." (66) Later, the charlatan priest thanks God effusively for serving and redeeming his people, and for bringing back Sozabory from the land of the spirit as He brought back Lazarus from hell (152). Thus, Barika is no less superstitious than the other villagers, who, thinking that Sozaboy died during the Iwoama raid, are afraid to accept him back into the community. Barika, too weak, too shallow, cannot save the poor boy from those desirious of making him a human sacrifice to appease the gods of death and Sozaboy is compelled to abandon his village forever.

When the village is bombed, Barika and Birabee, supposedly respectable leaders, "cry like a baby" (13) and run away like rabbits. Much worse still, at the refugee camp, they resume their shameless roles as government stooges and unarmed robbers. It is Birabee, "smiling his idiot smile always" (40), that denounces Sozaboy as enemy soldier (158). And he does what he seems to do best: "Chief is no chief nowadays. Only to tief, chopping money from poor woman plus money wey dem collect from village." (41) At the camp, he and Barika are put in charge of collecting and distributing rations of stockfish, gari, rice, and clothes supplied by the Red Cross. The old man, Terr Kole, informs the newly arrived Sozaboy of the dastardly acts of the two "bellymen": "He said that it is very bad for young man. Because some people have sold their eyes and their ears to the big sozas for their belly.... Because they want to chop for today, tomorrow and even for many tomorrows to come, they even hear things which nobody have said." (156) These two wicked men, spies, of a useless government, prevent Sozaboy from staying in the camp, especially when he asserts that he is less interested in the war than in finding his wife and mother. Birabee, ever the fool and the fraud, retorts, fabricating the lie of "a new country": "And Chief Birabee said that I should remember that all young men are wanted to go and fight in the front so that theenemy can be defeated and we win the war and then we shall all return home and we shall be in a new country where nobody will tief, there will be no hungry again, everything will be free... In short, after we win the war, there will be life more abundant." (154-155)[12] To this spurious call to patriotism and this mendacioius optimism are added Barika's own hypocritical preaching of commitment, that Sozaboy should think less of finding his mother and wife and more of "taking care of everybody." The two men do the exact opposite of what they preach. The "new country" remains a perfect mirror of the old. "Fat like a pig" (158), the leaders resume their decadent, lecherous lives and, with the forced departure of Sozaboy, their sole vocal critic, they stand a chance of perpetuating evil.

As for the secondary characters in this dance of death—Duzia, Bom, Zaza, and others—the critic, Helen Chukwuma, opines that Saro-Wiwa's sympathy "is with the cripple, the downtrodden and the marginalized of the society. The author casts his lot with the downtrodden. He makes Duzia and Bom survive the war, feeding fat from the abandoned farms while the people die of starvation in forced exile." (*Critical Essays*: 50) This assessment is definitely erroneous; for, Duzia and Bom's parasitical and opportunistic ways are not at all supported by the author. Indeed, these bums are not redeemed by their role of comic relief in an increasingly tragic scene. To a lesser degree than the Chief and the Pastor, they, too, are their people's enemy. Bom, Duzia and Zaza exploit the war situation to spread rumors and make money: everyone calls Bom "BBC [British Broadcasting Corporation] because na him sabi the news of the war pass, is everyday saying how our sozas are killing the ENEMY like fly." (66) Zaza, the Burma veteran, accompanies the Chief to his rounds of telling lies to people about how, through his efforts, the name of Dukana is being made famous on the radio and, therefore, they should reward him the communal fame. When, later, Sozaboy meets Zaza at the refugee camp, the latter has lost his swagger and superiority complex; he bursts into tears, and reveals his real self, a common coward who "just dey run like foolish idiot." (145) Duzia and Bom's survival in the village hs to be seen in the light of their irresponsibility. Duzia, a cripple, cannot even walk, and Bom, lazy, hides in the nearby bush. Duzia's claim to be "living like a king these days" (134) is an expression of his selfishness, insensitivity, and readiness to exploit others' problems. With that knowledge, one can only sneer at his seemingly remorseful comment, that "the war have buried our town." (134) Duzia and others incessantly tell Sozaboy lies about the fate of his wife and mother, thus maintaining the atmosphere of rumors and confusion beclouding the social landscape. At that juncture, Saro-Wiwa crafts a point of collusion between the big "bellymen," Birabee and Barika, (victimizers) and the small players, theeir victims. Duzia claims tht Agnes has become a 'war wife" (135), while Barika says that she and Sozaboy's mother went away in a soldier's lorry. Bom, not to be outdone, says that there was no lorry, that a soldier walked off with Agnes. Such fabrications, in addition to the propaganda, and the details of killings, and robberies by all sorts of people (140), help to implicate the whole community in the war-crime.

It is usual to call the mass of the people innocent victims of war, particularly when, as in *Sozaboy*, the authorities do nothing to educate them. Sozaboy laments the fate of "innocent people like myself [who] have already dead because of nonsense war." (169) Saro-Wiwa's narrtive offers possibilities for debate on the matter. Innocent? Yes, as victims of the original cause and perpetration of the conflict; but, as (ignorant) collaborators, these people are not immune from culpability. That is the dilemma of the governed, this majority of numbers but a socio-psychological minority in the power-play among the elite of the neo-colony. Mene keeps criticizing and condemning officialdom; yet, he does not stop obeying: "I must follow when chief call." (6) Duzia, too: "You are the Chief, so we must believe you." (7) The People grumble about levies for the war-effort, but they pay up, "cursing as they are paying." (9) Mene, caught, tortured, and only miraculously saved from being shot by Manmuswak after the Chief has denounced him, condemns war as "useless nonsense and all this uniform and everything is just to cause confusion and make porson fine like goat that they have make fat and ready to kill for chop during Christmas." (127) Surprisingly enough, almost immediately after, he resumes his dream of becoming "a very rich man with very big belly and walking all over Dukana nd everyone will be following me and asking for help to send their picken to school and for money so that they can buy food to eat. And they will be begging me to allow them sweep my house or be apprentice in my lorry or driver. And I will be driving away those that I do not like while I will give some fine thing to those that I like and everyone will be talking about me how I am good man to those who are good and bad to those who are bad." (165) This mixture of optimism and pessimism, of vain and vile materialism and deep-rooted, refreshing humanism (e.g. p. 155, the episode in the refugee camp when Sozaboy asks old Terr Kole to go sit down while he helps him take his food ration from the Red Cross representative); this flux between cowardliness and courage, comedy and tragedy, accord *Sozaboy* a complexity and a comprehensiveness that make the text a viable mirror of Nigerian society.

The hero's change of uniform from one side to the other -and he easily fits into both camps- adds to the drama. "Enemy" is defined in the final analysis, as whoever or whatever is unacceptable to the group controlling a particular spot and to the population under their control. When he is compelled to flee into exile, Sozaboy metaphorically becomes the greatest Enemy, a situation which underscores the tragedy of the story and the society.

SARO-WIWA'S SATIRE AND IRONY

Saro-Wiwa's satirical art saves the narrative from the morbid mask of death. Satire is most effective when there is a psychological distance between the satirist and his subject, and, simultaneously, a commitment by him to change regarding the condition or situation that has led to the criticism of the subject. As an intellectual and an admirer and a user of good English, the novelist is able to use "rotten English" to laugh at Mene and the Dukanans. On the other hand, the events being described, being beyond these people's control, serve as a means of laughing with them as victims. Thus, both victims and victimizers are ridiculed as members of a foolish society.

The Village characters, Duzia, Bom, Zaza and Terr Kole, serve as clowns and social critics, telling hilarious tales, "nacking tory" (23), and making everyone laugh. They are Mene's "masters" (61), the ones who give him his nickname, Sozaboy. Together, they represent a culture of happiness and simplicity and, in conjunction with Mene (they also enjoy the first-person narrative), they symbolize a certain empowerment of the lower classes, still unaware of their potential but already whispering against their elitist tormentors. That potential is, of course, not intended to be recognized as such; for, the novelist is mainly engaged in holding up to ridicule the foolishness and failings of these comical characters. Like *confusion*, the word, *prouding*, is very recurrent in the text; at each point, it is well used as a marker of satire[13]. As the story draws to its tragic end, as Sozaboy becomes disillusioned and more mature and sober, there is less use of the word.

Overall, satire in Sozaboy is most adequately used in speeches, and conversation between characters. Here, Saro-Wiwa shows his dramatic skills, in scenes such as the call to combat by military and civilian leaders and the people's reaction; Mene's chat with fellow Dukanans during his search for his mother and wife in the refugee-camps; his encounters with Manmuswak; his discussion with Duzia and Bom in his first visit home from the war-front, and his final, aborted return and exchanges with the superstitious villagers. On each occasion, the novelist gives his characters freedom to perform, like actors coalescing with the dramatic personnae; thus, they enjoy a certain credibility before the reader. A certain conspiracy, or confidentiality, or complicity, too, so that, within the scope of the plot, the reader does not just recognize their ridiculous, foolish ideas and actions but does so with an understanding that he or she, or someone else in real life, may also entertain such stupidity.

Mene's familiar style of telling his story also encourages the complicity and lightheartedness. It is as if we are witnesses to the events, or participants, or the audience enjoying complementarity with the actors on stage. The narrator uses various expressions referring to shared experience: *As you know; I think you know; You remember; I think you remember; Look, you know*. Other expressions solemnly address the authenticity of Mene's narration: *I will not tell you a lie; God in heaven; Believe me; yours sincerely, if you see as those people were looking you will sorry for them; I am telling you; I will not tell you a lie; If I tell you I was happy, know that I am telling a lie; My dear brother, you have not seen the type of confusion tht I see that morning; And my brother, if I tell you that I begin chop fresh snail make you no surprise; If I tell you that I sleep well, I am telling lie and God will punish me*. At no point is this style more successful than when Sozaboy, more perspicacious, arrives at the refugee camp and finds his village leaders acting like predatory animals. Pastor Barika is there praying for the dead in whose graves he and Chief Birabee have hidden money made by selling the refugees supplies and by acting as spies for the military rulers; and he is asking God to save those still living and to take them back to Dukana. The pathos is negated by the knowledge of the man's insufferable hypocrisy. Sozaboy, too, sheds tears, and more so when he sees his people, "how all their eyes have gone inside their head, and all their hair have become palm oil colour and they have dirty dirty rag shirt and all their bones are shaking inside their body." (151) After they have finished praying and have opened their eyes, one man recognizes the supposedly dead Sozaboy, and exclaims that God has worked a new miracle. The pastor praises the Jehovah for the miracle, but he and the Chief soon connive to hand Sozaboy over to the authorities as an enemy soldier.

The irony in the above episode is quite compelling. Sozaboy respects the two men as elders and leaders of the community. Although he wisely deists from telling them categorically that the war is meaningless and stupid, -"I just tell them some of the things that they will like to hear" (153)- they still do him in. According to the critic Ezenwa-Ohaeto, "the ironies in *Sozaboy* are both thematically interwoven and artistically contrived. These ironies revolve around the basic irony associated with the change of government which degenerated into a civil war. The replacement of the civilian with a military regime is expected to introduce a well organized system of administration." (*Critical Essays*: 54). That, and much more: the "new government" is supposed to solve all problems, to immediately transform the people's living hell into heaven. Saro-Wiwa's novel paints a picture of this misplaced expectation, the frustration and the fanciful pretexts that the civil war creates, cultivates and, subsequently entrenches s a burden that the population is constrained to struggle to shed. At both the personal and communal levels, irony prevails. The Enemy, as already explained, turns out to be living right in the midst of the people. Mene is betrayed by the leaders of his community. The evacuated village of Dukana is left with only two inhabitants, Bom and Duzia, "the two idiots," while "those with safe legs and safe mind come to Nagwa [the refugee camp] to suffer like hen and goat and ant." (145) A villager, afraid and ready to show absurd hospitality, offers his daughter to the captain who rejects her and, disappointed at not being taken by the "big man," the girl bursts into tears, unaware as she is that the man is a harbinger of death, and not the good life. The war that is supposed to solve problems, only increases chaos. And Sozaboy, arriving at his village after spending many months in search of his wife and mother, not only learns of their death soon after his departure, but of his own death in the rumor-prone superstitious minds of his people. The irony is more striking when we recall that one of the reasons why Mene joins the army is to be able to protect his wife; by going away, he actually exposes her to death and, while it is true that he becomes wiser and better prepared to survive after his war travails, his final exile is the culmination of the very irony of the whole war.

Sozaboy's satire and irony are highlighted by humor beginning, as we have seen with the "rotten English" of the narration and the narrator's lack of understanding of certain concepts and words. For example, his ignorance of the expression *mambo-jambo* used by Manmuswak, makes for a laughter-inducing scene describing the latter's wickedness and Sozaboy's unknowing acquiescence to his own oppression. "Mambo-jambo. I like that word. Mambo-jambo. And that is what I was talking when I came to the hospital the first time." (119) He thanks Manmuswak for being so nice to him. He adds the expression to his vocabulry and, henceforth, that precedes some patients' death. And death occurs quite often there: "Those who die, they just carry them throway like dead cockroach. And the whole hospital is smelling one kain, one kain." (120) Such dark humor is not unusual in the novel.

There is a great deal of laughter. Basically, there are two kinds, one, an expresion of joy and a reaction to something funny. This "laughing small small" is spread over the novel, particularly the section before Mene's war-experience. Two, there is laughter as a sign of derision, spite, or pity; this occurs especially during the war, when disaster and death increase; when friends remove their masks and show their faces as foes; when life is all too suddenly overtaken by death. One noteworthy quality of Saro-Wiwa's novel is, that even if he has not succeeded in maintaining an equilibrium between the two types of laughter, he has been able to retain elemtents of the first.

Saro-Wiwa's ability to use metaphor and simile to vividly describe scenes and capture features and movements of the human body is an important piece of his humoristic arsenal. The Chief Birabee, "king of Dukana," is an old man with a bald cowardly head. "Not completely bald-oh. It is like bird have been chopping his hair." (4) The Chief and the elders, sitting in the village square, are "serious like boxers." (6) Urging the noisy crowd to be silent, the headmaster explodes: "You want fly to fall inside [your mouths]? Small thing and you begin formfool." (7) The man that will metamorphose into Manmuswak finishes eating at the bar and "belched one big belch—etiee!" (17) Mene comments on the scarcity of salt as the stories of war increases: "Suffer suffer chop beans without salt... country don spoil." (23) Zaza, proudly weaving his tale of this travel to Burma: "The ship was dancing in the ocean, left right, left right. Quick slow, quick quick slow. And the belly of many of those sozas was turning, slow, quick quick slow, quick. They were vomitting like no man business. Haba. But not myself, man picken!" (28) And Duzia and others are eating every lie from his sweet mouth, "with thier mouth open like *mumu*." (30) Zaza continues, describing "aeroplane shitting proper bomb, heavy heavy bomb (...) As the aeroplane shit, na so person dey die." (31) When Mene is hit by a policeman, his head begins to ache: "I keep quiet with several people shouting little shouts inside my head from the policemen's stick blow. I said to myself, 'trouble don begin.'" (46) The visiting District Officer, there to engage in war-propaganda, keeps a serious mien, his "face tight like Post Ofice." (51 As he continues to encounter one tragedy after another, Sozaboy becomes overwhelmed; he declares, "water don pass gari." (104) Led to the captain when he is captured by enemy troops, he is scared to death: "I am like dead goat only I never begin smell, and blood did not come out of my body." (122) Manmuswak, his living nightmare, tells the captain "that he picked me like snail from bush." (123) And, "my teeth were shaking like truck on the road and my feet were dancing on the ground. I am telling you, fear catch me *helele*. I was shaking like idiot *mumu*" (123)

All these examples, and many others, combine laughter with a tragic pathos. They show Mene's naivete, ignorance, excitement and anxiety to be a full-fledged soldier, while not eliminating his engaging innocence, simplicity and goodness, and a desire to improve himself. They also offer a multi-faceted picture of a population that is basically happy, humoristic, and melodramatic.

CONCLUSION: OF DEATH, SURVIVAL AND THE NIGERIAN DILEMMA

In the blurb of Sozaboy, the novel is described by the Lagos newspaper, *The Guardian*, as "one of, if not the BEST book on the (Nigerian) civil war... the sort of book one is proud to own." One would imagine tht such high accolade is due to the novelist's choice of subject, that is, the first-hand experiences of a *common man* 9to use the traditional, aestablishment language explicitly expressing the fascist under-pinnings of society), described in ordinary language and in an earthy atmosphere where the majority of the audience would feel at home. Other novels have recounted the civil war,[14] but none has given the victim's viewpoint in the first person, and in "rotten English." Having said that, however, one must noet that Saro-Wiwa's very original artistic choice, by giving freedom to the hero, has also created apotentially dangerous chasm between author and narator-protagonist and, indeed, between author and reader. No doubt that Mene-Sozaboy's ideas are, to an extent, Saro-Wiwa's, too. Nonetheless, the first-person narrativ eused here, not being autobiographical ficiton, and presenting as it does a lower-calss position, leads to questions on clas stratification and relationships. Saro-Wiwa, a bourgeois, places importance on thinking. He makes Mene think, but the level of the effort is so low, so pristine, that one too often laughs at his stupidity. The author's position would appear to be that, higher education would have helped the hero out of his naivete and made a better ma out of him. In that sense, Mene would not be apositive character, as long as he has not has that training. The theme of thinking will be dealt with in other chapters; for, Saro-Wiwa also mentions its absence at other levels of the Nigerian society.[15]

A corollary to the education issue is the conflict between life in the village and in the city. Mene, the traveling apprentice-driver, feels superior to his fellow Dukanans who have never left the village; on the other hand, he feels inferior to Agnes, "the young beautiful Lagos baby with J.J.C." (60) whom he must marry. He believes that marrying the girl would be expensive because she is a Lagos girl. And, to his naive mind, there is a "Lagos style" of making love (62). This complex-factor goes hand in hand with the class stratification: the military and police, symbols of power, are revered by the cowered population. The District Officer, too, as well as the Chief. In other works, we shall see that Saro-Wiwa thinks much less of Lagos than does his hero. As for traditional society, the village Chief may be important, but he has to earn the respect. Birabee does not; hence, Mene lambasts him throughout his narrative. The myth of military government is debunked, and Mene quickly learns that corruption is not eradicated by the Uniform.

In assessing Mene's character, one is left to vacillate between sympathy and criticism. His evolution, his maturation, from boy to man, remains incomplete. The air of superiority that he exhibits vis-a-vis other Dukanans hardly changes. They are still "stupid" (141). He is still farcically ignorant: when his master-driver, who has become a drunk, tells him that his people have gone to a *camp*, he asks "Why camp? Are they scout or what?" (142) When a man informs him that the Red Cross are treating patients dying of kwashiokor in the camp, he comments: "Kwashiokor. K. K. I am telling you, I like that name Kwashiokor. And you mean to say it is disease. If it is so, it will be a very good disease to kill somebody. Wait oh. So praps my mama and my Agnes can be suffering from this K.K. When I think of that, I begin fear bad bad." (143) Mene's stunted growth would be adduced to the psychological confusion that he undergoes in his life as a civilian and a soldier. Mene transformed into Sozaboy entails a confusing process; the human being remains part of the military persona, and both struggle for supremacy. Unfortunately, the soldier boy corrupts the human being's character. Fortunately, the corruption is not complete.

The description of, and reaction to, death demonstrate the surviving human side of Mene's character. Death is experienced at close range in its most horrible configurations. Tortured by the monstrous Manmuswak; dragged along the road by a vehicle to which he is tied after being beaten to a pulp, and left for dead in a ditch; standing face to face with death popping out of the executioner's gun and saved only by a stroke of luck; witnessing the bombing of his battalion, with limbs flying and decapitated bodies of his comrades keeping him company in the trench; watching sick prisoners of war speaking "mambo-jambo" before dying and being thrown into mass graves; combing through "the compost pit" called refugee camps and learning that "refugee is somebody that they just throway like rubbish" (147), and that that is his people's status, Mene is not always sure whether he wishes to live or die. Firstly, he thinks that he would be better dead, thus finding peace and happiness, like his friend Bullet. Secondly, he thinks he is fortunate to be alive, particularly with the thought of seeing his wife and mother again. "And it is not a good thing for young man to die when he have not enjoyed and he have not done anything that he can show to his children and his mama. And after all the world is very nice place with very many nice things that God have made for enjoyment of man and there is no need for man to die just like that like ant or goat or chicken. So I said no, I must not die..." (164) The will to live, to survive, is thus stronger than the resignation to death. But Mene is no revolutionary. No commitment to any common cause. No ambition beyond the widespread selfish and self-centered objectives of many a survivor. Always Self, never Society. Would this be Saro-Wiwa's criticism of his hero? "Praps!" And would it be reason enough to say that his vision of his society is "pessimistic"? (*African Literature Today*, 20, 1996: 43) Probably not.

Humor, satire, and irony have been crafted in the novel in such a way as to keep novelist and narrator, and the reader with them, a few steps away from pessimism. Evil and death may triumph, but not always. As for the selfishness exhibited by Mene, it is not particular to him; and, having survived, he would still stand a chance of growing, and changing for the better. The pathetic image of returnees to the village at the end of the war, does not make for optimism: they are trudging along the roads like ghosts, "even some of them jsut drop for ground as they are walking and die" (170). The war, one might say, is not really over. And death is still lurking around, when not taking another innocent life.

The emphasis on self-survival is lessened by Mene's oblique but credile love for his village, starting with his wife and mother. Of course, the irony in his hopeless hope of finding them long after their death in a bomb-raid, subsumes the dilemma of the hero's quest, and of his very existence. It also brings to our attention the theme of ethnicity in the Nigerian setting and, in particular, the minority question, which became Saro-Wiwa's life-long commitment. A most tragic moment in the novel occurs when Mene arives at his devastated village: "When I see my own home town, I begin cry." (129) Yet, the Self fails to coalesce with the Community. Mene, after surviving death in the war, is dealt the cold hand of obliteration by his own people. To die physically would be better than to live in death, as is his destiny. As he runs away from the village, he states, with despair, "in fact, I did not know where I was going.(...) The war have made me like porson wey get leprosy because I have no town again." (181) Note the past tense, an affirmation of survival, and continuity, and some hope for the future even with the harrowing reality of forced exile. If nothing else, Mene's story would serve as a lesson to others (the linkage between fact and fiction), most significantly, to Nigerians who have never sat down to analyze the facts of the civil war that devastated the country and set it back on its road to development. It is interesting that the poor man is declared dead by his people, suffering from backwardness, superstition, ignorance, microcosmic of the diseases of the larger sociey.[16]

It has been stated that, one conclusion adduced from *Sozaboy* is, that "most people of Mene's level of education—and these were in the majority in the Nigerian civil war—were being mindlessly reckless with their lives" (N. Inyama, *Critical Essays*: 107) That is but a very dislocated conclusion. For, if the Menes were "mindlessly reckless," the faceless war-mongers who urged them on to their death, and with themselves staying a very safe distance away to profit from wages of war, those "big men" should earn, first and foremost, the laurel of culpability. Mene and millions of others remain victims, deserving of an explanation from the likes of the pompous Chief Commander. His statement is good enough as the final word: "I do not know why we are fighting the war." (114)

NOTES TO CHAPTER II

1. Mene, the narrator-hero in Ken Saro-Wiwa, *Sozaboy*, Port Harcourt: Saros International Publishers, 1986: 114. Further references to this novel will be incorporated in the body of the chapter.

2. *Sozaboy*: 17. The speaker is the "tall man" that Mene meets in the Diobu bar at the beginning of the novel, and whom he meets later in the war-front as Manmuswak.

3. See N.F. Tuyama, "Saro-Wiwa: Maverick Iconoclast of the Nigerian Literary Scene," *African Literature Today*, 20, 1996: 38- 39.

4. Saro-Wiwa's position would seem to place "good English" on a pedestal of superiority which would, by extension (language as repository and vehicle of a culture) mean that a certain supremacy inheres in the civilization to which the language belongs. That superiority would then be attained by those able to immerse themselves in the language-culture. Later in this study, we shall delve more into Saro-Wiwa's ideas on Western education among Nigerians.

Another remark on the "rotten English" of this novel: it is at times reminiscent of some episodes in Wole Soyinka's prison diary, *The Man Died*, (Penguin Books, 1972). See, especially, the prison superintendent's comical speech to the Ibo prisoners, pp. 102-104: "This rebellion must. Be nimp in the bond." (104) Did Saro-Wiwa read this book? There are other interesting details for discussion later (see Ch. 2).

5. Later, in his activist writing, Saro-Wiwa traces the history of the Ogoni as an ethnic group priding itself in resisting enslavers and even colonial invaders. This kind of pride is visible in Mene.

6. This word, *confusion*, and its various derivatives, appear very often in the novel. A rough list of pages: 2, 8, 9, 19, 21, 34, 35, 38, 39, 40, 42, 45, 46, 52, 72, 80, 90, 92, 93, 98, 99, 112, 113, 114, 118, 166, 175. This

shows that, at a point when Mene is more or less convinced of the futility and senselessness of war, his confusion abates; but only to re-surface towards the end, when he is declared dead by his people. Note that this element of confusion becomes a constant in Saro-Wiwa's other novels in contemporary Nigeria. Significantly, the state has evolved, from that of an individual and his village (Mene and Dukana) to engulf a whole country of confused people--a sad comment on Nigeria's "development".

7. The issue of Mene's age is problematic. The war veteran, Zaza, says that Mene "be small picken" at the time of the soldier's exploits in Hitler's war (p.26) That would mean that Mene was already born by the early 40's; now, how old would he be during Nigeria's civil war fought in 1967? Would this be one of the novelist's chronological lapses, or, could it be that this "boy" is one of those older "boys" so called in relativity to the age of their elders? In real life, it is not unusual to find apprentice drivers, "boys", more or less of middle age.

8. p. 69. The novel is full of such lewd references to the sexual act. In his hilarious tales of Hitler-search-and-destroy, the veteran Zaza boasts that he "fucked Hitler's daughter from morning till night for three months" (68). He also brags of "fucking [his white wife] well well" (33). Duzia tells Mene: "I am sure you are fucking that girl well. Please don't tear her thing, oh." (62). The consensus among the villagers is, that being a soldier affords one ample opportunity to sleep with women; it is the soldiers that "fuck pass" (62). Zaza wonders, "which kain war that will stop a man from sleeping with a woman? Is it not during war that someone will sleep with plenty women? Especially brave man like myself?" (32).

The propensity to sleep with many women would partially explain the acceptance of polygamy in this community. Mene, dreaming of a war experience of Hitlerian proportions (thanks to Zaza), imagines himself marrying Hitler's daughter--"Win-the- war-wife"--after Agnes. He also subscribes to the idea that marrying a new wife reinvigorates man: "It is good for young man, like old man [old Kole] to get new wife, proper J.J.C., every time so that his blood can change" (81).

In criticizing this aspect of Saro-Wiwa's novel, one must not forget, firstly, realism: men's interest in the female figure as a sign of beauty, as well as the common lusting after the overwhelmingly sexploitative picture would pose the question of author-character and communal relationship, and readers would have various reactions. Suffice it so say that Saro-Wiwa seems to both laugh with and at his characters. He is at once high-handed (the superior, "civilized" observer looking down upon his creations) and even-handed (a member of the community, participating in the common life through his main character, Mene). This duality, or, indeed, this dichotomy is visible in all of Saro-Wiwa's work (and, one might say, life). At its best, to become the springboard for commitment to create and cultivate the community; at its worst, it can serve as the root of conflicts and contradictions.

9. p.20. The word, *trouble*, appears very many times in the novel. For example, see pp. 3, 4, 5, 7, 9, 12, 15, 16, 17, 19, 20, 22, 36, 43, 45, 46, 50, 51, 55, 63, 64, 67, 71, 74, 88, 89, 103, 104, 108, 111. The reduction in use is understandable, as the story progresses; when trouble becomes full-scale war.

10. *Thinking* is a very important aspect of Saro-Wiwa's philosophy of life, as will be seen in later chapters of this study. His most positive heroes are those who think; not to think is a sin, and thoughtlessness is one of the most significant elements of the Nigerian tragedy. Regarding Mene, he does evolve in the novel, from a non-thinker to a thinker, that is, one that questions, refuses to accept things as they are, that struggles for change. Although that process is not clear at this level, due to the hero's lack of western education, the *Prison* novels (see chapter II) give us a better view. The subject of debate would be, the adequacy of that education.

11. p.146. Note that this is the theme of minorities' oppresion in the hands of a majority, a theme that later became the most poignant reality of Saro-Wiwa's life: the Ogoni struggle. Reading the episode of Sozaboy where Dukana villagers are taking to their heels at the sight of soldiers, one is struck by the strange resemblance between that fictionalized past and this factual present, when soldiers and other agents of Nigeria's end-of-century dictatorship are doing a merry, ethnic-cleansing dance of death over Saro-Wiwa's people. See chapter on Ogoni.

12. The idea of "a new country" will again be subject among the elite. See chapter II: the same lies, the same hypocrisy, the same players in the macabre theater of destruction.

13. pp.3, 12, 16, 18, 19, 20, 21, 23, 25, 27, 29, 30, 31, 32, 39, 44, 46, 51, 53, 54, 59, 60, 65, 68, 71, 72, 76, 77, 78, 81, 88, 93, 99, 104, 113, 125, 126, 132, 135...

14. Other novels on the Nigerian civil war are: Vincent Ike, *Sunset at Dawn* (1976); Phanuel Egejuru, *The Seed Yams Have Been Eaten* (1973); Cyprian Ekwensi, *Divided We Stand* (1980).

15. The psychological distance between author and subject is balanced by their pysical resemblance. Like Saro-Wiwa, Mene is a short boy, so short that he is refused enlistment into the army and that he has to buy his way in. Zaza, Mene'a first military model, is also considered too short for the army, and he has to beg and bluff his way in. This habit of including himself in his fictional and theatrical work was to become much more visible in latter works, as we shall see in chapter II of this study.

16. Further discussion of the superstitious declaration of the death of an undesirable element in the village is found in Saro-Wiwa's short story, "A Family Affair" (see chapter IV).

III. PRISONERS AND THE PRISON: THE *JEBS* NOVELS

—"The artist has always functioned in African society as the record of the moves and experiences of his society and as the voice of vision in his own time." (Soyinka in Per Wastberg, ed.: 21)

—"In Nigeria, honest men were prisoners and the thieves free men." (*Prisoners of Jebs*: 19)

—"They [the military] have been without a vision for the country. They've failed to fight corruption and disorder, which is the only reason their intervention has been welcomed." (*Prison*: 201)

—"[The satirist] holds up a distorting mirror before people. Some people look into the mirror, see their reflection and get scared." (*Jebs*: 103)

INTRODUCTION:
LOOKING INTO THE MIRROR, DARKLY

Saro-Wiwa's two novels on Nigeria's—and by extension, Africa's— socio-political and economic realities in the mid-late 80's, owe their existence to his *Vanguard* newspaper column, with weekly instalments running from November 1985 to January 1987. He explains in his "Author's Note" to the first novel, *Prisoners of Jebs*: "My initial plan was to use the inmates of Jebs Prison to examine weekly events in Nigeria, and possibly Africa. I had also the *mischievous* intent of sending wrongdoers who escaped the arm of the law to the Prison to serve time." Nigeria had just welcomed a new leader at that period, its very first self-named military Executive President, Babangida, the beneficiary of the latest *coup d'état,* whose most popular platform was "human rights for all" and who, blessed with a sweet smile and a brain fit for genius (he would later call himself an evil genius) immediately set free many of the political profiteers imprisoned by his military predecessor.

The content and thirst of that first articles-turned-novel were altered by another event, "when," as the writer explains in his Note, "a young 'journalist' on *Vanguard* (Peter Okute is his name) wrote an incompetent and rude review of my award-winning novel, *Sozaboy, A novel in Rotten English*. Pita Dumbrok became a character in the story..."[1] So, here we have the ingredients for a satirical stew concocted by a wronged writer determined to punish perceived sinners and criminals, including the young "journalist" who had dared to pan his award-winning novel. The punishment, no doubt, is not meant to be serious. An elite prison would be built for "politicians, professors, journalists, bureaucrats, judges, smugglers, the military, [all] the stuff of Nigerian life in 1986." Fact and fiction come together; indeed, the fiction had been so forceful that the Air force had to respond to one of the instalments!

In the first novel, *Prisoners of Jebs* (1988), we learn that Jebs (the name is chosen by the Nigerians, out of the blues, and nobody knows its meaning) is created by the Organization of African Unity (OAU) "in its accustomed wisdom" (1). Their reasoning is noteworthy: "Africa needed political unity, economic unity, and general unanimity... Each member-nation had a surplus of prisoners who ate too much food and embarrassed the big bosses. To off-load them was sheer relief." (1) Nigeria, celebrating its twenty-fifth anniversary of a meaningless independence, seizes the opportunity to celebrate something concrete. It therefore offers, in its now legendary largesse, to supply the land and construct the prison, which it does with its usual flair and profligacy. So as to have a truly continental prison, an artificial land was created offshore in the Atlantic; the contract is executed by the Dutch at twice the cost they themselves offered to do it. The contract for constructing the Prison is awarded to the Bulgarians. Some Nigerian "patriots" complain about the necessity for "indigenization"; hence, the contract is newly awarded to one of their members, Popa, "mobilized" with millions of naira that he uses to celebrate his great fortune, to buy a chieftaincy title, and to finally engage the services of Bulgarian engineers. The Bulgarians, proud and wise men, reject his offer. The government is therefore forced to re-award the contract to them at three times the original price. They executed the contract and laughed off to the bank with Nigeria's petro-dollars. Chief Popa disappears, but he later surfaces as a prisoner of Jebs. "The Nigerians were proud of their contribution to the erection of Jebs. They bragged about the numerous millions they had spent on it. But everyone knew the true story, so no one listened." (3)

Of all the African countries that send their elite prisoners to Jebs, Nigeria is the most visible, with its rowdy, irresponsible representatives from both the majority and minority groups. The Director chosen is more or less Nigerian; the governing policy, too, as it is marked by dictatorship and demagoguery and every iniquitous manifestation on mainland Nigeria. Jebs, one might say, is Nigeria. The Director is assisted by several shady characters, particularly, his right-hand man, the infamous Chief Popa; Joromi the Kangaroo, an Australian-born judge sent to the Prison after visiting Nigeria; and the Professor, a Nigerian that arrives mysteriously on the island Prison, and becomes the symbol of wisdom and the master of the Prison's destiny. Pita Dumbrok, the pseudo-journalist, is sent there by the Nigerian government to report on its governance. He is soon arrested by the Director and placed in a cage atop a pole in the open yard. Released by the Director, Dumbrok becomes the Professor's student. He learns to think and is ready to return to Nigeria to use his knowledge to change the society. Meanwhile, the Prison is sinking to the nadir of corruption and chaos, with the Director becoming more ambitious and more fearful of his island being destroyed by Nigeria (where the President is afraid of being overthrown by the Director)which sends a ship for that purpose. Professor, casting a spell over the Prison with his magic wand, finally sinks it before the mission can be accomplished. Only Pita Dumbrok is saved, because he has recently been returned to his cage from where Professor has spirited him away. The journalist's tiny body is discovered by the Nigerian naval force and taken ashore. He is shown to the public at a Presidential press conference announcing that the Jebs mission has been accomplished. Mr. President recognizes (surprisingly) Pita. He then asks the Navy Commander the whereabouts of "the enemy Jebsian you captured" (176) and, smiling, takes a gold watch from his wrist and presents it to Pita with a "welcome to a new Nigeria" greeting.

The second novel, *Pita Dumbrok's Prison* (1991), is a continuation of the first. The title is that of the file opened by a journalist, Andizi, with European reporters' stories on Jebs. Since his famous return, Pita has been in demand to tell his incredulous story on the existence of the Prison and the characters therein. The Nigerian government is also being hassled by European nations, its creditors in the Jebs project, to produce the Prison, and repay the loan for its construction. To punish Nigeria and push it into action, the Europeans send in the army of Sap to fill the country with misery. Pita's serialized articles appear once in the newspaper and is then stopped by government agents, especially because he has been embarrassing the Naval Commander who was in charge of the mission of destroying Jebs. Pita's insistence on the existence of the Prison, and his "Letter to My Compatriots" expressing his desire for people with like mind to come together and search for a new society, convince other journalists who become committed to finding the island. Pita himself ends up being blown away by a parcel-bomb, a la Dele Giwa, a journalist that suffered a similar fate in Babangida's real Nigeria, allegedly for holding information on a drug courier, supposedly dead but living in London and in the services of big drug barons, including Babangida himself. For his quest, the journalist, Andizi, is also killed by a sudden explosion after he and a younger colleague, Biney, have visited seven strange islets in the Jebs region. The parcel-bomb is delivered to Pita by Miss Kokane, one of the notorious inhabitants of Jebs. Biney, saved from death, is captured by Jebsian forces patrolling the borders and taken to the Director-turned-President, His Excellency Babeena Baboona, bestriding his island kingdom "like a colossus." (279) The Nigerians say nothing of Andizi and Biney. "A rotten corpse, a missing youth, were not new in a country where robbers regularly cut down men and women in broad daylight, where hired assassins moved into homes and decapitated their victims, where security agents regularly carted off people to oblivion and received the blessings of courts operating draconian decrees and where a hundred men could, after a show of a trial, be lined up before a firing squad and shot without a simple voice of protest(...)And the army of Sap marched triumphant over the face of the Nigerian nation flaunting its undisputed supremacy while it patiently awaited final orders from ovoviviparous Imf." (280)

    Saro-Wiwa deliberately engulfs his Prison and everything about it in mystery, and confusion. Questions of identity are constant, in regards to people and places, the only certainty being the bad character of Nigerians. Is Jebs Nigeria? One of two professors speaking at a book-launch in Lagos, says that Jebs is "a mirror of Nigeria (...) and what he had read of the Prison made him want to laugh, cry, lament and mourn. He went on to describe the beauties and merits of the Prison and also its demerits, defects and blemishes." (*Prison*: 58) According to his colleague, waxing more philosophical, "every man lives in a prison." Vacuous intellectualism? These professors have never visited Jebs, but do they have to? And, the novelist, as mischievous as ever, calls Nigeria, "a prison, sorry, country" (*Jebs*: 166), while mentioning those among them who, disgusted "escape from the Nigerian nation, or rather, Prison." (145) On the very first page of *Jebs*, it is categorically said that "Nigeria was a veritable prison, although the prisoners, sorry, citizens did not know it, and did not indeed care." One might then wonder why the need to create another Prison. The OAU's vaunted wisdom, one is well aware, is only a mask for its stupidity or, more appropriate, a euphemism for its ability to replace subject with shadow, to exchange good with bad, to foist thralldom on people who go on exuding joy at the freedom carved out for them by these their saviors, the masters. OAU's stated reasons for constructing Jebs lacks reason. How would criminals proffer solutions to problems created by them when they are living in luxury on an elite island?. With Nigeria in charge, who needs a thinking cap? From the beginning, therefore, the reader knows that this mirror, viewed darkly, will throw up monsters and madmen, patriotic vultures and their hapless preys voiceless and without the will to protest. The artist holding up this mirror, a master-portraitist, knows his subject very well; for he also is one of the men in the mirror. He himself affirms his lack of seriousness by believing in OAU's good intentions. But does he really think the whole exercise is not in futility? Is he (not) an agent of the wise men? It is left to us to see whether, with honesty of purpose and the love for his people, he will go beyond the mirror and provide a vision. The story-line's evolution, implied in the two titles, from *Jebs* to *Peter Dumbrok's Prison*, may be considered as a sign of encouragement. The search, as with all serious quests, would be traumatizing, entailing death. Whether anyone would have enough perspicacity, and commitment to persevere, that is another question. For now, we shall look at the mirror, darkly.

Now, Saro-Wiwa's sequencing of his two novels constitutes a major problem if, in truth, some lessons are to be learnt by his audience. For, since Pita Dumbrok is the hero, and since historical events and persons—with delimitations in time and space—the glaring anachronisms when the two novels are combined, would reduce the thrust of the message. Firstly, Pita Dumbrok's sojourn in Jebs would have lasted about nine months, going by statements alluded to another journalist, Andizi, who has just returned form a nine-month leave of absence abroad, and only two days before Pita's re-appearance. Pita disappeared after Andizi's departure for further studies.

THE PRISON, OFF-SHORE AND MAINLAND

Whether it is called Jebs or Nigeria, the author, "a wicked wit" (*Prison*: 19) if ever there was one, presents a catalog of crimes and sins committed singly and collectively. The journalistic style is mostly visible particularly in the first novel, with episodes upon episodes of maneuvers to maintain the status quo, or, to worsen the social conditions so that the oppressors may benefit more. Jebs' journey into the darkness is, of course, set in motion by Nigeria. Nigeria creates the Prison, builds it, keeps it going and, finally, decides to destroy it. Not surprisingly, in choosing the Director, the Nigerians, allowed to decide "because after all, the Prison was in Nigeria," (8) and laying down other complex criteria for sharing this "national cake," after categorically disqualifying all ex-convicts, pull out the name of an ex-con from a hat. This is a very Nigerian way of doing things. The man is a near-illiterate considered a Nigerian until it was discovered that he was born elsewhere, in Niger. This first confusion spreads to all other people and events in Jebs. The Nigerian authorities are very pleased with their choice of Director and are convinced that he will run Jebs "in true Nigerian style." (9), and, yes, he does. The Nigerians vote millions for running Jebs, just as they do in running their own country. As expected, the millions are immediately embezzled by the Director, leaving the Prison in beggardom. Becoming smarter by the day, the man blames his "host country," Nigeria, for his tribulations. He claims that since Jebsian stolen assets belong to Nigeria, he cannot do anything "because in their country assisting millions to disappear is no crime." (21)

The Director hates to read. He loves to sign documents without reading them. He is arrogant. His ignorance is exploited by opportunists such as the fraudulent contractor, Chief Popa, who becomes his henchman and "grows fat on the Director's ear." (9) With Popa's help and his own forays to the host country, the Director becomes an expert in the games the Nigerians play. "Operation Show Your Certificate," preferably forged documents to be shown as proof of one's qualification on the job. "Tribunals of Inquiry," with millions wasted to amass useless information and memoranda, and report, and white paper on innocent people whom, at times, they may not punish. "Magical documents," known as "Local Purchase Orders," presented to obtain fat contracts that need never be executed once the money has been provided up front. In four months, Jebs has begun to look like Nigeria, which does not please the Director; for, he knows full well that the Nigerians hate to have anyone in a highly-placed position for long enough to master it and make an impact. And the man, at least in some pronouncements, appears to be principled, as in this statement to Popa: "A government should mean what it says, say what it means. And act deliberately, after careful thought." (*Jebs*: 70) Pity that talk, as they say, is cheap. The narrator informs us on the very next page that "the Director himself is behaving very much like a Nigerian—criticizing and condemning in public what he is doing in private, and hoping that no one would catch him out." From his very appointment, he fits perfectly into the Nigerian model of corruption and profligacy and incompetence, all of which high qualities give him an excellent chance to remain in the post for life. Besides, he has precedents in Nigeria, and Africa at large: "When you are President, the people love you, clear the streets for you. But just stop being President and see what will happen. So, the only thing is, be President for life." (42) Firstly, the Director will work at mutating from a Prison officer into a nation's leader; then, finally, with the kind help of his newly found European mentors, he will declare himself President of "the kingdom of Jebs."

Some of the details of the Prison's life are debatable. Saro-Wiwa's vituperations are sometimes not borne out by his narrative. The Director's competence, for instance, is in doubt from the start and, the idea that he is a student of the Nigerians, smirks of excessive vilification. We already know that the Nigerians are bad; the Director, too. There is therefore really no need to try to convince us of the man's evolution, or growth. "His ancient depravity" (72) is enough of a springboard to stardom. Perhaps the configuration of his gradual training for perfection is used by Saro-Wiwa to justify Pita Dumbrok's later lessons under the Director's tutelage. That, again, would not be necessary: it is a stated fact that the Director's lessons in socio-political wisdom are being taken from Professor, before being passed down to Pita. It is noteworthy that the Director does seem to be less intelligent than one might think. Once in a while, one is reminded of *Sozaboy*; and the Director does speak some form of rotten English (71). When Popa tells him that Nigerian civil servants "like to dramatize things during military rule," the Director shouts in surprise, "Drama! Are they having a concert party or what?" (68) Always ambitious, the Director entertains the hope that, maybe by 2000, he might walk into Nigeria and assume its presidency. But, then, Saro-Wiwa may be satirizing the man's warped logic and stupidity: if Nigerians have given their country "the final baptism of fire" (66), there would be no Nigeria to rule. And, in the true Nigerian tradition of setting buildings, particularly important ones, on fire (usually to destroy evidence of corruption), the Director has given thought to playing arsonist on his Prison. The only problem: a shortage of matches!

So, he continues to make Jebs a carbon copy of Nigeria, depending on information supplied by the likes of Popa, and the omniscient narrator-critic continues to detail Nigerians' most commendable negative qualities. The elite's pastimes: chasing after what they call "essential commodities...which they do not need but which are, to them, most essential." (2); change of government and abuse of former leaders and praise of new ones. "They love excitement. They hate to question." (2) The Nigerians love to grant their treasury-looters reprieve, "to show that stealing is a human right granted by God to man since time began." (27) The Director loves this wisdom and humanism, and hopes that they will use it to forgive him for emptying the Jebsian treasury. Indeed, given the fact that honest men are prisoners and the thieves, free men, he is expected to be praised for his crime. Public servants love to travel so as to claim daily travel allowance ("estacode") in foreign currency; impressed by this habit, the Director travels to Nigeria, to check on their culture of dirt. The Nigerian prisoners of Jebs live up to this cultured dirt. They refuse to clean up the prison and Popa's assertion that cleanliness is "contrary to Nigerian behavior" (34) is borne out by the Director's visit. After going to the land of dirt, he orders the prisoners to keep Jebs dirty, and the Nigerian prisoners, having once again proven their supremacy among Africans, celebrate with an all-night party.

There comes a time when the Director claims to be fed up with his Nigerian prisoners, because they appear to have all the vices in the world. "How did God ever create this race of human beings? (...) The Nigerians have driven me mad," he laments. (35) They are untrustworthy; are always lying; speak so many languages; have so many religions; make so much noise; are undisciplined; fight to do everything... And the Director bursts into tears. The outburst is humorous, but unconvincing. The Director is already in the know of the Nigerian character and, he, too, shares in it! The other prisoners of Jebs, it must be noted, do not exhibit any better behavior than these Nigerians, which supports our contention that Jebs might as well be Nigeria. The other African prisoners are also criminals, to a certain extent. The manner of their choice is further display of Saro-Wiwa's critical outlook on African affairs. For example,

South African President Botha offers his country's entire black population, but the Nigerians say they are only interested in Nelson Mandela[2]. The Liberian Dictator, Sergeant-turned-General Doe, sends his political opponents after the Nigerians have refused to take his first offer, that is, all the other Liberian tribes and the corpse of his erstwhile ally-become-opponent, General Quiwonkpa, whose corpse he had displayed in the center of his capital city. And other prisoners came, all opponents of their countries' Heads of State.

For each vile group from another African country, there is a Nigerian counterpart, either at Jebs or on the Nigerian mainland. For example, Ghanaian judges, drunk, idolatrous, corrupt, are to be sent to Nigeria, "alleged headquarters of judicial corruption in Africa." (60) The Nigerians, ever ready to claim their supremacy in corruption, affirm that they have their own corrupt judges, and they therefore dump the Ghanaian contingent in Jebs. They are welcomed by Joromi the Kangaroo who has arrived from Nigeria where he headed Kangaroo courts[3] based upon the principle of injustice. Kangaroo tells the arriving Judges a "contemporary drama" (61) about the trial of the polygamous "bright, singing bird" (in reality, the renowned Afro-beat musician, Fela Anikulapo-Kuti) accused of contravening the foreign-exchange decree by having on his person at the airport a few pounds. The Nigerian judge sentences him to five years in prison. The bird has left behind his twenty-four wives. The judge visits the convict while the latter is sick in the hospital, and asks to borrow some of his now idle wives while confessing that the bird, innocent, was jailed as per the advise of Kangaroo. The Nigerian government, embarrassed by the story of that encounter, asks the judge "to go to bed" (63), retires the Chief Superintendent of Prisons with full benefits, and sets the bird free. The Ghanaian judges applaud Kangaroo excitedly. They toast each other with champagne and wine. The Director, so happy about the prison official's fate, orders more champagne and wine for all prisoners. Everyone celebrates "the wonderful way of eminent men who have turned the law into an ass." (63) Meanwhile, it is reported that the judge in the famous case is not a Nigerian, but a Sierra Leonean. "A Saro man."[4] This sends the Sierra Leonean prisoners into ecstasy; for their compatriot's achievement of such fame.

Note that the "twist in the tail" (63) at the end of the drama underlines the absurdity of the whole Jebsian life, and the Nigerian. Everything is based on rumor, fabrication, injustice, and lack of logic. More often than not, one is unsure of the true identity of a Nigerian official, which is a tragedy; for, how does one expect commitment from someone who may be a foreigner? Time and time again, Saro-Wiwa satirizes this problem in his novel. Worse still, other African countries do not challenge the vices so outrageously flaunted by Nigeria. For example, the Sierra Leonean Vice-President visits Nigeria to ask for oil and help in training his country's customs and tax officers, because news has spread that Nigerian customs officers have "magical powers (...) to obtain from their monthly salaries such expensive items as palatial homes" (39). Also, revenue officials deliberately create tax loopholes, from which fall "bloated forms, bloated houses, bloated cars, bloated wives, and bloated bank accounts— straight into the waiting and welcome arms of tax officials and their friends." (40) The Sierra Leonean prisoners criticize their government for wanting to send those officials for training in Nigeria, because they believe that the men already know how to create loopholes. Little do they know that the Vice-President, mesmerized by the magnificently trained Nigerian officials, has decided not to return home. The President, curious and anxious to go to Nigeria himself, has to promise his Vice the Presidency before the man agrees to return to Sierra Leone.

If other countries' politicians are hurrying to go to Nigeria to share the sweet "national cake," Nigeria's military authorities, as they are holding a meeting of the Armed Forces' Ruling Council (AFRC), receive a "celestial message" from "the Holy Spirit" (98), that they "ban" all politicians from politics for "ten years." One member thinks he heard "a hundred years;" another thinks, it is, "banish." The Council agrees that they are to be banished. No wonder, since "a Nigerian politician is venomous. A Nigerian politician of the Second Republic is a curse. The Nigerian politicians of the Second Republic in one body add up to an epidemic." (99) The matter is tabled by Nigeria before the meeting of the Economic Council for West African States. All the Heads of State reject these "terrible animals," and the Sierra Leonean Head advises the Nigerian President to send them to Jebs. There they arrive, "these eminent men who had supervised the ruin of their country." (107) The Director is exceedingly happy to have them, thinking that they will offer him all the millions they have stolen from Nigeria. Unfortunately for him— and for Nigeria!— these prisoners are only the poorest of the lot; "the biggest of fish had slipped through the net and went safely in exile abroad."[5] Thus, the Nigerian military machine has tricked the Director, and everyone else.

The confusing message from "the Holy Spirit" might make one think that Christianity is the accepted official religion in Nigeria. Nothing could be further from the truth. "The Holy Spirit" comes after the invocation by a civilian member of the AFRC, a Christian "Prince of peace." The Nigerian masters accept "the message" as a matter of expediency, the way Nigerians do when they are desperate. As a matter of policy, however, the regime places the country as a member of the Organization of Islamic Conference, without informing anyone, neither the non-Moslem members of the AFRC, nor the general public. As usual, the Nigerians do not complain. As the Moslems would say, it is the will of Allah! Whether Christians or Moslems, or whatever, Saro-Wiwa describes Nigerians as being interested in religion, of course, to ridiculous extent. Witness the group massed at the Lagos Bar Beach, *salaaming* and praying (Moslems and Christians, that is) to God for deliverance from their Nigerian Prison, and also to "the Good Director" to admit them "to the happy and safe Prison of Jebs." (143)

The Director's interaction with other Jebsian characters is a pointer to his own reprehensible traits. Saro-Wiwa may have meant to depict him as such, but it is not clear, because of the expressed objectives for creating Jebs. The Director's best friend is Chief Popa, the Nigerian crook, and it is not at all surprising that, when the Chief Executive becomes desperate about the danger posed by Nigeria to his kingdom on the ocean, Popa suggests himself as a replacement for the embattled man. (168) Joromi the Kangaroo, another confidant, is adored by not only the Director but by Presidents all over Africa. "Only the masses of the people abhorred him and complained bitterly after his visits." (54) Of all his critics, journalists and cartoonists are the worst. When he sees Pita Dumbrok in Jebs, Kangaroo begins to tremble, remembering how he has sentenced his colleagues to unwarranted jail-terms. Again, one may fault Saro-Wiwa's reasoning here, because he has already informed the reader of journalists' fondness for "brown envelopes" (55) containing wads of dollar and pound sterling bills that Nigerian officials use to bribe them to publish lies on their behalf. In addition, Pita's presence on the scene, being due to Saro-Wiwa's wrath against the real-life journalist, Pita Okute, it is strange that the journalist would make Kangaroo shake with fear. Maybe, however, the fictional Pita is being made to evolve towards the committed citizen of the second novel who will stand up against the military, in the name of the people. Whatever explanation is made about the journalist, it is indubitable that Kangaroo deserves to be treated with opprobrium. Soon after his arrival at Jebs, the Nigerians (true to their character) forget him. So also does the Director who lavishes attention upon the epitome of injustice just long enough to make asses of his critics. Saro-Wiwa is wrong to claim that Kangaroo is languishing in Jebs "to the delight of the common people of Africa," but right to mention the delight of the Director. Kangaroo also deserves to have his foreign currency seized, but definitely not by the Nigerian prisoners who do so under the pretext that they have to pay off their country's debts and to import goods into Jebs. Even though thrown into disrepute, Kangaroo continues to be available as the Director's and everyone's favorite judge-referee-chairman. His misjudgement is forgotten; they all prefer to remember that in Nigeria, he presided over the centenary celebrations of the Nigerian Bar Association; a strange collaboration between bench and bar only imaginable in Nigeria. Nigerians constitute more than eighty percent of Jebsian population. Kangaroo is therefore naturally at home among crooks. He "supports the Director's incompetence and skulduggery to the hilt" (*Prison*: 193). The latter rewards him by making him the referee of the football matches on which we shall comment in a later section.

Two characters symbolize an element of wisdom and integrity in Jebs. Firstly, the Guinean prisoner who makes an explanation on the disappearance of the Prison's millions. He says that the money has disappeared, not by magic but that those supposed to take care of it stole it. He recommends detecting theft by checking accounts monthly, by imprisoning any thief, and by making anyone living above his salary-level to account for his unearned wealth. These he calls "basic truths" (23). In his lecture entitled "*Ex Africa Semper Aliquid 'Stupid'*" (From Africa, there comes always something stupid), the Guinean analyzes the African's propensity to tolerate evil and to subject him to idiocy. He pays particular attention to Nigeria, apparently created by God "to be an object lesson to black people everywhere." (11) He is disturbed by Nigeria's abject failure, her squandermania, her inability to do anything concrete with its "black gold," oil. He asks Nigerian prisoners to bend their heads in shame. They all comply, including Popa. Now, the question arose regarding what to do to eliminate Africa's *aliquid stupid*. The great lecturer promises to address that in a future lecture. The Guinean warns his fellow Africans that the road to success is very difficult but, to achieve success, "the individual [has] to take himself more seriously. The individual [has] to think. Because thought [is] very important to the process of eliminating all 'aliquid stupid'. At the mention of the word 'thought', the Nigerian prisoners [become] restless." (11) Popa, who absolutely detests thinking, walks out of the meeting.

The Guinean wise man never gives the promised second lecture. And one notes that the first lecture is attended by only several prisoners because the Director has warned people to stay away from a speaker interested in abusing mother Africa, "and anyone who [abuses] his mother [does] not deserve life itself." (10) It would therefore be preposterous to believe that his words of wisdom would have much impact. While the lecture is in progress, the Director is busy counting his millions. The Guinean's "basic truths" are common knowledge to anyone among his eminent audience, that is, anyone willing to be honest to himself. The importance of *thought* has been mentioned by Saro-Wiwa in *Sozaboy*. It re-surfaces here as a major lacuna in the Nigerian psyche. It is significant that the Guinean philosopher does not expatiate on the subject. There are quite a number of references to it. "The Nigerian government was averse to thinking; she did not mind other people thinking for her." (119) This remark is made in regards to the hordes of Nigerians running away to England and being sent back by the British government. The Nigerians, we are also told, being lawless, assert that, instead of politics, everybody practices "bellytics," that is, the art of using every means to find something to eat. Many people do not understand this line of reasoning, and do not wish to understand "because the Nigerians have given up every right to be taken seriously as a nation of thinkers." (64) Obtuseness is the country's hallmark and the few wise men have been forced to consider themselves ignorant.

More light is thrown on Saro-Wiwa's definition of *thinking,* in *Pita Dumbrok's* Prison. During the attack on Nigeria by Imf's army of Sap, the Commander exudes joy at his troops' effortless depredations of the country. He splits the Nigerian enemy into "their natural groups—the thinkers and the un-thinkers," and says that the latter number less than one per cent. His strategy is to concentrate the power of the Brain Drain Brigade on this group. "A nation devoid of thinkers is no nation at all. A people who do not think are the plaything of history. They are mere toys. Worse, they are as brutes, merely eating, sleeping and reproducing." (83) Thinkers are therefore all those using their intelligence for productive purposes within the nation. Some of these thinkers escape the attack of the army of Sap and go to Saudi Arabia and other foreign lands (an allusion to the eventful exodus of Nigerian doctors and nurses to the Middle

East). The country's educational system is reduced to rubble by the Sap army's Stagflation Brigade that has raised book and equipment prices. There is little or no learning in the universities. Professors fly away in search of greener pastures. An insignificant group among these "thinkers" remains in the country to resist against the invading army. They are "a great challenge," according to the Commander; "however, they are an insignificant group, incapable of fighting back successfully or thwarting our war efforts" (86) In the face of such affirmations confirmed by the devastation visited upon Nigeria, one may safely conclude that the thinkers stand no chance and that their efforts are inconsequential. One might ask, of what use is a group of thinkers (professors, doctors, nurses, technologists, etc) standing against an army with unparalleled strength such as Sap? Saro-Wiwa's definition still remains unclear!

To further confuse issues, we also note that thinking involves exchange of ideas, debate, putting heads together to seek solutions to problems. That is exactly the advice given to the Director of Jebs by the Nigerian government. "He had to keep the prisoners debating, maybe Nigerian fashion." (*Jebs*: 24) Loans, politics, religion, Jebsian foreign affairs, everything is debated in Nigeria; most importantly the people's opinion does not count in the government's final decision and action. The debate concerns their choice of government, military or civilian. After heated arguments, all the prisoners agree that Jebs should not have a military government, which, of course it does not. In essence, their thinking is an academic exercise on who is misruling, or should misrule, in Africa; for, as the prisoners also agree, both the military and the civilians are engaged all over the continent in killing their countries. Saro-Wiwa knows the Nigerian fashion very well: it is the period of Babangida's famous Conference on the constitution when, after lengthy debates, memoranda and all, the conferees propose a socialist state, and the government, most patriotically, threw the proposal into the garbage and produced a White Paper containing its own particular thinking.

Still regarding thought, one would expect that Professor, "something of an institution in Jebs" (5), the most important and most respected of the prisoners, would help to unravel its mystery. Professor it is that the Director consults in apparent desperation over the missing millions: "Disappearing was a magical trick. The only magician in Jebs was Professor." (14) Without using his professional stones (magic), using traditional methods of inquiry (brains), Professor advises the director to pay attention to *details,* as a competent leader does, that he should search his, the Director's, bedroom ceiling, mattress and garden where he, Director, has hidden the money. The Director later informs Professor that he has found out how the millions disappeared, that "they were eaten up by a little bug called DETAIL which the Professor had planted in Jebs Prison(...) He pleaded with Professor to conjure away the bug." (20) Professor laughs at him for behaving like a Nigerian and blaming his misfortune on everyone but himself. Integrity is therefore an essential aspect of thinking. The problem with Professor is his magic. His co-prisoners call him "professor of magic," "a real jujuman" (6). He himself enjoys the magical powers, which he places at the service of the corrupt Director: when he is convinced that the Nigerians will attack the Prison, the Director appeals to Professor to remove the spell on the Generals who have been sleeping since their arrival in the Prison one month before. The military men go to Nigeria, infiltrate the Police, and obtain guns which they bring back to Jebs. Once the guns are securely in Jebs, Professor sings the Generals back to sleep and makes the Director bullet-proof. Professor's readiness to serve the Director attains other, more complex and more compromising dimensions when the magician's identity is confused (deliberately?) by Saro-Wiwa with that of "Wole Soyinka, Nigeria's Nobel Laureate [who] declared the Government the finest thing that had ever happened to Nigeria." (162) Weaving further this "factional" intrigue, the novelist has government appoint Soyinka Commander of the Federal Republic (a naval ship) to go and "end the obnoxious rule of the Director of Jebs" (167).

Meanwhile, Professor, inside Jebs, has listened to Pita Dumbrok's prayer to destroy Jebs. Professor begins to chant strange songs. He conjures a boat-like Sarcophagus beside the Prison. He casts a spell over the Prison. He has decided to destroy it and rescue "only those elements which would ensure the emergence of a new generation, a new entity shorn of the inanities which the director's administration had bred over the year of existence of the Prison of Jebs." (169) And "the Professor" (Soyinka), leaves for Stockholm with his troops of assorted friends—"a powerful force of admirals, captains and lieutenants"- and admirers and officers, to purchase dynamite and go on to destroy Jebs, "leaving no trace of its disorganized existence." (170) When the Prison is finally destroyed, no one is sure of who does the deed: Professor or the Professor, or both coalesced into one?

Saro-Wiwa is, of course, satirizing Soyinka's friendship and compromising relationship with Babangida, the military "prince of the Niger" (title of a biography by a Nigerian opportunist bourgeois, Chidi Amuta). A thinking person that calls a military regime a democracy is making the mistake of his life. A thinking person that wines and dines with a dictator is a potential political prostitute. At the fictionalized lunch held to honor the Nobel Laureate, the unnamed President exults in having "captured an eminent lieutenant. Had not that great General Napoleon, said that men are led by toys?" (168) Significantly, we read that, upon watching the merry friends on television, "the Director of Jebs wept." Why? Possibly because he realizes even he, the colorless pseudo-dictator- that the one percent of Nigerian thinkers have been dealt a decisive blow. The metaphorical command crafted by Saro-Wiwa refers to the national honor given to Soyinka by the government as a face-saving reaction to the Nobel Prize; as a further sop, he was provided with a presidential plane in which he and his entourage gloriously jetted out to the award ceremony. There was an aftermath to the tragicomedy. A consolation, impossible to use in Saro-Wiwa's novel: Soyinka came to understand that Babangida was a self-styled "evil genius" ready to smile his way through mass murder, death of democracy, and absolute dictatorship of his planned life-presidency. On an eventful day of celebration of his own sixtieth birthday, the Nobel Laureate marched in protest on the streets of Lagos and stomped upon the medal awarded to him by the people's murderer. That, symbolically is the triumph of thinking.

Saro-Wiwa deserves to be congratulated for making himself an integral part of this confusion called Nigeria, sorry Jebs. He does this combining fact with fiction. Already, from his Author's Note, we know that the novel, *Jebs*, is a transformed newspaper column, and that certain individuals objected to the columnist's acerbic comments on Nigeria. A fictional Saro-Wiwa is therefore brought into the Jebsian affair, firstly, as a rumor (what else?). It is said that this Saro-Wiwa is in the pay of the Saro (Sierra Leonean) prisoners and that, indeed, he himself is a fake Nigerian, really a Sierra Leonean settled in Port Harcourt, home of old Saro families. "He had a way of caricaturing or magnifying what Nigerians said or did in Jebs, while hiding what the Saro in particular, and others in general, did (...) *The Nigerian prisoners promised to deal with the Saro prisoners. Some day.*" (*Jebs*: 38, emphasis mine) The rumor about the "loud-mouth and trouble-maker" substantiated later by the most laughable, real occurrence of 1986, when, in response to one of the articles in the Jebsian column, when the Director lamented of the Nigerian pilots' knack for crashing planes, the Nigerian Chief of Air Staff vehemently defended the Air Force's patriotism and "ability to perform its primary function which is the defense of the nation by air. It sounds naive to think that a trained pilot would deliberately crash an aircraft simply because he does not want to fight. What then is he in the NAF to do?" (179) The Chief's naivete, or perverted patriotism, is simply mind-boggling. He forgot that Saro-Wiwa was writing satire, that Jebs was a figment of his imagination even though it was fed by facts and based upon realities. Fear is one useful result of satire; hence, the air-man, aware of his force's incompetence and disabilities and inability to fly a kite, was perhaps jittery that someone might decide to turn the writer's imagination into action or, that some pilots had actually been turning the shameful trick. It is a fact that, in Nigeria, an Air Force plane carrying an alleged coup-plotter crashed in 1986, and there have been mysterious plane-crashes, including one, in 1990, of a Hercules C-130 in which some two-hundred (you are never sure of exact numbers, including the population of the country!) young military officers lost their lives.

For writing his article, the real-life Saro-Wiwa was an unwilling guest of the Air Force authorities who interrogated him as an unpatriotic trouble-maker. The occurrence is included in the *Jebs* when the Director, the author of the anti-Air Force statement in the first place, expresses his fear of the Air Chief who might bomb the Prison and of Saro-Wiwa, who has been writing negative stories about the place. The Director is also informed of another side of Saro-Wiwa which refers to the Nigerian civil war: the death in a plane crash of the writer's bosom friend, Dan Ato, an Air Force pilot. "Since then, every plane crash has affected him badly," affirms Pita Dumbrok. (104) Thus we perceive a serious side to the satirist. He could be called a *thinker*, one who wishes to use his art to bring about change in the society. The danger for the satirist, the thinker, is that the un-thinkers would cavil at his well-intentioned criticism or, in the extreme, kill him. The Nigerian Jebsian prisoners' promise to deal with the Saro prisoners, some day, makes a shiver rush through one's body. It rings a bell of reality, the reality of what has now happened to Saro-Wiwa.

Would fear for his life explain his statement in the cover-pages to his second Jebsian novel, *Pita Dumbrok's Prison*, that "all the characters in this book are fictional and bear no resemblance whatsoever to anyone, dead or alive, known to the author"? Was it out of simple subterfuge, or carelessness that he claimed, in the Author's Note to *Jebs*, that "the main thrust of my story had nothing to do with the government of the day"? Both pronouncements add to the confusion emanating from the novelist's fictional universe, and questions about his intentions and achievements. For one thing, all the characters in the second novel cannot be fictional if it is to be accepted that the story is a continuation of the first novel. For another, the main thrust of the story cannot but include the government of the day if the basis for it is the life and the living of Nigeria. The writer's criticism of the Second Republic politicians is understandably a major interest, those looters and leeches having been booted out of office by the men in uniform. However, the latter, the current rulers at the time of Jebs, the creators and colonizers of Jebs, as it were, are also major players, even if they do not don jerseys and participate in the football match. Saro-Wiwa's encounter with the Air Force, mentioned above, is an example of the military's action in the satirical game. The activities of the ever-smiling President (why does Saro-Wiwa not call him by his name, Babangida, when he so does with many other characters?) And his henchmen are well chronicled in both novels, particularly in *Prison*. If the first novel satirized the off-shore prisoners as complementary criminals to their counterparts on the mainland, the second text places the latter at center-stage.

And the Nigerian military regime figures prominently in both prisons. Discussions in Jebs include the meeting of Abuja ECOWAS Heads of State, all "debtors-hunters" and "treasure-hunters," (91) searching for their debts which, according to Professor, are hidden at Abuja. The prominent military Heads have signed off their countries to the International Monetary Fund (IMF). The hunters, after failing to find the hidden billions, adjourn for one year and, meanwhile, commission a "palace of debt [costing fifteen million naira] as befitted the profligacy of Abuja." (*Jebs*: 92) Abuja, where Nigeria's money is sunk, is a sight to behold: gigantic five-star hotels, a plethora of badly constructed government buildings, and a surrounding wasteland so prominent that most of the billions must have been buried underground or spent removing any recognizable signs of development. Abuja is the fortress of the Head of State, his haven which he is ever afraid of leaving. "In Africa, you do not step out of your domain if you are the boss. Some have been caught napping at OAU meetings. Ask Gowon. Others were caught praying in Mecca. Ask Idiagbon."[6]

Saro-Wiwa also satirizes the Nigerian Military's game of "musical chairs" (139) of whimsically changing postings, especially important ones, and retiring officers sporadically and as suddenly as they are promoted. Upon their retirement, these most patriotic officers are duly rewarded with the pastime of political positions in parastatals or on various boards where they continue to grow physically and financially. Or, as is often the case, our retired political generals become great farmers. "Thus does Nigeria waste her sons. No tears for the nation," asserts the narrator. (139) Other African countries copy Nigeria in offering fast promotion to their military men; sent to Jebs are many young but highly-placed sergeants-turned-generals, a mutation best done by a coup. And these progressive generals are bejeweled with medals. "In Africa, medals are given for battles lost." (116) Example: Ojukwu, the Biafran leader who promoted himself general after losing all major towns to the federal forces during the civil war. That, according to the narrator, is "his very valuable contribution to military history." (116) Ojukwu is clearly abhorred by Saro-Wiwa. His botched secession is ridiculed by Popa who advises the Director to "separate" from Nigeria, and to do it right, unlike Ojukwu who did it "just to have his name in history." (132) Saro-Wiwa also sneers at the real-life Ojukwu's announcement in a Nigerian magazine that he was "ready to fight again if Babangida, the smiling dictator, was said to be putting together a special corps for his personal protection and use, called the National Guard. The Jebsian Director surmises that Ojukwu might be chosen as head of that secret reserve army. "As a General, Ojukwu was not much to write home about... But he had the ability of leading a suicide attack against any enemy, and he did not care how long it lasted or how many people died in it, so long as he himself survived it all. His leadership of Biafra two decades earlier had demonstrated that amply." (144) In preparing for the expected Nigerian invasion, the Director makes a glorious speech compared to Ojukwu's, with Nigeria being accused of wanting to exterminate his country in a "war of genocide;" that the Nigerians wish to steal their great wealth; that Jebs is better than Nigeria; that, like Biafra, they have friends and, that if Biafra armed only with dane guns, could resist Nigeria for almost three years, Jebs, with its superior arms, will do better. Unlike Ojukwu, however, the Director vows not to desert Jebs. And, when the Nigerian naval ship, *Ambe*, captures "the first foreign enemy soldier, Pita Dumbrok" at the blow-up of the Prison, it is stated that the achievement is "more than Ojukwu, General of the People's Army [ho! ho!], had been able to do." (175)

Remarks are made about the Nigerian military's professional incompetence; the soldiers are too busy with politics and government to get involved in such dangerous pursuits as war, except, naturally civil war in which they can kill off one another, or a coup where the winner takes over ownership of the land. Their incompetence and lack of professionalism are patriotically imitated by others in uniform, such as the Police. Saro-Wiwa uses a historical event at the University in Zaria where students were wantonly murdered by the police, to cast aspersions on that very uncivil force. News reaches the police that the university has been invaded by South African marauders: the university has been closed, and students sent home. However, the Police verify what they have suspected, that the invaders have killed all the students. Then, parents begin to complain of finding their children in the mortuary. Lo and behold, the Police now admit that there were no South-Africans anywhere close to the campus, only policemen using students as targets in a shooting practice! And the Nigerians, proud of their Police Force, praise the brave men for felling so many targets and using live bullets, in preference to rubber bullets or tear gas which are considered too cheap and ordinary for the police of the great nation. Other uniformed patriots, prison warders, are known for thoroughly torturing prisoners, to teach them a lesson. Which does not stop these prisoners from escaping from time to time, given the warders' love of freedom!

Saro-Wiwa is not always critical of the forces; he sometimes praises the leadership and explains their incompetence. When some police officers are caught co-operating with criminals, he blames it on their poor salaries and their having to support "jumbo-sized polygamous families." He is also full of praise for the Inspector-General of Police and his deputies "who had, by self-improvement, obtained University degrees and disciplined training. But they had under them what amounted to a rabble. Poorly-housed, poorly educated, badly-equipped and poorly-paid policemen." (136) He tacitly praises the Nigerian President for promising to re-organize the Police Force. Can we therefore claim that Saro-Wiwa is pro-military, or pro-good government? It is hard to answer this question. His satire on the military is very broad, very general, rather unspecific when certain individuals are concerned. He easily could have attacked the marauding military with the same vigor as he does Ojukwu. The veneer with which he treats the Uniform may be explained by his belief in the Nigerian federalism at the time of the civil war. His take on the events of the 80s is less easy to explain. *Pita Dumbrok's Prison* makes the novelist's stand even more controversial. The Nigerian President is now given a name, Abudu Malik, with a mysterious, confusing identity: Pita Dumbrok, the recipient of Mr. President's unexpected generosity in the form of a gold watch, is unknown to the young man who has been away from his beloved Nigeria for only about one year. Pita remembers meeting the President at the State House once, almost two years earlier, but this is not the same President he saw then. "So had there been a new coup installing a new President, or was he in an altogether different country?" (*Prison*: 13) So, has Pita missed another game of the Nigerian "musical chairs" with leadership changing hands as quickly as the military messiahs change girl-friends? The narrator's chronicling of Malik's life-history weaves more confusion. He tells us that the man is a World War II veteran, became a General and seized power when the politicians proved their inability to rule the nation. He returned the nation to civilian rule two years after, but the politicians again proved incompetent and were thrown into prison in large numbers by a young colonel, Badiya. With the new leader's refusal to deal with their matter with dispatch, he himself was overthrown in a bloody coup by a young Major Laya who promoted himself General, freed the thieving politicians and began a reign of despotism abhorred by a young sergeant who assassinated him and became Head of State. The unnamed Sergeant was summarily removed within one week by some Majors who invited Malik, "the only surviving military man with a reputation to rule the nation." (76) Malik's only condition for acceptance is that he be called President (a la Babangida). "This was in line with his democratic bent." (77)

It is this democratic bent that leads to the setting up of a Defense Council and a parallel Council, the State Security Council, whose membership the President rotates regularly among the young coup-makers. Now, the whole group (*they,* according to the narrator) is responsible for promising to "clean the Aegean stables that Nigeria had become." (77) They suspend the constitution and promise to return the country to civil rule after some years. But these redeemers of the nation have fallen for money, women, the bureaucrats' sycophancy and the business men's obsequiousness. In short, they are now as corrupt as their predecessors. Coup-plotters rear their heads and the rulers hack them down as fast as they appear. As President, Abudu Malik is not blamed by the narrator; rather, he is pitied as being "trapped" between his warlord-lieutenants and the other colleagues outside government: "He had become a prisoner to his desire to see the return of democratic rule and to the young hawks in the junta who needed his reputation to justify to a restive population, the continuation of military rule. He could neither resign nor was he in effective control of the ruling clique." (77) Again, the question, does Saro-Wiwa have a soft spot for the military, or for certain military men? His Malik, so pitiful, so ineffective, comes across as a tired, old war-horse best retired to pasture, and redundant in the equations of a country being misruled by gun-toting goons. Why can Malik not resign? It is because he himself enjoys power and its requisites. Besides, Malik is not interested in democracy. Witness his handling of the controversy over Jebs, the prison built and bombed out by his country, and which the European Creditors and other African countries are anxious to find, or at least, know the truth of its fate. Malik sends emissaries to the Europeans on bended knees, with a load of lies, as they seek to have Nigeria's astronomical debts re-scheduled. He himself attends the meeting of the Organization of African States (called, in the first novel, Organization of African Unity, which is the real union of African misrulers), holds a secret meeting with the overwhelmed Secretary-General whom he orders not to place the Jebs issue on the agenda. Given the fact that Nigeria is the only paid-up member of the Organization, and therefore his employers, the Secretary is compelled to comply. The African leaders are not at all concerned about principle, they are only anxious to save faces, to present to the world an image of responsibility and accountability, and peace and progress. Jebs, the narrator reminds us, is their prison, too; "human life means nothing to African leaders." (48) And they will do Nigeria's bidding any day.

Malik's Nigeria, "The Giant of Africa, The Sleeping Elephant, The Hole of Africa," (41) is a veritable hopeless place. The President is so helpless in the face of the disaster over which he is ruling that he secretly agrees that the Europeans should punish his country and -surprise, surprise!- "that the arrival of the goddess Imf would direct the attention of his captors from the power game to the real task of national redemption which they had undertaken of their own volition." (78) Malik, figure-head, or headless Head of State? Saint surrounded by devils? One cannot find sympathy for the neo-colonialist fool colluding with the colonists-turned-imperialists from almighty Europe. Malik's government actually puts the country up for sale; only, no willing takers! It turns out that Malik's government is not really sure of what has happened to Jebs. Malik is bluffing, pretending to be anxious to get to the truth but preventing anyone from making the effort. His navy Chief, most concerned with his personal image, and "afraid to make an ass of himself for the second time before his Commander-in-Chief" (80) who has already asked him about the prisoner taken from the ambiguous first attack on Jebs, is determined to keep Jebs a mystery forever. When a young female journalist, Asa, after going on a personal search for Jebs, finds a prison off the Lagos coast, the Malik regime quickly informs their European masters that Jebs has been discovered. The Europeans are not deceived however; the discovered prison is Ita Oko, whose establishment as usual in Nigerian affairs, is the subject of rumors. In their investigation, the Europeans affirm many a truth about Nigerians "known to be one of the most mendacious people on earth— 'mendacity' being a Nigerian word which had been appropriated casually by the ubiquitous English language." (64) The Nigerian government denies owing some of the debts listed by the Europeans. In Nigeria, the meaning of "developing" is "look forward. Never backward." (66). When the Europeans announce their decision to send the goddess Imf to Nigeria, Malik instructs his Ministry of Finance to inform the members of the Paris and London Clubs that Nigeria has run out of paper and is therefore unable to issue visas to Imf.

The satire of the goddess Imf is most tragi-comical, a brilliant portrait of European imperialism in Africa. This powerful, relentless, unforgiving goddess is the creation of the Americans who use her to control world economy and compel borrowers to suffer like slaves, and to live according to the dictates of the United States. Imf reproduces children identical to her, hydra-headed, with a trillion feet, a trillion eyes, a trillion hands." (67) They are called Sap and accompany her on the journey to nations slated for punishment. Together, they easily reduce these nations "to beggardom, to the wearing of rags, to the eating of left-over food from rubbish dumps, to ignorance and illiteracy. And the debts grew as they were collected, forcing the goddess Imf to send more of her dreaded children to the devastated battlefields." (67) Notwithstanding the Nigerians' prayer for Imf not to arrive, or their President's attempts to stall, the monster and her children descend from the skies. The monstrous army is divided into seven Brigades, of "Hunger, Disease, Brain Drain, Theft, Stagflation, Riot and Chaos." (70) They attack the unwary Nigerians from all angles and, soon enough, the country is brought to its knees. The land is devastated; with an incompetent military, Nigeria, even if it were to try, could never be a worthy opponent to Imf and her Sap Army.

Saro-Wiwa's creations no doubt are personalization of the International Monetary Fund (IMF), and the Structural Adjustment

Program (SAP), which have almost sapped Nigerians' energy to survive the hardship imposed upon them. Several of the events satirized in the novel actually occurred. For example, there was a SAP riot (130) in Lagos that led to the cancellation of Babangida's trip to France in 1991. Armored tanks were rolled out to quell the riots in which the rioters burnt some government buildings, and some of them were killed by the angry military. In reality, all the allegorical Brigades of the Sap Army were very evident in the lives of Nigerians. The President kept smiling and promising better days. In Saro-Wiwa's story, Europe gives Nigeria reprieve and re-schedules its debts. Imf's army withdraws, but the devastation is done. Just as in today's Nigeria. The story of Imf is an excellent example of Euro-American sadism, as well as their complicity in Africa's destruction by dictators whom they prop up for as long as they dance to the imperialists' tune. In an interesting twist to the story of Jebs, France and Britain vie for a place of honor with the Director-turned-dictator (in "the new Jebs," the man now wears a faded khaki uniform). Britain invites the Nigerian Malik to London, while France welcomes the Jebsian Baboona (baboon!) To Paris. Both countries send ambassadors to Jebs. Thus, they establish their influence over a new land, before the imperialist competition arrives.

"This new Jebs" is Professor's magical creation, on a new spot in the ocean, with seven islets. Professor has acted thus, to give Nigeria another chance. But, Nigeria does not know of the new Jebs led by the President and Savior Babeena Baboona, where Kangaroo is Chief Justice, and Chief Popa and other famous prisoners have been given new life. Professor is tagged "the spirit of Africa." (117) By resuscitating Jebs, he may be desirous of giving Nigeria, and Jebs, a second chance; unfortunately, neither of the two prisons shows any signs of improvement. Baboona's "new Jebs" is worse than the original model. With the seven new islets, Professor highlights this evolution towards the nadir of iniquities. Baboona signs away, to Britain and France, the mineral rights of his unexplored kingdom, concerned as he is with only the promised payment into his coded Swiss account.(133) He has graduated from drinking beer to Remy Martin cognac happily supplied by the French ambassador; he regularly lubricates his brain with the potent brew. To perfect his governing skills, he studies the *African Handbook on the Torture of Political Opponents*. He has placed Popa and other Nigerians in "preventive detention" (240), to prevent them from causing problems for him; then, he releases Popa to collaborate with him in eliminating Pita Dumbrok who has been reported to be writing negatively about Jebs.

The "new Nigeria" is similarly worse than the old, as Pita Dumbrok has found out. In his opinion, the main culprits for the degradation, are the military. During his interrogation by Captain Ita of the State Security, the journalist comments, "They [the Military] have been a great betrayal... They have been without a vision for the country. They've failed to fight corruption and disorder, which is the only reason their intervention has been welcomed; indeed, they have immersed themselves in corruption and caused confusion enough to benefit by it. They have now formed a dangerous club of wounded men, alas, and am afraid that if they are not stopped from further infecting the body of the nation, they will lead us all to perdition." (201) Saro-Wiwa's portraiture of the journalist attests to our contention that Pita's is a correct assessment.

PITA DUMBROK, OR THE JOURNALIST AS THE VOICE OF VISION

Pita Dumbrok's evolution from the verge of Jebs Prison to the catalyst for change in the Nigerian prison is excellently depicted in the two novels. Saro-Wiwa uses the character of the young journalist to express the importance of the profession, as well as the necessity and possibilities of thinking. Pita arrives in Jebs as "a semi-literate hack" (*Jebs*: 27) of no consequence. He is quickly caged on a pole from where he keeps chirping "silly plot!" as his comment on the debate over Africans' corruption and incompetence. He learns to become responsible, gradually with the help of the Director and, particularly Professor. The lessons stem from the satire on Nigerian journalists whom, according to Saro-Wiwa, are mostly stone-stupid. The few good ones are "either very busy writing themselves into the hearts of the new humane regime or writing themselves into jail for criticizing the judgment which kangaroos "blessed animals hand down to men." (27) For the first lesson on honesty and integrity, the Director shows Pita a brown envelope. He grabs at it only to find it empty. The Director assures him that "the pen is mightier than the sword," that an intelligent writer can always parlay his knowledge into the necessities of life. He urges Pita to think, to read good books, and to become wise. For the second lesson on commitment to development, the Director says that while Nigeria has done well to give millions of dollars to the anti-apartheid ANC, it would do better to use intelligence and self-reliance and to attain technological development. Meanwhile, Pita, ever more alert, notices that the Director's governing methods are policies which merit condemnation. He wonders whether the man is expressing his own ideas or those borrowed from others. Pita finally realizes that the real thinker is Professor. Professor shows a soft spot for him and, as we have stated, saves only Pita when Jebs is sunk.

Pita begins to appreciate people's feelings, such as the pain of the Guinean prisoner-philosopher. He thinks incisively of the Director's dishonest speech urging the Jebsians to fight to save the Prison against Nigerian "genocide." He recognizes Nigerians' potential for greatness through the Nobel Prize won by Wole Soyinka, even though his zeal is temporarily dented by news of the parcel-bomb that killed the journalist, Dele Giwa. Upon reading a secret memorandum by Northern Emirs and Chiefs on the necessity to keep political power in the North, he decides to return to Nigeria, "a blessed country endowed with a rich soil, mineral wealth, a strong and vigorous population." (*Jebs*: 146)

This Nigeria of his dreams, one notices, is hardly seen or experienced by himself or anyone else in Saro-Wiwa's novels. The journalist's description of Saro-Wiwa as "a mean, spiteful little wretch, and (...) learning to be a satirist," (103) is, to all intents and purposes, merely humorous reference to the quarrel between the Nigerian writer and the young journalist. Essentially, the fictional Pita is no longer the moronic journalist rebuked by Saro-Wiwa. Studying pays off for Pita. Whether any of that is relevant to creating and nurturing the new Nigeria is a matter for long debate. He vows to dedicate himself to "action backed by thought, in concert with like minds [and] set an example for others to follow." (147). His return from Jebs to Nigeria becomes a spectacle for rumor-mongers, with that gold watch from the President making him a hero, albeit one who, given his dirty appearance, ugly face and unusual ideas and behavior, is suspected to be mad by many. His *researched* ideas on the Nigerian leader as a great man must shock even the most naive observer. His famous "Letter to My Compatriots" (*Prison*: 103-114)[7] is a rehash of Nigerian history and the betrayal of the people by the military rulers. His detailed description of Africa's glorious past represented by the great Empires, would be a master-piece of history. So also is the story of Africa's depredation by the foreign enslavers and colonizers. His condemnation of "our people [who have been] willing tools in the hands of the enemy (*Prison*: 110) is a convincing example of a mind prepared to do self-criticism and to compel others to join him in solving the nation's problems honestly and thoroughly. His final proposal: "search for the Prison! Look for the Professor! He holds the key to the truth of the Prison, and he is real." (113) His description of Jebs as quintessence of misrule, can only lead to confusion. For, were those heeding his call to succeed in finding the Prison, what would be the use? Perhaps such successful quest is to conscientize them to be like him; nevertheless, that would still not inform anyone categorically of the revolutionary *action*.

One positive aspect of Pita's personality is his ability to arouse others' commitment to a cause. The paradox of such an ugly man blessed with "a voice like honey," (149) is captivating; by deduction, it may be said that Pita is an artist acting as the voice of vision for his people. The visionary diagnoses the country's problem and, in spite of the gravity of the current dilemma, he is optimistic enough to predict a new Nigeria. He is heard by other young journalists, Andizi, a Features Editor, and Biney, who follow his call and embark on the search for Jebs. The old guard, the Publisher and the Editor, discourage their decision: "Who needs patriotism in Nigeria?" is the latter's rhetorical question.

If the reader is supposed to believe in the future as belonging to the youth brigade, then Andizi and Biney's quest for Jebs should be accomplished. On the contrary; firstly, Jebs is a "new prison," worse than what Pita experienced; secondly, the wise Professor has added seven new islets, unknown to Pita or to anyone else. It may be true that the process of the search itself, and not the end (discovery of Jebs) is the important aspect in this whole matter. It may even be opined that the optimism aroused in the two men by Pita, is of significance, and not the actual journey. All that would be elements of patriotism, that is, the will to act selflessly to ameliorate the country's destiny. For instance, Andizi recounts his dream of Biney as a middle-aged man living in "a strange country where everything works to near perfection." (139) The big catch is that, in addition to that dream, there are the fictional realities of those islets to which an unseen hand appears to be directing the two men's rented boat.

The islets constitute an allegory of vices already described at length in the two novels. They are, "the land of laziness, misery and hunger," where the people always beg for food and, after eating, fall asleep; "the land of happiness," whose inhabitants dance and make love all year long, and are extremely dirty; land of religious fanatics, with two groups at each other's throats. Land of thieves, where the judges always find the innocent guilty, and where robbers are honored. The land where the obese oppress the thin men and where aliens came and took over mining of the thin people's gold, forced the Fat and the Thin to live together in disharmony, and passed the mineral wealth to the Fat[8]; the land where the illiterate govern the literate and have eliminated all but one of the latter; land of Moolah, an iron-piece valued by the god, Moolah, worshiped by the ignorant people who have transformed the piece into a god, like money.

The seven islets, note the searchers, have a great deal of resemblance to Nigeria. They hope to see Jebs, and Professor, and to return home so that they may begin to work to eliminate the vices there. They suddenly sight another land. Then, as suddenly, their boat is enveloped by mist. Biney becomes grumpy, complaining about everything. Andizi tries to calm him down. A sound explodes, and the bullet kills Andizi. Thus have the two failed in their quest.

Biney survives and is captured and taken to Jebs. His fate strangely similar to Pita's. Would that be an ingredient for hope? Nigerians give no thought to the decomposed body of Andizi washed ashore at Lagos. He is buried and forgotten. Biney, too, is forgotten. Any contribution he might be able to do remains buried with Saro-Wiwa in his unmarked grave!

WOMEN AS PART OF THE PROBLEM AND THE SOLUTION

Now, in the Nigerian, or Jebsian prison, Man is master monster. Saro-Wiwa's Nigerians are, in their vast majority, men of mean character, in whatever profession, at whatever level, inasmuch as they are catalysts for social, economic and political rape of their unfortunate country. A chauvinistic society this is, without any doubt. Saro-Wiwa is, however, careful to portray a realistic reflecting in the dark mirror. Looked at closely, the reflection reveals some female figures. These few women complement the men, perfectly. They bring out the worst in men who, grateful for the favor, fawn upon the women, showing that the two cannot live without one another.

The female prisoners' arrival in Jebs is an occasion for festivities; the caliber of women, commensurate with the high level of criminality of the civilian population. The most prominent arrivals are Madam Kokane and her daughter, Miss Smuggle Kokane. Madam is "the precursor of a special breed of women being reared by excellent skills of observation of the female anatomy" (a skill well exhibited in his other creative writings, too). It is all graphic, lewd, caricatured, and darkly humorous. Madam is "appropriately large. Her breasts hung pendulously in front of her and her posterior stretched behind her like the wooden bodywork of a five-ton truck." Her daughter is beautiful, "slim, comely and dressed in superfluous finery." (81) At the sight of these two cocaine-laden bodies, their male hosts, particularly the uxorious Nigerians, become excited; they wish to touch their irresistible bodies, their urge for female companion having been renewed by these black beauties. The Director is not exempted from their charm. "Starstruck," he is overpowered by their personalities and does everything possible to keep them for himself, unsuccessfully. His discussions with Miss Kokane, a graduate, on the why of her drug-smuggling, is an example of hypocrisy of a leadership mired in the mud but claiming to be as clean as cocaine. The Director keeps wondering how "an educated girl couldn't find a decent job;" (84) not at all bothered by the man's strange pinch of morality, the young woman retorts with a reference to the Bible's injunction to children to obey their mothers, and to the necessity to make money by other means than the measly salary from a regular job. Miss Kokane's position is proudly supported by the egregious Chief Popa. He, the acclaimed expert on Nigerian matters and manners, tells the Director that it is not against the law to smuggle cocaine, that, besides, "Nigerians do not obey law," and that the two women are "very enterprising women," just like most of their sex: "Women are contractors, and traders and lawyers and business entrepreneurs in Nigeria. Yes. After all, it is money that matters." (86) Popa, impressed, would like to marry both mother and daughter. The Director is convinced of their extraordinary qualities. He welcomes the women officially to the Prison. He reserves to himself the right to examine their anatomy for drugs...

Saro-Wiwa depicts the two women as not only ingenious in matters of drugs, but as experts in the ways of men. They are "women of the world," (92) and as expected by the Nigerian authorities that sent them to Jebs, they entertain, and are entertained by, the men. "As Napoleon said, women are the pastime of warriors, the occupation of idle men." (92) Military men are the greatest beneficiaries of the women's attention. On this point, Saro-Wiwa definitely is being very realistic; for, in military-misled Nigeria, the Uniform, symbol of power and wealth- both exaggerated and exhibited in their ugliness- always attracts a bevy of beautiful bodies ready to do his bidding.[9] While investigating Pita Dumbrok's activities, Captain Ita of State Security meets the female journalist, Asa; he thinks she is very beautiful, and he is surprised that a senior military officer has not taken her for his girl-friend (*Prison*: 152) Actually, Ita is only ignorant: true to his expectation, Asa has been taken by the Chief Naval Officer, Viko. Some women's readiness to jump into bed with the Uniform must not be considered as a characteristic of their *nature*, which is sometimes implied by Saro-Wiwa's descriptions of "the Nigerians" as a whole. Journalists are also enjoined by their editors to "enjoy themselves" whenever they can: In *Prison*, Andizi, assigned to cover the African Heads of States' meeting in a foreign capital, is advised by his editor to find one of the famed beauties of that city and to spend the night in her boudoir (36). And an element of inferiority complex comes into play when, for example, Nigerian women are compared to their foreign counterpart: Chief Popa says that Margaret Thatcher, the British Prime Minister, "uses her brain, whereas Madam Kokane and her daughter believe in their equipment." (148) This, it should be noted, is sometimes an extension of men's badly veiled colonial mentality: The Director visits Thatcher in London, and he accepts, as a matter of course, her superiority, since she is white and Prime Minister of Great Britannia ruling the waves. "He was so black, she did not see him throughout their meeting. This suited the Director fine. She did all the talking, well, most of the talking." (150)

Examples of women being used for dirty jobs by men, include the investigation of the foreign currency stolen from his country by the Sierra Leonean President, Siaka Stevens. (*Jebs*: 43) The authorities choose the kind of woman who is dazzled by money and material, such as the Nigerian girl who falls for the ugly Kangaroo carrying foreign currency in his pouch. (51) Saro-Wiwa, never one to miss an occasion to satirize, recounts that episode with the girl taking her father to court for objecting to her wish to become Kangaroo's wife. The judge in charge of the case is sympathetic to the girl's beauty; he therefore sentences her to "twenty minutes' imprisonment in a dark chamber." (52)

The most insidious action by a woman in the Jebsian novels is Miss Kokane's delivery of the parcel-bomb that kills Pita Dumbrok

(*Prison*: 246). Her choice for the action is made by Popa. Here is the kind of collaboration visible between politicians and prostitutes. Miss Kokane's murderous journey also arouses the reader's confusion with regard to Saro-Wiwa's position on resolving the Nigerian dilemma. Andizi and Biney' catch a glimpse of the woman on their way to Jebs. If they knew of her and her objective, they might be able to divert her route, to delay her, to make her desist from her inglorious collaboration.

The most commendable action by a woman is being depicted as part of the possible solution to the country's problems. With this character, Saro-Wiwa presents a multi-dimensional, female persona combining beauty with brains; human, in the sense of not being perfect; proving that a woman is capable of living (being productive as a career person) and loving a man. A male chauvinist would not see beyond a woman's role as wife and mother. Biga, the Security Chief in *Prison*, admonishes Asa: "You are a woman. Why worry about politics? Leabe politics por 'ze men. Marry, settle down, habe your children. Enjoy yoursep. Is zat not all you want in life? And you are a bery beautipul girl. Many men will want to marry you." (171) This encounter, in Asa's house, shows her as being both woman and human. She does not discourage the lecherous man's flirtations but, at the same time, she refuses to be relegated to playing the roles of a man's bed-mate baby-machine. Biga invites her to dinner; pompous and presumptuous, he also offers to spend the night. Rather than being rude and revolted, she is courteous and cautious.

"Many thanks for your very kind invitation to dinner. I'm sorry I don't accept it this time." (171-2)

Asa must be enjoying the attention of these two powerful men, the Security and Naval Chiefs. She is a proud woman, given, however, to some exaggeration. Her behavior towards Biga at no time makes one imagine her virtually shooing him out of her house. In fact, that is not the man's only unannounced visit. Asa is aware of her beauty. She insists on her independence, but one doubts whether she can lay claim to that. Her relationship with Viko gives us an insight into her character. She first met him when, at age twelve, she lost her money in a shop and a young lieutenant, Viko, paid her bill and gave her and her friends a ride in his jeep. Five years later, they met again at her high-school graduation ceremony, when Lieutenant-Commander Viko, special guest, presented to her the five prizes she won. Then, after graduating in journalism from university and joining the newspaper, she was sent to interview the new Navy

Commander Viko. Details of that third meeting underline the realization of a dream carried within Asa since she was twelve. Viko is the "very subject of her fantasies" (153). She confesses to missing a few heart-beats, even though she tries to be professional. He does not hide his interest. He asks whether she has a boy-friend. She does not give a direct answer, but her laughter is enough of an encouragement to him. He informs her of his marriage and divorce, with three children. Her soliloquy is indicative of her happiness that the man is free. Viko starts phoning her every day for a dinner-date; after holding out for a while, Asa accepts the invitation.

Asa's comments on men are interesting, to say the least. They are, in part, the chauvinistic contention of a bourgeois woman and, also, the notions of a progressive woman with an understanding of her rights within the society. And in this complex persona, there lies a woman subconsciously accepting the submissiveness of her sex in a male-oriented society. "There is hardly a man who wakes up in the morning and looks at himself in the mirror who doesn't immediately conclude that he is an Adonis and that no woman dare refuse him. When that man has power and influence, he probably considers himself irresistible to all women... In pursuing my relationship with [Rear-Admiral Viko], the physical was not the first thing at the back of my mind... I've often been told that I'm proud, haughty, unrealistic, idealistic and more... I always consider myself a career woman... I didn't ever accept that being a woman was a disability. Quite on the contrary, I consider my gender an added advantage: it enables me see things from a perspective different to the bulk of those with whom I interact. This makes my contributions, I reckon, a bit more refreshing."(157-8) Then, in praise of her father, Asa continues: "I think he believed that the worst thing any woman could do was regard her femininity as a way of sponging on men or subordinating herself entirely to the whims and caprices of men or to the mores of a society which thinks of women as sex objects or as bearers of children or cooks and helpmates, housewives, some second class citizen." (158) Note, however, that her mother, even though educated, was a meek housewife.

The supposedly independent Asa is immediately attracted to Pita, the "decidedly ugly" man with a voice "as of vintage palm oil, smooth, a spangling colour, the rainbow across the sky, a gurgling stream flowing gently over the rocks, clean, clear water. Its effect upon me was so gripping." (166) "The ugly man with the voice of liquid gold" (168) replaces Viko in Asa's heart, but not by a process of active pursuit on his part.

Saro-Wiwa is too aware of the sublimity of Pita's philosophy and the subject of Jebs, to allow for such triteness. The new love-affair contrasts very convincingly with the Viko one. Mutual interest, appreciation of the mind, commitment to a popular cause, these are the bases for the Pita-Asa love; with Viko, there are disharmony, physical and material interests, conflict of interest between a military leader (military gun) and a woman and a journalist (military/government, gun/pen). It is therefore not surprising that Asa easily takes to Pita, the visionary.

Her single-handed search for Jebs is a sign of her heroism and her role as responsible citizen performing genuinely her patriotic duty. Her discovery of the Ita Oko prison cannot be viewed simply as failure; on the contrary, the very effort is praiseworthy, and it makes her all the more attractive to, and respected by, Pita Dumbrok. Saro-Wiwa uses the affair between Asa and Viko to unmask the military's political penury. Viko is always hedging when Asa asks him questions about the running of the country, because she believes that the people have a right to know. She criticizes the military for copying, and surpassing, the civilians in corruption. "The discipline which entitled them to claim political power was often betrayed." (156) Viko's decision to leave Asa after finding Pita in her sitting-room (181) signifies the victory of true love over lust. Together until death, the two journalists, man and woman, prepare to chart the course for a better future for their people. Asa is aware that Pita may be eliminated; yet, she stays by him, because his ideas cannot be killed. What she has learnt from him is "a way to understand myself, my society, a way out of the dilemma in which I find myself as a member of my society." (213) Before Pita is blown up by the bomb delivered by Miss Kokane, Asa informs him of her pregnancy with their baby:

"All I could do was give him what was essentially good news. 'Pita,' I called to him softly.
'Darling.'
'I have good news for you,' I said. 'I'm pregnant.'
'How wonderful!' he said in his honey-sweet voice...
The warmth of our bodies glowed into our hearts and the agony of the seven days melted in the afterglow of indescribable pleasure. And then we slept."(215)

Pita wakes up to his death. Asa will continue. She will bear the fruit of their shared commitment. That fruit may be symbolic of some hope, for Nigeria. For the present, Asa makes another statement on the hydra-headed dilemma: "The worst enemy of truth and freedom in our society is the ethnic majority."(209)

THE MINORITIES AS VICTIM

One would be justified to state that, in a general fashion, Saro-Wiwa is a defender of the underdog, and that his concern for the Nigerian minority groups stems from this sympathy. This general statement has to be very well clarified, however; for, the novelist does not appear to show as much clear-cut attachment to the under-class as he does to the ethnic minorities. This would explain his use of the term, *the Nigerians*, in his constant condemnation of the Nigerian people, without distinguishing between the victimizers (military and civilian rulers and their bourgeois collaborators) and their victims (the governed who, due to their ignorance and internalization of their inferiority complex, have misconstrued the cult of corruption as a virtue that they must worship and imitate once the opportunity presents itself).

There is no such grey area where the minority issue is concerned, specifically that of Nigeria's oil-producing areas to which Saro-Wiwa belongs. His satire on the subject is based upon a general, all-inclusive division of Nigeria into two groups, *the majority* and *the minority*: from there follows an almost absolute dichotomy between bad and good. Oppressor-Oppressed. The Robbers-The Robbed. Consumers-Producers. Powerful, Undeserving Beneficiaries-Helpless, Unwilling Benefactors. Developed-Undeveloped... In Jebs, there is an argument over the Nigerian "national cake." The narrator explains: "The three biggest
Nigerian groups, the Was, the Zos and the Bias, ganged up and said the Director would have to come from among themselves, the Wazobians. The small Nigerian groups... began to scramble to take a place beside one of the big three, because the national cake is delicious, and he who has no big brother is likely to be starved of it altogether." (8)

The allegorical football matches played in the Prison delve more deeply on the matter; the distinction between the oppressive and repressive Wazobians is more or less absolute. At this point, Saro-Wiwa also expands the notion of majority-minority disharmony to include other African countries, but also briefly. These matches are suggested by the Nigerian authorities to the Director as a way of deflecting the prisoners' attention from the important matters of state. The British Prime Minister Thatcher also advises him to use the same diversion, to stop the prisoners from thinking. Ironically, the diversion turns out to be a means of bringing to center-stage (albeit only as far as we, the readers are concerned!) the nagging problem of ethnicity. There are three matches. The first one is played between the Nigerians and the Rest (other Africans). After using all sorts of silly illogicalities to have the referee, Kangaroo, allow them to play twelve men against the other team's eleven, the Nigerians finally remove the "constitutionally irregular" player. But they are still big crooks, those Nigerians. With Kangaroo's complicity -it is a "new constitution" (156)-, the excessively heavy and slow Nigerians celebrate goals scored by their opponents. The referee agrees with them. Their President, too; for, he sends a message flashed on the scoreboard: "Spell all the initials of my name!" (Saro-Wiwa's reference to a real incident at Lagos) and the opponents comply on behalf of the slow-footed Nigerians. The oppressed Africans, the Rest (think of the dregs, the left-overs, the forgotten, the second-class citizens), disgusted by what the match commentator, Pita Dumbrok, calls "a travesty of justice and truth," (157) walk off the field. The Nigerians are declared winners by Kangaroo. The referee's explanation is, "that in Nigeria, the men who scored the goals never took them, the men who baked the cake did not have a right to eat it; the areas which produced oil were left poor and destitute while the non-oil-producing areas had all the dams, special educational funds, irrigation schemes, electricity, unfailing telephones... During the civilian regime, for all the thefts committed by officials, the only Federal Minister jailed was the one from the oil-producing area. The Kangaroo said this showed that the men who owned the oil did not even have the right to steal it. All others could steal it, if they so wished." (157) It is noteworthy that Kangaroo, the favorite judge of the unjust, is the referee of these matches; also of significance is the fact that only Pita openly disagrees with him. The farcical scenario could justify the general opinion, that it is only a match; but Kangaroo's explanation makes that pretext, showing that, in Nigeria, the absurd can and will be used to denigrate or destroy the sublime. Of course, Nigeria has been known to play big brother to other African countries. It is also an open secret that, due to its pomposity, it is often despised by brother countries which, nonetheless, do not mind benefitting from its famous, misplaced magnanimity.

At the end of the first match, the other Africans decide never again to play football with the Nigerians. An artistic error would be detected in that decision: with the non-participation of these others, the *expressed* objective of the football matches would be non-existent.

Indeed, the non-Nigerians begin to whisper and plot against the director. Nothing comes of it. Pita earns another trip to the cage in the yard and according to Popa, if the Nigerians, as majority are happy, then there is no problem. Anyway, the second match is played between two Nigerian teams, the Majorities (Wazobians) and the Minorities. They display their excellent sense of confusion and disharmony. The Wazobians score first. Using the "old constitution" that served their united team against the other Africans, the Minorities jump for joy. Unfortunately, Kangaroo says it is the Wazobians' goal. When the Minorities score the second goal, the Wazobians claim it, and the unjust referee again agrees with them. "Bullied and humiliated," the Minorities play the game to the end and are declared loser. The winners celebrate noisily; the real winners are cowered into silence, or timid grumbling. Translated into Nigerian reality, this portrait lacks two ingredients, the presence of the willing collaborators, the stool-pigeons, among the Minorities, as well as sympathetic resistance in the oppressors' camp. In the chapter on Saro-Wiwa's Ogoni struggle, these factors will be addressed in-depth.

The third and final match is, naturally, between the three Majority teams, Was, Zos, and Bias, all entering the field at once and claiming the right to play the game. They keep making new alliances, two against one, for one whole week, with mutual recriminations galore based upon Nigerian history, politics, and economics. The impasse remains unresolved. Doing what they do best, the three recoil into their alliance of negativity, to subdue Kangaroo. They go in pursuit of the Director who locks himself in his office. Popa, erstwhile the Director's main weapon of protection, leads them there, and they all cry triumphantly as it happens on Nigerian Television, "cries meant to show that Wazobians were as much the owners of Jebs as they were of Nigeria." (17!) Soon after this episode, the Prison is blown up. Another show of unity mentioned elsewhere, at the highest level of Nigerian society when the President holds a luncheon to celebrate Soyinka's Nobel Prize. The "Nigerian unity meal" contains dishes, specially prepared by Mrs. President herself from the Efik, Igbo, Yoruba, and Hausa menus. (168) At least, in this example, Saro-Wiwa includes a fourth ethnic group.

The novelist considers as purblind and superficial one configuration of Nigeria that was established by the colonizers and that has not ceased to enjoy currency in contemporary politics: the North-South "incompetent division." (*Prison*: 74) In the novel, the division is the handiwork of the trillion-legged, hideous goddess Imf and her Sap army, during their preparations for the war of attrition on Nigeria. The deadly Sap Brigades are located in cities of the majority groups, with the North having four, and the South, three. None is placed in the areas of the minority peoples. The narrator further informs us: "Thus, the majority ethnic groups in Nigeria... hosted the Brigade headquarters. The Commander had correctly surmised that in the unlikely event that the Sap Army should finally be defeated, [the majority groups] would be inclined to treat the defeated Army and its Commanders with leniency." (74) One is astonished that Saro-Wiwa, normally very thorough in his knowledge of history and logical reasoning, has, in this instance neglected historical content and turned logic on its head. For, the North-South division being the convenient operative set-up of the colonialists as part of their divide-and-rule tactics, cannot be condemned as the invention of Nigerian politicians. In addition, since Imf and her army have "perfect understanding of Nigeria," it might have been interesting to have them change the politicians' "incompetent division." It could be argued that the allegorical war is meant to portray the Nigerians' deserved defeat. However, the very fact of that annihilation is a decisive proof of the competence of that division. Contrary to Saro-Wiwa's belief, therefore, there are, in Nigeria, "a preponderant 'North' and a lesser 'South'." (74) That does not disprove the presence of other permutations. The careers of two characters in *Prison* attest to this.

Chief Biga, Chief of Security, and Captain Ita, one of his subordinates, are both engaged in the "national duty" of investigating Pita Dumbrok, to specifically stop him from continuing to spread the story on Jebs. Biga is known to be Hausa (from the North). He plays the man of the preponderant group to the hilt, by his outlook, and by his speech-patterns. Significantly, he is the only character whose conspicuous diction is consistently satirized. Ita is Efik (a minority). He went through military school in Zaria and became an Intelligence Officer. Imprisoned for participating in an alleged coup, he was retired and later employed in the State Security, where he came under Biga's supervision. Ita's best friend at school was Alade, a Yoruba who was also later charged for the alleged coup. Alade was condemned to death by firing squad; on his way to face the gun, he gave his watch to Ita to pass to his father in Akure. When Ita visited the old man, the latter gave him a newspaper cutting of Alade tied to the stakes. Ita, from his days at school, has been "well known for sudden bursts of anger whenever he was wronged" (87). He always insists on his rights and justice for all. No wonder he has kept in his mind the injustice done to his friend, Alade. His investigation of Pita is done with justice in mind. He is immediately impressed by the ugly but honey-voiced journalist whose words he is "forced to drink." (150) He admires Pita's courage and equanimity and, in reading the latter's "Letter to my Compatriots," Ita is struck by the injustice in Nigeria, including the official murder of his friend Alade. The "letter," contrary to Biga's claim, has no destabilizing effect on Ita; instead, it speaks to him, "tells me things that I did not know before," about Africa's problems, and Nigeria's stunted progress. Besides, Ita is most concerned with performing his duty, and wishes to "earn money and train [his] brothers and sisters." When Biga orders him to arrest Pita, Ita refuses, because he is convinced that the man "has nothing but love for Nigeria." (204) Biga calls Pita a criminal, a liar, a mad-man, and Professor's accomplice. Ita ends up murdering Biga and Viko, the Navy Chief embarrassed by Pita's story and jealous of his affair with Asa. After shooting the two corrupt men, Ita hands himself over to the police. He is satisfied: "I don't bloody care what anybody thinks. Duty is Duty. I had to do my duty." (268)

During Ita's trial, it is revealed that Biga is not Hausa, after all, something that the intelligent Asa already suspected the very first time she met him. (163) Biga was "an Ishan man, a Christian from the midwest of the country who, *to protect his career in the State Security Department*, had assumed Hausa speech habits and the Muslim faith." (278, emphasis mine) His fraudulence has helped him to succeed and survive in a position of power. The crime is not detected until his death. Ironically, it influences Ita's final act, because Ita expresses hatred for the system that empowers Northerners such as Biga, "catapulted into a high position because he comes from some place called the North, is a Muslim, is half-educated, won't bother to study, all that rubbish. If Pita Dumbrok had been a Northerner and a Muslim would they put him under detention?" (275) That irony categorically underlines the importance of being a Northerner.

We must emphasize, however, that that does not make it right. The characters of Pita and Ita show that all manners of ethnic exclusivity are wrong. Ita, Efik, has as his best friend a Yoruba. Pita is also from a minority group but this fact is mentioned only once, when he is being interrogated by Ita, who reveals that ethnocentricity is a part of the education in Intelligence School.

'You are Nigerian, of course. Born of Isoko and Itsekiri parents. Right?'

'Does the second part matter?'

'Oh, yes. To judge any Nigerian rightly, you must know his roots. Different communities, different beliefs, different gods, different languages, different psyches. We've learnt that in Intelligence.' (190)

Pita refuses to subscribe to any ethnic distinctions. Rather, he believes in class particularities, as we find out in his response to Ita's question on the origins of Popa:

'Which part of Nigeria did he come from?'

'I would not know. What I do know is that he betrayed all the traits of a Nigerian of his class. He was greedy, cantankerous and disloyal.' (191)

The problem with Nigeria is, that Pita's philosophy does not take cognizance of the complex entity. The journalist is being progressive; he proffers a viewpoint that, if implemented, could resolve the national problem in favor of the power-mongers. The fifth islet willed into existence by the magician, Professor, populated by Fat and Thin people, offers a fact that Saro-Wiwa has not adequately dwelt upon in his novels, that "an alien people came... and forced the Fat People and the Thin People to live together in one country." (25) In other words, the artificial entity called Nigeria still has a long way to go to transform into a nation. And the Fat People, in particular, are far from being a cohesive group. More analysis on the Nigeria confusion will be done in the chapters on the civil war and Ogoni, respectively.

CONCLUSION: FEAR, QUEST, AND CONFUSION AS METAPHORS OF NIGERIA

Saro-Wiwa's attempt to transform a series of newspaper articles into a novel (*Jebs*) has been only partially successful. His use of satire in the two novels, on the other hand, is quite impressive. It is more frank, more frontal, more far-reaching, more fierce than in *Sozaboy*. All of Nigeria is revealed in the satirist's mirror, and the picture is almost perfectly pitiful. The body politic is rotten; the ship of the nation is listing dangerously and it runs the risk of capsizing. (*Confusion,* as well as its derivative, is one word that the novelist uses over and over again.[10] Another oft-used word is, *rumour*.[11] They both underscore a problematic situation; for, if one does not know the truth and the facts of a problem then, confused, one is liable to live in limbo and in darkness, unable to find the way forward.

Saro-Wiwa himself is victim of some kind of confusion caused, initially, by the limitation of changing his articles of motley substance and style into a cohesive novel. There are many unnecessary repetitions and variations of the same themes.[12] There are also examples of bad sequencing (*Jebs*: 49, 54, 92) and contradictions (66, 80). One sometimes has the feeling that Saro-Wiwa is guilty of over-kill, using every opportunity to discuss Nigerian history and to condemn the Nigerians. These shortcomings are made up for by the novelist's skill for use of dialogue, an aspect of the dramatic genre which is his forte. The force of this dramatic expertise is, to engage the reader's attention so that he enjoys the satire without being aware of the discrepancies.

In *Prison*, Saro-Wiwa uses the device of five different narrators (the general narrator-Andizi-Commander of Sap army-Captain Ita-Asa). Does that remove the element of confusion? Does it present different points of view, thus increasing the authenticity of the tale and, therefore the novelist's credibility? To some extent, yes. However, the narrator's view begins and ends the novel; besides, information is often repeated by the narrators. Certainly, this artistic device lends more clarity to the story. There is also deeper discussion of issues. But overall confusion remains.

That confusion is endemic in the Nigerian context. Witness the debate on government by the Jebsian prisoners. The conclusion: "Once people wore the mask of government, they did the same things, whether they were military or civilian." (*Jebs*: 30) Saro-Wiwa proposes a farcical reason for the Nigerians' love of military regimes: their civilian Head of State was allowed to take pictures in the Uniforms of all the arms of the military, Air Force, Army and Navy. Being geniuses, the military in power use civilians as nannies for the sick baby, Nigeria. Patriotic cooperation, some might say. Saro-Wiwa depicts the two groups as collaborations in confusion and corruption.

In his Author's Note to *Jebs*, he dismisses any idea of "grave fears for [his] personal safety" consequential to the subjects of his biting satire, and prefers to entertain the possibility that his work would "continue to scare a few people, [given the fact that] fear is an important theme of the story." The various aspects of fear, fraught with confusion, do not appear to give much hope for resolving the Nigerian problem. The Director is one person shown to be scared about the Nigerian authorities. He uses all sorts of machinations to pre-empt an attack. Finally, his fear proves to be unfounded. Jebs is spirited away by Professor and, then, revived in even larger dimensions. The Director also becomes larger. The small-time executive is re-born as a President aspiring to absolute dictatorship. In Nigeria, there is no sign that the villains have any fear at all. It is their victims that need to be scared; from the real Dele Giwa to the fictional Pita Dumbrok, they can be blown up into smithereens with hardly anyone daring to ask a question. Like the fictional Andizi, and the real Kudirat Abiola and Alfred Rewane, they live in the diurnal fear of being on the receiving end of a bullet to their brains; or, indeed, like Saro-Wiwa himself, they may find a noose tied round their necks and wondering why it should be sin to seek one's rights and to express love for one's country.

The experiential and essential presences of Saro-Wiwa's novel help the reader to consider several possibilities for understanding, solutions, hope, cooperation, and commitment. In each instance, there is the other possibility of failure. This is most poignantly expressed in the trope of the quest, in *Prison*. We have already noted the encouraging commitment the two journalists, Andizi and Biney, who set out together in search of Jebs. From their conversations, and Andizi's comments, it is clear that the journey is arduous, not to mention their strange encounters on the seven islets. Communication between the two men becomes increasingly limited. Andizi is somewhat bothered, but he consoles himself that, perhaps, "the ease of [their] situation" (233) explains the lack of communication and, that if they had difficulties to share and solve, they would certainly interact better. As it is, each is left to his own thought. An unusual and inexplicable comment, to say the least, because their quest for Jebs presents the perfect occasion for sharing. Andizi would appear to prioritize the individual experience. "What we were going through was an experience which, to make maximum impact, had to be individual. One digested it against one's background, one's psyche... So as I say, there might have been a difference between the way Biney and I were reacting to each situation." (*Prison*: 233-4) This logic is confusing. It pales before the philosophy of Pita who is supposedly the catalyst for the quest being undertaken by the two journalists. Andizi's remarks arouses in this critic a temptation, that, just maybe, Saro-Wiwa is subtly injecting into the discourse his idea of ethnicity, or ethnocentricity. The question would be, that given the inevitability of the individualized experiences, as well as the differences (if not oppositions) they may engender, how would we create and cultivate real commitment and unity?

Hope may be seen to persist in the personas of Pita and Professor, the two symbols of *thinking*. Two points of peril, however: death, and magic. Pita's disciples are either murdered (Andizi), accused of murder (Ita), or sent into exile and oblivion (Biney). Ita has already expressed his disillusionment after an act generously described as confused commitment. "I look into tomorrow," he says, "I see nothing. No future." (87) Hope may rest in Asa and her yet-to-be-born baby. Regarding Professor, his magical persona can only make one cautious of all the philosophy about thinking; after all, everyone and everything could, with one incantation from the mouth of the master-illusionist (?), be nullified.

Saro-Wiwa's contrived confusion of Professor with Wole Soyinka may be the final consolation of this fictional (and factual?) universe. Think of the real Soyinka's evolution, from friend of the Nigerians to their most famous foe. Think of his activism, his combination of thought and action. One recalls the Nobel laureate's "A Letter to Compatriots," in which he quotes like Soyinka a victim of totalitarian oppression. In the letter are set out three phases of a victim's evolution into true commitment: humiliation; (humiliation of) fear; solidarity. "You begin to live with the daily humiliation of fear, and you begin to loathe yourself. And then, deeply wounded in your conscience as a citizen, you begin to feel a solidarity with the people to whom you belong." (*The Man Died*: 14) At this stage of evolution, one rejects humiliation and fear. At what stage would the Nigerians be? At the first, for sure, with the exception of Pita Dumbrok, and Professor (Soyinka). With these two in mind, one may join Andizi in saying, that "learning lends hope to man that good may finally triumph." (*Prison*: 256)

NOTES TO CHAPTER III

1. One notes here a certain superiority complex, or pomposity on the part of Saro-Wiwa, a trait that must have rubbed some people on the wrong wide and may have made for abhorrence of him on their part.. At the socio-political level (see chapter on Ogoni), such an attitude no doubt created the animosity that led his opponents to seek his destruction.
The evolution of the fictional Pita Dumbrok character in the two novels

is proof enough that Saro-Wiwa respects the profession of journalism, and that he means well in his criticism of the journalist's write-up on his novel. Nonetheless, by castigating a critic for daring to make negative comments on his novel, is Saro-Wiwa not displaying the sort of fascistic tendencies that he himself would condemn in our Supreme Commanders and dear dictators, self-chosen messiahs claiming to be God's appointed leaders to the promised land?

2. Of course, Mandela was still in prison when Saro-Wiwa wrote his novel. Nigeria was one of the world's leading supporters of the anti-apartheid movement. At the United Nations, Nigeria headed the Anti-Apartheid Committee. It also gave millions of dollars to the African National Congress. Interestingly enough, during that same period, certain Nigerians were doing shady deals, most importantly in oil exportation, with apartheid South Africa. Today, after those millions spent in liberating South Africa, Nigeria is being treated with contempt by the Mandela-led government for its fascist regime and its inhumanism reminiscent of the worst elements of apartheid hell.

3. Kangaroo courts, where the judges are corrupt and are stooges of the unjust government, and arrive at decisions to find the innocent guilty before hearing the case. Many of the Nigerian courts have become such scenes of absurdity during the unending military regimes. See chapter on Ogoni.

4. *Saro*, a play on Saro-Wiwa. This artistic legerdemain will be discussed later, in the section on minorities.

5. The Nigerian Second Republic was the second coming of civilian politicians (1979-1983), when the government of Shehu Shagari ruled and ruined the country economically. The mis-government led to the 1983 coup that brought the Buhari regime to power. "The biggest fish" of the corrupt politicians that escaped into exile included Umaru Dikko whom the Buhari-led military regime tried to smuggle back home from London in a crate that was discovered by British police and seized before it could be put on the plane.

The military junta that sacked the Buhari regime (actually, these new messiahs were members to that old order), later (1994) flew the "big fish" back in a presidential plane, a new patriotic and wise hero, to offer his wisdom to the discussions on a new Constitution already prepared and printed by the most knowledgeable dictators.

6. *Jebs*: 92. References to Nigerian Generals Gowon and Idiagbon, respectively. Abuja is Nigeria's controversial new capital that replaced Lagos. Chosen ostensibly for its geographical centrality, it has become another Norther city where successive heads of State find refuge among their feudal subjects.

7. Could Saro-Wiwa have been influenced by Soyinka's "A Letter to Compatriots," in his prison notes, *The Man Died* (pp.11-15)? Although Soyinka does not outline Nigerian history as does Saro-Wiwa's journalist, the expressions of commitment (dedication to revolutionary changes), the call to action, and the condemnation of power profiteers, are similar.

8. This is most likely an indirect reference to the minority issue in Nigeria; the gold would be oil.

9. *On A Darkling Plain* details activities of the occupationist forces of the military among the civilian population. Rape is one of the most patriotic pastimes. *Sozaboy* also makes the point.

10. See pp. 10, 14, 23, 80, 100, 136, 141, 148, 151, 184, among others.

11. Pp. 24, 32, 47, 62, 63, 101, 278.

12. For example, *Jebs*, pp. 70, 101: the episode of the ex-military governor given an honorary Ph.D. for misusing state funds; 74, 89, 101: story of soldiers becoming farmers. Repetitions of phrases and sentences are also common; 129, 149: the Director's experience on a plane-trip to Harare when he sits beside a Nigerian lady eating her own personal food; another lady behaves similarly on another trip to London.

IV. THE *MR. B* SERIES, IN PRINT AND ON TELEVISION

—People like them [Saro-Wiwa's characters] are created to amuse and warn us.
—We were creating an awareness of our predicament. This was the most important thing. We were in trouble as a nation. And unless people realise this, they would not be able to change their habits." (Saro-Wiwa, in *Topnews*, 14, *1988)*
—Anyone who has knowledge has power. (Professor, in *MR. B*: 76)

ON STAGE, IN PRINT, AND ON TELEVISION

Before becoming known for his Ogoni socio-political activism, Saro-Wiwa was a popular celebrity, as the creator of the weekly television comedy series, *Basi and Company*,[1] of which the main character was Mr. B (Basi), with a surrounding cast of five average-Nigerian types. This cast regaled a very appreciative audience of all ages and conditions, with their mixed bay of humor, from slapstick to a satire bordering on the sad and serious sides of our sick society. The series has been variously described as Nigeria's hottest comedy show; displaying "the classic wit and humour of Ken Saro-Wiwa's writing;" "flawless characterisation;" and "always topical, witty (...), good clean fun generated by clever dialogue." (blurb of *Basi and Company*)

Saro-Wiwa has used the series' popularity to broaden his audience, to include readers of plays and novels. This, to say the least, has not only consolidated the show's legendary status, but may arouse criticism about Saro-Wiwa's double role as author and publisher. The same story lines have been presented on television, as a novel, and as a published play; there is also one play, '(The) Transistor Radio," that has been published in two editions. On the complimentary side, one can see in the various genres and editions, how Saro-Wiwa's skills developed over the years as well as the problems and possibilities of each genre. For example, the play just mentioned was first performed as a sketch when the author was a student at the University of Ibadan, in 1964. It was broadcast on BBC radio in 1972, and was performed on stage that same year at the Nigerian Festival of the Arts. In 1985, it was adapted for television as the first episode of "Basi and Company".

One is also struck by Saro-Wiwa's descriptions of the Basi works. The television series, usually shown on the Wednesday 8:30 p.m. slot, was a prime-time event watched by both children and adults. The first edition of "The Transistor Radio" leads off a collection called *Four Farcical Plays*. The second "Transistor Radio" edition appears in the collection, *Basi and Company* (four television plays). The novels, *MR. B* and *MR. B is Dead*, are described as children's books/novels, and are published in the Saros Junior Series[2]. The latter text (developed, according to the author, for the entertainment and moral instruction of youths) includes questions on each chapter at the end of the story. The television-play text also has questions; in the introduction, the author says that the scripts are presented "for classroom reading," and that "children in secondary schools—and even adults—will find the plays particularly interesting to read and stage." (vii)

We shall discuss this matter of audience by examining the style, themes, and characters of the works. The television series was definitely not geared to any specific audience; hence, the necessity to know why Saro-Wiwa would call the written works children's books[3]. A further comment on the genres: *MR. B*, the first novel, is precisely a collection of episodes involving the same characters, which is an adequate format for the TV series or one-act plays; each chapter's title describes the topic of a given episode. The first paragraph of Chapter VI gives the author away: "Segi met very often with MR. B, Alali, Dandy and Josco. They would sometimes meet at Dandy's Bar or at MR. B's palace. Segi found all of them very funny. They did and said things which amused her a great deal." (73) The only reason for calling the book a novel would be that, besides the same characters, certain facts link the episodes together, to give the idea of continuity, of "one plot." With regard to the TV plays, Saro-Wiwa moved away from "one-act plays" to plays divided into "Situations" (not scenes). The choice of words appears to be inconsequential; but, perhaps, the author meant to assert the particularity of television, as opposed to the stage. As we shall see when comparing the two versions of "The Transistor Radio," dividing the play into "Situations" is practical; it facilitates a better understanding of the plot, gives both actors and audience a more logical and convenient perspective of the action, and allows for a more relaxed theatrical atmosphere. Of course, on television, commercials are placed at the end of each "situation."

The basic story is simple enough. One evening, "a tall, handsome man wearing a faded blue jacket, a cap, worn shoes and carrying a grey faded shoulder bag," (*MR. B*: 1) arrives at Iddo Motor Park in Lagos. We do not know where he came from. His cap bears the name, Mr. B. By which he is known henceforth. He sleeps in an empty lorry which takes him to Ibadan, a hundred miles away. He dismounts and finds his way back to Lagos in a bus. Penniless, he has to lie and run from the conductor. He wanders into Adetola Street, rents a ramshackle room that he calls his "Palace," from Madam, the landlady living upstairs and a business woman excited by the words on his singlet, "Think like a millionaire." (7) Mr. B meets a young man, Alali, upon returning to Iddo to try and pay the Ibadan-Lagos fare with money that he borrowed from Madam. The conductor is gone. Mr. B. and the ever hungry Alali become friends. Alali moves into his Palace, to Madam's disapproval. Thus begin the adventures of the two men as they try to survive on the Street, and to make their first million, through shady deals and in competition with other supporting characters, Dandy the barman, Josco the ex-convict, and Segi, the beautiful, soon-to-be college student. The crooked but comical adventures include the episode on Segi's new transistor radio which she gives to Dandy for safe-keeping, but which the latter and Josco try to use to make quick cash by pretending to give it away as a prize to anyone owning an empty Saros beer bottle, and then making the "winner" pay a bribe for not having a licence for the radio while having it seized by "the licencing officer." The prank is played on Alali; as usual, Basi saves the day, claiming to be a C.I.D. officer. The radio is later given back to Segi who unveils Basi's identity; she, however, has to make Dandy and Josco go to Basi's Palace to own up to their crookedness. Basi, still triumphant, plays the winner and wise man to the hilt. Another episode involves a fake letter being circulated by Josco, purporting to offer a shipload of rice at a very cheap price; the contract-owner will sell it for an exorbitant price. Each of the characters tries to win the contract. Again, the winner is Basi after he has managed to convince Madam that he has the contract and needs a down payment from her to purchase the rice. By the time she realizes Basi's trick, the latter has spent part of her down payment. To force Basi to pay her back the money, Madam seizes his mattress and pillow, an action that leads to another series of tricks on Basi's and Alali's part, to get back the two items without paying a penny. Each of these episodes is adapted into a television play.

In his Introduction to *Basi and* Company, Saro-Wiwa tells us that the plays "tell splendid comic stories and are enjoyable as such. But they also portray comic characters and situations and offer social comment on familiar attitudes and actions." (vii)

Segi's role in the series is interesting. In the original edition of "The Transistor Radio," she is not present at all. When she is later introduced, she serves as a kind of external observer of the Basi-led comical clan (*MR. B*: 77-8). She does not feature much in the episodes; she seems to pass briefly on the scene, and then leaves. She is used by Saro-Wiwa to introduce another interesting character, Professor, her next-door neighbor and "teacher," who appears in *MR. B* and explains to her the behavior of the characters on the Street. Professor is "the wise man" amused by the foibles of these money-hungry individuals. Nobody knows the man's name. "Professor was a learned man... The most notable part of his house was the library which was full of books... Professor laughed a lot; and whenever he laughed in his boom voice, the sound echoed and re-echoed..., spreading laughter all over as it made other people laugh as well." (74) So, Professor is the catalyst for the humor and the philosophical lessons to be learned in the work. Professor says these characters will make mistakes and amuse the world, just as Segi is being amused by their very looks and habits (77). Her reactions may, indeed, be considered as representing that of many a reader, or audience. What is intriguing about Segi's reaction to the other characters is her objective "to make sure that they did not do anything that was against the law. She knew that it was the duty of a good citizen to stop others from doing things which could cause harm." (78) This and Professor's lecture on Basi's character, sound like Saro-Wiwa's subtle way of emphasizing that we are dealing with *comedy*, that light-heartedness, the ability to laugh at the crooked behavior of Basi and company, these aspects are of greater interest than any deep philosophy; and that these characters are not criminals, just ordinary folks trying to cut corners. It is also interesting that Professor's role is similar to that of his namesake in the Jebsian novels. The element of *thinking* is noticeable in both; it is a characteristic that the author continues to highlight as essential to everyone's life. And Professor (Saro-Wiwa's alter ego) has a soft spot for Basi who, the absurdity of his dreams notwithstanding, stands out for his thinking like a millionaire...

Professor does not appear in the novel, *MR. B is Dead*, in which Mr. B becomes fed up with the Lagos people who spend money only on the dead, not on the living. He travels to Ibadan and sends a telegram to Alali that he, Mr. B., is dead. He then sneaks back into Lagos, reveals his secret to Alali and the two capitalize on their friends' generosity towards the dead by spending the large amount contributed towards B's burial by Madam and Dandy. Exposing his own greed, Mr. B gives the cash to Josco who promises to make a fast deal for him before the money is returned to its owners. However, Josco returns it to the latter, to Mr. B's disgust. Meanwhile, Mr. B. Cooks up another plot, pretending to have files on the fraudulent actions of Josco, Madam, and Dandy. He demands money in return for keeping their secrets secret. Madam and Segi offer B, the great gourmand, a delicious meal. He accepts. He gives up the fake files only to discover that the dishes form Madam are empty. The two "thinkers," Basi and Alali begin another plot: when Mr. Dada, the stationary-store owner, from whom B. bought the blank files on credit, comes asking for his money, Alali tells him Mr. B is dead and that he has to pay to get near the corpse...

This story of death and resurrection is a move away from the others in the series. It reveals the meanness of the characters, and a general harshness that has crept into the usually light-hearted milieu. The hate expressed for the "dead" B by Madam and Dandy, is almost credible. One begins to perceive the ease with which the comical side of life can reveal the tragic, particularly where money is a god. Professor's absence from the scene is significant. One misses his even-handedness, his wisdom, his reassurance that these are good people just foraging into the realm of the criminal, not hard-core villains deserving of condemnation. With Professor's departure, one cannot avoid noticing the negative side of Basi and Company. Between the first text, *MR. B* and *MR. B is Dead*, there are quite a few changes. Mr. B remains hungry, penniless and in debt; now, he is unhappy; he drinks on credit at Dandy's bar, whereas before, he used to drink gin obtained by guile from Madam. His friend, Alali, continues to yawn out his hunger, as before; his credit worthiness has sunk so low that he is even more disliked by the *suya* seller than by Mama Badejo, the food-seller. In the later novel, Madam has taken only the epithet, "Madam the Madam," and she is admired by Basi, for whom, ironically, she shows a rather hard spot. Basi, thought still penniless, surprisingly buys a newspaper and pays the vendor; he likes to read, to keep abreast of the news and to learn new ways of making money[4]. In the past,

Segi was an observer maintaining a certain distance from the rest of the gang. In *MR. B is Dead*, she becomes "Segi the gossip." In short, the characters have become more selfish, worse off materially while becoming more material-minded, and worse human beings, with the exception of Basi whose superiority over the others is more marked than before.

MR. B AND HIS "FRIENDS"

Saro-Wiwa offers a portrait of each of his characters in the introduction to *Basi and Company* (xi-xiii). The descriptions are useful to children for a better understanding of the plays. However, for adults, they represent the author's opinion; it is left to us to decide whether that viewpoint tallies with ours. Given the fact that Basi is the focus of his societal microcosm, the author describes him as "a confidence-trickster [who] although unscrupulous in his methods (...) is not really a bad person. He has a soft heart [and] is an eternal optimist." The other characters also combine a soft heart with their materialism. They are not as good as Basi, however, with the exception of Alali, "Basi's most devoted friend [who] serves as his unofficial A.D.C."[5]

Is Basi good, or wicked? Saro-Wiwa thinks he is good; on the contrary, Madam, Segi, Dandy and Josco say that he is "wicked" (*MR. B is Dead*: 124). He "looked wicked" (119). He is described "with a wicked glint in his eyes" (124) as he waves the fake files at Josco's face. The wicked trait, we must admit, is revealed only in the later text. Hence, we should address the question to the earlier works. This man arriving in Lagos from an unknown destination, uses his wits to catch a free ride on a bus after having been mistakenly taken to Ibadan in a lorry. The day after, he returns to pay for the bus-ride, but the conductor has gone. Basi also eats on credit, always with the good intention to pay later, just as he keeps owing rent to his landlady; unfortunately his poverty does not allow him to pay. A catch here, though: his promise to pay is for "as soon as he earned his first million naira," (*MR. B*: 8) which may be never. He is likeable. Children on Adetola Street take to him immediately, like fish to water, because he is easy-going, jovial, a dreamer making others believe in his dreams. He promises to take the children with him to the moon if they pass their examinations. So, Basi believes education is a very important trait admired by both his creator and the Street's wise man, Professor. Basi brings the impressionable Alali into his dream world of millions, and his Palace: "If you imagine that you are now living in a palace, if you dream that this is a palace, you will own a palace of your own in the near future." (29-30)

This would be an aspect of the optimism mentioned by Saro-Wiwa. The dream realized by one's imagination. The notion that everything will turn out well. "To be a millionaire, think like a millionaire." Pity that this millionaire-on-the make thinks! He is cunning, quick-witted, adaptable, and almost always a step ahead of others. When Josco, the fake licensing officer, collects money and the transistor radio from Alali, Basi steps in as a police officer and arrests Josco "in the name of the law." Indeed, more often than not, Basi seems to be more on the side of the law than others, for, he plays upon, and off, their weaknesses and misdemeanors. He outsmarts them every time. In the case of the shipload of rice, he succeeds in obtaining cash from the tight-fisted Madam. After Madam has seized his mattress, he, with the collaboration of his fellow trickster, Alali, makes everyone believe that he has stashed money in the mattress. Hence, there is a scramble to obtain the items from Madam. Meanwhile, Basi has spent the woman's cash to buy another mattress and pillow. To all intents and purposes, only Basi and Alali think; not the others. After Madam has refused to pay him for helping her to file fake documents for a government contract, Alali makes sure that, with Segi's help (Segi is the one character who, in earlier scripts, insists on people obeying the law), Madam's approved contract is nullified. But others do think, too. Josco always offers ideas to Dandy, for example, on how to make quick money from Segi's transistor radio. Madam is always thinking of some business deal. Maybe the difference would be that these other characters are not as smart as Basi and Alali. More likely in this critic's view, it is because the latter are the author's favorites, the major players upon whom all the account is focussed.

With regard to Basi's optimism, one is hardly pleased by his unwillingness to work. "Hard workers do not earn a lot of money," he tells Alali. (*MR. B*: 24) According to his unconfirmed story to his angry, unemployed, hungry "slave," (26) he looked for work in Lagos for a long time. Meanwhile, we have been informed by the narrator that Basi has spent one month in Lagos; he meets Alali on the day after his arrival (15). Such a discrepancy in the plot is only a minor weakness. More serious is the fact that, from the very beginning, Basi has been depicted as a man with a fixation about Lagos and the millions waiting to be made there, without working. Alali calls such people thieves (26). Basi ought to be included among them. Upon arrival on Adetola Street, Basi immediately decides that "this is [his] type of street [because] money is the message on the Street." (9) He studies the young, inexperienced Alali and notices his intelligence and active mind, and decides that he will make a good friend. The latter worships Basi who easily succeeds in making him his "slave," educating him in the crooked ways of survival, and to accept joblessness as a normal estate, which is contrary to what Alali's father taught him. We are told that Alali does not believe Basi, yet his behavior proves that Basi leads and he follows. "Alali did not believe him. He believed what his father had told him long ago. .. He had said that a good name is better than riches. Alali said so to Mr. B. "Wrong. Your father was wrong. You will see. When I have my millions, everyone will hear of me. Just wait." (24-25) Basi makes sure that Alali, rather than get a job, becomes his assistant. Alali, we are again informed, likes Basi because he is funny, but does not like the fact that Basi hates to work; as usual, the latter is not made action. While Saro-Wiwa presents other characters' bad actions in a negative light, he appears to condone, or encourage, those of this thinking duo. And Basi's regular dream is quite an interesting flight of fancy: he is in the V.I.P. lounge at an airport. He enters the plane which takes off. He is treated like royalty, called "Your Excellency, Your Majesty," fawned upon and feted with the most sophisticated food and drinks, such as caviar, champagne, and liqueur. Then, he has a dream within the dream as he falls asleep in flight: the plane suddenly flies into a storm. Basi is frightened out of his sleep. The plane lands safely, at a palace where His Majesty is driven in a convoy of cars and with highlife music and children dancing exclusively for his pleasure. The palace is guarded by lions and men armed with swords and shields. The walls are gold, with an array of flowers and plants. There is a swimming pool, an artificial lake and a yacht. There is a vault full of gold and diamonds. In the dining room, he is given a sumptuous meal of the most delicious Nigerian dishes. Madam's call rudely cuts short Basi's dream; "he wished it had not been a dream... There were tears in his eyes, but he did not cry." (40) Anyone in his right mind (a shrink's services would only be professional superfluity at this point!) would advise this dreamer to go get himself a job, to work hard, honestly, to live here on earth and not on the moon, to couch his dream in realistic dimensions. Saro-Wiwa does not do that, however, because the dreams—and the more fantastic they are, the better, for comical effect—are a great ingredient for entertainment. Thus, in the comical universe inhabited by Basi, he is given occasions to live still dream-like, some of those fanciful notions. At the local restaurant of one of his creditors, Mama Badejo, he asks for breakfast: "I could do with cereals, fruit juice, scrambled eggs, French coffee (...) I would prefer wine, but water will do for now." As should be expected, the woman is confused. She has never heard of such things before. (*MR. B*: 7) She is sympathetic of the "poor" man's plight; she thinks, perhaps, "hunger has made him mad." She also thinks that he is "confused. He likes to eat *dodo* and stew. Yet he asked for strange food at first." (7) In the original edition of "The Transistor Radio," Basi, assuming that he has made his million, plays the role of master, with Alali as his servant, Hezekiah. The situation is among the funniest in the script; the master humiliates the servant, calls him names, generalizes about all servants' stupidity, and flaunts his superiority like a peacock. It is breakfast time at the millionaire's mansion.

Basi: Boy!
Alali: Sah!
Basi: Come here. What is your name? I always forget it.
...

Shut up! Are you not afraid of your master? D'you think I pay you one hundred naira a month so you can speak to me anyhow you like?...
(They both laugh)...
That's not bad at all, Alali. I can really swank it when I mean to. We'll try again. Boy!
...
Go and get some food.
Alali: Here, sah.
Basi: No wine?
Alali: But there is beer, sah.
Basi: Nonsense! Go and get me some wine. And what is this? Fresh fish? Good. I love fresh fish. *Poisson sans boisson c'est poison.* Understand that? Fish without wine is poison. Ah, good fish... (*Four Farcical Plays*: 21)

While one appreciates the artistic effectiveness of such episodes, one also wonders why the comic hero must place a premium on "civilized" attitude and behavior. In spite of the comedy, Basi would fit well into the mold of the *confused* Nigerians, the types already found in Saro-Wiwa's other fictional writings. Furthermore, his claims to superiority might be less of a virtue than a vice. On occasions, he is as crooked as they come; as criminal-minded, too. Witness his collusion with Alali in the episode on "ghost-workers," when both of their names are placed on the lists of government workers for pay without work; "the contract," when, after his forms have been rejected for lateness, he makes sure Madam loses out, too. Basi is always the first to pass judgment on others. To Segi, who, angry that her radio has been lost by Dandy and Josco, he puts the rhetorical question, "You see the sort of friends you have?" (*MR. B:* 70) About Madam, he declares: "She's a very bad woman. She does not keep her promises. She is greedy and wants to have all the money in the world." (117) This criticism, as usual, is corroborated by the author: "Madam was a bad citizen. All good citizens always pay their taxes promptly to the government. But Madam did not ever pay, although she had a lot of money. And she also encouraged both Dandy and Josco to forge documents... Dandy and Josco, being bad men, did not mind. They hoped that they would not be caught." (115) The didacticism might be good for children, although thinking children are likely to retort that Basi himself is a culprit.

The script, "Comrades All," in which Basi returns Segi's radio to her (*Basi and Company*: 23-29; also, "Segi Finds Her Radio," in *MR. B*: 62-72) recounts how all the six become "friends." We have noted how everyone gravitates towards Basi, the central figure. The radio plot is the first instance of his control over others and situations. Friendship as defined among these people is not the ideal taught to every child; it is not the relationship of equals, or of like, selfless minds, mutually committed to helping one another and improving their conditions based upon harmony and understanding. "The six people became friends, but they were not very friendly with one another... because they did not agree with one another all the time. They were even jealous of one another... Although Segi enjoyed the company of Basi and his friends, her real friend was Professor." (*MR. B*: 73-4) Thus, Basi, whenever he talks of being "equal to all problems," (*Basi and Company*: 25) whenever he thinks "what he could do to help his friends," (*MR. B:* 120) is thinking of himself before anyone else. Each of the characters, as selfish as a miser, believes in using others, except for Alali who calls Basi "boss" (99) and remains absolutely devoted to him. It cannot be overemphasized that Basi sets the tone, the standard. He is so smart that, many a time, his victims do not realize that his selflessness is actually a ruse, a mask for his selfishness. In the radio episode, Segi is all gratitude when Basi, playing the good Samaritan, brings out her radio from under his bed. He is all smiles, "a light dancing in his eyes." He proposes a toast to friendship with empty glasses and, before anyone can begin to ask where the drink would come from, there comes Madam with the gin she promised Basi. Once again, the millionaire-dreamer has won the day: "I think we should all have a drink in celebration. You see, I am going on a journey. I want to earn a lot of money, become a millionaire in a very short time. I cannot afford to make enemies. A man like me needs a lot of friends." (71)

In the earlier episodes of the Basi series, the theme of friendship is still relatively marked by a certain innocence. Self-survival and selfishness do not drastically reduce the loose bonding among the characters. There is no animosity. They are "useful to another" (*Basi and Company*: 38) There is no desire to destroy even those that they call enemy. Thus, to an extent, we may say that this is not a mirror of the Nigerian society at its worst; references to the ills of society are made, as it were, from the outside. The characters are victims, forming a microcosm of the larger mass, and mess. On the other hand, they are part of the problem, since they are guilty of those common crimes and sins that have the cumulative effect of destroying the moral and material fabric of the society. If we can talk of a mean streak attendant to the distorted definition and actualization of friendship, we should also affirm that it is on a low scale, occurring over meager issues; consequently, comedy is upheld as a situation in which the characters laugh at , and with, one another, making a fool of one another, over mundane matters. They lie to one another constantly, but they laugh it off as another expediency of living. The novel, *MR. B is Dead*, changes this perspective.

In this novel, Madam and Dandy, in particular, express their spite for Basi; they would rather deal with a dead Basi than the living being. Basi wants a little loan, but Madam and her American Dollar Club friends are preparing to spend money on a friend's grand burial. Basi has not eaten for two days; Madam does not care. If he dies, she promises to give him "a befitting burial." (16) For his part, Dandy refuses to lend Basi money to bury his great-uncle. Josco shares that opinion. Dandy declares:

'Lend money for the burial of MR. B's great-uncle? Not on your life! If it was MR. B's burial, I'd pay everything. I'd even sell my bar to raise the money.'
'Why?' asked Alali, a little confused.
'Because I don't care for MR. B alive. I should love to see him dead and buried...'
Josco adds:

'MR. B's a very bad man. He's wicked. He's better dead than alive!' (27-8)

The story reveals how these characters have descended towards outright meanness. Madam is more greedy, more materialistic, more inconsiderate and more insensitive than before. She feels that Basi might as well die of hunger so that she may take back his room and rent it to someone who will pay. "Madam thought him [Basi] to be a bad man." (17) Basi's behavior complements that of his friends; for, the very idea of announcing his own death is quite bold, if not extremist. Regarding his character, one is tempted to agree with the others that he is wicked (cf the case of Saro-Wiwa, "a wicked wit," in the Jebsian novels), prepared to go to any length to abuse others' intelligence and to achieve his goals. To every selfish action by his friends, Basi comes up with a more selfish one. At the end of the story, he and Alali are still using the death ruse to cheat people out of their money.

All in all, the Basi texts depict characters that are likeable for their humor but, when it comes to the moral lessons to be learnt from them, there is ambiguity, confusion, too. Professor's comments, ostensibly Saro-Wiwa's, do not help to clarify the portraits and events in the texts. They serve a purpose as didactic statements; unfortunately, they are hardly supported by the projections on screen and in print. There is a mystery about Basi that makes his character dubious in *MR. B is Dead*. He seems to be a living example of the *rumor* that is Nigeria. He is described as being "away from the place of his birth for so long that he did not remember anything about it. At least so he said." (23) Up till Maja's burial party, nothing has been mentioned of Basi's guitar-playing and singing abilities; now, suddenly, we see him displaying those skills and Madam says that he used to play and sing for her. (80) When Segi claims that all his business deals have failed, Madam counters that some have succeeded; yet we never know which ones. In essence, the author, and Professor, would like us to have a positive opinion of Basi, without a proper portrait of positive action.

Saro-Wiwa has succeeded in making them amuse us, but not in warning us. The Professor's comments of their behavior needs to be read with that in mind. Professor laughs a lot at Basi. He is convinced that the man will never make his millions, not because he is lazy. Let us quote his discussion with Segi: "Mr. B is not lazy. He works pretty hard. But at the wrong things." (*MR. B:* 151) Does Basi work hard at all? The texts do not show it. About Madam's greedy and shady character, Professor tells Segi: "She still wants more money. She will get it only if she stops trying to trick money out of other people. Next time, I won't save her from going to jail." (152) Professor says Mr. B., Madam, Josco and Dandy will never be successful. The question remains: how do we learn to avoid the mistakes these characters make? Professor, philosopher, hardly bases his statements on what is being played out before the theatrical, television and fictional audience.

LAGOS SOCIETY AND ITS VICES

Contrary to the status of superiority and civilization adduced to Lagos and Lagosians in *Sozaboy* (cf. Agnes, the Lagos girl being admired by everyone), "this God-forsaken city of sin" (*Basi and Company*: 31) is viewed with mixed feelings in the Basi series. Lagos people "are always on the lookout for 'easy money'." (*MR. B is Dead*: 92) It is the reputation of the city as a source of easy money that attracts Basi to the place; and as a place to find work easily, that makes Alali go there. Basi hears of Lagos before going there.

"He had traveled to several towns in search of money, but did not find it. One day, he heard from some people... that Lagos was a city full of rich men and women... They said there was so much money in Lagos that the people did not know what to do with it... 'That's where I should be,' he said to himself. 'Lagos is my type of city. I'm sure that once I get there, I will be a millionaire." (*MR. B*: 4-5)

Basi's lesson, passed to Alali, is an eye-opener to his skewered beliefs about the city. "There are no jobs in Lagos. Only money. You should have been looking for money, not a job." (24) It is this generalized, negative, exaggerated character that is emphasized throughout the Basi series. A further generalization takes place: Adetola Street, or simply, the Street, is depicted as a special place. A world on its own, with everybody ("People") behaving in the same manner, that is, bad. Basi asks: "Why is everyone on this street so cruel to us?" (*MR. B is Dead*: 9) Alali reads obituaries in the newspaper, and the author declares: "Adetola Street obituaries were impolite to the dead and a mere show-off by the living. They lacked dignity; they were crude." (22) And Basi declares: "The people of Adetola Street? They're all mean and petty... They all want to see me dead." (29) Yet, these are the same people that the two ever-hungry men owe money for food eaten on credit, and for articles bought on credit. (Mrs. Badejo, the *suya* seller, and Mr. Dada, the stationary store owner). Basi and Alali include Madam and the others (but not themselves) in their generalizations about the Street.

Adetola Street, at another level, is a symbol of Lagos, and Saro-Wiwa uses it to satirize institutions and people. Some policemen are corrupt and lazy and incompetent.

"Some of the policemen... were very dishonest and corrupt. They were fat and lazy and did not like to do their work... It was the laziness and corruption of the police that made Adetola Street a dangerous place to live in... Sometimes robberies were committed in the daytime. Yet very few robbers were ever caught. Some residents believed that some policemen were robbers too." (82-3)

Not all police are bad: Basi's impersonation of a C.I.D. officer, Segi's constant statement about the force's responsibility in protecting the people, these are signs that the institution consists of competent officers. The opinion would then appear to be that Lagos has a corrupting effect on people.

Taxation is another matter where satire is used. A good citizen pays his tax. On Adetola Street, however, people do not want to pay. Madam is one of the worst offenders—she "did not ever pay, although she had a lot of money. And she also encouraged both Dandy and Josco to forge documents." (*MR. B*: 115) Basi does not pay either, but he uses his state of joblessness as a reason. Meanwhile, the unwillingness to work is not mentioned. As sanctimonious as ever, he criticizes government for its incompetence: "What do they use the tax for, anyway? There are no drugs in the hospital, the roads are full of pot-holes and the schools have no books. I won't pay my tax unless they supply all these things." (82) Alali, often the voice of reason and responsibility, is not given enough force by the author to prove the author's desire to truly let his audience learn lessons from his characters' misdeeds.

The lack of attention to the living is another example of Lagosians' vices. Madam and her Amerdolian friends display the insensitivity and senselessness of a society long on materialism but too short on humanism. The description of the long, careful preparations for their friend's "befitting burial" party, and its execution with fanfare, are skillfully contrasted with the short funeral service. The gaiety makes many people think that it is a birthday or wedding ceremony. The food is so much that passers-by stop, eat and drink for free.

The lack of interest in helping to heal the sick is complemented by the desire to see others suffer. Basi and Dandy's argument in the latter's bar is most welcome by an audience ready for entertainment; they have no sympathy for Dandy who will surely be ground to the dust if attacked by Basi and Alali. "The people were like that. They liked to see others suffer... They were enjoying themselves. The quarrel... was an entertainment for them. They wanted the excitement to go on." (*MR. B is Dead*: 75)

The greed of the main characters of the Basi clan are only a mirror of Lagos society. For example, Mr. Babalola, the lawyer contacted by Madam in her efforts to get back her money from Basi, only offers her silly advice based on posturing. At the end of the short session from which Madam has learnt nothing new, the lawyer charges her a consultation fee of one thousand naira. "She knew that Adetola Street lawyers were greedy. She paid Mr. Babalola who received the money with bulging eyes and cheeks." (*MR. B is Dead*: 56)

A pinch of male chauvinism is thrown into this society of "mean and petty" people. Dandy's jealousy of Madam is due to "the foolish reason that he thought a woman should not be richer than a man." (*MR. B*: 74) Basi, once he sets his eyes on Segi, is convinced that she "is a luscious fruit that must be plucked." (*Basi and Company*: 35) The women are not innocent of biased thoughts and actions. Segi, thinking that Dandy may be colluding with Basi who is trying to keep the cash collected from his friends for his burial ceremony, tells Madam: "They are men, which means they can't be trusted." (*MR. B is Dead*: 83) Which does not mean, however, that these women are members of a feminist organization. They become opponents as soon as their personal interests are at stake. For example, convinced by Alali that Basi likes them both, they start to compete, to show jealousy, to get each other out of the way. (*MR. B*: 102-106).

Segi is always ready to exploit her man. She is well connected "with the Police Bosses, not just the sergeants." (*Basi and Company*: 35) "As vain as a peacock," (*MR. B:* 92) this woman symbolizes the young society woman, superficial but charming, selfish but generous in some matters involving people's rights (cf p. 107, on tenants).

Segi's character (Basi's, too, from the author's, and Professor's, standpoint) would thus be a redeeming factor for sanity and decorum "in Lagos [where] anything is possible" (*MR. B*: 23). She is what Madam could have been if she had not been materialistic, and if she had been better educated. In spite of the widespread corruption; of the pervasive black-market in its various connotations, Lagos remains attractive because of its potential; of those very possibilities that can be used for good. In Lagos, you learn to be, you have to be, smart in order to survive. The challenge is, how to use the existing energy for positive objectives. As it is, the people on Adetola Street, react to the potential personalized by Basi, but for the wrong reasons. Indeed, they are, by and large, depicted as stupid people: most believe that Basi is really a millionaire, and a magician. "All of them agreed on one thing: he had made Adetola Street very famous throughout Lagos and the world." (*MR. B is Dead*: 47) Here, Saro-Wiwa, ever so witty and confusing, subtly brings us back to the essential, reminding us that the TV series and its popularity matter more than anything else. Still, his ambitious comments (see top of this chapter) on the impact of the program has to be criticized as a misinterpretation of the content.

ON THE TWO VERSIONS OF "(THE) TRANSISTOR RADIO"

"The Transistor Radio" (original title; second edition bears only "Transistor Radio") is without doubt Saro-Wiwa's most successful play in terms of critical acclaim, and awards. It won a prize in the 1972 BBC African Theater Competition, and another in the same year's Nigerian Festival of the Arts. From its first performance as a sketch in 1964 to its adaptation as the first episode of the television series, it has undergone significant changes. The two published versions (interesting that the later edition precedes the former in print) can be used to study Saro-Wiwa's development as a dramatist, as well as his skills as a television producer. The first version, "The Transistor Radio," is the only play in the Mr. B. Series (specifically the first and only at the time) contained in the collection, *Four Farcical Plays*, in the introduction to which Saro-Wiwa writes: "The plays represent my early concern as much with the social problems of our time as with an adequate language of communication of a Nigerian theater aimed at the broadest possible public." (7) If this statement sounds familiar, it is because the author expresses these same notions in his introduction to *Sozaboy*, his first novel.[6] In the first version, Madam, Basi's landlady, uses pidgin English; in the latter, she uses standard English. This shift is significant. The original Madam comes across as uneducated, cantankerous, easy to hate; but her language, with its local color (the use of popular terms, such as *wuruwuru, wayo* = dubious) and earthiness definitely adds to the farcical situation. By regularizing the language of all the characters in the later edition, Saro-Wiwa succeeds in creating a socio-psychological equilibrium, leveling the field of play, so to speak, with no character being disadvantaged. It also helps him to remove the focus from Madam and place it upon Basi, his main character. Whether the change in language has not reduced the comical effect, is up for debate.

The character, Segi, is absent from the first edition. There is therefore no explicable source of the transistor radio that Dandy and Josco are trying to use to make quick cash. By introducing Segi in the television version, Saro-Wiwa makes the story more plausible and more interesting. Segi adds to the human factor and, as the series progresses, she continues to blend into the cast. Of course as an intelligent young woman, she brings a critical perspective to the program; she is also the character that introduces Professor, her neighbor, used by Saro-Wiwa to contribute a philosophical outlook to the comical community. In short, the second version is more logical and more deep than the first.

However, the removal of other episodes in the later version could be construed as lessening the depth of the discourse. For example, several discussions between Basi and Alali are absent: Basi's efforts to get a job (*Four Farcical Plays*: 14); Alali's insistence on committing suicide (15); Basi drinking tea, Alali chewing the leaves, and their discussion on the fraudulent rich (18); Basi's big talk on his millions and his play-acting as millionaire, with Alali as his humiliated servant (20-21); Alali's repeated complaints of hunger (22); their discussion on the beer-bottle left behind by Madam (23); a whole final section in which Alali repeats his desire to kill himself, to return home to the village, while Basi tries to convince him to stay, and the episode ends with a voice announcing *a million to be won playing* and Basi and Alali rushing out in search of a million (30-31). These scenes give a sort of dark edge to the play. Alali is rather serious. Instead of concentrating on laughter, the audience might spend time dealing with the man's miserable life in Lagos. The expunged scenes also reduce the length of the action, thus making it more adequate for the television time limits. The division into "Situations" as opposed to the one-scene format of the first edition has the same effect. It also makes the script less unwieldy.

Another note on the language: the later edition uses more colloquial English, more monosyllables, and more phrases, whereas the first edition's English is better structured and, therefore, less normal. Saro-Wiwa has certainly achieved the transformation of his text into a TV script. Bearing in mind that the image on the small screen gives much room for body movement and image manipulation, his later script contains less descriptions than the first. The setting remains simple, with just a small number of pieces in the decor. It is not surprising that the series was the most popular on Nigerian television for several years.

CONCLUSION: CAN LAUGHTER MASK THE TEARS?

The Basi series gives abundant proof of Saro-Wiwa's sense of humor. The overwhelming success of the television show is also proof that his compatriots, too, have a sense of humor. Now, years after the screen had seen the back of Basi and his cap and heard his trade-mark millionaire phrase, Saro-Wiwa was interviewed. He complained bitterly about Nigerians: "Nigerians lack a sense of humor. People take themselves too seriously. They should learn how to laugh." (*TELL*, Nov. 27, 1995: 11) Had he forgotten the mirthful past? Probably not.

At the time of the interview, he was on the point of being sentenced to death in a charade of a case, a tribunal misconstituted by the tyrants and chaired by the kangaroo. He must have been wondering where the laughter had gone. However, had he known his audience well, had he read properly the pulse of his volatile people, he would have realized that he himself encouraged their senselessness, because his comedy helped them to laugh and do away with thinking. And it had been so long ago that they laughed with him. In a neo-colonial society, comedy poses a grave danger of luring the audience to sleep. People forget to think. They not only take themselves less seriously, they do not take themselves to be anything at all! And, in Saro-Wiwa's then on-going trial, he ought to have realized, too, that kangaroos do not have a sense of humor. That, even though their unwieldy gowns and wigs make them better suited to be clowns in a circus using hare-brained performers like them, they love to pose as luminaries and repositories of justice, a very serious responsibility, indeed.

In that prison serving as his passage to the perdition specially prepared for him by his assailants (monsters that can only laugh when they see others die), Saro-Wiwa was possibly nostalgic for some light-hearted interlocutory, to take his mind off the tragedy of existence. Contradictions and confusion. Because he himself knew better than that. His favorite character, Basi, thinks, we are told. But he makes us laugh better than he does, thinking. Confusion. Professor laughs at the Basi clan, and he philosophizes. But his philosophy remains ambiguous, even with its high morals and idealistic statements. "Money is not the most important thing in life. Knowledge is(...)With knowledge, mankind can be made happier and human life better." (*MR. B*: 77) But nothing is said about how to attain that knowledge in a society where materialism and unabated merriment in the midst of material misery reigns. Confusion. As mentioned in the novel, *Prisoners of Jebs*, the Nigerians owe one of their most used phraseologies to Saro-Wiwa's series: "It was a matter of cash, as the Nigerians had learnt to say, thanks to the newest popular series on their television station, *Basi and Company*." (*Jebs*: 121) And everyone is busy running after his millions. And Alhaji Dollar is facing the front of Bristol Hotel, Lagos, buying and selling foreign currency in "a very confused scene" (*MR. B is Dead*: 88) with the authorities pretending not to know of such transactions. And members of the American Dollar Club are busy preparing for the next big splash of their wealth in their expensive clothes before a very appreciative crowd who can staunch their hunger for one more night. And, on Adetola Street, hunger remains the most prominent presence. Finally, Mr. B, the master comedian, is lying on his bed, rudely awakened by Madam from his beautiful dream. "There were tears in his eyes, but he did not cry." (*MR. B:* 40)

NOTES TO CHAPTER IV

1. In his novel, *Prisoners of Jebs*, Saro-Wiwa refers to the TV series. The Nigerian Attorney-General used to be "Leader of the Bar, not Dandy's Bar of the famous Nigerian comedy, *Basi and Company*. (98) In *MR. B*, Dandy is erected by Madam as "Leader and keeper of the Bar." (90)

Madam's stock statement showing off her materialism,, "It's a matter of cash!" (MR. B: 69) is recognized in Jebs as a general Nigerian mannerism (and malady?) "It was a matter of cash, as the Nigerians had learnt to say, thanks to the most popular comedy series on their television station, *Basi and Company*." (121)

2. Other novels in the series: *MR. B Again; A Bride for* Mr. B.

3. Saro-Wiwa has two other children's novels, *Tambari and Tambari in Dukana* (Longman's "Palm Library for Younger Readers"), for "students in the upper classes of primary schools and the lower forms of secondary schools. The novels relate the life of a boy from Dukana, Tambari, schooling in Umuahia and traveling home for holidays. The themes include, village life and people and culture; morals; growing up. The Tambari works are not nearly as popular as the Basi series, a fact due to television and Lagos, the scene of the comical events.

4. *MR. B is Dead*: 18. This new trait, of course is inserted to provide the opportunity for Basi to read obituaries, which would give him the idea of announcing his own death.
 If one is a stickler for logic and details, one can easily pick holes in the plots of the Basi series. But comedy (laughter) is first objective; hence, Saro-Wiwa's lack of attention to logic.

5. *Aide-de-Camp*, a military term, and a strange description for Alali's relationship to Basi. Note that Nigeria is under military rule. Saro-Wiwa's admiration for the Nigerian military will be discussed in the chapter on the civil war.

6. The other plays in the collection are, "Bride by Return," "The Wheel," and "Madam No Go Quench Again." The last play, as the title suggests, uses pidgin English. An interesting study would be, the comparison of this English to the much vaunted "rotten English" of *Sozaboy*, to discuss whether and how the two types of language facilitate communication with "the broadest public possible." For example, the lawlessness of Sozaboy's English mentioned by Saro-Wiwa, may not, after all, be much different from that of pidgin spoken in so many forms by so many people. In both Wiwan texts, one common effect is, that the language is very comical and apt for the satire excellently depicted by the writer.

V. *A FOREST OF FLOWERS*, SHORT STORIES

>-He cursed the earth for sprouting oil, black gold, they called it. And he cursed the gods for not drying the oil wells.
>*(A Forest of Flowers: 111)*
>-If God na man, some people no go chop. (20)
>-A good story will only feed the storyteller when the audience is large. (40)
>-What's our life her in Dukana? A daily death? An escape from death? (61)

INTRODUCTION: OF TITLES AND TALES OF TRAGEDY

Saro-Wiwa wrote "High Life," one of the stories in his collection, *A Forest of Flowers*, in 1966. It was his first effort in what he would later call "rotten English" in the novel, *Sozaboy*. Remarkable enough, that story, of a young cook's Christmas season visit to his brother at Aba, is the sub-title of the two part collection ("Home, Sweet Home" being that of the first part). This division has been used by the critic, N.F. Inyama, to analyze the stories along distinct, dichotomous lines of the village Dukana, on the one hand, and the cities (Lagos, Port Harcourt, Aba, Kano) on the other. Upon reading the text myself, I have found reasons to disagree with Inyama's analytic methodology. Although all the stories in Part One deal with Dukana, not all those in the second part deal with cities. One story, "Night Ride," recounting the ride in a car of an Administrator with a civil war widow, is also based in the Dukana (Ogoni) country. The grim realities already described in the earlier stories are revisited here, but with greater depth and sensitivity, by a narrator able to understand his people's psyche and to express their despair. Another story, "A Legend on our Street," while belonging to Part Two, does not have any definitive city atmosphere. The Street on which lives the narrator and a shopkeeper, and "the Legend", the extraordinary, wise old man, who becomes his and others' hero because of his resilience and survival through the generations of Nigeria's tumultuous and decadent history, is not a metaphor for any modern madness or mania, as is shown in other stories. My feeling is, that Saro-Wiwa made his division in order to highlight the two lead stories of each part. And, if "Home" is strictly a

Dukana tale, "High Life" may not be strictly an Aba story; for, the hero reminds us of Sozaboy in his village or small town mentality, zealous to "jollie" (have fun) in the city and, because of his travels outside the village, feeling superior to others around him.

The title of the collection has been satisfactorily analyzed by Inyama. The "forest" is "a metaphor for the rural, forest-bound world of [Mene's home town in *Sozaboy*] Dukana. The flowers that bloom in this forest village are *fleurs du mal*, of ignorance, superstition, filth and stagnation(...) Saro-Wiwa refuses to shield these negative elements under a fake, romanticized, rural innocence... The notion of a caring, mutually-protective rural populace is belied by the frequency with which the people of Dukana allow their ignorance to overtake and overwhelm them and find expression in the crassest of cruelties, inflicted with horrifying implacability on one or other of their members." (*African Literature Today*, 20: 46) Continuing, Inyama affirms: "Modern cosmopolitan Nigeria does not appear to be much different from superstitious Dukana; rather, the city gives the village a negative complementarity which anchors the author's perception of a different, ugly reality." (48)

There are other possible configurations of the title. The connotation of *forest* can be broadened as, indeed, Saro-Wiwa has done. Not only Dukana is forest ("a clearing in the tropical rain forest peopled by three or four thousand men, women, and children," 3); but also Lagos: after the shopkeeper in "The Shopkeeper and the Beggar" has closed his shop and sold off all his wares, he is invited for a chat by the bank manager, "the king of the forest [who] asked how he meant to settle his debts (...) The shopkeeper broke into a wild stammer as he saw the monsters of the jungle [metaphor for overdrafts, balances, compound interest, and other items dreaded by debtors] jump at his throat (...) The monster king of the forest smiled again, and all of a sudden, in that icy-cold forest, a sheen of sweat glistened on his forehead. The monsters howled and barked, wagged their tails, danced around him in a circle until the king bade them hold their peace." (140-141) Thus, the forest of the city, the Jungle, is also modern, and more murderous than the wild woods of the village. In the forest, flowers grow wild, out of control, with a beauty impossible to appreciate because of their habitat, and habits. These flowers, as a metaphor for human beings, populate and pollute the pages of Saro-Wiwa's novel, as they spread their nauseous odor through village and city, as they visit death upon God's other creations, using their poisonous, thorny petals as weapons of war on the wretched of the earth.

The irony is all-inclusive. Flowers, usually symbols of beauty, are, in these stories, quintessentially bestial. Fortunately, there are a few exceptions which give one a little bit of hope, that is if one is truly committed to the task of finding the lost or corrupted beauty and plucking them out to form enchanting bouquets. The titles of the vast majority of the stories underscore the irony of the forest of flowers. "High Life" describes an utterly low life. "Home, Sweet Home" portrays a sad, sour existence in an atmosphere of ignorance, superstition and selfishness. "The Overhaul" depicts the frustrations of a catechist caught in the web of a fraudulent religious establishment replicating the infamous human weaknesses of the secular society. "A Family Affair" shows the lack of love, harmony, mutual support and communality too often vaunted as the pillar of traditional society. "A Share of Profit" tells the story of a materialistic man ready to exploit another, less intelligent and less material-minded man, without sharing with him the profit that only the latter deserves. "Case no. 100" satirizes the incompetence and corruption of policemen proud to list the astronomical number of cases they have treated, but none of which is ever resolved according to authentic laws or logic. "The Stars Below" discusses the dilemma of a public officer forced to the verge by a corrupt, retrogressive system that has turned responsibility on its head. The stars are no longer viewed from above, in the sky, but below, in the sea, thus revealing the fleeting nature of happiness, its impossibility, its status as a mirage that may never be made real. "A Caring Man" chronicles the mutual lack of care of a profligate husband for his wife. When the man provides her with a Mercedes Coupe in wine color, she exudes with magnanimity, "The milk of human forgiveness welled up in my breast. Dani was always a caring man, you know." (133)

These stories either end tragically, or ambiguously. The narrator of "Home, Sweet Home" finally obtains an answer to her question, about the fate of her childhood friend who, unlike her, completed her education. Sira, her friend, had twins and, following tradition, was forced to leave Dukana. The narrator, dumbfounded, goes to her room where she lies, unable to sleep, hearing the rhythm of drums in the distance, the sounds of various night creatures, and "the spirits of my home, my sweet home." (10) These spirits, these gods and goddesses, are the very ones that dictate to the people their postures of backwardness, their murderous mien, their absolute bestiality. Ironically, the people are elated to have the narrator back home, to infuse some blood of progress into the community. Whether that would occur, however, is another matter altogether. "The Inspector Calls" ends with the Sanitary Inspector's arrival at an evacuated Dukana. He, "a plague" as detestable and as horrible as any other, such as influenza, is considered undesirable by the town lights, that is, the Chief and other leaders of darkness. When he does come, these corrupt fathers of the community satiate his thirst for alcohol, and send him off with money and foodstuffs, bribes that make him overlook the filth plaguing the town. "He took away with him, in the dust clouds following upon his now heavily-laden motorcycle, all those ill winds which, had they remained behind, would surely have plagued Dukana. And once again, Dukana returned to its accustomed peace, somnolence, tranquility, dirt and happiness." (18) Such happiness in ignorance and dirt, surely must be inviting to disease and death.

"A Family Affair" ends with the murder of a mad man by his family, ashamed of his state of mind and his action of going about naked and bagging for food. After burying him alive, and certain that he is no longer wailing out his being alive, "they looked at each other, turned upon their heels and picked their silent way through he secretive forest back to Dukana." (33) Nothing is whispered about his mindless murder. Nobody will ask questions, since the murderers have announced the death to the whole community. A similar ending of secret and silent murder is seen in "The Bonfire" in which Dukana youths, convinced that an innocent loner has a hand in the death of a townsman, set him on fire inside his house. "The youths, without a word, hurriedly disappeared in different directions." (39) In this community, collusion, conspiracy, complicity, those are the hallmarks of a way of life showing no signs of change.

In many cases, the apparent solidity of societal tragedy is consequential to the presence and promotion of bigotry couched in simplistic sermons of solidarity through diversity. Garga, a Hausa living in his native Kano, has as best friend Garuba, an Ibo who has changed his name in order to blend into the milieu. At the outbreak of one of those ethnic riots that the Nigerian leadership has never tried to address, Garga rushes from the walled city into the Sabongari, the strangers' sector, driven by selfless, sacrificial and, some would say, stupid love. He must save his friend from certain death. On the point of picking up Garuba's little daughter, Garga is decapitated by Okoye, Garuba's brother. Enough said for inter-ethnic friendship ("Garga").

A few endings are, however, more positive. "The Overhaul" shows catechist Daniel having a vision of his later life, as Pastor Barika of a new church, moving with power among his people, "receiving reward both in cash and kind [and praised] as a great messenger of the Lord." (26) But, then, one notes that this vision, "terrible in its beauty," is only a re-affirmation, or confirmation, of the decadence represented by the already existing churches and priests. Pastor Barika becomes a fixture of Dukana (see *Sozaboy*); hence, the vision is translated into reality in Saro-Wiwa's fictional universe. In "High Life," the narrator-protagonist, after his lust for "fine babies" has led him into a hilarious but horrible encounter with a woman-man, escapes from Aba in one piece and vows never to return there. Which does not resolve the repetition of such experiences; for, the narrator mentions having recently read of an identical event in the newspaper.

The unfolding of the "Acapulco Motel" fraudulent existence of Alhaji, shows his victim, the narrator's aunt, returning to Alhaji's motel one year after his promise to resolve the poor woman's land problem. The motel has been closed down and converted into living apartments. A solitary goat is standing up front, staring at the woman and her nephew "as though he had known us for ages. And among us, the goat is a symbol of foolishness (...) I did wonder if some charm had translated Alhaji into a goat. And given the disposition of matters in our time, the possibility did not seem remote." (95) The society that breeds the likes of Alhaji would appear to die hard. Superstitions, ever willing to accord viability to villains, it will welcome other crooks, and not all of them will become goats. Besides, the goat staring at the woman and the narrator may indeed be a human goat, pretending to be stupid but preying upon his new victims, the inhabitants of the apartments.

"A Legend on our Street" is probably the most optimistic story of the collection. Papa, the octogenarian Legend, survives the scare of an unexpected illness. He and the narrator-shopkeeper continue their blossoming friendship. The narrator's business continues to boom, and "Papa still lives on our street, a legend if there was one." (150) Pity that such a story of love, long life and happiness is not common in fact or fiction.

TRADITIONAL SOCIETY AS SYMBOL OF DECADENCE

Tradition, that body of beliefs, habits, attitudes, handed down through generations, is often regarded as sacrosanct, immutable, and immune to any change which, in the minds of the traditionalists, is tantamount to a crime of immense proportions. Saro-Wiwa has used his short stories to debunk the myth of tradition as a citadel of innocent, untainted happiness, depicting it instead as a monstrous monolith masking stagnation, inferiority complex, ignorance, and barbarity. He explains the complex psyche of traditional society, that mixture of fear of invasion and obliteration by outsiders and a trait of xenophobia fueled by the love of freedom, as well as a misplaced superiority complex that repels any foreign or strange elements.

The usual tendency in so-called civilized circles, is to draw an absolute line of distinction between Tradition and Modernity. Education-Ignorance. Science-Superstition. Progress-Parochialism. New-Old. Saro-Wiwa refuses to subscribe to such exclusivism; for, he realizes that, in a neo-colonial setting such as ours, the so-called Civilization is often rooted in a jungle worse than that inhabited by beasts, and that it often complements Tradition in acts and attitudes of repression and oppression of people either ignorant or too indolent to resist the power of both behemoths.

Dukana's tradition is the main object of Saro-Wiwa's criticism. The narrator of "Home, Sweet Home," a school-leaver returning home to settle and teach, dissects with both an uncanny objectivity and a sarcastic sympathy, her people's psyche in their condition of unrecognized underdevelopment. Symbolically, the town's only means of transportation and communication with the outside world, an old lorry driven by a "son of the soil" (a Dukana free-born), is named *Progres*, and the wrong spelling subtly emphasizes these people's half- or mis-education. The very first sentence sets the stage for this long adventure into ignorance and ill-health, conditions with which the people, paradoxically enough, are satisfied. "*Progres* spluttered lazily down the long, dirt road which stretched before us like the coated tongue of an ailing man." (1) The lorry is "proud witness to the progressive and cooperative, modern spirit of Dukana." (1) Without the lorry, she would have to make the journey from city to town, on a bicycle.

The girl states what every true Dukana daughter or son believes with pride, that "home is home," better than any place else on earth and she simply is compelled to agree so as not to be considered "disloyal to communal wisdom and to be disloyal to that wisdom so carefully distilled through the ages was arrogance." (2) As her mother has advised—and mother knows best—, she will try to understand her people. Making an effort not to be arrogant, or unappreciative, or unpatriotic, therefore, she lists what outsiders, "ill-informed malicious people," would condemn in Dukana and what insiders would show off with pride. On the former list: the town's topography as a clearing in the forest by a few thousand emaciated, illiterate people making a miserable living on farming and fishing; absence of basic amenities like health clinic, a good school, pipe-borne water, and electricity; presence of disease, and early death. In short, Dukana would be perceived by outsiders as "doomed in a modern world" (3) with its space programs and scientific control of the ecology. On the Dukana pride-list, made up of items whose identity and quality are determined by the people's confused and contradictory conceptualization: the Chief, a would-be king, lives in a Palace, to where the occasional official letter is addressed (images of Basi's hovel proudly misnamed as palace); the elders constitute a Council of Chiefs handing out justice according to pristine laws of an effete oral tradition; Dukana is a kingdom, having fought wars to preserve her independence and her self-sufficiency; the kingdom enjoys peace, tranquillity, and progress. From the list, it is evident that these people have heard about modernity; but, rather than accept their lack of development and the necessity of change, they are converting reason to irrationality, replacing substance with shadow, and positing vices as the acme of virtues. That is the narrator's tongue-in-cheek explanation of the people's definition of progress as retrogression or, at best, a tokenism in which the skeleton becomes the whole body, a single unit is configured as a whole network, and scientific control is embodied in a series of sacrifices to deities supposedly guaranteeing regular supply of basic needs. Their primary school is looked upon with the same awe as a university; their lorry, *Progres,* is like a plane linking them to all the civilized cities of the world; and the waters of Maagum resemble a vast dam that only dries up when the deities become angry.

The narrator herself, sharing a secret with the reader, but which her people must not know, tells us: "As I grew older and traveled, [Dukana's] delights had diminished in my eyes and comparison had dimmed its supposed qualities." (2) There lies one basic problem: These people have not traveled and, indeed, when they do, such as the driver of *Progres,* they still claim superiority over any other place described as "this bush town." The narrator's sarcastic tone is often a source of laughter, but the pathos, the potential tragedy, remains always close to the surface. For, these people, even though ignorant and illiterate, do have a confused idea of what good quality is. Witness, "the confusion of houses," described in progression qualitatively, from the majority of simple mud houses covered by raffia palms; to the handful of those covered with rusty corrugated iron sheets; to the rarest, a brick house, the construction of which is "the task of a life-time."(5) The owner, a rich man, indeed, goes through the slow laborious process of buying cement piece-meal, making bricks and adding them to the structured shell. Finally, he moves in, usually after ten years. Most commonly, those able to build a brick house are "sons of the soil" living away from home. One example is Alec in "The Bonfire." One of the few young men that attended school and ventured out into the outside world, Alec is considered to be doing well, although nobody knows exactly what he is doing. He must be doing well, since he writes his mother and sends her money not only for her upkeep , but to buy cement to begin to build a brick house. "And this was a sign of wealth!" (38) And in Dukana, wealth breeds fear in the wealthy, who believe that others jealous of them, may decide to harm them. Alec's poor, illiterate mother laments that she has to seek another person's help to send her son's letters, thereby having to reveal the secret of his wealth to the envious people. So, when it is reported that Alec has died and that his corpse will be brought back home, both mother and everyone else are convinced that he has been eliminated by an evil hand, right there in Dukana. "The world was full of wickedness. One had to be careful, very careful." (38)

Superstition and witch-hunt, the belief, and the behavior, the attitude and the action, the combinations are normal, daily ingredients of Dukana life. Death is never natural, someone has to be held responsible. The autopsy on Alec confirms his death from diabetes; on the contrary, Dukana is convinced that it is a result of "envy, magical spells, mumbo-jumbo and necromancy." (38) Rumors begin to circulate about who may have done it, and why. When the corpse's arrival is delayed, the anger against the evil-doer increased to a crescendo: he has caused the delay; he must be ferreted out and dealt with. An easy target: Nedam, a very successful farmer who single-handedly established his big cash-crops farm by careful planning and hard work, is, however, despised for being different from the rest. The very qualities that he saw in them and that made him decide to develop his farm and his life, alone, are the factors that precipitate his murder. Nedam has traced out a path to success and happiness, including marriage and a family at the right moment. A progressive mind, in spite of his lack of schooling, he has realized some of his objectives, that is, the material aspects; unfortunately, the other side, the communal, marked by mutual mistrust and misunderstanding, remains in limbo. The likes of Nedam are ahead of their time in a community of "a superstitious, rumor-mongering lot who truly did not understand much. Their limitations were many and to live among them in their way, was to drag oneself down." (36) Instead of living apart, but in the same town, Nedam probably would have done best to leave town; or, in the best scenario, instead of going it alone, he would have worked with one or two elements of like mind. He also should have heeded the narrator's words about the ugly rumors being whispered out of his hearing, that he was born wicked with mysterious supernatural powers, that he has been going into the forest to practice evil, and that he is a potential killer envious of others. In the event, his superstitious people -the youth of Dukana- pounce on him and make a bonfire of him and his house. One wonders why the narrator does not do anything to save Nedam's life; for, after all, he himself has studied the man, and is convinced of his qualities: "I was proud of him, very proud and I did wish there were more like him in our town. I told him so." (37) Instead of telling Nedam, he ought to have told the people. The narrator's disposition in "The Bonfire" is comparable to that of the female narrator in "Home, Sweet Home." Both lack the courage to criticize, to be different and to show the community that progress can only be achieved through a process of self-criticism, open-mindedness, and awareness of one's limitations, and an appreciation of others' qualities, particularly when they have something to offer. Interestingly enough, those two narrators are educated; thus, they represent the voice of progress being constantly propagated by Saro-Wiwa. Perhaps his stories are meant to serve more as mirror than vision.

In other stories, Dukana people are seen reveling in their superstition, squalor, and ignorance, characteristics that again lead to murder. "A Family Affair" depicts a family enmeshed in the town's superstition, as well as hypocrisy and shame for having a member that goes mad, (therefore deserving punishment) as if it was his personal wish to lose his mind. The various avenues used for solving the problem—the native doctor, the churches—show the people's readiness to opt for the irrational and the supernatural, over the rational and logical. And the efforts are made as a matter of desperation by a family concerned with their image, not with the well-being of a member that they claim to love. And the Dukana people encourage the family's decision to deal death to their own, because the people have been carrying rumors of the dubious and devilish origins of the sick Dabo's wealth. The insidious nature of superstitious beliefs is exemplified by the native doctor's treatment of madness: "he beat Dabo night and day with a big leather belt, leaving wicked marks on the man's back and bottom. The devil had to be beaten out of the madman." (30) When Dabo bolts from the famous healing home and heads back to Dukana, his family members decide that death is better than seeing the symbol of their collective shame walking the dusty road of their town. And they catch "the walking scandal," asleep in his house, and bury him alive.

The tragedy is, that the people still believe in the native doctor's excellence, just as they consider as sacrosanct the alleged powers of Oyeoku, the juju with the ability to give wealth, misery, or death, and the rain god, and the ancestors to whom sacrifices are given to prevent the Sanitary Inspector from visiting Dukana. When sacrifices have been done, every eventuality is attributed to their success. Hence, after a fatal bout of influenza had hit the town, "the worldly-wise man" (13) declares that it was not the medical team's intervention with injections that made the difference, it was the action of the gods. These gods, these genii, omnipotent and committed to Dukana, are always on the alert, guaranteeing the town's indestructibility. Dukana people are so enamored of their independence that they consider the Inspector a plague, that they believe that, once they pay their taxes to government, they should be left alone to rot and die in their disease-infested town. Dukana, as the narrator says, simply is wisdom of the ages, the conclusion is the same: the Inspector is an unnecessary intrusion that must be ejected before doing any harm to the "neat and tidy" town. "You would think the town was stinking with the putrefaction of the dead, or the smell of excrement, the way they are always nitpicking about sanitary conditions." That is the voice of Zaza, one of the jobless old bums whose only profession is rumor-mongering and indolence. The chief of the kingdom adds: "I'm sure it's all born of jealousy. All the surrounding villages have always been envious of the success of this town. From time immemorial." (13)

One of the successes is Dukana's form of government. They claim its originality, an invention that other places do not concede to Dukana because of envy. This great success resembles the kind of system visible in real-life, modern Nigeria, enslaving the people, stifling their minds and supposedly stultifying development. In that system particular to Dukana, everything is *decreed* (remember the Uniform?) by "the lords of the town." (15) The Chief and his Council, like a Supreme Military Council, meet behind closed doors, for as long as they wish; for there is no accountability, and they owe no one any explanation. The only elements that would distinguish this Council of Chiefs from that of the Military Chiefs is that, in Dukana, no records are kept. "Reading and writing is the pastime of children at Dukana's school. The elders cannot indulge in such child's play." (15)

When the dictator and his lieutenants decree that a special levy should be paid, sometimes people grumble; but they pay, slowly and surely. When the object of contribution is the prevention of a plague, such as the Sanitary Inspector's visit, everyone pays immediately, with alacrity. "It is either your money or the plague." (15) And the Chief, ever wise, ever practical, accepts foodstuffs in lieu of cash. Naturally, one of the dictator's great virtues is corruption. Chief Birabee collects the levy in cash and kind. Gradually, the money and food mysteriously escape, although the Chief does not forget to make an offer to the ancestors and to feed his fellow elders. They "ate and drank and Dukana continued to luxuriate in its accustomed inertia." (17) The remainder of the levy is, of course, used to bribe the Inspector.

As we have affirmed earlier, the line between Tradition and Modernity is very thin, and it is to Saro-Wiwa's credit that he has avoided mutual exclusivism in his portraits of Dukana beliefs and behavior. Belief in Oyeoku and other gods do not solve problems; however, prayer to the Christian God hardly does any better. Furthermore, the Church proves itself to be more corrupt than the Shrine. To cure Dabo's madness ("A Family Affair"), his family is advised to take him to every available place, including churches, particularly those "real churches where members see vision and heal the sick." (28) At the headquarters of the Brotherhood of the Cross and Star, an internationally flavored church with membership in Europe and America and everywhere, the excellent cure comes in the form of an order from above that the family sell off the sick man's great wealth, his "scourge," and deposit all the proceeds to the

Brotherhood. The order is obeyed to the letter; yet, poor Dabo continues to sing and dance relentlessly.

As catechist Daniel Dekor ("The Overhaul") is battling with bedbugs that have blotted his miserable bed with his blood, he realizes his undeserved poverty in a life devoted to Christ for twenty-five years. He views, with shame and sadness, his evolution from the past, when he was looked upon as bearer of the torch of enlightenment and herald of a new civilization, to the present, when his word is no longer law; from then, when the people of Dukana, his devoted congregation, used to give him donations and make him comfortable, even though his official stipend was paltry and sporadic, to now, when his congregation is reduced to a handful, many having moved to other churches, with nobody willing or able to give him any more handouts; and from that time when being a catechist was considered prestigious, to the present when Daniel's mates have moved on to better jobs and positions. To his dismay, Dukana has become materialistic and, indeed, modern. The nine new churches are all competing in prosperity, while Daniel's church has remained alone in poverty. From time to time, he has thought of owning his own church, but has dismissed the idea, continuing to believe that religious life is different from, and better than, the secular. Nonetheless, he cannot reject the reality of the bedbugs in his wretched grass mattress, and the necessity of an overhaul in his fortunes, something for which he has been praying. With the Bishop's impending visit, Daniel believes that God is, finally, revealing his goodness to him, and that, "in spite of the fact that in that country you do not get a thing because you merit it, but because you have someone to speak for you or you belong to a favored group." (20)

Daniel makes sure everything is done to welcome the Bishop properly. Everywhere is cleaned out. The congregation is organized to sing and receive the Lord's representative with glee and zeal. Daniel himself is decked out in his specially starched suit. Then, Bishop Okoro arrives in a lovely Mercedes Benz. He is in a hurry. He is not in the least interested in the items that Daniel and his congregation have spent long, hard days preparing for him. In his "booming voice loud enough to wake the dead," Mr. Bishop addresses a few words to the Committee of Church Elders: "Let your faith be joined with good works." (24) He urges them to follow Christ's advice to be charitable, to contribute generously to the upkeep of the Church. He holds Daniel responsible for the current low level of contributions and when the latter complains about his meager, irregular salary, God's High Official retorts: "You are only sharing in the general misfortune of our country. The times are difficult. Your parish has not paid its dues, remember." (25) Besides, according to the Bishop, earthly fortunes are meaningless; as the Bible says, "Lay not your stores on earth; for what shall it profit a man if he gain the whole world and lose his own soul?" (24) And the Bishop, pleased with his performance, drives away in his Mercedes carrying the goat and other goodies given to him by his happy church. And Daniel, finally fed up with the Bishop's disinterest in his decaying destiny, and angered by the injustice of a religious system that replicates the secular with highly placed and highly paid officials earning their salaries on time while the lowly paid suffer in silence, decides to resign. And after he has established his own church and metamorphosed into a modern man of God, rich and respected, performing miracles, Dukana comes to sing of him "as a great messenger of the Lord." (26)

The ambiguity of Saro-Wiwa's concept of *thinking*, via Western education, is seen in his total fictional universe, that is, both at Dukana and in the cities. "A Share of Profit" is but one excellent example of how negatively—in terms of attaining only personal selfish goals, and cheating the illiterate—the much propagated education can be used. Kara has gone to school. He therefore feels superior to Bom, illiterate and simplistic, through whom he makes a very profitable business deal. The setting is war-time Dukana occupied by soldiers, the new lords of the land. Bom is one of the town's wags, a lay-about living on charity. He has gladly become the corporal's servant because the association gives him a sense of empowerment. Bom's lack of education and poverty and stupidity would explain his inability to deal with the windfall facilitated by his master. He informs the smart Kara of the military's wish to buy crayfish at two hundred percent profit to the supplier. Kara provides the commodity and the corporal pays Bom an even higher sum than anticipated. He is overwhelmed by the smell and the quantity of the money which he cannot count correctly. The money gives him a feeling of importance. He hides the bundle beneath his mat and tries to sleep; but he cannot. Kara arrives, full of anxiety, torture and suspicions, as he blames himself for entering a deal with the ill-refuted, irresponsible Bom, "a rascal and a ragamuffin" (44) Here, Saro-Wiwa reveals to us the mind of a selfish and greedy man for whom money is a god. Kara goes as far as questioning his own good judgment. He imagines the simple-minded Bom doing all the dirty tricks that only a cheat like himself could do. Then, Bom brings out "the much-desired commodity." (45) Kara is stupefied, and relieved. He counts the cash. He shows no surprise that it is more than he was expecting. He stuffs everything into his shoe, offering nothing to Bom. The latter asks him for something for some gin and snuff; Kara gives him some change. Bom, pleased, thanks him. "You have made me more than rich," exudes Bom. (46) So, what are we supposed to make of this man who, obtaining pennies to barely survive, and living in his mother's house, feels happy? A story-teller nicknamed Stockfish, Bom believes that he is not made to count money: that a good story is as good as a good wife, a good house, a good bicycle; that he is therefore rich. Kara definitely knows the value of money; he exhibits a character common in today's society where the story-teller, the artist is reduced to begging, if he cannot adapt to the neo-materialistic community constituting his audience. Saro-Wiwa's comment is that "a significant good story will truly feed the storyteller when the audience is large." (40) Because the audience will remunerate the storyteller for his skills. The comment is also confusing because the audience in question may not always be appreciative, and the audience may not be the traditional society where money and materialism count for little. Bom has allowed time to pass him by; he is living in a society that no longer appreciates a good story, but deifies good money, the society belonging to the likes of Kara. "You should go to school," advises Kara, when Bom tells him of how he could not count all the money paid by the corporal. (46) If Bom were to go to school, would he learn to count money, to become another Kara, a crook, a cheat, an exploiter of the ignorant? Or would he learn to think and become responsible to himself and to his community? Saro-Wiwa's stories offer many more examples of the former than the latter.

OF MODERNITY, MATERIALISM AND CORRUPTION

Modernity in the neo-colonial setting is supposed to mean improvement, progress, the eradication of ignorance, and a move away from primitivity. Ironically, however, modernity has too often meant a move backwards into bestiality, a process of exacerbating the meanness of individuals in the struggle to be the master. Saro-Wiwa's stories are replete with many instances of the contradiction called modernity. We have already seen the elements of corruption in the church ("The Overhaul"), dictatorial tendencies in government ("The Inspector Calls"), and the false notion of superiority attached to a person living away from home ("Home, Sweet Home" and "The Bonfire"). One common factor is the absence of communication between the leadership and the people or, more precisely, a glaring unwillingness by the leadership to implement positive change. Modernity cannot be without a set standard for development and education. It cannot be when, at every level, corruption is the existential and experiential hallmark. And it really has nothing to do with life in the village or the city.

For instance, citizens are required to pay taxes so that the money may be used to develop the community, to provide amenities, and to improve their lives. On the contrary, in Dukana, taxes are arbitrarily levied by the Chief and his Council, as well as the government officials from Bori, whose visit to the town is similar to an attack by a plague. No one knows how the money is used. People are actually of the opinion that taxes are a kind of punishment which, once served, would give the victim peace of mind. The tax clerks pursue everyone in the town, with gusto. You either pay or escape into the bush. Or, you are welcome to bribe them or, on the rare occasion, you may protest their levy. Adda ("A Death in Town"), a hunter, uses the money he has been keeping for his desired burial in a gold coffin, to bribe a tax clerk, but that does not save him from the paws of other prowling collectors. Adda once trekked the fifteen miles to Bori to seek an audience with the District Officer. After refusing to be turned back by the rude messenger, he forced his way into the big man who was always too busy but never on tax collection day. The visit was a shocker for Adda, unaware of the modernization process at headquarters. Kole, one of Dukana's wags, entertains his audience with the details: "Well, Adda goes in to see the D.O... And he's confused when he sees a black boy fresh from school sitting on the D.O.'s chair. 'What are you doing here?' asks Adda... 'So black boys are now D.Os. Is that why the taxes have risen? Is that why they chase us round at odd hours of day and night?' Adda never got over it." (59) When Adda dies, there is no money to buy a coffin. His corpse is buried in a shallow grave as his townspeople seek consolation in the fact that, in death, he has finally escaped from the tax gatherers, "the big liars." (62) Later on the night of his burial, the tax clerks arrive in town. They leave a summons to the tax office in front of his shut door.

Not only do the townspeople pay tax. They also provide another, more profitable way to the budget of the uncaring government, with "the black gold," (111) oil. The narrator of "Home, Sweet Home" views with sadness the contrast between the wretched people, farms and houses on the landscape of her home and the possibilities of better life symbolized by a few traits of modernity. "Once in a while, a building of modern construction... would peep out of the bush, a reminder of other possibilities. Now and again we would drive past a gas flare reminding us that this was oil-bearing country and that from the bowels of this land came the much-sought-after liquid which fueled the wheels of modern civilisation." (4) The gas flare itself is a sign, not of civilization, but of exploitation. The narrator of "Night Ride," charged with rehabilitating the area after the devastation of the civil war, recognizes this fact which, on the contrary, his former lover, a war widow, considers as the villagers' good fortune. "A village basked beneath the flare. Some of the houses had no roofs. They had been removed by heavy shells during the war. The village, ugly, squat and untidy, had gone to sleep. 'Lucky villagers. They have light all night. No need for electricity,' she said. 'None.' And he laughed a hard, merciless laugh." (114) She does not realize that this artificial, eternal light is useless and unhealthy; that the gas is disease-laden; that the light has transformed the people's lives into a timeless existence in squalor and misery.

The narrator-administrator underscores the government's materialism, exploitation of the people, insensitivity, and general corruption. He also affirms that oil was the main reason for the civil war. "His role [in the war] had been to bring education, food, drugs, and succour to the war-weary, battered communities living on the flat scrubby plains where oil wells gushed night and day; the wells which were the main argument of, and fuel for the war." (110) He meets women whose farms were destroyed by oil prospecting companies, without any compensation or consideration for their survival and their labor. An old woman's lament: "They mowed down the toil of my brows, the pride of the waiting months. They say they will pay me compensation. Can they compensate me for my labours?... Oh my son, what can I do?" The narrator's response is, that he will look into her complaint later. Then, in a fit of rage, he accepts his lie to the poor woman. He expresses his disgust at the oil prospectors and the government. "He cursed the earth for spouting oil, black gold, they called it. And he cursed the gods for not drying the oil wells. What did it matter that millions of barrels of oil were mined and exported daily, so long as this poor woman wept those tears of despair? What could he look into later?... He should have told the woman to despair. To die. Not live in death. That would have been more honest and respectable." (111)

Corruption. You find it in all spheres of life, not only in matters concerning the black gold (or god). Alhaji ("Acapulco Motel") is a true Nigerian, "a man of the world, a man of ideas," (88) a Chief living large in Lagos, the owner of a brand new Mercedes Benz, symbol of success. He is a middleman for landowners whose desire is to sell the same land to several buyers. Alhaji finds the unsuspecting victims, all necessary fake papers to have the land registered under each one's name, and makes sure that, when the matter invariably becomes a law-suit, no winner emerges. In short, Alhaji is a servant and savior and blood-sucker to all parties concerned; he collects his commission from each buyer, from the land owner, and from the judge "to ensure that one of the buyers proved willing to buy the judgement whenever it was to be handed down. Negotiable." (87) Alhaji is a big man, naturally, with his hands in every kind of shady business and the support of all those saddled with the responsibility of protecting the people and maintaining law and order, including the police.

Corruption. The policeman called to the scene after the hilarious encounter between the sex-starved narrator and a woman-man ("High Life"), unashamedly asks for money "so that he will look for the person who have played me that trick." (71) Another story, "Case no.100", uses a day in the life of two policemen to detail the structure of an institution built upon bribery and corruption, class stratification, incompetence and nepotism. A Lagos police station is the scene. Sergeant Ikime and Private Okeke are sleeping soundly on the job. The former uses every occasion to show that he is Okeke's superior. He even berates him for sleeping on the job, as if he, being a sergeant, has the right—or privilege—to do the same. Ikime is proud of his promotion, although we know that he bribed his way to the higher position, having been rewarded for "real qualities" by paying a hundred pounds to those that matter. When His Majesty, Sergeant Ikime, sends him out in response to a burglary report from Abeokuta Street, Okeke, alone on his motorcycle in the frightening darkness populated by monsters threatening him for taking bribes, the superstitious underling confesses his crime and implicates everyone in the miserable country: "No, no I am not the only bribe taker in this country; look at the Ministers of State and of religion, the chiefs and all... Everybody in this country is corrupt." (78) Upon his return to the station after listening to the tall story of a single-handed "savior of the street", a plainly arrogant landlord aptly named the Pot who claimed to have shot some armed robbers, Okeke is asked by Ikime whether he caught the burglar or brought back some booty. The negative response angers Ikime. He is bitter against "these professed 'big men' who did not know how to make people comfortable and willing to do their duties." (83) These policemen would therefore not do their duties if the people they are supposed to protect do not bribe them; besides, their sense of duty would be aroused first and foremost by the rich who are able to provide the commodities essential for their comfort. The poor citizens are left to pray and hope for the best somehow.

Corruption. In the foreign office, incompetence and indiscipline are the order of the day. A senior officer interested in improving the system and in providing useful service to the country, finds himself absolutely powerless ("The Stars Below"). His boss, the Permanent Secretary, expected to offer competent, professional leadership, is not concerned with such secondary issues as administration and the government's foreign policy; rather, he peruses the files for "the award of contracts for the construction of houses for officials, the purchase of furniture for various embassies throughout the world." (98)

Materialism is an aspect of the culture of corruption. Saro-Wiwa is, however, not always precise on the role of materialism in the modern state because, as a businessman, he favors a capitalist system. The narrator-shopkeeper of "A Legend on our Street" would appear to be the writer-businessman's alter ego. He is a competent and honest shopkeeper. He is always seeking to improve his operations; hence, he follows the advice of the old man, Papa, to adopt the idea of keeping a stock abstract which makes his shop prosper. (147) On the other hand, the protagonist of "The Shopkeeper and the Beggar" first achieves immense success by carefully using a book, *How to Run a Shop*, but later decides to close down his shop after losing his customers to his new, next-door competition. According to the narrator, he has "stopped thinking," consulting his book "in the way oracles are consulted," instead of reading and implementing its ideas intelligently." (139) There is the other intriguing subject of the three beggars that left the front of his shop after he had refused to give them alms. He believes that the absence of their usual morning prayer, "Allah bless master," has had a fatal effect on his business.[1] Superstition and lack of intelligent, professional planning have therefore led to the man's failure. Nonetheless, the coming of the beggars appears to be peripheral to the business's success. Before their arrival, the shopkeeper has already established a reputation. What is striking in the narrative is, the shopkeeper's one-man-shop, similar to others depicted in the aforementioned "A Legend on our Street," in "A Share of Profit," and in "The Bonfire." With the exception of the first story, all the others reveal a success smeared by greed (Kara in "Profit"), or cut down by people's envy (Nedam in "The Bonfire"). In another story, "Acapulco Motel," we also witness the one-man empire of Alhaji in which, for fear of robbery by unreliable employees and lack of trust for his compatriots, the man decides to hire only Ghanaians. All these examples prove that, in spite of the possibility and, indeed, reality of success through hard work, capitalist enterprise in the neo-colonial setting of Nigeria is full of corruption and materialism. Saro-Wiwa has done well to provide us with the positive exceptions, but the negative remains overwhelming. The picture of the victims of corruption remains fixed to the mind's eye. Saro-Wiwa does not suggest a clear way out of their resignation. Duzia, the Dukana wag, stares at the corpse of his townsman, Adda, and laments: "Lie there and watch us slowly live this death in life, our life a burden and a terror. But see us smile like sunshine, singing like the cricket through it all... Then watch us succumb at the touch of nature, watch us die a happy death, the final death." (62) The artist's plaintive tone is heart-rending. In the city, another member of the class known as the wretched of the earth,[2] Robert ("Robert and the Day") takes matters into his own hands as he watches with anger the comfortable life of his master's dog, Bingo, "more important than himself," (107) far better fed and cared for than his children, living in filth with their distended bellies. His pathological hate for Bingo ends in the decision to "show" the dog some day. His chance arrives when his master and his wife leave on a six-week vacation and leave the dog in his care. Robert locks up Bingo and leaves the house, forever, taking with him the dog's delicious food to be eaten by his children. Bingo dies.

Robert's action may be construed as a symbol protest against the bourgeoisie represented by his liberal, kind-hearted master and his wife. The pity is, that such a protest could be no more than a victim's violent act of rage, which would in no way ameliorate his status. Robert's children would eat the food meant for a dog. Exhausted, the food would no longer be available, but it would have established their status as being inferior to the dog. In the meantime, Robert, and Duzia, and others, would continue to live and die in filth.

WOMEN IN SOCIETY

As has been confirmed in his other writings, Saro-Wiwa is concerned with women's problematic condition in his society. The stories in the collection being studied express that concern.[3] They affirm categorically that women must be educated in order to function properly and contribute fully as members of the society.

Women in Dukana suffer mostly from a chauvinistic tradition that discourages the education of girls. Note, however, that, contrary to common belief in certain feminist circles, this chauvinism is the culpability of both men and women. The invaluable consequences of education is seen in the female narrator of the very first story, "Home, Sweet Home." A rarity among Dukana girls, she has gone away to continue her schooling upon finishing at Dukana's only school that offers no more than primary education. Even though there is ambiguity about how far she has gone (high school, teacher's college, or university?) the consensus is that she has come back home to contribute positively to her people's progress. The whole community is gathered in her mother's house to welcome her. They are filled with "pride that I had gone out to the world to acquire the new knowledge, new treasures, and that I had returned to plant some new seeds on the Dukana earth." (7) Her perspicacious remarks on the wretchedness and underdevelopment of Dukana and its people are due to her training and traveling. In a much more significant way than *Progres*, the only lorry facilitating communication with the outside world, she is now Dukana's pride, the medium of communication with the modern world, opening up new vistas and leading her people out of their state of anomy. She herself confesses the improvement that going away has made in her life: "As I grew older and traveled, [Dukana's] delights had diminished in my eyes and *comparison had dimmed its supposed qualities*." (2, emphasis mine) Without the opportunity to compare one's life with another, without seeing other people and places, one would remain imprisoned in one's small world. Thus, Saro-Wiwa has broadened, ever so subtly, his definition of education. Traveling not only affords one the occasion to compare; it also helps out to appreciate one's culture and tradition. When the heroine of "Home" affirms that Dukana's qualities are more imagined than real, she is exhibiting the sort of honesty and integrity that many others, parochial and close-minded, would reject. In the final analysis, she is a trail-blazer who, unfortunately in Saro-Wiwa's story, does not go the whole distance to make a statement directly to her people about her observations. This reticence is due to her age; for, tradition demands that the young respect the old, and that they show circumspection in their attitudes and actions in regards of societal belief and habits. The young narrator's style in "Home" is less critical and more laid-back than that of the older narrator in "Night Ride."

Parallel to the uncommon life of the narrator of "Home" is that, very common and unfortunate, of her best friend, Sira, "Like most Dukana girls, her education had been terminated abruptly; she now had four children and was again pregnant when last I had seen her." (2) On this particular trip back home, her final return from school, the narrator is very anxious to see her friend again. She asks her mother about Sira, but the mother is not forthcoming with an answer. Then Sira's mother, Waale, comes to welcome her back home. The narrator notices how emaciated and aged Waale has become. Waale informs the narrator that Sira has traveled but that she knows neither her destination nor her expected date of return. After Waale has left, the narrator insists that the mother tell her exactly what happened to Sira: Sira had twins and was therefore compelled to leave town. Sira was also a brilliant student. When she was forced to abandon her education, the reason given was, that the parents could no longer afford the school-fees. "But that was an excuse. Her parents had wanted her to have children, to procreate so that the family would not die off. *And she had had to obey them.* She had not married and her four children were by four different men. I suspected that the fifth pregnancy was by a fifth man." (8, emphasis mine) Being an only child, Sira is pushed to ensure continuity of the family-line. One may safely say that hers is a special case of a family's fear of obliteration (cf. Dukana people's pride in their indestructibility).

Tradition demands that one obeys one's parents, and most Dukana parents, men and women alike, subscribe to the belief that procreation for women is a priority. Witness the exchange between Waale and the narrator's mother:

> "'The baby of yesterday is today's elegant woman,' said she half to me and half to Mama.
> 'It's incredible,' Mama said with a hint of pride. 'She's going to make a grandmother of you sooner than you realize.'
> 'The sooner the better. I've waited long enough as it is. I should love to hold a grandson in my arms before I die.'" (8)

In Dukana, mothers have the greatest influence on their daughters. The narrator of "Home" tells us that "mother's counsel was law" (2) against which she could not argue. "The Divorce" recounts another story of a mother instructing her daughter about life. "Like most children in Dukana, [Lebia] had grown up doing what her mother asked her to do." (48) She helped on the farm, planting and harvesting, learning at her mother's feet, growing up to be a woman. Her mother's hope was that, one day, Lebia would marry, or at least find a man to take care of her. "For that was the ultimate aim of a Dukana woman. To be the only wife of a poor man. Or one of the many wives of a rich man.(...) The favour of such a one, would go a long way to satisfy the upbringing of a girl, any girl... A husband did a girl a favour by marrying her." (49-50) In short, poverty coupled with tradition leads to Lebia's being used by her mother to make money. The husband is a driver who, struck by the girl's beauty, expresses his interest. The two mothers discuss it and the girl is coerced into the affair, "a good bargain for her mother who is paid a nice sum." The man is, however, disappointed when Lebia does not become pregnant, because he has married her primarily for having children. After three years of futility, he simply packs her belongings, returns her to her mother, and demands his money back. The mother, we are told, is "proud of her daughter." A matter also of honor, she works hard, sells off some of the land she owns, and pays off the man. The story shows both the blight of male chauvinism and the mother's materialism. When man and woman cannot make babies together, the latter invariably stands to be blamed, a tradition showing up male pomposity and presumptuousness. As for the mother, her survival is more important to her than her daughter's fate in society. In Saro-Wiwa's Dukana, it is significant that women are engaged in farming; they therefore need the help of their children, and there appear to be more girls than boys. Yet, it is interesting that, where there is a choice to be made, marriage seems to be preferable to education. As we have already stated, a mother's pride at her daughter's education ("Home") goes hand in hand with her anxiety for her to get married so that she may become a mother.

With regard to education, the need for the daughter's help on the farm poses a problem to many a mother. Such is the dilemma discussed in "Night Ride." The narrator-administrator, charged with rehabilitating the people after the civil war, is very much interested in promoting education, including that of girls. He drives past the newly-planted farms and ruminates about the people's future: "These farms will be the death of you, my brothers and sisters, he thought." (110) The narrator cannot offer an acceptable response to the peasants' questions. One is left to guess the consequences of that conversation. On a general level, the narrator himself shows his commitment to his people's cause; but, whether his own position would be enough to convince others to change age-old traditions, that is another matter altogether. In all likelihood, mothers would still use their daughters as pawns in a struggle for survival which, by its very conditions of misery and wretchedness, is doomed to be long and impossible to win. Daughters would still follow mothers' law and marry young. Some mothers and fathers, progressive and therefore exceptions to the rule, would send their daughters to school and thus sow the seeds for a future society brighter and better, and more human, than the present. Papa in "A Legend..." is one of such fathers. The narrator mentions Papa's past action regarding his daughters. "He confessed to me how he had once been foolish. He had done what all his friends did: he had refused to train his daughters. Daughters were only good for marriage, he had thought... Though much *against his better judgment*, he had educated a number of his daughters." (147, emphasis mine) The contradiction in this statement is probably to be adduced to Saro-Wiwa because if Papa had once been foolish by not wanting to educate his daughters, how could he claim to have educated them "against his better judgment"? Be that as it may, the point is that Papa has taken the wisest action. He is now enjoying the fruits of his labor, and the migratory birds are now useful in their faraway nests, as they welcome the visitor and give him a comfortable and happy life. One of Papa's daughters is the cleverest lawyer in the country, according to the proud old man.

 Papa's progressiveness in matters of education cannot be viewed as being totally out of context, culturally and traditionally. As we have seen above, by educating his daughter, his own benefit is also highlighted. After all, Papa is a shrewd business man always thinking in terms of his investment. The narrator has been astonished to learn that the eighty-year old Papa's youngest daughter is only three months old. He later discovers that the man is a polygamist, his policy being to employ women as shop assistants and to convert them to wives. From experience, he is convinced that young men are untrustworthy, that young women are only a shade better but, as wives, they keep it all in the family. "A very wise investment policy, Papa said. If your wife stole from you, it remained in the family. But you had to ensure she had children, otherwise your wealth would be siphoned off to her lovers." (147) Business acumen, or male chauvinism?[4] Papa's materialism is not uncommon in a society desperately and confusedly engaged in a process called modernization, and where corruption has become a culture. At least, his brand of materialism is based upon honest, hard work from which all those concerned would derive ample benefits.

It is noteworthy that Papa's character is not depicted as part of a so-called traditional or modern society. His persona would fit into what may be simply called Nigerian society. Saro-Wiwa maintains a high level of realism in his narrative. For instance, while propagating the education of women, he reminds us that the educated woman, in most cases, does not choose career over motherhood or marriage, and that, as a wife, she is still supposed to obey her husband. Duzia, Dukana's glib storyteller, advises the narrator of "Home": "'Daughter of mine,' says he, 'you don't know what your arrival means to us. We are poor and we are ignorant, but we know a good thing when we see it, even though it is beyond our reach... The advice I give is good and it's free. *I say I hate all wife-beaters and I hate beaten wives.*'" (6-7, emphasis mine) Conservative and chauvinistic, some would no doubt call this word of wisdom. The author's position would appear to be, that husband should not beat wife, but wife should not do something that would provoke him to beat her. Yet, it is an aspect of life in both city and countryside. And educated women are mindful of its importance.

Saro-Wiwa's text includes two stories about bourgeois women living in the city. Both stories underscore these women's belief in the importance of marriage; one woman ("Love Song") has been married for ten years, and the other ("A Caring Man") for twenty-six. Both women also play the role of housewife to the hilt, their careers notwithstanding. Noteworthy is the fact that, the wife in the second story, being saddled with the impossible double duty of mothering and housekeeping, decides to take a house-girl. The husband is soon discovered to be sleeping with the girl, Ayo. This worsens a relationship that is already problematic; for, the husband has had a child out of wedlock and, although the wife was willing to adopt the child, the mother-in-law made it impossible. The quarrel over Ayo is followed by the husband's departure to London on a business trip. He returns a changed man, with his hair in "jerry coils, like a miserable, cocaine-sniffing West Indian on the crumby streets of Brixton (...) a vulture wearing glass beads."[5] She becomes profoundly placated and consumed with newly-oiled love when he presents her with the keys to a brand-new Mercedes Coupe. Love here is very modern, very shallow, very materialistic. Marriage becomes a matter of profit and loss, and the woman is shown to be a villain, not a level as qualitatively low as the man, but in a manner that makes one understand that the blame for failure is more shared than singular. If the husband is a "miserable wretch" for "dancing" on the side, the woman is a miserable leech for grabbing the keys to the Mercedes, and a pitiful fool for not suspecting that her already infamous husband would be "dancing" with the house-girl. As for the mother-in-law, Saro-Wiwa has not dwelt upon the matter enough to allow us to comment upon his views. We would derive from the little revealed in the story, that the mother-in-law is a thorn on the side of a bourgeois wife who is concerned with her exclusive rights to her husband; for her part, the mother seeks to maintain her hold on her son.

"Love Song..." also comments on the superficiality, or ambiguity, of love, as well as the confusion, in many a bourgeois relationship. The woman soliloquizes upon her supposedly absent husband's whereabouts when he ought to have returned home for dinner. She expresses her rejection of polygamy, preferring the European way. "When you are fed up with each other, you cut the links, share the responsibilities and go and start all over again with someone else. But the male beasts here just want it all their way. The pigs!" (128) But, it is the same she who admits that, if she hears that her husband has had a child outside, she would "get into [her] very best clothes, call up his dearest friend or his assistant in the office and offer to make love to them." (127) And she admits that other women are ready to accept polygamy. The irony is, that as she sits there worrying and wondering, after ten years of marriage, the husband is already home, asleep. It means that she came home rather late; that she did not prepare the food she is so anxious to give him, on time; that, rather than she asking about his whereabouts, he ought to be asking the questions.

The speculations, suppositions, and premonitions filling up the woman's mind, as well as the drama of "A Caring Man," demonstrate the difficulties of couples trying to combine, or straddle, cultures, with a particular desire to live the modern life. Saro-Wiwa does not delve into the background of those two couples. One can only speculate that, being educated, they would have had a chance to authenticate love; which, in truth is the contrary. Another story, "Night Ride," proves the reality of true love. Unfortunately, circumstances prevented the two young lovers from getting married: the girl fell prey to a young man who took advantage of her innocence and put her in the family way. She got married, but the husband died in the war. Now, together again, the lovers have a second chance. Or, do they? She admires and loves that "elemental goodness in him" (115) which he is now putting to excellent use in his actions to rehabilitate the war victims. She would love to have him back, but, afraid, she kills the thought. He does likewise. He looks at her and sees the imperfections, the loss of beauty, the fact of a first marriage, and a child. Finally, he takes her in his arms. Here we have love being rooted in reality, combining sentiments of the heart with an appreciation of the human beings' communal activities; thus, the couple's relationship stands the chance of growth as they engage in their efforts to help others while helping themselves.

SARO-WIWA'S DRAMATIC EYE

Artistically, perhaps the most prominent aspect of this short-story collection is Saro-Wiwa's eye for the dramatic. Bringing into play his immense and engaging skills in presenting a realistic picture to his public, he captures the essence of a scene and brings it to life, as if we are witnesses to the event. He facilitates this by concentrating on people as living human beings engaged in action, and motion. Part of the actions and motions is speech; and the Wiwan monologue and dialogue must be among the most captivating and hilarious in Nigerian literature. Furthermore, the living people are seen in their habitat, either in city or countryside; thus, colors, sounds, and smells, as well as essential elements of nature, are described at length as they determine and affect human lives. "Garga," the story of the outbreak of a Kano riot, makes a graphic portrayal of violence and death by means of the changing colors of the scorching blood-red sun which, after disappearing at night, is replaced by "a halo of deep red" (122) in the darkness. Garga hears his heart beating, first slowly, then more rapidly, in unison with the low moans at dawn rising to the tumultuous sound as of violent waves breaking on the shore, as of a lion moaning in agonizing pain." (123) Fear and violence come together. Frightening shrieks burst upon Garga's ears and his blood, cold, runs down his spine. "The evil smell of excrement" (122) adds to the horror of coming death. By the time he reaches the scene of the mini-war, all the components of death have come together; the mob's blood-curdling chants and their bedeviled faces: the wild, murderous swing of the machetes and the flight of missiles, and the smell of blood oozing from dismembered bodies.

In several stories, Saro-Wiwa describes the filth of both city and countryside, thus linking the physical to the psychological. "The quagmire of Ikeja" (186) is appropriate breeding ground for a phenomenon like the crooked Alhaji. The rickety, ugly mud houses of Dukana, and the general putrefaction are adequate conditions for a people wise enough to despise the coming of the sanitary inspector. And Lagos, the confused metropolis where the most progressive clash with the most retrogressive, and electricity is forever irregular, is an excellent metaphor for the people of Nigeria: "Lagos, disorganized as ever in the sweltering heat, was already breaking into its accustomed fever. Harsh sunlight fell dully on rusty rooftops. Houses, thrown together in clashing confusion, reminded him of a garbage heap (...). Big, luxurious cars belching forth thick suffocating smoke sat satirically beside dirty, ill-looking houses where people swarmed like maggots." (98)

A few examples of human beings in action, and in conversation, would suffice as proof of Saro-Wiwa's powerful description hinged on both the ever-observing eyes and the ever-awakened sense of humor and satire. Bom, the simplistic buffoon, is trying to count the huge fortune of five hundred pounds paid by his master for Kara's crayfish. He decides to share the cash into twenty places, to facilitate the arithmetic. He begins to build each bundle. Then, a noise outside distracts him. He begins again. He is almost done; "and then horror of horrors. A light wind came all of a sudden, sweeping the notes here and there. Bom gave chase. He picked up a note on his right and dashed to the left for another note... Bom went round and round in a circle until he turned giddy and fell on top of the currency notes." (43) It is easy to imagine the fool chasing flying notes, in exasperation, desperately, in fear of losing one, and escaping the jealous eyes of the townsfolk.

The suddenly mad Dabo ("A Family Affair") is taken to a native doctor in Ko. The man is very famous and his reputation is guaranteed because the government has given a certificate with a long number of it. "The notice on the board said so. Those who could read, and there were not very many of them, had said that his number was very long, beginning with several noughts... This native doctor's potions were the mortal enemy of witchcraft and necromancy... In short, he was the one to whom all could turn when everything else in heaven and earth had failed." (30)

Members of Dabo's family are no doubt greatly impressed, convinced that, at last, their son and father, the source of their shame, will be healed and thus save their pride. The man with the government certificate shows how powerful his hands are by beating Dabo to a pulp.

When Dabo escapes from the hell at Ko and returns to Dukana, his family, mad, decides to send him to real hell, or heaven. The exchange between the determined murderers and their quarry exemplifies the unequal conflict between victimizers and their defenseless, hopeless victim.

> "'I am not yet dead, oh God.' [comes the voice from the hastily dug grave]
> 'Then you must die today, you eyesore, you disgrace of the family. You must die today.'...
> The relatives were surprised at the amazing clarity of the man. Was he not mad? How was he able to distinguish between life and death?... Each asked himself the question. Each resolved within himself to bury the answer with the mad beggar." (32)

They hope that the silence of their victim would bury forever their murderous action.

A most comic scene is that in "High Life" when, as a result of his half-education, an ugly drunk visits violence upon the hedonistic narrator. The victim should have known better than to exchange New Year greetings with an unknown man with eyes "red like palm oil" and reeking beer.

> "'Happy New Year.'
> And I replied: 'Same to you.'
> 'What!', he shouted, 'why you curse me?'...
> 'How did I curse you?,' was my next question.
> 'You said, "Shame to you"'...'
> 'I did not say "Shame". I said "Same to you".'
> 'Idika,' he called, 'do you hear? He has repeated it again. Shame to me. Is it so? Do you think I am a thiefman or what?'" (69)

An exhibition of mis-education coupled with superstition and the deadly skills of an experienced crook, is found in "Acapulco Motel," where Alhaji is trying to cower the woman he has defrauded into giving up her right to the land sold to her under false pretenses. Alhaji feels "achamed" (ashamed) over the land; as a "sheef" (chief), he cannot be a cheat; he wishes to resolve the problem, but the common use of "sharms" (charms) by everyone is making him hesitate about further action. Observing his dexterous moves, the narrator chimes in:

"'You are very wise, Alhaji,' I said.'

'Thank you very much, my brother... These people will do anything for money... Yes, I have to wear my "sharms" to court everyday.'...

I could see that Alhaji was very impressed with me. He stared, mouth-agape at the huge ring on my third finger...

'Madam, that land is in trouble,' he said. 'But it is not my fault. Believe me yours sincerely, it is not my fault. I did not make them take this case to court; I do not know the judge... Beg Madam for me, my dear friend. I am doing my best. I will do my best. I am on her side. You know as an Alhaji, I have to be on her side. Allah.'" (93-4)

Of course, he knows the judge; and the woman is aware of his chicanery; but her nephew's (the narrator) smart jab at the irresponsible man has lessened her suffering. When, at the Alhaji's use of the name of Allah in vein she bursts out laughing, with the two men joining in, the reader arrives at a point of fully understanding the character of that godless, colorless crook.

A galling level of lewdness and sheer bestiality is reached in "Case no.100," when the two policemen give an inmate permission to urinate and excrete inside the cell.

"'I wan shit,' the voice repeated, briefly and menacingly,"(75) as the two policemen go into a combat of competitive sleeping on the job. After the repeated plca-threat, one of the law officers gives the order: 'Awright, you can fit to shit dere.'

It is significant that the policemen are not bothered by the stench, that they actually have no sense of smell; instead, it is the prisoners who feel offended by the foul odor filling the air. An effective metaphor for Nigeria, one would say, because the authorities, the leaders supposedly aware of the people's needs, supposedly enlightened enough to show the way out of the tunnel of decadence, have proven themselves totally incapable of thinking. The policemen in the station are satisfied with the surrounding stench. They love it. As long as they can enjoy their sleep, and take their bribe which they will use in the morrow for merriment in the neighborhood bar, the prisoners can fill the precinct with excrement! Yet, the corporal, the superior officer, has the audacity to proclaim: "We are different from you civilians...We believe implicitly in method." (77) There may, indeed, be a method to the madness of this senseless system, but it is still madness.

CONCLUSION: OF COMMITMENT AND SOLIDARITY IN A HOPELESS STATE

It has been stated earlier in this chapter that Saro-Wiwa's interest in business would explain his capitalistic tendencies, and support for materialism which we consider, in the larger perspective of Nigeria, the bane of the society. It need be asserted that the materialists and capitalists are not nearly the most engaging figures of these stories. With the exception of the legendary Papa of the final story, the other characters in that mold are negatively depicted; they exhibit either the extremism of selfishness and corruption, or, the short-coming of superstition, both of which traits constitute a barrier to success.

More than those tendencies encouraging the characters' individualism, the call to commitment and solidarity with the people is the most reverberating message of *A Forest of Flowers*. Returning to one of the possible configurations of the title, one would say that, in the forest, few flowers stand out for their beauty and sweet scent, for their ability to arouse in us the desire to appreciate their beauty as potential components of a bouquet. Such flowers are, the female narrator of "Home"; the male narrator of "Night Ride," the male heroes of "Garga" and "The Stars Below."

What all the four characters have in common is the consciousness to commit themselves to the amelioration of their community, as well as the belief that they must be at one with the people. The solidarity is best enunciated by the young heroine of "Home" being warmly welcomed back into her community by the very people that her knowledgeable mind has seen reason to condemn.

> "And as they sang, they danced their prayers, their wishes and their hopes. In the twirling and twisting of waists and shoulders,... I heard the call of nativity and I saw what united me with them inextricably, a bond which neither education nor distance nor time could destroy. And I leapt to my feet and joined them in their expression of joy." (7)

That "call of nativity" can only be interpreted as a form of atavism, deeply embedded in the soul, latent, and awakened by the thumping drums and the tantalizing turnings of the body, and the sublimity of prayers to gods that she herself, the educated one espousing reason over superstition, must mistrust. No wonder that solidarity remains problematic; it is a passing fancy, a fictitious, "spontaneous outburst of joy" almost immediately dislodged by the facts of underdevelopment of both mind and material, and the nagging questions regarding her mysteriously absent friend. In the circumstances; the young woman, still inexperienced, just arriving back home with the tools, may be said to stand some chance of actualizing her commitment and solidarity. She would thus represent a bright future. The big problem is, that those very tools are ambiguous, just as is the education, precisely Western education, propagated in many a Wiwa text.

On the other hand, one cannot forget that there are other youths in Dukana, uneducated, caught in the web of superstition and conservatism even worse than that of their elders. Those are the youths of "A Bonfire," suddenly unleashing Dukana's pent-up anger in a united murderous action against an innocent man believed by everyone to have used his evil power to kill a townsman. They murder the suspect in cold blood and disappear in different directions. This misguided, murderous energy is, of course, a sad vision on the possible future of that community; these youths symbolize the continuity of a tradition frozen in a time that has refused to evolve. It rejects the normal dynamics of human existence. It stands firm against change. And the young ones, proud children of their fathers and mothers, heartily become the hand that deals death to a man's dream simply because he has dared to be different. If there is any consolation in this horror, it would be that, given positive leadership, the youths can move together, in a different direction.[6] The narrative of Nedam's murder is also significant for the acquiescence of the adults, or their failure to react to the youths' violent act.

The narrator-administrator of "Night Ride" is definitely more experienced than the young heroine of "Home;" nonetheless, his take on the tragic existence of his people is not much more gratifying than the girl's. In fact, his companion in the night ride [night, symbolic of a reality of disease and death, and an overwhelming dilemma], his former lover, calls him a cynic for his almost totally pessimistic and discouraging comment on everything. This negativity is a result of his deep love and sympathy for his people. But, when the administrator, the one appointed by the authorities to rehabilitate the downtrodden, the wretched of the earth, when he, supposedly the symbol of hope, confesses that there is no hope, and that he is a blatant liar, the gravity of the situation is truly at its nadir. "He should have told the woman [wondering about her mowed-down farm by oil prospectors] to despair. To die. Not live in death. That would have been more honest and respectable. He tapped his foot on the floor, agitated." (111)

His agitation, it could be said, is a sign of a desperate desire to seek a real solution to his people's problems. Thus, his plea to his former (and new?) lover at the end of the story may be read positively: "You will have to teach me to live with death." (116) To live with death may be a subtle acceptance of the responsibility to face death and to snatch from it some sense of survival. This character resembles very much Saro-Wiwa himself who was administrator at Bonny and who underwent similar experiences as the narrator's. Saro-Wiwa's depression and agitation were necessary preparation for his Ogoni struggle. With the woman, another war victim, another example of the wretched mired in living death, by his side, the man may be ready to actualize solidarity, and commitment, through revolutionary action.

Garga, the eponymous tragic hero of the story about a Kano ethnic riot, is one more example of the hopelessness of commitment, when the individual is acting alone, without reciprocity from others. The theme is the problem of ethnicity and ethnocentricity in Nigeria, one of the catalysts of the civil war. Garga is an exception to the rule, a Northerner living in Kano who has for best friend a Southerner, precisely an Ibo business man named Garuba. Important note: Garuba is the man's new name: "He had changed his name from Sylvanus Okeke to Garuba, when he had adopted the Muslim faith. It mattered to him that he was a Muslim and his first name was Hausa. He had thought it would make him feel different but the change of name had done nothing to him basically. He still remained Sylvanus Okeke essentially... But his business moved more briskly. It was compensation enough, he often thought." (118-9) In other words, Garuba is no longer considered as a *stranger*, (therefore, potential enemy, and a *Kaferi*, pagan) because he has changed his name and religion. Another important note: although Garuba distinguishes between the Sabongari (the quarters in Kano occupied by Southerners) inhabitants, stating that they come from different *countries*, Garga sees no distinction;

for him, they are all *strangers*. Garga's open- mindedness is not complete, but his love for Garuba is genuine, and therein lies the ray of hope.

As he himself realizes, the city wall is a barrier, both physical and psychological; if you live inside, you belong; if outside, you do not belong. "It [the wall] took on a more sinister aspect as a wall erected in the hearts of men by language, religion and custom. Behind both sides of the wall was something more permanent, an almost ineradicable suspicion, a refusal to come to terms with each other, a refusal to understand, to communicate... The wall remained real, forbidding and powerful." (119-120) Besides Garuba, the only other Southerners with whom Garga interacts, once in a while, are prostitutes, who make him reach "the acme of joy; [for] there was such a difference between these outlandish, modern, sometimes young women who ogled you as you passed by them, smoked, drank and danced happily, and the women one kept at home in purdah." (120) These women are like their Sabongari, with its "speed, the modernity, the brash crudity." (119) Such private joys, stolen on the run, in the secrecy of the Sabongari, outside the wall, are not to be taken seriously. Garga remains a man of his people, accepting the established norms of behavior, the way of life opposed to that of the strangers.

When, at the outbreak of the riot which does not have any immediate explanation—besides the seeming hatred, the tension boiling just below the surface of uneasy tranquillity—Garga rushes out of the walled city towards his friend's house, he is driven by love, by a certain ambiguous commitment, but there is no solidarity here beyond that potential existing within his deep love. His duty to his friend, and to his friend's daughter, making him rush headlong to his death, must be encouraging in a milieu reeking of hate. He is decapitated by Okoye, Garuba's townsman (his "brother"), who has never hidden his envy of Garuba's success. That action reduces the element of hope to a minimum. Garga's death, therefore, may be meaningless in the circumstances.

The above story, more than any other in Saro-Wiwa's collection, poses an essential question: is there hope for Nigeria in the face of ethnic hate and violence, and myriad fundamental differences? Garga's character, laid-back, resigned to his fate, lacking the drive to achieve anything beyond his basic needs, is almost diametrically opposed to Garuba's, driven by material success, dynamic, enterprising, and cautiously selfish. Symbols of two opposite cultures, one might say, like the walled city and the Sabongari. To those who might think that Garga's action is, at least, a sign of what can be, let us note that, outside of the walled city, in faraway Lagos, there are men of business, men of the world, men of ideas, brilliant men, like the great, corrupt Alhaji, who, to maximize his profits in his slew of shady businesses, lays down this battle plan for engaging honest and capable workers: "All Yorubas were out. No Yoruba man respected another Yoruba man... All Nigerians were out. Ever since oil money poured into the national coffers, every Nigerian was determined to procure as much of this unearned income as possible... He said he was going to hire Ghanaians... well trained and hungry... They would accept any salary he offered. They would work hard because they knew that if he sacked them, they would have nowhere else to go." (90-91) Now, in real, rotten Nigeria, the Ghanaians have found somewhere to go: back home, to Ghana.

The last hero that attracts our attention on the matter of commitment and solidarity is Ezi, the foreign affairs officer in "The Stars Below." Taking a night walk after another meaningless day at the office, he has a vision. From the confusion of Lagos with its beauty and squalor, and its component parts of progress and retrogression,

"there pressed forward a great crowd surging and dancing towards him... And soon he felt himself in their very midst, engulfed by their radiating energy, swept off his feet and floating with them to that point where earth, water and sky met... And he knew then that he was only one of the crowd pressing forward with one aim, and that it was necessary to ensure that they all -the beggars, the lame, the deaf, the dumb, the weak and the strong alike arrived there safely. And his effort alone would not do it, but it would help and it was not to be denied that crowd, otherwise he might not get there when all others did."[7]

This powerful vision, however, must be taken for what it is: a sudden, sublime experience by a lonely, frustrated man. Ezi's vision, we are informed, "faded as abruptly as it had begun." (104) He is brought back to the reality of his life. Dawn is already breaking, and he will soon return to that dreadful office, and its squalor, and monotony, and irresponsible workers, both high and low.

So, where is the hope? Perhaps it lies in the psyche and potential of individuals such as Ezi, incessantly knocking on wood; and the narrator of "Night Ride," telling his people the truth and thus beginning his revolutionary journey as their true leader; and the young woman in

"Home," feeling "the excruciating pain which knowledge confers on those who discern the gulf which divides what is and what could be." (4)

NOTES TO CHAPTER V

1. "The Shopkeeper and the Beggar" reminds me of the Senegalese novel, *La Grève des Battù* (The Beggars' Strike,) by Aminata Sow Fall. But in that story, the beggars' presence to receive alms is the necessary means to the end, a politician's ambition to become Vice-President.

2. cf. Frantz Fanon's masterpiece, *The Wretched of the Earth*, on colonized people's past, present, and future.

3. Another Wiwan text, *Adaku and Other Stories*, largely concentrates on the theme of women's fate in their relationships with men. Women are once again seen as victims that contribute to their own victimization, as a result of societal constraints, particular circumstances and personal weaknesses, and human qualities.

4. Papa's policy is very much a part of reality in Nigeria. For example, the late Hubert Ogunde, the foremost name in the traditional theater, used to marry the actresses in his company. Reputedly, he finally had some twenty wives at the time of his death. The great Afro-beat musician, Fela Anikulapo-Kuti, married his many wives for a similar reason.

5. *A Forest...*: 133. Jerry *coils*, or curls? Is it Saro-Wiwa's error, or is he deliberately laughing at the woman's mis-education?

6. We shall discuss the role of Ogoni youths and their relationship with Saro-Wiwa in the chapter on Ogoni. Part of the accusation used to convict him had to do with the action of the Youth wing of the Movement for the Survival of Ogoni People (MOSOP). It was stated that those youths had followed Saro-Wiwa's order to eliminate "the vultures," that is, all those opposed to the Movement's alleged militancy and violence. The four murdered Ogoni leaders were proclaimed victims of that order.

7. pp. 103-4. Ezi shares much in common with the heroes of two Ghanaian novels: Ayi Kwei Armah's *The Beautiful Ones Are Not Yet Born* (1968) and Kofi Awoonor's *This Earth, My Brother* (1971).

VI. *SONGS IN A TIME OF WAR*[1], POETRY

> -*Songs in a Time of War* may seem to refer to a
> particular time but it speaks for all time,
> especially in Nigeria's circumstances.
> (Theo Vincent, Intro to *Songs*: 11)
> -Ye bakers and hawkers of lies
> Who bare your jaws and call for wars,
> Inviting the lame, the blind and the deaf
> To the merry ways of guns
> Where shall ye find the lotion,
> The balm to heal the wounds? (*Songs*: 24)
> -Ogale is a ravished woman. (*Songs*: 29)
> -To laugh, you see, is to show my teeth
> And to cry is just the same
> And well, I choose to laugh. (*Songs*: 35)

INTRODUCTION: POETRY AND THE PAIN OF EXISTENCE

Out of his vast production of more than twenty books, Saro-Wiwa published only one poetry-collection. This does not come as a surprise, because he himself affirmed: "My forte, if there was such a thing, was, I always thought, either short-story writing or the drama." (*Plain*: 111) As the title confirms, *Songs in a Time of War* is a period piece, brought to life by circumstances and conditioned by the writer's lived experience. The trauma of the Nigerian tragedy, war and its shocking sights, the stench, and the deafening sounds of death symbolized by the bombs and bullets dismembering human bodies and buildings alike, these are the components of a poetry that captures one's attention and refuses to let go until the very final word.

The introduction, written by Saro-Wiwa's Ogoni compatriot, Theo Vincent, points out most of the collection's qualities: the brutality of war contrasted with the beauty of love; nature as symbol of peace suddenly transformed into the setting and victim of war's devastation; the poet's fanciful play on social situations by means of imagery, which is an element of his comical art; the final poem, "Dis Nigeria Sef," using pidgin English to playfully pummel a people seemingly resigned to a life of decadence, disease, and death. Theo Vincent rightly mentions the poet's ability "to adopt various attitudes: the cynical, the symbolic, the harshly critical—all these underscored by a mind that can mock the foolishness of man in sardonic poetry that can make the mind ping." (*Songs*: 10)

Where one disagrees with Vincent, however, is in his claim that the love poems in *Songs* "describe a tenderness and longing, a yearning for life which *sharply contrast* with the harshness and death-wish of the war poems [and] an intellect *that would distill order* from the cacophonous sounds of different emotions..." (emphasis mine) Saro-Wiwa documents in his war diary, *On A Darkling Plain*, the genesis of a good number of the poems. One easily gathers from his account that, if, indeed, there was an attempt in the love songs to "distill order" from the unfolding disorder, it was only short-lived, only a natural, human emotional search for a haven away from the surrounding hell. Such search may be successful, but definitely temporarily; for, the mind embarking upon the search is caught in the continuing conflagration, and, given Saro-Wiwa's avowed commitment and courage, the peaceful cocoon offered by love must cede space and sensitivity to the existential and experiential pain of war. In fact, the love poems do reveal the impact of the tragedy spreading death and destruction. Saro-Wiwa, a man that loves to spread and share laughter, is pained by its absence as people die around him. So, the love poem, "For Maria," is crafted to relieve the pain and the loneliness" (*Plain*: 167) Yet, he himself quickly realizes that love is really a memory, a past that cannot compete or conquer the present: "For Maria" is followed by "Were You There," which describes the sight of a sergeant's leg blown off by a bomb.

WAR: THE SOUNDS AND SCENES OF DEATH

Saro-Wiwa's *Songs* would be an excellent text for defining the meaning of poetry (literature); for, it states and describes the poet's search for "music to soothe my troubled soul" (p.24), and the reality of causes and effects of "trouble." Just as we have seen in the fiction, *trouble* and *confusion* are constant in the Nigerian landscape. Ideally, the poet, a singer, loves to sing beautiful songs. Saro-Wiwa does make the distinction between the poet and the purveyors/ protagonists of war in the first poem, "Voices" (*Songs*: 13) They are the political animals, the opportunists, interested in material selfishness as patriotism, using the highfalutin and hypocritical language of honor. While they speak, the post is

still able to restrict his song to that of love for his beautiful woman:
> They speak of taxes
> Of oil and power
>
> They speak of honour
> And pride of tribe
>
> They speak of war
> Of bows and arrows
>
> They speak of tanks
> And putrid human flesh
>
> I sing my love
> For Maria. (13)

The poem can be divided into two sections, the final two lines being the second. Love can easily be contrasted with the other, mundane interests; the last two verses, in their sheer simplicity and soothing joy, cast opprobrium upon the preceding lines describing issues of politics and economics, tribe, and the horror of war. However, by the very length of that first part, and the imagery of "putrid human flesh," one knows that the song of love cannot but succumb to the sounds of war. *They*, one also notes, are opposed to *I*, a fact that Saro-Wiwa always emphasizes: he was opposed to the civil war, convinced that it was being used by the Biafrans—particularly, Ojukwu, whom he absolutely detested—to stake their claim to the oil-rich delta area of Eastern Nigeria. It is no surprise that, the poet's opposition notwithstanding, the voices of war succeeded in obliterating that of love and peace. The poet, one might say, is thus compelled to vacate the escapist cocoon of the "nuptial chamber" (*Songs*: 28) to elements of division, disintegration and death.

The sounds of war. The sound of silence: it is presented by the poet in two different forms. First, as the silence of sensible thought and truth, as resignation to war, as collusion with war-mongers who are ready to eliminate anyone that dare oppose their hawkish position.
> The vows of silence
> They must be kept.
> For you cannot speak

> While the guns roar
> And you cannot cry
> Where you'll not be heard
> For the loud resonance
> Of an empty lie.
>
> Silence.
> And the vows of silence
> Must be kept
> Or else...
> Where silence will be kept. (14)

The last two lines subtly imply the threat of death (the silence of the cemetery) against any critic of war. That loud threat, "the loud resonance of an empty lie," is made more frightening by the roar of the guns drowning the human voice.

This second sound of silence, actually a corollary to the first, is the very absence of the human voice, the voice of children's laughter, the voice of people expressing the joy of being alive. The sound of silence is, indeed, the sound of death. The chief of the village is dead, and the community, normally exuberant in celebrating life with music and dance, is reduced to nothingness by the forces of war.

> The old year is dead
> And the new, unheralded
> By shouts of laughing children
> Seeps sadly into empty homes
> And the mortar falls at dusk
> In the empty bridal-chamber
> Where lovers twined like snakes
> Made soft music to silences. (18)

The silence of collusion, added to the silence of death, corrupts the silence of love now poisoned by the landscape reeking of death.

As is to be expected, the sounds of silence are finally overcome by the sounds of Death in the form of bombs and bullets, and human beings groaning as they fall.

> Earth echoes with alien sounds-
> Stuttering rifles, weird moans-

And the harsh face of war
Fills the land with abomination. (18)

The poet personifies Death, as well as other participants in this process of human victimization and destruction. The triumph of Death and its collaborators, symbolized by the "alien sounds," is diametrically opposed to the human tragedy traced through the many absences and silences depicted in Saro-Wiwa's verses. Tears are the commonest sight and sounds here. The chief, leader of the community, is deceased; fathers and mothers are dead, leaving "the orphaned land" in tears. "Empty homes" welcome the new year, as dead as the old one because of the absence of "shouts of laughing children." "Weird moans" fill the stinking air.

At times, Saro-Wiwa also contrasts the silence of night with the clang of boots. "Near the Forest" (17) was composed on a sleepless Nsukka night, before the war began, as Biafran soldiers were being trained. Normally night is a time of peace, when human beings sleep and prepare themselves for a bright, new day. Not at Nsukka, however; for, these are abnormal times. The poem's persona is angry at the noises disturbing his sleep, perhaps, forever: "The clang and clamour" of "harsh boots" "snap the silence, sap the soul." The brutal din is exacerbated by the harsh, tropical heat. Suddenly, the poet realizes that war is imminent and "you hear the curse of doom on man." The poet now understands that there is no music to soothe his troubled soul; that war marches to its own music of horror and harshness, far removed from the rhythm of life and forever tainted by the tunes and tones of Death. In such circumstances, Nature, loved by the poet, also becomes victim, overwhelmed by the messengers of the Master Destroyer, Death. The "monotonous rhythms of rain "is superseded by "the bumping thud of bombs" (24). "While balls of fire" fall into forests "where the youthful enemy lay." (22)

The greatest tragedy of war, as depicted in *Songs*, is that of the youths, innocent, inexperienced, committed and credulous, following their fathers and leaders with the understanding that the latter are preparing for them a future full of hope and happiness. On the contrary, that future is being obliterated by a present peopled by lying, lecherous leaders. The death of the present is graphically painted in poems, such as "Were You There":

Were you there to see the stump
Of the sergeant's leg borne dutifully

Into the young doctor's room.

Were you there to see sticking out
Of the shallow sandy grave
As though in supplication
The bony palms of the bombed soldier,

You would not smile at the radio account
Of victories and smashed battalions. (22)

While many are being killed and maimed, the radio, official arm of the well-oiled propaganda machine, keeps proclaiming with apparent pride, phantasmal victories which, interestingly enough, the people heartily cheer and spread abroad.[2]

The poet debunks patriotism and other shallow words as blatant lies for which the leaders must, sooner or later answer to the people. His reasoning is at times surprisingly mild-toned, showing his intellectualism, as well as a cynicism that would later blow up into venom spitting outrage.

Perhaps they [the young men] must die,
So we live for ever.
For this have we told the lie
The famous lie about the sweet and honour
That lie in dying for one's country.
But death is a taskmaster
And only the living can know
That honour and sweet we preach
To them that are to die... (24)

Here is one of the ironies of war: the combatants have no say in deciding whether or not to fight. The policy-makers are not the ones condemned to facing the fire of bullets and bombs. And, even if a soldier survives, he is often left to live with nameless, endless traumatizing after effects, while the leaders, Master-manipulators of the people, bask in the glory of sham victories. Saro-Wiwa, hard-core pacifist, condemns these leaders.

Ye bakers and hawkers of lies
Who bare your jaws and call for wars,
Inviting the lame, the blind and the deaf

> To the merry ways of guns
> Where shall ye find the lotion
> The balm to heal their wounds?
> How untell the lies
>
> How pray for forgiveness
> When the departed made wise
> Demand restitution? (24-25)

The imagery is immersed in common, essential practices, thus highlighting the deep effects of war on the people. Bread is common foodstuff in Nigeria, and the bakery constitutes one of the constant elements of daily realities, just as are hawkers of bread and other food items. The leaders' deceit is thus underscored by their symbolic accessibility to the people. Unfortunately, instead of providing the basic source of living, these leaders hawk lies; and, as war-mongers (*hawks*), they also reveal their hypocrisy, having hidden their murderous mien behind a mask of peaceful suppliers of bread. Moreover, rather than provide protection for the weak and innocent, and succor and scare for the sick, they deliberately send them to die, as if war were a place for dancing and merriment. The questions asked by the poet are rhetorical; for, there is no balm to heal the wounds perpetuated by these false patriots on helpless, innocent victims. Lies told cannot be untold. When the departed souls return—according to traditional belief—to ask for restitution, the guilty leaders, nameless murderers, would have nothing to say in their self-defense, except, of course, to tell more barefaced lies.

Meanwhile, among the living, the lying continues apace. "Moratorium" describes one other element of the "empty lie" called war. The title sets the tone of this ironic poem. It connotes delay, suspension of activities, a period of reconsideration, a re-think, a possibility of change for the better, indeed, for a final resolution of the problem. However, Saro-Wiwa, ever so subtle in his cynicism, immediately implies the presence of hypocrisy in the whole process. Emotion, he reminds us, too often overcomes reason. Moratorium is proclaimed, not to re-affirm, or re-establish reason, but, tragically, to replenish and reinforce war supplies and strategies, and to entrench lies, so that the murder and mayhem may become more massive.

> Objective detachment
> Sound judgment
> And charity
>
> Prove too high, impractical...
> So we proclaim a moratorium—
> For the meantime.
> *Only the meantime.*

In other words, moratorium is another arm of propaganda, used to pollute and "pervert consciences." As a result, people assume roles, they posture, and propagate high-sounding theories. Saro-Wiwa, the renowned manipulator of language never fails to exhibit his clever play on words.

> My friend,
> In mean times
> We assume coats
>
> Which become us
> As we become them
> During the meantime and
>   After the meantime
>   We have a system. (15)

The link between meantime and mean times is not only brilliant in its simplicity, but also striking in its subtle commentary on Nigeria's sociopolitical life. It combines the meanness of the civil-war period with the temporary nature of moratorium, and its meaninglessness: *during* and *after* the meantime, we have a *system*, of lies, just as before the supposed break in action. Significantly, the fact is, that there has never been a break at all! The *status quo ante*, publicly placed in abeyance, has always been in place. Loss of conscience and consciousness. Corruption and compromise. That is the system in our dance of death.

"Ogale—An Evacuated Town" (29) captures the dance with an eye for the dehumanization of everything in sight. Saro-Wiwa again displays his talent for using a few words to tell a whole story.[3] Again, the imagery is of most importance. In order to emphasize the pervasiveness of death, Saro-Wiwa personifies everything and paints a picture of their having lost life. Of course, the absence of human beings is already stated in the title, the town having been evacuated before the arrival of Federal troops. Objects replace human beings as victims. Lifeless objects are thus given useless life.

> Cars cannibalised
> > Amputated
> Lie by the roadside
> > Abandoned
> > Forgotten (29)

Animals, normally with life, now hungry, become scavengers, feeding on dead humans.

> A lone lean dog
> Scrounging for food
> Reaps human skulls
> In a shallow gutter.

Houses, like human beings, "gape forlorn" at wet angry skies. And Ogale, broken out of her senses, helpless, stripped of her children, ravaged, is no less than a widow, raped by the dastardly, rampaging troops.

> Ogale lies in broken images
> Astride the narrow tarmac
> Moaning insensate
> Her lost sons and daughters
> Whose wails I hear
> This eerie night
> For Ogale out in the dreary rain
> Her legs apart like a cheap prostitute
> Exposed, utterly exposed.
> Ogale is a ravished woman.

Ogale is symbol of her inhabitants, looking askance, unable to understand the reality of this undeserved punishment heaped upon her by Nature and by human beings. The picture is made more heart-rending by the imagery of the woman, either the mother or the woman being forced into sex by a rapist. Either way, the act castigates the absent—but ever-present in our imagination—perpetrators of these crimes who have done everything to bestialize woman, the repository of continuity of the society. And the prostitute is the quintessence of this bestialization: What is sacred is made cheap, shallow, bared naked by the brutality of idiots. In conjunction with other poems, this piece also calls attention to the emptiness of the war. Far from being a show of patriotism, it is a shocking epitome of prostitution.

"Epitaph for Biafra" (33) summarizes the poet's condemnation of the Biafran leaders. He asks questions, and gives answers that are actually questions. His concern remains the destiny of the young soldiers doomed to the "dance of death."

> Where will they go now?
> Nowhere, nowhere.
> Where can they go now?
> Nowhere, nowhere.

Resuming his play on words, he contrasts *where* (a place,) with *nowhere* (loss of place, the war-front), with its agony. It is Life, as opposed to Death.

> Where the young men lost their bones
> In lonely trenches
> In a plain of agony.
> Marching to nowhere
> Where nothing waits upon nothing
> Where the bones await the bones
> In a dance of death.

Saro-Wiwa once again uses down-to-earth images and actions to express the nothingness and nowhereness of war. His people, the Ogoni, being farmers and fishermen and women, he refers to the dearth of food as one of the harrowing experiences. One is thankful and fortunate to have anything at all.

> They'll have toads for supper
> They had snakes for lunch
> And lizards for breakfast.
> Reptiles are a delicacy
> On the survival menu.

Reptiles, slimy, creeping, creepy, unpalatable, and poisonous, have become a delicacy on a menu meant to keep one alive, by all means possible, as a matter of desperation.

The poet then, for the first and only time in this collection, comments upon an aspect of the war which is often forgotten when people think and talk of *peace*, and other perplexing aftermaths: the role of Europe.

> The cooks of Europe will praise
> Their ingenuity

> In the survival game!
> They will play at Rebels
> And Vandals
> Fill the nation with blood
> And scandal.
> Then they will return as agents
> And angels
> Laughing and weeping and begging
> For minor mercies.

Continuing their game of imperialism and colonialism, those collaborators, as the poet rightly affirms, are only out to fleece the country, to "pacify" it as a means to emptying its resources. Saro-Wiwa's use of the third-person plural, *they*, may be considered ambiguous -is he referring to European "cooks," or Biafran "eaters"? -but, in my opinion, such ambiguity expresses the collaboration of both sides, as well as the duplicity of Biafrans who, at the end of the war, returned as agents and angels, begging for and obtaining minor and major mercies, claiming to be committed to peace and progress after pompously prosecuting destruction. No example of such two-faced fiends can be worse than that of the Biafran leader, Ojukwu, whom Saro-Wiwa hates like the plague.

The poet vilifies Ojukwu and his followers especially because, in his opinion, all the facts available should have shown them that they could never win the war, and that only a miracle could have made it possible. His rhetorical questions are:

> Didn't they test the hardness of the egg
> On the skin of their teeth
> Before dashing it against the rocks?
> Didn't they know that water turned wine
> But once in days of yore?

Since miracles are a big rarity, and since the war-mongers are brimming with absolute confidence in their propaganda of lies, the poet has nothing but contempt for them:

> They should stop their foul breath
> From infecting God's good air.

A similar contempt is spat out at the staff and students of University of Nigeria, Nsukka, for students of their blind commitment to the war, in a poem, "Foul Mouth," published by Saro-Wiwa in *Plain* (114):

>No business to mind you dirty pig?
>With the loudspeakers
>And microphones
>And the coarse voice that shrieks
>And calls to war and cries
>'Kill that man, he's your enemy!'
>No business to mind, you brute?

The language, uncharacteristic of the style of *Songs*, blends better into the tone and rhythm of the war diary where Saro-Wiwa does not hide his absolute scorn for the secessionists.

OF LOVE AND FRIENDSHIP IN A TIME OF WAR

We have noted earlier that Saro-Wiwa's love poems cannot be fully comprehended outside the horizon of the horror that befell Nigeria. The poet's treatment of a theme that could be considered as being diametrically opposed to the surrounding, suffocating realities, can be explained as a sign of his own humanity, threatened but obstinately sought and nurtured. To some extent, his opposition to the Biafran secession is underscored in this thematic oddity; but, his stylistic approach, and the details of the love enunciated, would be deemed to enhance his human sensitivity. Love and friendship, while being preferred to hate and violence, cannot but be affected by the murderous presence of the latter. Besides, Saro-Wiwa does not forget to laugh at himself, and to reveal that, even in matters of the heart, he himself is no saint. "Courtesan" (32) attests to this fact. The short poem tells the story of a drunken "late bird" returning to find a "nest too full, and the door shut in [his] face."

>And live on lively memories
>of the cries on entry,
>The ease of re-entry, while, I
>Tired and breathless spaceman
>Toil on for the pleasures
>Of the final splashdown.

One immediately thinks of a man turned back from a busy prostitute's door. Drunk, his head is swinging with images of love-making, the hard breathing; the joyful cries, ecstasy of orgasm, the fatigue after the superhuman effort; the peaceful pleasures of two bodies become one, for a passing period.

Saro-Wiwa takes the imagery much farther, into space—the fantasy of a brilliant imagination, or the hallucination of a drunkard?—, thus arousing in the reader's mind other ideas about our unfortunate society. The space technology introduced into an apparently simple poem of crass sex, proves Saro-Wiwa's interest in the body politic polluted by political animals and prostitutes. While Nigerians are busy killing one another, others are exploring space. In light of the sophisticated title—courtesan, a highly-placed, refined prostitute—, the notion of "spaceman" could be a mockery of the poetic persona playing the "civilized" among the "savage."[4] But, then, on other occasions, this contrast becomes a real indictment of a society with feet of lead marking time while others are racing into the next century. Witness the final poem of *Songs*, "Dis Nigeria Sef," and its images of trained people inventing nothing (40); white man on the moon (41), and prostitution become fashionable among young men obsessed with money (41).

Saro-Wiwa opposes to such dastardly act, genuine love between man and woman. "For Maria" (26) was written when he was Administrator at Bonny. It was a difficult period, when he and other Rivers leaders were afraid that the Federal government might be coerced into negotiations to end the war and might therefore have to "bargain away Port Harcourt [the Rivers capital] in its search for peace" (*Plain*: 166). "On these occasions [of certainty]," writes the poet, "it took a turning to softer, personal and more intimate matters to bring me some calm and send me back to sleep." Yet a close reading of the poem reveals that sleep is but temporary, or a thing of the past, a dream at best difficult to attain, only beautiful as something cherished. The poem is filled with elements of softness, sweetness, contrasting the breeze of the river-bank with the storm of the sea; the peace of dusk with the pandemonium of a day spent dodging bullets; the moonlit and starry night perfect for lovers with the dreaded darkness of the trenches hiding from the invisible enemy; and the dream of youth with the nightmare of imminent death. It is all a matter of *memories.*

> Walking over old memories
> In the gentle breeze of a Bonny eve
> I have thought of you

In silent extasies (sic).

The poet's love, his Maria (his teenage wife), has a "voice soft as silk," the gentility of that Bonny breeze, the freshness of a "cob of maize in May." She is the only one capable of quelling "the storm that flays [his] heart." She is the only hope in a horizon darkened by the specter of death.

> When clouds invade my sky
> And stars cannot peep out of doors
> Ascend th'empyrean of my soul
> Be the moon and the stars
> And let me play still
> In the softness you shed.

And there is the catch: the woman is absent. The moon and the stars too. She, the heavenly element of his soul, can only be conceptualized through imagination. The idea of playing "in the softnesses" she sheds also remains that, an idea, hidden in his heart, because, if revealed, it risks being snuffed out by the demons populating the night. In that atmosphere of fear, the past remains the most reliable means of contemplating happiness. The question to be answered: can the past bliss be given new life?

If the love expressed in "For Maria" stands a chance of being rehabilitated, the contrary is true of other relationships. In "Corpses Have Grown," everything, including love, falls victim to the implacable terminator.

> And the mortar falls at dusk
> In the empty bridal-chamber
> Where lovers twined like snakes
> Made soft music to silences. (18)

Even before they disappeared from the bridal-chamber, answering to deadly duty, these lovers displayed the characteristics of poisonous partners capable of slow murder. One might therefore say that the war only served as a means of activizing their latent power. Here, one's thought would go to realities of pre-war Nigeria, a country slowly but surely advancing on the path of the final conflagration.

Saro-Wiwa refuses to give in to the vagaries of war, and that would be symptomatic of his aversion to the whole madness. "For Her" (27) complements "For Maria." It details both the physical action of making love and, most significantly, the unity of two souls coalescing into one, eternally. Yet, here again, it is a matter of memories sharpened by the trauma of war.

> I see you soft as the twilight
> That now caresses our soul
> Uniting us in an eternity of love.

The lover wonders whether his woman is on the same plane as he.

> Darling, do you dream the dreams I dream
> And do you walk the gardens of suave redolence
> Through which I walk as I think of you?
> And do you remember that day
> When the dying sun shot gold-tinted arms
> And we swam the river from shore to shore?
> Do you remember the words I said to you?...

Doubt? Desperation? Fear of death? All these are subtly revealed in the above lines. The love's very absence and the depth of the man's love, make for the concentration of thoughts, the realization of his dream, the ability to roll back the hands of the clock and make the past present.

> Swiftly, swiftly, my skein of time unrolls
> When from the deep well of your being
> I slake the thirst of my love.

This ability to slake his thirst, this unity of two souls in eternal love, do they mean that the problem of absence, and the danger of death have been forever resolved? At best, one can answer in the conditional. For, the questions posed by the poem imply the strong possibility that the absent woman may, indeed, be living a nightmare, not a dream; that the garden of love may, in reality, be a field of mines and military men mowing down innocent victims.

"Midnight" (23) is an excellent proof of the ephemeral nature of the dream. The same poet that celebrates the ecstasy of love, with its orgasmic zenith leading down to the equally subliminal post-copulation rest, now laments his inability to sleep. He is tormented, tortured like a boat on a stormy sea. Combining anger and envy in lines marked by irony, he addresses the young brown eyes:

> How I envy you, brown eyes,
> That you can laugh and sing
> And sleep in bliss
> While I, I'm storm-tossed
> In tormenting billows that lash me
> Furiously from shore to shore.
> My smile a quirkish mirthless grin
> My sleep a garish closing of the eyes.

He, "the listless insomniac," tossed helplessly in the turbulent sea populated by sharks, then offers a prayer for the young woman's "eternal bliss." One notices that the prayer may be a curse:

> May you always laugh and sing
> Young innocence, e'n when storms
> Towering high wash me down
> Cavernous chasms of despair
> Then turn their fury on your tenderness.

As he chides the woman for her indifference to the storms tormenting him, as he warns her that, contrary to her feeling of immunity, she is next in the line of attack by the implacable enemy, Saro-Wiwa inadvertently calls our attention to the lack of realism in his own poems of love. This is the point where the war impacts most poignantly the life of everyone caught in its flaming belly. If love, real love, exists in such circumstances, it must take cognizance of the presence of death. It must be involved in the struggle to survive, to overcome death. Which is what Saro-Wiwa does by escaping from Biafra to Lagos, capital of Federal Nigeria, where he engages in activism, to keep Nigeria one and, more importantly, to affirm his people's autonomy and rights.

In order to make his commitment meaningful he sees fit to establish friendship with the soldiers. In "Night Encounter" (16), the poet adroitly uses irony to introduce the birth and growth of friendship between himself and a soldier. The title implies darkness and disharmony. The poem begins with the terse description of an accidental meeting between civilian and soldier in the night. The two parties, poles apart, indeed, considered enemies in the reality of Nigerian life, symbolize their respective groups, with the latter being the oppressor-aggressor. Monster meets man. Victimizer towers above victim. The potential for disaster is truly powerful. Significantly, they meet on a staircase, as the potential victim is coming upstairs, and the symbolic monster blends with the darkness.

> ...I met him
> One with the darkness.
> I stopped for a moment
> Frighted,tense

But tension is immediately deflated by the soldier:

> He laughed gently and I relaxed
> happy to find
> In spite of the gun
> He was still a man.
> It lit the dark
> That gentle laugh
> In the pith of night...

The soldier's laugh is enchanting. It turns darkness into light. It exudes the humanity shared by all, even those hiding their fears and failings behind the power of a gun. Pity that the fraternity shared by the two sides--civilian and military—hardly ever lasts. Firstly, the soldier brightening the darkness with his ray of hope, is doomed to die.

> But it was only the low laugh
> Of one who was soon to die.

Secondly, the meeting-point of soldiers and civilians will not always be a staircase; more likely, they will meet in villages being bombed and being hurriedly evacuated, or in refugee-camps closer to concentration-camps than to anywhere fit for human congregation, or, at best, on a boat en route to Lagos. "The Escape" tells the story of Saro-Wiwa's escape from the war-zone. It is now clear that the civilian-soldier friendship forged in the dead of night is particular, distinguished by the latter's affiliation to the Federal side. Biafran soldiers, hated to death by the poet, are bloodthirsty "beasts," (19) turning everything into the color of blood, spreading fear. The only human reaction is to flee. The movement is symbolic: the poet and his entourage leave by night and, by dawn, they are on the waters, the rains coming down as an "evil wild storm" threatening to last forever. "But after the storm came brilliance." (19) A lone fish swims by, in all its majesty, and white birds stand by, shining in all their beauty. Thus, hopelessness is replaced by hope. Fear, by confidence; war, by peace. The flight "from the stink of war/The stain of greed and bitterness," (20) is proudly rationalized as a necessity, as the sole means of survival in order to continue the struggle.

At Bonny, the poet meets another soldier; only, now, instead of the earlier "encounter," there is a relaxed atmosphere. The soldier, watching over the bay, begs him for a cigarette which he gladly gives. (20) As the boat plods on towards Lagos, the poet's mood vacillates between joy and despair. He thinks of the war raging behind him and the complex process of attaining peace. He knows that the flight to Lagos does not mean that the war is over. Hence, upon arrival at Lagos, the expected mood of relief and total happiness is missing:

Ariya! Ariya! After the storm-tossed night
The sands of Lagos
And cohorts of bathers
Peace? (21)

Ariya, meaning enjoyment, merriment, is a common epithet used for Lagos and Lagosians. It implies nonchalance before tragedies, irresponsibility, lack of seriousness, a hedonism envied by some, abhorred by others. To be at the Lagos beach is to wonder whether this is the capital of a country at war with itself. In his diary, Saro-Wiwa underscores the fragility of the peace, or its sham, by reporting the bombing of the city by a Biafran plane: "Within that same week [of his arrival], laconic Lagos was to be shattered by a bomb attack on placid Ikoyi." (*Plain*: 142)

With regard to Lagos, Saro-Wiwa must be criticized for telling only one side of the story. His poem and diary fail to mention the fact that the city's placidity and hedonism are nurtured by officialdom as part of the propaganda, to make the world believe that the war is nothing more than skirmishes in a section of an otherwise peaceful society.[5] In the period under discussion (1967-1970), Lagos was the seat of government whose highest members wined and dined and womanized to their hearts' content, while the soldiers were killing and being killed on the war-front. Saro-Wiwa's *Songs* castigate the Biafrans. It is noteworthy that, after fleeing to Lagos and observing the easy life there, he never wrote any poems to describe the rot. The consolation, if it be considered as such, is his long poem on the macrocosmic confusion called Nigeria.

"DIS NIGERIA SEF"

"Dis Nigeria Sef" (36-44) is by far the longest poem of the *Songs* collection. Unlike the others, it is not, strictly speaking, a "war poem." Written in 1977 (see *Similia*: 97), it is a satire on Nigeria, its past and present, its people, its politics, its cultures, its underdevelopment, in short, its confusion. Another significant point: instead of the standard English used in the other poems, Saro-Wiwa experiments, as he has done elsewhere, with popular, pidgin English. It is the aspect of confusion that links the poem to the others: here, the poet traces the country's history, thus indirectly explaining the reasons for the civil war and the meaninglessness of the tragedy.

In a manner similar to a scientific experiment, the poem's first stanza, Saro-Wiwa states the problem to be addressed: Nigeria, the body of confusion.

> "Every time na de same wahala
> Moving to night plenty palava
> Na so dem all den dey hala
> Nigeria don spoil
> Water wey dey boil
> No hot like dis Nigeria
> ....
> I beg, which trouble be dis Nigeria? (36)

Remarkably, this is the only poem with a semblance of rhyme-patterns: The pidgin offers possibilities for a regular rhythm, with onomatopoeia and humor used to arouse the reader's interest. In addition, popular proverbs and imagery, both aspects of pidgin, contribute a philosophical depth to the discourse. For example, Nigeria's uniqueness is subsumed in the imagery of boiling water and black pot: Nigeria is hotter than boiling water, and, black pot that it is, it becomes blacker when you attempt to clean it.

Given this shocking uniqueness,, this recidivist badness, the poet poses to Nigeria the simple but complex rhetorical question: "Why all your tings na soso confusion?" Reverting to a style used in the earlier poems, he personalizes everything, from the country (the body politic and the people) to the socio-economic system as well as the policies, to show the totality of *confusion*, a word used in various forms at least twenty-four times in the poem. In Nigeria, nothing works. The towns are full of filth. The whole system is stuck in stagnation. The people are wallowing in corruption.

Saro-Wiwa contrasts this "dirty confusion" with other peoples and places. There, everything is well organized. Workers are competent and committed. There, countries have been transformed into nations through genuine nationalism. Not in Nigeria, unfortunately, where disorganization and alienation and underdevelopment are the hallmarks of Nigerianism. And, in Nigeria, internecine warfare is the people's pride, as they make enemies of one another.

> For yonder, soza dey shoot enemy
> Nigeria soza dey shoot him broder
> Not one day. Not two. Every time. Wetin?
> Oder people police na gentleman propa
> Nigeria police na wuruwuru wayo tief
> Oder people nurse go smile person come well
> Nigeria nurse na soso post office face
> Sotey sick man wey see am don die quench

Images of the civil war, and of the peaceful times: soldiers kill one another, without knowing why; soldiers turn on the people, just to prove that they are in power, and that the people can do absolutely nothing about it. The soldiers' irresponsibility is complemented by that of the police, scoundrels supposedly interested in people's safety, and that of the nurses, agents of death disguised as soft and sweet providers of succor to the sick. Saro-Wiwa's hilarious humor is as strong as ever in this picture of Nigerian chaos as opposed to other people's constructive character.

> Oder people dog dey drink milk
> Your own dey chop propa shit.

In matters of religion, vanity and materialism are the Nigerian's strong suit. The Moslem goes on pilgrimage to be able to use the title of *alhaji*, and to buy gold for his teeth.

> You no see as him obey proud
> Him be alhaji, double alhaji

> Dey put gold for all him teeth
> Sake of him don go mecca return
> God don punish you foolish man
> You don forget your own religion. (38)

The other symbol of religious alienation, the catholic priest ("fader") is accused by the poet of going against the natural, human law:
> Him talk say him be fader
> Dey make him pillow him wife
> Na lie lie you lie foolish man
> You no fit! How man fit stay
> No sleep with woman, no born pickin?
> Dis fader work no be for Nigeria man.

Celibacy, belief in Christ's miraculous birth, these, in Saro-Wiwa's opinion, are foreign cultural tenets that Nigeria should not imitate. This call for indigenization of culture sounds quite interesting; however, when one considers the totality of the poet's work, there is a lack of conviction, and a certain ambiguity. This criticism of foreign cultures is followed by that of the proliferation of languages, local languages, from which the country has failed to choose one, instead borrowing another people's language.
> Nigeria, you too like borrow borrow
> You borrow money, cloth you dey borrow
> You borrow motor, you borrow aeroplane
> You dey borrow chop, you borrow drink
> Sotey you borrow anoder man language
> Begin confuse am with your confusion (39)

And name: "Name sef you no get (...) Common name you must borrow borrow." The humor here is infectious and the reader could laugh until tears run down his face. Yet, there is that very confusion for which the poet is castigating his people. For one thing, by using English, standard or pidgin, he himself is committing the same crime as all others. For another, it is simplistic to lump together every facet of life as part of the "borrow borrow" syndrome. By not being specific, Saro-Wiwa fails to affirm categorically the areas and modalities for necessary action.

His comical style could also be problematic. This is apparently why he refers to the accentuated laughter emanating from his poem and warns his reader not to forget the serious nature of the facts.

> Look as you dey laugh as I dey talk
> You tink say I dey joke?
> Na true word I dey talk
> My friend, better no go follow you
> Because na soso laugh you dey
> You no dey tink, you no dey shame
> Your laugh na cry, foolish man (39)

After the first salvo of insults and curses, the poet reverts to begging, to expressing his patriotism.

> Because true true I no fit tire for you
> Nigeria and myself na one belly
> If 'e get headache, me I get bellyache
> If 'e no get to chop, me I go hungry qua
> Nigeria and myself we be prick and blokkus:
> Prick get up begin dey go
> 'E go tire after some time
> Because agaracha must come back
> Agaracha must come back
> When 'e return, blokkus dey wait for am
> Person no fit tire for dis Nigeria. (42)

A positive point, one would immediately say: Here is a Nigerian determined to stick with his country, even with all its confusion. Not for him the exile of the uncommitted and the weak-minded. The metaphors are, as usual, very down-to-earth, if not downright dirty. Saro-Wiwa displays his interest in the human anatomy, particularly concerning male-female copulation.

He goes on to list Nigeria's good qualities, such as its natural resources; the beauty of its women;[6] its crops and fruits; its animals and insects, and their characteristics for survival; the competent and committed workers, exceptions to the rule laid down earlier.

> Some of dem na better man
> Dey work from morning till night

> Weder soza nurse or police
> Or farmer wey dey cut bush plant
> Or trader dey sell petty petty for market
> Or akowe dey sidon for him office
> ....
> Dey help him country people
> Oh yes, some Nigeria pickin get sense
> And better go follow dem all. Amen. (44)

Two facts lessen the positive impact of the above portrayal. One, the good qualities being praised by the poet are not widespread among the people. Two, the praise-singing is done as an after-thought and as a sign of contrition; for, the poet, as critic, is afraid of repercussions meted out by a sick society complacent in its corruption and never prepared to take correction. In such a situation, the poet's expression of love may be a lie; his approval of certain good qualities may be met by deaf ears. The critic's life is always at risk in a society where it is taboo to tell the truth. One notes the pathos of the following lines:

> But I beg you oh, Nigeria
> No talk say I dey cuss you
> True to God no be say I no like you
> Because I know as you dey do your own
> You no dey like make person talk true
> Small time now you fit send your pickin
> Weder soza police or kotuma ash bottom
> Make dem wahala my life small
> Come lock me for one dirty shit prison
> Or you fit send anoder wicked pickin
> Like hernia come blow my blokkus
> Or smallpox come make pit for my face
> ....
> Make you no vex sake of my song (41-42)

The fear of the truth-teller prostrating himself before his monstrous country is not to be seen as absolute, however, because he refuses to be silenced. The fear goes hand in hand with love of the country, with that commitment that gave birth to the poetic message.

Indeed, that is the crux of the matter, as the reader tries to sort out the complexities of Saro-Wiwa's views on Nigeria:
>Dis Nigeria sef,
>You too bring confusion!
>How person no like you still 'e like you
>Dis no be grade one confusion? (44)

The final portrait, of both the poet and his people, has to be one of pity, which is exactly what Saro-Wiwa seeks from his reader:
>So I beg make una sorry me small
>Because I don confuse well well at all
>Sake of dis I-love-I-no-love Nigeria
>
>I TIRE. (44)

The pity comes from the presence of the country's endless potentials, both at the natural and human levels. When Saro-Wiwa says, "ah, Nigeria, you to fine for my eye," (42) one imagines what might have been, what could be. Which deepens the feeling of frustration and anger at the "stupid confusion" that is.

CONCLUSION: THE CONFUSION, THE PRISON

Confusion remains the overall quality of one's thoughts after reading Saro-Wiwa's poetry. Thus, one could rightly describe the work as an expression of the Nigerian character. War is an imposing presence. Peace and the joy of living, that is the dream desperately desired, and prayed for. "To Sarogua, Rain Maker" (30) is such a prayer, to "wash the stain of strife away," so that
>We'll speak no more
>Of coups and colonels
>And raids at dead of night;
>We'll forget the bombs
>And bury the dead.

Prayer, or promise? Possibility, or pipe-dream? Saro-Wiwa has not proffered a means for realizing the dream, besides praying to a god, Sarogua, the rain-maker, who, already, has refused to accede to the people's request for rain; who, instead of rain, has brought down a thunderstorm, and blood.

The love poems, and "To Palm Wine" (31) also show the poet's preference for peace, and his abhorrence of war. He enjoys his palm wine and his pipe; dead, his spirit will return to add to the people's joy. But, again, the idea remains enmeshed in ambiguity; for, if palm wine is used in libation to the ancestors, it would be contradictory to imagine his spirit breaking loose "the bondage of ancestry" in order to fulfill the traditional notions of linking the dead to the living. The mythical, as it were, would thus be linked only with difficulty to the material, except one clearly accepts an African world-view, which is absent from Saro-Wiwa's conceptualization of Nigerian society.

The confusion pervading the horizon is an important aspect of the *prison* described in detail in Saro-Wiwa's fiction. "The Tail of a Tale"[7] comments on the prevailing dictatorship of the powerful (tiger) over the weak (tortoise). The latter uses cunning to survive; problem is, that survival does not destabilize or dislodge the former from his position as predator. One possibility is, the collaboration between both, in a manner similar to the relationship between the military and the civilian observed in *Songs*. Would that lead the country out of the tunnel? Saro-Wiwa's collection is "dedicated to the officers and men of the Third Moving Commando Division of the Nigerian Army." The Division, one notes, was directly involved in liberating the poet-activist's people. In our analysis of *Plain*, we shall return to the whole story of his strange love for the military.

Although, in *Songs*' war-poems, there is no sign of cleavage—the honeymoon was just beginning!—, "Dis Nigeria Sef" reveals an aftermath of *trouble* (cf. preceding chapters). Not surprisingly, the Nigerian confusion culminates in the following poem, "The True Prison," written prior to Saro-Wiwa's ultimate murder in 1995, by which time the civil war had become particularized in the one-sided war against Ogoni in the person of their diminutive leader.

It is not the leaking roof
Nor the singing mosquitoes
In the damp, wretched cell.
....
It is the lies that have been drummed
Into your ears for one generation

It is the security agent running amok
Executing callous calamitous orders
The magistrate writing in her book
Punishment she knows is undeserved
The moral decrepitude
Mental ineptitude
Lending dictatorship spurious legitimacy
Cowardice masked as obedience
Lurking in our denigrated souls
It is fear damping trousers
We dare not wash off our urine
It is this
It is this
It is this
Dear friend, turns our free world
Into a dreary prison.
(*A Month and a Day*: 221)

Nigeria, the prison wallowing in confusion, continues to be the scene of tragedy. The people continue to be collaborators in the destruction being perpetrated by the dictatorships. What the poet affirms, the activist confirms in *Plain*, tragically, with that very confusion upon which the country was created, still threatening to foul the air forever.

NOTES TO CHAPTER VI

1. Ken Saro-Wiwa, *Songs in a Time of War*, Port Harcourt:Saros International Publishers, 1985.

2. We shall address the issue of war-propaganda in the next chapter. Since this is an account of a raid on Biafra, it would be a way of chastising observers against believing the lies of victory commonly reported on radio. However, such proclamation of false victories, was also a part of the war-ammunition on the Federal side. Saro-Wiwa's anti-Biafran standpoint may be criticized as a form of obsessive, hardly objective partisanship, a matter to be closely examined in the next chapter.

3. This descriptive talent is somewhat surprising, when one considers the long-winded style of his novels. The poetic style is in total contrast.

4. This idea comes up from time to time in Saro-Wiwa's work.

5. For a long period, the Nigerian government did not talk of a civil war; rather, it was "police action," to discipline an unruly mob and to bring them back to their senses. Of course, the complacency back-fired. Biafra, Nigeria's leaders learnt to their dismay and disgrace, meant business. Any sensible assessment of that tragedy must address the matter of government irresponsibility; a pipe-dream, one daresay, since the post-war attitude has been to pretend that there was no war at all.

6. These references to women's beautiful, shining black skin "like ripe mango," their backside "dey shake like milk," their "fine breast dey stand like hill," and their "plenty s.a." (sex appeal), make me recall L.S. Senghor's famous poem, "Femme noire" (black woman). Saro-Wiwa's portraits of Nigerian women are sometimes condescending and restrictive, as if women are only good for their physical beauty (a criticism also made of Senghor). Feminists would have a hard time accepting these graphic descriptions of the anatomy, and of the sexual act. Note that, in Saro-Wiwa's opinion, making love is nothing to be ashamed of; it is an ecstatic experience, a union of two bodies fit for celebration.

7. *Songs*: 35. A version of this story is included in the children's novel, *Tambari in Dukana*: 31. In the poem, the tortoise explains to the tiger that his laughter and his crying are the same since, in doing both, he shows his teeth. The tiger is angry and turns predatory. In the novel, Totonika tells his friend, Bukana, the story: as the monkey laughs at the leopard's stupidity, Totonika seizes him by the tail.

VII. *ON A DARKLING PLAIN*[1]: A PERSONAL CHRONICLE OF A MEANINGLESS WAR

-The writer's responsibility is to tell the truth as he sees it.
(*Plain*: 13)
-Indigenous colonialism and the blind materialism of international capitalism which prospects for oil in the belly of the delta ring the death knoll of these [minority] peoples."[2]
-Ojukwu is the only one [Nigerian leader] who tried to steal a country! (225)
-A war of solidity (...) There will be victors, of course, but not the sacrificing masses of Biafra or the rest of the nation.
(Wole Soyinka, *The Man Died*: 181)

INTRODUCTION: ONE WRITER'S TRUTH ON THE SKELETONS IN NIGERIA'S UNDERBELLY

As has become usual in a Wiwan text, *On A Darkling Plain* carries an "Author's Note" in its opening pages. This note, we are made to believe, explains the author's position, his perspective, how he tells "the truth" which, he incessantly affirms, is the writer's responsibility. Never one to shy away from controversy, always determined to express his opinion, and as vociferously as possible, Saro-Wiwa's does exactly that here. His emphasis on the "personal experience" immediately leads to caution on the reader's part: Saro-Wiwa's truth may not tally with those of others.

An overview of the "Author's Note" would be useful in critiquing the text. Saro-Wiwa informs us that the bulk of the book was written shortly after the civil war (which ended in 1970), and that he delayed its publication "in deference to the process of reconciliation in Eastern Nigeria." (9) According to him, "reconciliation has ben achieved and the scars of war have largely healed." He believes that, in order to avoid future wars, the civil war "must be fully detailed, analysed and understood. Hence this publication at this time."

Regarding the Ibos, and the war, Saro-Wiwa contends that, up till now, the majority of books on the war have been written by them,[3] thus presenting a skewed viewpoint of the events. That "biafran propaganda"[4] has tried to convince the public that Ibos were the victims. Saro-Wiwa's claims the contrary: Although Ibos were at the centre of the crisis, "the real victims of that war were the Eastern minorities who were in a no-win situation. They are the oppressed in Nigeria." (10) This affirmation is, finally, Saro-Wiwa's major position, particularized in the case of the Ogoni people. In other words, his account of the war is meant to remove the Ibo from the centre, symbolically, and to replace them with the minorities.

Rather apologetically—and, one might say, uncharacteristically—, Saro-Wiwa takes some pain to explain that his generalization on the Ibos does not mean that he holds them "as a group responsible for the cruelties of the war." (10) The Ibos as a group are to be distinguished from "Ibo LEADERS," particularly Ojukwu, whom he accuses "of exploiting Ibo suffering for their private purposes and of destroying the community that was Eastern Nigeria." (10)

Saro-Wiwa also condemns exploitation, deceit and sleight of hand in Nigeria; and expresses the notion that competition between the majority ethnic groups (Hausa-Fulani, Yoruba and Ibo) brought about the civil war. Oppression of the minorities by these "indigenous colonialists" must stop if Nigeria is to survive and progress. Oil is the big bone of contention. Going beyond the period of the civil war, Saro-Wiwa sketches the plight of his Ogoni people, "one of the most destitute in the world," (12) raged and ravaged by ugly international capitalism represented by the Shell-B.P. Addressing this minority issue, so states the author, is the main objective of the book. He believes that his narrative has taken on "the high and mighty in Nigerian society." (13)

This last point is quite interesting; for, it implies, on the writer's part, a certain courage, a certain objectivity, that would set him apart from others. My own objective has been, to assess those qualities as exhibited in *Plain*. Furthermore, I am struck by the writer's attempt to distinguish between the Biafran leadership and the people, and to use this to show his admiration for the Ibos as a people. As a Nigerian, I am also surprised by Saro-Wiwa's statement that reconciliation has been achieved; that there is a three-way, indigenous "majority" collaborative exploitation of Nigerian minorities; and that, once this exploitation is stopped, Nigeria would be able to proudly march along the path of progress.

In analyzing *Plain*, I have seen fit to read another, non-Ibo account of the civil war era, Wole Soyinka's *The Man Died* (London, Penguin, 1972). Soyinka's book, subtitled "prison notes," is an account of his personal experience during the period leading to the civil war, as well as an analysis of Nigeria's socio-political situation. Of most importance is Soyinka's assesment of Colonel Gowon's government, that took over power in July 1966 after the assassination of Ironsi by northern elements avenging the elimination of their revered leader Ahmadu Bello, the Sardauna of Sokoto, in the first coup in January 1966. Soyinka, an avowedly independent mind standing firmly against the Gowon Federal regime's refusal to negotiate with Ojukwu, entrenched in Estern Nigeria with the threat of recession, was arrested at the beginning of the civil war in 1987. His crime was the allegation that he was Ojukwu's accomplice whereas, according to him, he was working for a solution through dialogue. He spent over two years in jail. In *The Man Died* the reader is presented with another perspective—often diametrically opposed to Wiwa's—of the Nigerian dilemma and the players in the murderous and suicidal game. Soyinka's book was published in 1972; it is therefore interesting, to say the least, that Saro-Wiwa's book neither alludes to it, nor pays attention to the clearsighted viewpoints expressed therein. And, maybe, that ought to be so; for, without a doubt, Saro-Wiwa's text is pro-Gowon, pro-North, and pro-Federal government.

Saro-Wiwa is right in stating thus: "Government in Nigeria is an instrument for managing the affairs of the wielders of power." (*Plain*: 135) Where one disagrees with him is in his tendency to make facile and spurious statements on the components of *government* and *the wielders* of power. From the first chapter of his book to the last, this flaw is visible. His artistic talent as humorist, of course, makes the written text very entertaining; unfortunately, facts are often twisted, or tarnished by his own biases (what Nigerians call "hidden agenda"), to keep Nigeria one which as the popular civil-war saying croons, "is a task that must be done." When the first, symbolic event leading to the war occurred, that January 15, 1966 coup when five Majors eliminated some political heavyweights, including the Federal Prime Minister, Tafawa Balewa, his master-mentor, Ahmadu Bello, and their ally, the Western Region Premier, Ladoke Akintola, Saro-Wiwa was a graduate student at Nigeria's premier university, Ibadan. His description of events and people is, as usual, dramatic and full of both light and dark humor. From the "relentless Yoruba woman" in the rickety taxi spitting venom on Akintola with support from the taxi-driver clapping boisterously and thus endangering the passengers' lives in his potentially murderous carrier, (16); to the university students celebrating the coup by carrying a mock coffin; to the local and foreign radio stations' conflicting reports, finally confirmed by Kaduna Radio (17), Saro-Wiwa proudly displays his eye for details and, more significantly, for the deep confusion underpinning Nigeria.

His notions on Nigeria's history, on how the country arrived at the state of confusion, are difficult to support. A few items that the reader might wish to explore: the colonial experience and the programme of the British; the position of the North (the Hausa-Fulani) in the Federal dispensation, before and after the 1960 independence; the rapport between the three majority ethnic groups, Hausa-Fulani/Ibo/Yoruba. In Saro-Wiwa's opinion, the civil war is one more aspect of the struggle, or competition, among the majority groups, for the oil-wealth produced by the minority groups of the delta. He dismisses the popular North-South dichotomy as an attempt to sidetrack the real issue of oppression of the monorities. He sees Ojukwu, the Biafran leader, as an ambitious, pompous idiot ready to sacrifice everyone and everything for his power madness.

Saro-Wiwa fails to give adequate background to the January 1966 coup. He sketches the complicated situation marked by political complots and connivance, but leaves out the fact that Ahmadu Bello ruled Nigeria from his northern throne: It is an open secret that, during negotiations for Nigeria's independence, the man known as the descendant of the mythical superman, Uthman dan Fodio, insisted that independence would be acceptable only on his terms, that is, the central power would belong to the Hausa-Fulani. Bello himself was too proud, too superior, to condescend to go down south (a symbolic descent from his throne on high) to govern personally; hence, he sent his surrogate, Balewa, who became Nigeria's first Prime Minister. In describing the infamous mid-66's impasse in Western Nigeria where the Premier Akintola—formerly Obafemi Awolowo's political lieutenant and finally, and fatally, ally of Balewa—, was declared victor in a rigged election, Saro-Wiwa misses the point about Balewa's powerlessness. "The politician in him [Balewa]," he writes, "overcame the statesman, and Sir Abubakar declared publicly in an interview that nothing was wrong in the West." (24) In actuality, Balewa, as Bello's handmaid with a commitment to continuity of the Hausa-Fulani stranglehold on power, could not, and would not, have done anything to lessen that power, even if, as it occurred, it meant bloodshed.

Saro-Wiwa's comments on the January 1966 coupists is also lacking in insight and evenhandedness. He lists the names of participants that he picked up from the grapevine -Nzeogwu, Ifeajuna, Obienu, Onwuatuegwu, Udeaja- and comments: "It is not surprising that I should have heard only of the boys from Umuahia [his secondary school] or Ibadan University [where he did his undergraduate studies]." (26) Why not surprising? Because, as the whole book shows, Saro-Wiwa believes in the superiority of both institutions and their products and, he shamelessly flouts this feeling in the face of anyone unfortunate enough to have attended other, inferior schools. As for the character of the coup-makers, his soft spot for them is hardly disguised; which, again, is quite interesting in a writer always claiming to be more objective and more perspicacious than others. In one breath, he criticizes Nzeogwu and company for their political shallowness; in another, he showers praises upon them, especially on Nzeogwu, for courage and patriotism.

One point that Saro-Wiwa makes with conviction is, that, contrary to the thinking in certain quarters, the coup was not an Ibo plot (27). However, that did not stop those convinced that it was, from carrying out a counter-coup in July 1966, that eliminated Ironsi, the Ibo Head of State, and Fajuyi, the Yoruba Military Governor of Western Region who was hosting him at Ibadan, the regional capital (36). Saro-Wiwa does not address the well known fact that the July blood-bath was clearly an act of revenge by Northerners. He accepts the fact of *tribalism* in Nigeria (26), but refuses to admit that "the cankerworm" has remained an essential aspect of the country's existence. He writes at length on Ironsi's performance as Head of State—"He was a good man and he did his best under the circumstances." (35) Again: "We must shed a tear for Ironsi, for he was an honest man." (36) He mentions Ironsi's lack of firmness in taking decisions, for example, in dealing with the January 1966 coupists who were in prison. "The choice was indeed an impossible one for the Major-General...Ironsi had to try to satisfy everyone." (29) Now, Saro-Wiwa does not see why Ironsi could not be firmer: His own weakness was exacerbated by the complication of dealing with northern elements. In addition, Saro-Wiwa condemns Ironsi's Unitary System of government (Unification Decree), by which civil servants, employed on merit, replaced politicians who were, naturally, absent from the scene. "Many [civil servants] appeared intoxicated by their new-found power [and] as Ironsi himself proved pliable, the Permanent Secretaries [especially the Ibo ones] moved in on him in one fell swoop. They led Ironsi to the slaughter." (32-3) Thus, Saro-Wiwa indirectly blames Ironsi's assassination on the Ibo civil servants, as well as on Ironsi's malleability. He also downplays the reported massacre of Ibos in the North after the July 1966 coup, thus pouring cold water on the authenticity of Ibo anger and ultimate decision to secede, while positing his own theory of their desire to corner the oil-wealth of the Rivers area.

Soyinka's *The Man Died* gives us a totally different picture, however. He does not see any sign of Ibo domination in the civil service, nor their influence on Ironsi. He addresses the role of Gowon, Chief of Staff in Ironsi's regime, and in charge of investigating the January 1966 coup and giving a report. Soyinka points out Gowon's dubiousness. He delves into the Northerners' refusal to cooperate in implementing a progressive, detribalized policy. He sees the Unification Decree as a bold revolutionary decision. According to him, the decree is, indeed, the first step in detribalizing Nigeria, which Saro-Wiwa also wished to do. Soyinka affirms:

"The unification decree was only one possible beginning among many, and it had the approbation of all except the feudalist monopolies in the North and the status-conscious functionaries of the nation who saw and dreaded the disappearance of grandiose and overpaid civil service positions... Some [voices of dissent] held genuine fears of motivation that were not idealistic, such as Ibo domination. On this atavistic distrust the Mafia of the North were already at work, aided by their Southern allies, many of whom had moved into the North loaded with money for the dirty work at hand. We were not after their vendable territory but after a supposedly different generation of enlightenment." (165-6)

It is that generation, "the new North" (163), that Soyinka and his comrades wanted to work with, in order to create a new Nigeria. To his dismay and disappointment, Soyinka discovered that the line between the old and new North, if at all it existed, was—and remains—blurred, and that only Western Nigeria "remained scrupulously committed to the revolutionary ideals." (177) Where Saro-Wiwa sees Yoruba confusion and collusion, Soyinka sees progressive policy poised for real change for the better, as witnessed by full restitution of the politicians' misdeeds, without compromise. While Saro-Wiwa summarily dismisses the 1966 Northern massacre of Ibos, Soyinka details it in all its gory bestiality, as a "pogrom" (177) choreographed by the Northern Mafia, continued in, and complemented by, the Gowon regime's efforts to build a nation on a successful genocide. Here are some relevant questions unanswered by Saro-Wiwa: if "Ibolization" of government was wrong, was "Hausa-Fulanization" right? Was the government right to seek "free mobility of skill and power" (33)? In the past and present, is it true or false that the North has always preferred expatriate workers to southerners whom they treat at best as inferior foreigners?

Saro-Wiwa states that, in a fashion similar to Ironsi's, Gowon, his successor, also foisted a Unification Decree upon the people in 1970. However, Saro-Wiwa's bone of contention is the centralization of the oil-wealth (34). His statement, "apparently, Gowon could do it, but Ironsi was not allowed to do it!" (34) is left unexplained, as if he does not know why: Ironsi was Ibo; Gowon, the northern Hausa-Fulani oligarchy's representative, was their instrument in holding on to power.

SARO-WIWA'S OJUKWUPHOBIA, AND THE RISE AND FALL OF BIAFRA

Saro-Wiwa chronicles the passing of the baton of power in July 1966, from Ironsi, the assassinated Ibo Head of State, to Gowon, his erstwhile northern Army Chief of Staff, in a conspicuously low-key style. He does mention the element of surprise in Gowon's choice, since there were other officers senior to him; but, in Saro-Wiwa's words, "Yakubu Gowon became more acceptable, *at least in certain quarters*, as a man who had a mission to accomplish, *more so as it appeared to the public that a lot of bargaining had ben done behind the scenes*." (*Plain*: 40, emphasis mine) Saro-Wiwa does not dwell on the identity of those quarters to whom Gowon was acceptable. He does not deem it necessary to comment on the horse-trading. A major error, one would say; for, those very facts and the personalities involved, contributed in no small way to the eventual blood-letting. Saro-Wiwa's oversight is restricted, however: He remembers Ojukwu. His words:

"One man who certainly did not like the emergence of Yakubu Gowon as Head of Stae was Lt-Col. Ojukwu... The pain of the Ibo people, we thought, mattered to him; but his pride was wounded when Gowon who was a young officer now superseded him. It appeared that Ironsi's death might even have been overlooked if Ojukwu had been appointed Head of State after his death. Besides, Ojukwu had not for one moment imagined that Gowon whose intelligence he grievously underrated could ever be his boss." (40)

The amount of speculation here is odd, considering that Saro-Wiwa prides himself in being objective, being sure of his facts, and in not engaging in shallow-mindedness. Did the pain of the Ibo people not matter to Ojukwu? Why, indeed, was Ojukwu overlooked in the choice of Head of State? Was Ojukwu right in underrating Gowon's intelligence, or ability to rule? Saro-Wiwa is satisfied with Gowon's choice, particularly because the latter, in his inaugural broadcast to the country, revokes the Unification Decree which Saro-Wiwa detests. (39) Saro-Wiwa also affirms that Gowon's enthronement unleashed "the process whereby large numbers of Ibos were encouraged to leave their places of work, particularly in Lagos and Western Nigeria, and return home to Eastern Nigeria." (40)

Here, one can accuse the author of bad faith and sleight of hand, because, in 1966, the exodus back to the East was actually most prominent in the North. Saro-Wiwa claims that, yes, indeed, Ibos in the North "either fled or were sent away." He thus implies that the Northerners were considerate, and the Ibos living there, realistic. On the contrary, those living in Lagos were "weak-minded," and the Lagosians and Ibadanians (Yoruba), xenophobic. He reserves the last word of opprobrium for Ojukwu, symbol of secession, quintessence of the egomania that produced Biafra. In Saro-Wiwa's opinion, Ojukwu is the personification of everything that is bad. Even before addressing the Biafra debacle, the author reveals his aversion for the Ibo leader. Commenting on the four regional Military Governors appointed by Ironsi after the January 1966 coup, he says that all the four governors are acceptable to their people in each Region, with Ojukwu having a significant advantage. "Except for Ojukwu who basked in the limelight of his millionaire father's name and his Oxford degree (points which carried extremely well with the Ibos of Eastern Nigeria), the other Governors were little known (...) This probably made them more acceptable. Not being known, there was, surely, very little to object to in them." (29) One need not comment on the shallowness of this statement. One may note, nonetheless, that while Saro-Wiwa's writings underscore the quality of hard work and pour encomium on the struggle of the underprivileged and the impoverished masses, they also flaunt the superiority of certain educational institutions (University of Ibadan, Government College, Umuahia, both Saro-Wiwa's *alma maters*). Maybe, just maybe, he abhorred the acclaimed superiority of the Oxonian experience exemplified by Ojukwu.[5] The reputation and respect infused by wealth and special education were apparently so great that the Ibos became sheep, and Ojukwu, their shepherd whom they followed willingly to the slaughter-house. Throughout the text of *Plain*, hardly do we read of anything positive about this monster of a man, driven by pride and personal ambition. And it all dates back to the Ironsi days: Ojukwu is the antithesis of Gowon, whom Ironsi "trusted." (39) Also before the war account, Saro-Wiwa recounts the release of Obafemi Awolowo, the Yoruba leader imprisoned for treason during Balewa's civilian regime. The event occurs just after Gowon's ascension. Meanwhile, Ojukwu sends Awolowo a telegram claiming that the latter's release was Ironsi's last decision before his assassination. Saro-Wiwa asserts that Ojukwu is a blatant liar, that he has been courting the North by making the Emir of Kano Chancellor of the University of Nigeria, Nsukka. "Credit for the release of Awolowo," writes Saro-Wiwa, "went solidly to Gowon." (41) It is hard to imagine that Gowon himself was not playing politics in the matter.

Saro-Wiwa emphasized Biafran propaganda before and during the civil war, and Ojukwu, we are made to believe, is the choreographer of everything. From the reports of "rampage and carnage [against Ibos in the North] meant to incite feeling against the perpetrators of these acts" (42), to the formation of a Consultative Assembly (79), to Ojukwu's speech proposing to the Assembly a provincial system of government, Saro-Wiwa sees the working of a devious mind, and the development of "petty dictatorship and tribal politics." (59) On the Aburi Conference, held between the Federal and Eastern Nigeria governments in early 1967 as part of the efforts to resolve the country's problems and to avoid secession and the eventual civil war, Saro-Wiwa also sees Ojukwu's evil nature and his desire for "a separate country. He accordingly rejected the Aburi accord." (63) The author fails to tell the public whether Ojukwu is right or wrong in insisting that, at Aburi, agreement was reached to create a confederation, with a loose, weak center and strong, autonomous regions. Members of the Eastern Consultative Assembly are described as "political thugs and touts" (79). On the other hand, their counterparts on the Federal side, called "Leaders of Thought," are not similarly written off, although, in his assessment of the political situation at the time of the first coup (January 1966), Saro-Wiwa condemns the politicians' general thuggery and thievery. Saro-Wiwa continues his lampooning of Ojukwu and the Ibos by commenting on Ojukwu's promotion to the rank of General during the war. "When he had lost enough towns, he finally did promote himself to the rank of General." (80) Meanwhile, no such comment accompanies Gowon's similar rise to the same position in the Federal Army.

One must admit that Ojukwu is, indeed, egomaniacal, immensely ambitious and repulsive. Saro-Wiwa documents these qualities with conviction. For example, in his speech to a national Reconciliation Committee sent to him before the war, Ojukwu beats his chest with pride, with guarantee of victory in war, lacing his words with blatant lies, and the hypocrisy that he is interested in protecting the South against Northern invaders. "I am no longer speaking as an underdog, I am speaking from a position of power," (83) he declares. Here is "the braggart soldier" relying on nothing more than his delusion of grandeur, ready to sacrifice his people for the power that he cherishes with all the madness in his bloated bones. And, the most damning act of all, is Ojukwu's flight to Abidjan when Biafra has been brought to its knees. He claims, not to be running away, but to be going in search of peace. Saro-Wiwa's words, correctly harsh, merit being quoted: "Ojukwu's message to the biafrans (sic), as he fled, must rate as one of the highest exercises in casuistry. ... The captain had fled, like a coward, leaving millions of those he had pressed into war to face that deadly fate which he had assured them would be theirs in the event of their losing the war." (222)

Saro-Wiwa's reference to others' views on Ojukwu is very well used to support his own opinion. According to Wale Ademoyega, one of the January 1966 coupists, Ojukwu "a bigot (...) pretended to be a soldier-statesman." Nnamdi Azikiwe, Nigeria's first, figure-head President, calls him "a confirmed coward." N. U. Akpan, Secretary to Ojukwu's Administration, soundly condemns him as a manipulator of minds, a compulsive liar, a blackmailer, a terrorist, and a murderer. Akpan writes in his book, *The Struggle for Secession* (1971), that in 1968, as the Biafran Army was disintegrating, Ojukwu kept assuring everyone of his commitment to the cause and his determination to fight, if necessary, alone, as a guerilla. "His action drew much respect, admiration and sympathy." (Quoted in *Plain*: 224) Yet, too soon, Ojukwu fled in a plane loaded with his family and friends, and provisions for a life of luxury in exile.

Saro-Wiwa's analysis of Ojukwu as a persuasive actor, is no doubt credible. Nonetheless, the notion that the Biafran leader is all-evil, and that his followers are all-credulous, remains curious, at best. Of the other views to which we have alluded above, let us take the example of Azikiwe, to show that those individuals themselves may have personal reasons for condemning Ojukwu and that their own characters may make one question the genuineness of their position. Azikiwe it was that composed Biafra's national anthem (218). He was with Ojukwu at the Organization of African Unity conference in Addis Ababa, in 1968. Then, suddenly, the old man disappeared. And reappeared, just as suddenly, and strangely, on the Federal side in 1969. Saro-Wiwa pours encomiums on Azikiwe for his "enduring prestige," his "great presence and charisma" (218). Most likely, the author overlooks the negative aspects of the man's demeanor and actions because Azikiwe apoligizes to the Ogoni on a 1969 visit to Port Harcourt; he is "a great man(...) [making] a public apology for wrong (...) This act has set Dr. Azikiwe apart from other Ibo leaders. Nigeria is the better for having had him." (220)

Now, what one cannot comprehend is the unreasonable absoluteness of the Ibos' followership of Ojukwu as related by Saro-Wiwa. Ojukwu, he tells us, is surrounded by "sycophantic intellectuals" (85), and this support is explained by Ojukwu's education. Ojukwu's potent propaganda machine is also able to make any doubting Thomases change their minds. Saro-Wiwa is enraged at the dexterity of the purveyors of Biafran lies as opposed to the ineptness of the Federal side. Hence, when Radio Kaduna, finally, succeeds in "paying the rebels back in their own coin [with] a foul-mouthed, slanderous campaign as virulent as anything the rebels were putting out," Saro-Wiwa is overtly elated: "The efforts of Radio Kaduna deserve comendation. That radio station was a great encouragement to those minorities who had chosen to resist the biafran regime." (92) Propaganda, made of deliberate lies, deceit, lack of dignity, manipulation of everyone and everything for a purpose, all that stands acceptable to Saro-Wiwa, as long as it is being done by the Feds! No wonder his denigratory mien vis-a-vis anyone against the Gowon government, starting with Ojukwu, and the Ibo people.

Saro-Wiwa was employed at Nsukka during the months leading to the civil war. In his opinion, "the co-ordinated schizophrenic activities of the faculty and students" (63) of Nsukka encouraged Ojukwu's decision to reject the Aburi accord. He goes on to contrast the newer university with the older Ibadan. He inadvertently condemns the integrity of the Nsukka founder, Azikiwe, and the institution's propagandist image. "Born with a bang, it maintained that bang in football matches, sports contests and the number of first class degrees it awarded. It challenged staid, old Ibadan." (64) Infiltrated and programmed by Eastern politicians, Nsukka faculty and students easily gave in to the myopia and paranoia emblematic in the Biafran cause. They were easily bamboozled by Ojukwu into the suicidal decision to secede. All possible? Saro-Wiwa, meanwhile, simultaneously describes Ojukwu's efforts to disgrace Azikiwe while wooing other "old politicians." Whoever was pro-Ojukwu becomes victim of Saro-Wiwa's venomous satire. Nsukka intellectuals are "academic prostitutes;" (65) Eni Njoku, a Minister, is "the moon-headed doctor of leaves." On the entire campus of Nsukka, "there was, indeed, little good sense." (66) When secession is declared, Saro-Wiwa decides to leave Nsukka and its war-mongering, senseless intellectuals. His cold-hearted comments: "I sincerely prayed that the University people should see war, should taste of its bitter fruits for their own edification... I was happy to leave Nsukka. I hoped it would receive a deserving baptism by fire. My hopes were not to be disappointed." (93-94) Would this be a sign of cynicism? or inhumanism? or a simple comment on what a senseless people deserve? Anywhere one finds Biafrans, the author describes them with such disdain, that one wonders whether he considers them as human beings at all. There is on those pages an astonishing glee, as Nsukka's befuddled lecturers and students flee (96), as bedraggled soldiers run from Bonny like "beaten dogs, their tails between their legs," (97) pursued by the triumphant Feds.

Saro-Wiwa certainly disagrees with Gowon who, at the end of the civil war in January 1970, magnanimously declared to the whole world, "No victors, no vanquished," and claimed to welcome back the Ibos into the peaceful nation. *Plain* expresses the writer's anger at any such thought. The Ibos, to his mind, deserved what they got, and much more. Saro-Wiwa, we must also recall, avows his high respect for certain Ibo attributes; the problem, however, is that he does not specify those attributes that he recommends to other Nigerian groups. (10) Rather, what one reads is a catalog of their belligerency, intolerance, selfishness, oppression and repression of others, and a superiority complex that is a cover-up for their inadequcies and inferiority. Saro-Wiwa, as he often does in *Plain*, uses the war situation to recount some of the history of Nigerian ethnic relationships, with particular attention being paid to the plight of the minorities. For example, the evolution of Port Harcourt, created in 1913, shows the arrival of Ibo settlers in 1937. The land was bought by the British from the Ikwerres. While the latter spent years trying unsuccessfully to reclaim their land from the government, while they never benefitted from the city's phenomenal development, the Ibos became the major beneficiaries; by 1953, they constituted 80% of the population. In short, unlike other immigrant groups (Ogoni, Ibibio, Edo, Yoruba, Sierra-Leoneans), the Ibo took over control of the land, so much so that, in the 1949 Town Council elections, they won hands down, using their education and wealth. Saro-Wiwa uses this example to affirm the Ibos' cunning: they claim, as Azikiwe once did, that "suffering is the label of our tribe," (176) whereas, it is a persecution complex used to sneak up on other unwary people who end up conceding everything to them. The Ibos have consistently frustrated other Rivers people, not only the Ikwerres. Saro-Wiwa asserts that they infiltrated the Rivers State Movement in the 50's. The Ibo State Union was used as instrument. Under the leadership of Z. C. Obi,[6] a Port Harcourt-based merchant, the Union claimed that Rivers was "part of Ibo land," (178) and that, even if a new state would be created, Port Harcourt, "predominantly Ibo," must not be part of it, since "the area was developed by the Ibos and the land owned by them now." (181) In short, Saro-Wiwa considers the Ibo inhabitants as colonizers of the Rivers people. When the Union, along with others of its ilk, was banned by the Gowon regime in 1968, the designs in Port Harcourt fell upon Ojukwu, who was absolutely uninterested in constitutional means and who did not even express himself in 'rotten' English." (186) Of course, Saro-Wiwa has already sneared at the dictator's Oxon English.

The Biafran temporary take-over of the Mid-West region is another example of Saro-Wiwa's refusal to concede anything to the Ibos. Historians of the civil war would remember that short period in 1967 when the Biafrans overran the Mid-West, succeeded in bombing Lagos, and threatened to bring the capital to its knees. That probably aroused the merry-making military leaders from their booze-and-bed induced hangovers. For once, they realized that a war was going on, not some "police action" that they had proclaimed against some defiant underlings. The perspective in *Plain* is biased and speculative, all in an attempt to denigrate the Biafran achievement. First, the author says that their victory was facilitated by the affinity of their kin in the region; second, he blames the neutrality of the region's governor, David Ejoor, who was betrayed by his senior Ibo officers, shameless collaborators with Biafra. Reference to reports supposedly heard on "the rebel [Biafran] radio," thickens the plot further. The radio painted "pictures of gallant biafrans swooping down on merry-making Yoruba soldiers caught as they slaughtered and ate cattle and drank themselves into *delirium tremens*. This stereotype of the Yoruba as pleasure-loving and cowardly had always been assiduously propagated by the Ibo elite.(...) It did not matter to them that the leader of the so-called "liberation forces" that had successfully overrun the Mid-West was Victor Banjo, a Yoruba." (105)

Apparently, we are expected to give kudos to Saro-Wiwa for his own objectivity and ethnic tolerance in the face of Ibo Yorubaphobia. The only problem is, that he never mentions the Yorubas' courage. In fact, a section of this chapter will prove beyond doubt that he either agrees with the very stereotypes ostensibly reported by Biafra radio, or thinks that the Yoruba are almost as repulsive as the Ibos, for other reasons...With regards to Victor Banjo, Saro-Wiwa fails to understand that the Yoruba man was the epitome of the nationalism which he, Saro-Wiwa, might wish to emulate, that is, a de-tribalized state of mind, a political philoshopy rooted in the people and committed to ameliorating their destiny together, not for the good of any one group. Soyinka's *The Man Died* (174-180) depicts Banjo in that light. To uderstand why Banjo, and Nzeogwu, and the renowned poet, Christopher Okigbo, fought and died on the Biafran side, one must read the Nobel Laureate's analysis, not Saro-Wiwa's prejudiced, particularized piece. Contrary to Saro-Wiwa, Banjo believed that, during those dark days of 1966, the Ibos were victims, not vandals; that the Federal regime, in its refusal to face the facts of Hausa-Fulani domination and the rising process of elimination of others, was entrenching genocide and tribal chauvinism and acting as potent arm of a profit-motivated massacre. Banjo understood why Biafra seceded, beyond the personal ambition of Ojukwu, a born reactionary. "In fairness to him [Ojukwu]," said Banjo to Soyinka, "I would say that there was little else he could have done. I saw the demonstrations. If he hadn't given in he would have been physically toppled." (*The Man Died*: 178) And Banjo's prophesy of the outcome of the war has come to pass, thus showing up the limited vision of Saro-Wiwa. Banjo affirmed: "The nation is not faced even with a choice of two evils [Gowon and Ojukwu]. Whichever way this sort of war goes, the only results will be the entrenchment of the worst of both evils(...) How do we get rid of the alliance of the capitalist adventurer and a bourgeois military after the war?" (179-180)

Saro-Wiwa's main interest in Banjo is, to show how the mad terrorist, Ojukwu, desperate to maintain power when the Feds were running over his army, cooked up stories of sabotage against Banjo, Ifeajuna and others, and had them killed. Without mentioning Soyinka, Saro-Wiwa lambasts "starry-eyed intellectuals in the West" (106) for supporting Ojukwu. Besides, he seems to forget too quickly his own statements, such as the following on the Yorubas: "As the noise of war threatened to disturb the peace, merry-making as well as the economy of the Yoruba, the Government of Western Nigeria suddenly took note of the gravity of the situation." (*Plain*: 106) Perhaps he was influenced by the rebel radio, after all!

Saro-Wiwa calls Ejoor, the Mid-West governor at the time of the Biafran take-over, "one of the best Nigerian military officers" (73) It is the same Ejoor who attained fame for, according to his truly riveting story of extraordinary will to survive, rode a bicycle out of the capital for well over a hundred miles to the safety of Lagos. In a show of humaneness and forgiveness, the author makes light of Ejoor's cowardice as a normal, Nigerian coincidence. He even praises the man for riding off "on a lowly, cranky bicycle," as opposed to other Nigerian rulers "riding in noisy, pompous, arrogant motorcades." Then, finally, without pulling punches, Saro-Wiwa reveals his real reason for exonerating Ejoor: Ejoor is a hero who played a key role in preserving Nigerian unity "by spearheading minority loyalties to the nation when the major ethnic groups were busy looking for ways to destroy her." He also rebukes "those who have heckled [Ejoor] as much because he is a minority man as because they desire to kick a great man who has fallen." (74) In Saro-Wiwa's estimation, whoever is for the Feds is a great man; whoever is against them is a goat; whoever goes as far as being on the Biafran side, is deserving of what he gets: genocide.

The author cannot understand why intelligent men, such as Nzeogwu, the coupist, could ever have fought for Biafra. He simply states his conviction that Nzeogwu "had not supported rebellion." (102) More importantly, he chronicles Gowon's act of patriotism for ordering that Nzeogwu, mowed down by Federal troops, be buried with full military honors at Kaduna, his northern birth-place. We are supposed to forget that Gowon had a far better chance at patriotism when, after the January 1966 coup, he was given the responsibility of investigating Nzeogwu's action and exonerating him by helping to put Nigeria on the road to true nationalism.

The life and death of the poet, Christopher Okigbo is given some space in *Plain*, but not because he fought and died valiantly as a commissioned Biafran officer. Saro-Wiwa laments the loss and expresses the opinion that Okigbo, an Old Boy of Umuahia -"a common background... at once binding and absolute" (123)- would have done best to write poems about Biafra. The author recounts his pre-war meeting with Okigbo and their discussion of Saro-Wiwa's play manuscript submitted to Okigbo's and Chinua Achebe's Citadel Press. He recalls Okigbo's comment, "that most of the best works of art emanating from Nigeria came mostly from the East, as he put it. It was a matter of pride, he felt." (124) Interesting remark, to say the least. We shall never know Saro-Wiwa's reaction; we do read, however, of his criticism of the Ibos' knack for thinking they are the best.[7]

It remains astonishing that Ojukwu waited until Saro-Wiwa's death before commenting on the unmitigated vilifications of both *Plain* and the Jebsian novels. The ex-Biafran's own *Wiwaphobia* strikes hard in a 1996 interview: "Saro-Wiwa deserved to die for allegedly betraying the Biafran cause." He accuses the Ogoni leader of "always biting the fingers that fed him (...) We gave him a position in Biafra and he subverted the country." (*Tempo*, Feb. 9, 1996: 16) Ojukwu thus remains the blatant liar with the bloated ego. What he shares with the departed Saro-Wiwa is that affinity for Nigeria's self-perpetuating masters, a privilege that permitted a shameless villain, having fled from a struggle for which he boastly vowed to sacrifice his life, to return home a hero. As if nothing had happened. As if millions of lives had not been wasted. As if Nigeria had not been set back many years by forces prepared to kill off everyone, just so that they may remain as supreme oppressors. The irony would nauseate any reasoning mind; for, while Ojukwu is basking in the sullied, midnight sun of the new, retrogressive Nigeria, Saro-Wiwa, the one that vehemently and relentlessly condemned Ojukwu's crazy quest, the one that stood firmly with the Feds, met his death at the hands of the same -for him, former- friends.

THE NIGERIAN MILITARY, AND
THE ISSUE OF HAUSA- FULANI DOMINATION

Saro-Wiwa's civil war account is based upon the premise that the notion of a North-South division in Nigeria, is nothing more than a figment of some shallow people's imagination, or, at most, a myth used by some devious indiviuals to hoodwink the people. Whether fact or fiction, this idea has remained very contentious since the country's birth and, Saro-Wiwa's forceful assertions notwithstanding, the issue must be addressed before one can begin to talk of a truly free and progressive Nigeria. A close look at Saro-Wiwa's work lends support to this statement; for, he himself unwittingly mentions the presence of certain privileges enjoyed by certain personalities whose right to such derive from nothing more than their ethnic affiliation and place of origin: Hausa-Fulani from the North. The belief is spread across the length and breadth of the country. It is so strong that many people lie about their place of birth and religious belief. (cf. Chapter III, the character of Chief Biga, the Nigerian Security Head, known at first as Hausa and moslem, only to be later unmasked as an Ishan, a minority, and Christian).

Before further analyzing this controversial perception as expressed in *Plain*, let us point out other views. For example, Gani Fawehinmi, a very popular and progressive Nigerian attorney who represented Saro-Wiwa at his final trial,[8] has stated in an interview: "When you see the attitude of some of the northerners, you will see this North-South problem really is the making of the military. The masses are not tribalistic." (*TELL*, Dec. 9, 1996: 14) Fawehinmi is commenting upon his recent experience as a detainee in the North where the controller of prisons instructed his deputy to provide an electric bulb in Fawehinmi's cell. Could one generalize such individual actions? Would they represent the masses' viewpoint?[9]

On the opposite side stands that other group, the self appointed owners of the land, the Northern leaders, claiming divine power. At a book-launch in 1993, and in the presence of then Military President Babangida, a one-time Minister and Permanent Representation to the United Nations, Maitama Sule, declared to his besotted audience: "Everyone has a gift from God. The Northerners are endowed by God and have leadership qualities. The Yoruba man knows how to earn a living and has diplomatic qualities. The Igbos are gifted in commerce, trade and technological innovation. God so created us individually for a purpose and with different gifts. Others are created as kings, servants, teachers, students, doctors, etc." (*The News*, July 29, 1996: 6) So, some are born to lead; others, to follow. The magnificent Sule goes further to explain the military supremacy (note: not on the battlefield, but in snatching and securing political power) of the North. He praises the foresightedness of the omnipotent first Premier of the North and scion of the Dan Fodio royal-house, Ahmadu Bello. Sule states that, after the first Iraqi coup that caused the death of the Prime Minister, whose body was tied to a vehicle and dragged round Baghdad, Bello reasoned that "we [contain] this type of development now by fixing our boys in the military (..) But for his foresight, our situation would have been worse (...) Today, we are reaping the fruits of that foresight." (*TELL*, July 15, 1996: 11) The fruits are, of course, military and political power, and a stranglehold on the country's destiny.

According to Saro-Wiwa, the most viable dichotomy in Nigeria is that between *the majority* and *the minority*, this thesis is aggressively advanced throughout *Plain*. The majority consists of the three main "tribes," Hausa-Fulani, Ibo, and Yoruba; the minority, all the others, particularly, the groups whose soil has been blessed with oil, the beautiful black gold that has made monsters of men in their desire to make millions, and become billionaires on the backs of the helpless rightful owners of the oil. The intra-majority collusion and competition, we are told, began since Independence: Azikiwe (Ibo), Awolowo (Yoruba), and Bello (Hausa-Fulani), "by their actions, gave the impression that Nigeria consisted of three ethnic groups instead of three hundred or thereabouts. Indeed, for Ahmadu Bello, Nigria was 'North' versus 'South'—a very erroneous concept, *as we shall soon see*." (21, emphasis mine) The unfortunate fact, unknown to Saro-Wiwa or, perhaps, known to him but unacceptable—therefore deemed untenable—, is, that Bello's view was, and remains, respected, widespread, real. For, as SaroWiwa himself admits, the man was a god among his people and, pitted against the two other so-called national leaders, he won the psychological and political war of independence. From that analysis, we never see the error in Bello's concept; on the contrary, events in Nigeria have proven his power. Saro-Wiwa often confuses issues; he mixes ethnic groups with regions. With regards to the political parties, he overlooks the fact that, if the Northern People's Congress (NPC) could be called essentially Hausa-Fulani, and the Action Group (AG), Yoruba, the National Council of Nigerian Citizens (NCNC) was not Ibo, because, it enjoyed strong Yoruba support.[10] Saro-Wiwa overlooks Nigeria's pre-independence which made provision for Bello's surrogate, Balewa, to go down South as Prime Minister. On the other hand, he describes with his usual humor, the independence day celebrations, to underscore the myth that "those who were once our masters are now our servants; [that] we are ruling ourselves now [and] the white men have gone home." (20) At Lagos, the capital, the Queen's colonial representative made a glorious speech, while Balewa was speechless. Saro-Wiwa contrasts the dull atmosphere of that day in 1960 to the buoyant, brilliant occasion of Ghana's freedom in 1957. He hits the nail on the head when he asserts that "Nigeria was a boiling cauldron;" but he misses the point by not realizing that the contending contents of the cauldron were not *majority* and *minority* groups, but the Northern oligarchy, versus the others who, in order to snatch a piece of "the national cake," metamorphosed into all sorts of strange shapes, sizes and symbols to suit the former's particular needs and desires.

Saro-Wiwa justifiably condemns the politicians' prostitute mentality: their lack of principle; their singular opportunism and craze for power and money, all of which led to weird political mergers. There, no doubt, lies the root of the corruption that has come to characterize Nigerian society. If he were as objective as he claims, Saro-Wiwa would address the role of minority politicians in this evolution towards the depths of venality, vanity, and bared-faced robbery. He does not. After establishing the notion of majority competition over the national booty, he tries to see everything in that light. As a graduate student at Ibadan University in 1966, he watched as the Ibo and Yoruba struggle for space. He claims that there were, in that university, "students and lecturers from all parts of the country." (34) One would like to know how many Hausa-Fulani there were; most likely, very few, just as Saro-Wiwa admits that, from his Ogoni area, there were very few college educated people. Once again, he keeps silent on a major fact, that the question of Western education—specifically, the lack of it among the Hausa-Fulani, traditionally uninterested in that training essential for development in the modern world—has contributed to the national problem: how and why should those without the training corner the reins of power and refuse to let go? If one can talk of nationalism in Saro-Wiwa's book, it can only be that emanating from his love for the Northerners, and the Military. At every turn, he presents us with a heroic Northern leader or military officer. Simultaneously, he praises minority leaders, and his school-mates from Umuahia. Exceptions to that rule include Awolowo, for his early statement and support for the minorities, and Azikiwe, for being the only Ibo leader to apologize to the Rivers people as the civil war drew to a close.

Balewa, Nigeria's first Prime Minister, is eulogized as "the Golden Voice of the North,"[11] a good man forced into evil by Bello. We are not told whether Balewa was a nationalist, or not; his "goodness" did not save him from the guns of the coupists.

With regard to the Military, Saro-Wiwa sets out by stating a fact known to everyone in the independence generation, that only the failures in the classroom and the uneducated chose the uniform. It would have been useful if he had gone ahead to identify the ethnic affiliations of the uniformed men. Would his failure to do so be construed as a sign of detribalization? Hardly; for, he is quick to complain about the absence of Ogoni in the army, even in the Biafran army which, in his opinion, deliberately refused to enlist his people. An incontrovertible fact is that, in 1966, most Northerners (largely Middle-Belt minorities), were in the rank and file, while the majority of the officers were Yoruba and Ibo (Southerners). After the coups leading to civil war, the officer-equation began to be balanced; Gowon, a Northerner, became Head of State. Since then, the position has remained there, in the hands of those "chosen few," whether clad in uniform or mufti, with the exception of Obasanjo, Yoruba, who reluctantly took over the post after Murtala Muhammed's assassination. Before anyone proclaims that as a real change, let it be known that Obasanjo was decidedly detribalized. Besides, his second-in-command, Yar'Adua, Hausa-Fulani, proudly noted that *they*—that is, he and his ethnic group—guided Obasanjo.

We have already seen how Saro-Wiwa downplays the massacre of Ibo in the North, a major prelude to the war. On the contrary, he discusses at length the harassment of Hausa in Iboland. Now, one may understand this action as the author's desire to be objective, to describe only those event that he witnessed. Such a position would only be partial, at best; for, Saro-Wiwa was not witness to all the events in his book; furthermore, the twenty-year period between the writing of the first draft and the final text's publication, gave him a rare opportunity to research his subject and change his position, accordingly. Which he does, on certain matters, but not on the subject of the North and the Military. The list of Federal military heroes is endless. Firstly, the non-Hausa: Alani Akinrinade, Yoruba, "Young, handsome colonel" (157) who liberated Bonny from the Biafrans; Beorge Amunguta, from Rivers, "that very fine man" killed at Bonny; Akindiji, Yoruba Major and medical doctor, an Ibadan alumnus; Benjamin Adekunle, the "brilliant officer" with tremendous success in the war, reputedly a terrifying personality but, in reality, a compassionate man whose *minority* pedigree (his mother was from Gongola State and he is married to a Rivers woman) is well documented by Saro-Wiwa; Olusegun Obasanjo, another Yoruba, Adekunle's replacement in the Rivers command, highly intelligent, cool and calculating, a reader of Saro-Wiwa's poems and, later his family-friend.

Secondly, the Hausa-Fulani: Major Hamman, "a tall, elegant and handsome officer, well-groomed, (...) Whose young wife (of Ibibio extraction)" (212) Saro-Wiwa knew; Murtala Muhammed, "one of the firebrands of the Nigerian Army and a leading hawk," (107) who would later become Head of State after the coup that toppled the sit-tight Gowon in 1975. Sanni Bello, another brilliant officer much loved by Saro-Wiwa, Ironsi's Aide-de-Camp who proudly asserts that he saved several Ibo officers after Ironsi's death, and a brave man getting into battle with a smile on his face; Major Abubakar, Adekunle's Public Relations man, a cool cat, unruffled by the shooting and bombing around him, going on with his duty calmly (138).

All those brilliant officers had "crack troops" (101) at their command. Where the author complains of the latter's indecent behavior towards the civilian community, he explains it as the result of their illiteracy. He prides himself in having ameliorated the relationship between the military and civilians during his tenure as Administrator of Bonny. Interesting, all the same, that he consistently condemns Biafran soldiers for raping women and girls, while readily forgiving the Feds for committing similar acts of bestiality.[12] Biafran officers are symbols of selfish ambition. Witness the example of Captain Ejiofor, a trained engineer and Saro-Wiwa's friend of sorts, based in Kone, Rivers area. He tells the writer that he joined the army because, afterwards, he would not be forgotten; he would certainly qualify for the diplomatic service, "particularly in important centres such as Paris and London." (116) His confession reminds Saro-Wiwa of the ambition behind the war-mongering of his Nsukka colleagues. The Federal military? They must have been great patriots, fighting to keep Nigeria one. Yet, the reality is, that those very patriots became the new political class, as members of succeeding regimes, as ministers and managers, and directors in the persistent dictatorship that sent Saro-Wiwa to his untimely death.

His assessment of Gowon, Head of State, is marked by the ill-conceived admiration for the Military. Gowon it was who appointed him Administrator for Bonny at age twenty-six (1967-68) and, upon the creation of Rivers State by Gowon's regime, Saro-Wiwa, now a State Commissioner (1969), was proud to welcome the Head of State to Port Harcourt. "Gowon's high spirit was infectious... I noted in my diary later that day, the idea of One Nigeria is right in his marrows. One could not but be impressed." (208) On the whole, Saro-Wiwa does not hide his joy at having been close to all those military men, to note "the dedication (...) to their profession and to the cause for which they were fighting (...) There was order and there was disciplinec but above all, there was that carelessness of danger which I admired." And he confesses: "My assessment of them as individuals and as a group has possibly coloured my indulgent attitude toward military rule in Nigeria." (209)

That may be why he does not see anything wrong in Gowon's return home as hero and professor after his ouster, and stint in Britain where he obtained a doctorate in political science. Why he blames Lagosians for their nonchalance and merry-making during the war, whereas the merriment was masterminded by the military leaders. Why he did not look forward to the ruturn to civilian rule in 1979. An additional reason: Saro-Wiwa feared that the civilians would return to the old, three-majority-group politics, as if, even in military times, the minorities were not being exploited, in the name of a nationalism representing the interests of the North. For example, Saro-Wiwa writes at length on the new capital, Abuja, created and cultivated with the billions from oil-resources. Yet, Abuja *is* in the North, notwithstanding the hot air regarding its geographical centrality. Since its creation, a Northerner has always been its Administrator, a mosque is part of the presidential complex of Aso Rock, (but no chapel!), and successive regimes have continued to build it up while simultaneously beating down Lagos.

SARO-WIWA AND THE YORUBA

In Nigeria's peculiar political equations, Lagos remains the most "national" city, in every aspect other than the geographical. Interestingly enough, Saro-Wiwa does not think of this in his largely negative comments on the Yoruba as one of the majority groups (read: exploiters of the minorities). The fact is, were the Yoruba as parochial and close-minded as their critics would have the world believe, Lagos would not be the cosmopolitian, open-to-all-comers' centre that it is. The saying, *Eko gbole, o gbole* (Lagos welcomes and harbors all sorts, including the lazy- bones, the lascivious, and the leeches, the prostitutes, the pimps and the pranksters), covers the field: Symptomatic of the Yoruba hosts, the city has become a true capital of a Federation, allowing everyone to prosper, which is contrary to the actions and attitudes of the Hausa-Fulani masters.

The major criticism of Saro-Wiwa's views on the Yoruba, is this inconsistency resulting from his obsession with the notion of the majority oppressing his minority people. Often, therefore, he simply tells one part of the story, or contemplates the picture from one angle. He depicts Ladoke Akintola, the Yoruba Premier of Western Nigeria at the time of the 1966 coup, as Prime Minister Balewa's "crony and new-found political ally." (*Plain*: 16) He also recounts the 1964 political situation in the West, when Awolowo was in prison, convicted of treasonable felony. "Akintola appeared to Awolowo's Yoruba followers as a traitor who had sought to subject Yorubaland to the Hausa Fulani rulers of the 'North' *who happened to be ruling Nigeria at that time*. Antecedents were found in history where a certain Yoruba chieftain had led his people into subjection to the Fulani." (22, emphasis mine) First, Saro-Wiwa eschews the fact that Awolowo's followers were not only Yoruba; they included among others, the Ishan, Tony Enahoro, and the Ibo, S. G. Ikoku. Second, the Hausa-Fulani's rule over Nigeria was not, is not, accidental; it was, from the very beginning, well planned and executed, with a view to maintaining its continuity by all means necessary. Third, the antecedent of the Ilorin chieftain, Afonja, remains one of the disgraceful episodes of Yoruba history; till date, the Yoruba Afonja royal house has been prevented from ascending to the Ilorin throne grabbed and held firmly in the grips of the Fulani descendants. The scenario is similar to that of the Military pretending to fulfill the messianic role of sanitizing society before returning to the barracks, only to entrench itself in the political arena, proclaiming itself the only patriots.

The question that Saro-Wiwa has not addressed is, whether Akintola tried to subject the Yoruba to the Hausa-Fulani. Many a citizen and critic would reply in the affirmative. The author's obsession with the majority-minority theory, is again played out in his belief in the Akintola's desire to have the Yoruba share in the national cake, as opposed to Awolowo's refusal to collaborate with the Hausa-Fulani and

Ibo. To some extent, that was true; however, the overriding reason is, Awolowo's insistence on his own supremacy within their political party, the Action Group, as well as his presidential ambition. Furthermore, Saro-Wiwa himself has affirmed, that Awolowo's qualities far exceeded those of Akintola or any other Nigerian leader. That makes for the tragedy of a country being misruled, raped and ravaged by incompetent leaders who succeeded in preventing the best of them all, Awolowo, from ever attaining power. In *Plain*'s final chapter, "Darkness Drops Again," Saro-Wiwa comments on the 1979 Obasanjo-regime crafted return to civil rule, the 1979-83 Shagari government of "the First Republic," and the same government's short-lived 1983 "Second Republic." He keeps silent about the well known manipulations and machinations to keep power out of Awolowo's reach, basically because the man was Yoruba, and not in the same league as his rivals.

When it is convenient for him, Saro-Wiwa showers praises upon "the sophisticated and highly cultured Yorubas." (22) On such occasions, he uses their qualities to pour opprobrium upon the Ibo who claim to be the best in everything. The author does not seem to perceive the strangeness of a situation where a group with "trained manpower unrivalled in any part of black Africa [and] quite capable of standing as a nation," (77) remains underlings of others. If he had recognized the Yoruba open-mindedness and their desire, despite the many odds against them, to help forge unity out of ever-menacing disunity, Saro-Wiwa would not have criticized what he calls their confusion. He even blames "the professional criers" among them, who, bemoaning the suspected demise of the Federation in 1966, sent a delegation to Enugu to make peace proposals to Ojukwu. For daring to hold out an olive-branch to the devilish Ojukwu, Awolowo and his delegation are described as unqualified stooges.

In the annals of the civil-war history, Awolowo's statement during that period of uncertainty, when negotiations were being done to try to avoid the impending doom, will always remain controversial. Saro-Wiwa quotes Awolowo: "If the Eastern Region is allowed by acts of ommission or commission to secede from or out of Nigeria, then the Western Region and Lagos must also stay out of the Federation." (79) Saro-Wiwa blandly asserts that the Ibo leadership's interpretation was, that the West would also go if the East seceded. He also mentions "the erratic parts of Awolowo's speech wherein he called for a peaceful solution to the problem and trenchantly opposed any war against the rest by the 'North.'" The author fails to give the reader his own interpretation of Awolowo's statement. Because he stands opposed to the Ibo cause, he papers over the issue of the West's possible secession, and the reality of the war as primarily a Northern campaign against the self-proclaimed Biafra. Saro-Wiwa expresses his zealous welcome at the advice to Head of State Gowon by the Northern Leaders of Thought, to suspend the ongoing Constitutional talks and to retain Northern soldiers stationed in the West and the departure of whom the Yoruba had demanded. (78) In short, Saro-Wiwa, at that auspicious period, was convinced that Gowon must deal with Ojukwu. Gowon followed the wise men's advice; the West was kept under siege, while action was begun against Biafra. It is noteworthy that, by failing to follow through with the threat in that fateful speech, Awolowo pawned off the Yoruba right to relevance in determining Nigeria's destiny. Awolowo died without ever realizing his presidential dream and, depending upon the observer's identity, he is remembered as either a patriot committed to keeping Nigeria one, or an over-ambitious individualist sacrificing his people's freedom for his lust for power.

Saro-Wiwa states that Awolowo, released by Gowon in 1966 after Ironsi's assassination, "appeared to owe loyalty" (77) to Gowon and the Army. To the Yoruba observer, that loyalty was a fact, beyond all doubt. And, after Gowon had used him up and failed to give up power, Awolowo resigned his ministerial appointment, some have said, in anger and disappointment. Saro-Wiwa pays little attention to this political marriage of convenience, precipitated both by Awolowo's patriotism and ambition, and Gowon's desire to use the man and his Yoruba people to keep Nigeria together under northern rulership. Saro-Wiwa is correct: "Without the West, the task would be difficult, if not absolutely impossible." (77) The author's favorable opinion of Gowon, particularly during the war, blinds him to much critical perspective. Hence, he gives a rave-review of the administration's actions. He is very pleased with the division of the country into twelve states, after Ojukwu's announcement of Biafran secession in May 1967. He is especially grateful that Gowon created Rivers State for the Eastern minorities. "For us who were protagonists of the creation of states (...), this proved too good to be true." (81) While Gowon is showered with praises, the Yoruba are blamed for their "factionalism," (53 not acknowledged for earlier cooperation in the creation of the Mid-West which, to all intents and purposes, was done to reduce the West's potency.

The Yoruba may derive consolation from Saro-Wiwa's consideration of their leader, Awolowo, as "probably the best political thinker Nigeria has ever produced." (27) Not surprisingly, the philosophy for which the author remembers Awolowo, has to do with minority rights.

THE MINORITY MATTER

Saro-Wiwa quotes copiously from Awolowo's 1947 book, *Path To Nigerian Freedom*,[13] with regard to each minority group's right to the same treatment as other, larger groups and an opportunity to evolve its own peculiar political institution. Understandably, that book became and remained Saro-Wiwa's bible. To propagate his anti-majority standpoint, Saro-Wiwa also quotes from the book's foreword penned by the Briton, Margery Perham. In her opinion, the hope for a nation lies in the possibility that the threee main groups would "come together at the centre to pool and share their traditions and resources," (in *Plain*: 51) thereby making Nigeria a leading power in Africa. Contrary to Perham's expectation, and to Saro-Wiwa's chagrin, the three pawns in the power puzzle quickly transmuted into monsters muscling the minnows and milking their abundant wealth for themselves. Saro-Wiwa deliberately turns history on its head; for, he forgets that, long before oil was discovered in those minority areas, Nigeria had other natural resources, much of which lay, not in the earth of the latter-day producers of black gold, but in the fertile lands of the majority, such as the Yoruba. The inference of the Perham statement is, that Nigeria might never achieve nationhood, a problem more vital, of far larger dimensions that that of the lot of the minority groups.

The more one reads of Saro-Wiwa's increasingly exclusivist views on the minority matter, the less convinced one becomes of the authenticity of his avowed commitment to a unified Nigeria. To my mind, the idea of Biafran secession was anathema to Saro-Wiwa, not out of a desire not to let the country "go to the dogs" (*Plain*: 39), but precisely because he suspected and abhorred the Ibo plan to monopolise the minorities' oil. On the matter of nationalism, there is also ample proof that the author's interest was Ogoni; Nigeria would serve only as means to that end.[14] Whoever makes the mistake of calling Saro-Wiwa an Ibo is lashed with his poisonous pen, as is the case with "a friend from [their] Ibadan days, Goke," who admits to having thought that Saro-Wiwa was Ibo:

"Enlightenment had taken a long time to come to Goke. How many other people still wallow in the darkness of over-simplification!" (147) He then claims that, if due recognition had been given to all ethnic groups, jobs would have been shared more equitably, and "the Ibos would not have been so preponderant in the foreign service as to present a diplomatic threat to the nation." Unfortunately, this line of reasoning is no less mired in the darkness of over-simplification than the ignorance of his friend. In fact, it might be worse, marked as it is by naive equation-balancing devoid of the real impact of particular conditions and qualifications. For instance, how does one explain the preponderance of ill-prepared, incompetent Hausa-Fulani in positions of power? Moreover, if and since Saro-Wiwa's ethnic group has not produced many trained people, how could they cover their allotted quota in a Nigeria meant to be a leading light in Africa? And what about the issue of their effective numerical strength?

Upon reading *Plain*, one is convinced of Saro-Wiwa's, and others', commitment to the Rivers minority cause. He traces the history of political awareness among the various groups. He writes passionately of his involvement in the process for the creation of Rivers State in 1967, through the Leaders of Thought Conference (47). Ijaws, Ikwerre, Etche, Abua, Odual, Etepeye, Engenni, Ogba, and Ogoni, all Rivers minorities, have been marginalized since the colonial period, and subjugated to the immigrant Ibo population. Saro-Wiwa asserts that, since the 40's, Ijaws for example, have been displeased with the provincial configuration that discountenanced the treaty signed with the British, guaranteeing Ijaw sovereignty. Rivers Province was created in 1947, but it lost its power upon the creation of Eastern Region in 1951. As a result of the Rivers' fear of political and economic domination by the Ibo, the people regularly voted against the Ibo Party, the NCNC, and for the Yoruba, pro-new states party, the Action Group.

Saro-Wiwa came to the forefront of the Rivers struggle in the civil-war years. He takes pride in the creation of Rivers State against the will of the Ibo in the East. In relating all this story, the author again reveals his bias for the North: He fails to see through the manipulative actions and attitudes of the Northern delegation to the infamous Ad-Hoc Conference set up by Gowon. He describes with flourish the Northerners' pleasure at finding that there was no unanimity in the East; he accuses the Ibo of being colonialists; he calls the minority members of the Eastern delegation "stooges and quislings" (55); yet he hardly sees anything wrong with the Northern configuration where, the aspirations of the Middle-Belt groups notwithstanding, Hausa-Fulani hegemony remained fiercely in control. He does not adequately analyze the events leading to the civil war, preferring to target only Ibo colonialistic tendencies, and not Gowon and the Northerners' even worse plans for dominating the whole country. The 1966 constitutional Conference showed categorically that everyone saw the solution in a loose center, a confederal system with each region having a large degree of autonomy. Gowon's decision to adjourn the deliberations remained without a clear and convincing explanation. Saro-Wiwa and other minority federalists were elated, because they felt that a confederation would mean their continued domination by the Ibo. Now, the question is, was Saro-Wiwa's federalist standpoint out of love for Nigeria? One would say, no; rather, it was out of fear of Ibo domination. In all his activities during and after the war, it is this fear, transformed into a firm Ogonism, that pushed Saro-Wiwa forward, from Nsukka to his home base, Bori, to Lagos, back East to Bonny where he served as the island's Administrator (1968) and, finally, to Port Harcourt where he became a member of the new Rivers State Executive Council (1969-1973).

Plain presents the reader with carefully documented facts of Rivers minorities' sufferings and underdevelopment, which tacitly explain Saro-Wiwa's ultimate commitment to the Ogoni struggle. (43-46) His ascendancy, from the early days as leader of the "One Nigeria Emergency Committee" (188), to his commissionership in the State cabinet, is phenomenal. As Bonny Administrator at age twenty-six, he must remain one of the youngest ever to hold such a position of authority. His achievements in education (re-opening schools and inculcating in parents and children the importance of education) and social services, as well as his efforts to eradicate corruption, are praiseworthy.

A 1957 episode at his Umuahia high school, when, after an election, the cooks and stewards called his people stupid for voting against the Ibo party (44), aroused the spirit of Ogoni nationalism in Saro-Wiwa. He spent months after that wondering: "perhaps Ogoni people were actually stupid?... I am afraid that the incident in the dining hall at Umuahia made me rather conscious of the problems of the Ogoni people." (45) Until his death, he was to prove over and over again that his people were not stupid. This obsessive "nationalism" pervades the pages of *Plain*. A certain confusion, too, between Nigerian unity and ethnic consciousness: quite often, the author mistakes his desire for Ogoni recognition as love for Nigeria. His stock would probably have risen much higher among the populace if he had fought for all minorities, not just Ogoni. As it is, Saro-Wiwa ended up expressing dissatisfaction with Rivers State, where the Ogoni turned out to again be a minority. He thus began the final struggle, for Ogoni autonomy, with the publication of his first book on the subject, *The Ogoni Nationality Today and Tomorrow* (1968).

Oil, discovered in Ogoni in the 50's and the source of Nigeria's phenomenal wealth, has, on the contrary, not been used to the Ogoni's benefit. "The Ogoni people," laments Saro-Wiwa, "remain one of the most destitute in the world." He continues: "if Nigeria considers itself a part of the civilised world, it must show concern for its minorities and treat them fairly." (12) He is hurt by the government's opinion, that the oil belongs to everyone, not just the Ogoni, and that the wealth should be allocated by government. He quotes, with contempt, the statement of an Ibo, P. C. Asiodu, one of the most powerful civil servants in the 60's: "It is not cynical to observe that even if the resentments of oil-producing states continue, they cannot threaten the stability of the country nor affect its continued economic development." (12) This "language of colonialism" is repeated and rejected several times in *Plain*. One muct commend Saro-Wiwa for courageously fighting against the autocratic exploiters until his death. A Revenue derivative policy was established as a result of his efforts, even though the percentage ceded to the oil-producers remained minimal and mismanaged.

The final two chapters of *Plain* recount the continuing plight of the minorities. Their post-war rehabilitation has been marked by recrimination for being "Biafran collaborators." Saro-Wiwa, ever awakened to the needs of his people, kept warning them of the long struggle ahead. In his opinion, the Federal government was less concerned with the minorities than with resolving "the Ibo problem [which] overcame everyone else's problem." (229) He makes a valid point about government's failure to address the matter of "debriefing of victims of Ojukwu's propaganda (...) The result, to my mind, is that the Ibos have become even more inward-looking than ever." (230) Yet, in the same breath, he praises Gowon's own return to Nigeria as a hero years after his ouster for irresponsible governance marked by a profligacy for wastage. Gowon is remembered by many as the Head of State that proudly proclaimed the dilemma of Nigeria's being so rich that she did not know what to do with the money!

CONCLUSION: "A RETURN TO CIVILIZATION," OR TO SAVAGERY?

Saro-Wiwa describes his escape from his besieged Ogoniland to Lagos as "a return to civilization." (138) The irony must have been lost on him; for, the remark is made at the sight of a copy of the newspaper, *The Daily Times*, which, deliberately, hardly makes any reference to the ongoing civil war. The same hypocritical silence pervades the rest of the society. The author himself often displays a surprising equanimity as if, once Ojukwu and his henchmen are beaten, Nigeria's problem is solved. And Saro-Wiwa's definition of *civilization* remains blurred, at best, when not caught in the confusion of Eurocentric ethics. On the escape journey, he enjoys a blissful sleep in a decent and comfortable cabin, and remembers a French poem (139). Many references to foreign cultures (writers, languages) are strewn across *Plain*, all of which would imply a mockery of African cultures: Still during the escape, his mind wanders off to "the idealist Decoud in the boat with the incorruptible Capataz, Nostromo." (226) "Biafra," he writes, "is something like Azania" (89; of course, not the Azania of the anti-apartheid South-Africans).[15]

Indeed, once in a while, this love of things foreign appears strange in a man so utterly taken up with his Ogoni people's cause. Saro-Wiwa never forgets the words of his foreign friends, such as his former professor who said that "nothing ever happens in Nigeria;" and the drama professor, according to whom, "most Nigerian dramatists think that the adaptation of a play meant copying the entire script verbatim, merely replacing 'beer' with 'palm wine.'" (102) In a similar vein, we read of the author's contribution, as state commissioner, to the successful visit of world figures, such as Harold Wilson, British Prime Minister, and his foreign minister, Lord Carrington, both of whom were "suitably impressed that the oil-fields were safe in Federal hands." (211)

With all those civilized, that is, reactionary, ideas in mind, one might be surprised to read: "In those days, I had a head full of revolutionary ideas, believing that Nigeria could be changed by the magic of revolution (whatever that meant)." (221) What this shows is, that Saro-Wiwa was confused, or uncertain, about the real meaning of revolution, as far as Nigeria was concerned. He was, however, sure of one thing: the need to change the Ogoni's condition. And, even at that time, he was already known for his forthrightness, his fearlessness, what some would perceive as rudeness and rashness. At a meeting with Rivers State commissioners, Col. Adekunle, the one they used to call "the Black Scorpion," for his reputed viciousness in smashing through enemy lines, noticed Saro-Wiwa's character. In the author's words, "he kindly opined that I was so 'thick-headed' I deserved 'to be shot.'" (207) Saro-Wiwa dismissed the remark as a joke...

We have already detailed his obsession with Ojukwu as Nigeria's devil incarnate. Perhaps that all-consuming hatred prevented Saro-Wiwa from seeing through the Hausa-Fulani machinations. To claim that "Ojukwu is the only one [Nigerian leader] who tried to steal a country!" (225) is to view events through jaundiced eyes. It would be more to the point to note that, where Ojukwu tried and failed, the Hausa-Fulani tried and succeeded!

In the final chapter of *Plain*, Saro-Wiwa reviews the situation of post-war Nigeria, twenty years after the Biafran debacle. Significantly, his own position has not changed much. Ojukwu's rise from grass to grace—his triumphal return from exile—is treated with well deserved disdain. Yet, Saro-Wiwa still has a soft spot for those that have given the warlord the chance to attain "iconic dimensions in universal imagination." (Soyinka: 44) Saro-Wiwa believes that certain lessons were learnt from the war: "There is optimism in the air about the future; the war has taught everyone several lessons, one of them being that secession of any part of Nigeria is an impossibility." (239) A few pages after, he states: "In the pursuit of the new wealth, all the lessons that have been learnt from the war are soon lost." (242) The ambiguity of these pages remains unfortunate; perhaps Saro-Wiwa was, at the time of writing, torn between his joy at the outcome of the war and his despair at the plight of his people. One could actually say that *Plain* says nothing concrete about any "lessons." Regarding a desire to secede, the chapter on the Ogoni struggle will show that the Ogoni demand of autonomy is not much different from that of the Biafrans. Saro-Wiwa failed to understand that, if the war had been a war of *solidarity*, and not of *solidity* (Soyinka: 181), the Ogoni struggle would either have been unnecessary, or have taken other, more harmonious and less acrimonious, dimensions.

In the last book published before his untimely demise, Saro-Wiwa again comments on *Plain*; that he wrote it as objectively as possible "in the circumstances," and that, "writing about [the civil war] is equivalent to walking a minefield." (*A Month and a Day*: 63) I believe that he has written subjectively -and rightly so- about the war; that he has negotiated the minefield and come out alive, but barely. Repercussions from the war, unknown to him, ironically contributed to the conditions that made his murder inevitable. In other words, his "return to civilization" was a fatal misconception. In truth, Nigeria was the epitome of savagery personified by the very people whom Saro-Wiwa called his friends.

NOTES TO CHAPTER VII

1. *On A Darkling* Ken Saro-Wiwa *Plain*, An Account of the Nigerian Civil War, London, Lagos: Saros International Publishers, 1989. Henceforth, reference to this book will be made as Plain.

2. *Plain*: 11. This statement is a refrain in the text (see p.12) and was to become the flashpoint for Saro-Wiwa's Ogoni struggle, indeed, an essential element in the very air that he breathed, and, ultimately, the reason for his murder.

3. Some of the texts on the war are:
Rose Adaure Njoku, *Withstand the Storm*; Vincent Ike, *Sunset at Dawn* (1976); Phanuel Egejuru, *The Seed Yams Have Been Eaten* (1993); Odumegwu Ojukwu, *Because I Am Involved*; Herbert Gold, *Biafra Goodbye* (1970); Nabo Graham-Douglas, *Ojukwu's Rebellion and World Opinion* (1968); Frederick Forsyth, *The Biafra Story* (1969); Arthur Nwankwo, *Nigeria: The Challenge of Biafra* (1980); Olusegun Obasanjo, *My Command* (1980); Alexander Madiebo, *The Nigerian Revolution and the Biafran War* (1980); Bernard Odogwu, *No Place to Hide: Crises and Conflicts inside Biafra* (1985); Jean Buhler, *Tuez-les tous! Guerre de secession au Biafra* (1968); Cyprian Ekwensi, *Divided We Stand: a Novel of the Nigerian Civil War* (1980); Nelson Ottah, *Rebels Against Rebels* (1981); Alain Renard, *Biafra; naissance d'une nation?* (1969); Ralph Uwechie, *L'Avenir du Biafra, une solution nigériane* (1969); Obafemi Awolowo, *Lecture on Financing the Civil War* (1970).
Some texts on the Jan. 1966 coup are:
Ademola Ademoyega, *Why We Struck* (1981); Ben Gbulie, *Nigeria's Five Majors* (1981).

4. To show his total disdain for the Ibo secession bid in creating the Republic of Biafra, Saro-Wiwa *consistently* uses the lower case for the breakaway country's

name: *biafra*. From the first mention of the name (p.10), till the last (p. 236), this symbolic condemnation to death, or refusal to accept a self-proclaimed nation's very existence, underscores a characteristic of Saro-Wiwa; a single-mindedness that may be read either positively or negatively.

5. Every reference to Ojukwu's background is meant to show his spurious superiority. On p. 42, we are told that he went to King's College, Lagos, and to a prestigious English public school, Epsom College, before Oxford. My analysis of Saro-Wiwa's own style and attitude reveals a similar sense of superiority. Witness his constant references to Umuahia and Ibadan; his use of the English language spiced with Latin words; his praise of mates as being superior for having attended those schools. Invariably, all Umuahia alumni are "brilliant Old Boys" (p. 67). The matter of language constitutes one more element of confusion and contradiction in Saro-Wiwa's philosophy; for, after all, he incessantly affirms his interest in using language as a vehicle for communication (cf. his use of "rotten English").

6. In an interview after Saro-Wiwa's death, Ojukwu claimed that the former was occupying the Port Harcourt house of Z. C. Obi who, before the civil war, was leader of the Ibo Union in the North. As we have noted in chapter 1, the issue of abandoned properties remained a bone of contention long after the civil war. Even now, there remains a great deal of dissatisfaction (see *Plain*: 237). Note, also, that Ojukwu is one of the most satisfied Ibo returnees to the Nigerian fold. His father's buildings at Lagos, the then capital, were returned to him, Ojukwu (the old man having died in 1966), through a decree signed by Nigeria's military Maradona, Babangida (see Soyinka, *The Open Sore of a Continent*: 46).

7. *Plain*: 77. For another view on Okigbo's presence on the Biafran side, see Soyinka: 156. Okigbo told him: "This thing, I am going to stay with it till the end."

8. Fawehinmi is perhaps the most detained person in Nigeria. Always a vocal critic of military regimes, he has engaged in a long battle against their dictatorship. It was he who drew the world's attention to the farcical unfolding of the Saro-Wiwa trial when he and his team withdrew from the proceedings, to protest constant harassment by the tribunal's (that is, government) agents and a badly hidden predetermination to condemn the accused to death.

9. In his prison notes, Soyinka alludes to similar experiences, although in greater details. (*The Man Died*: 55ff) He calls the reader's attention to "the confusionist tactics" in which the officials are trained, and their belief in "the dogma of power" stemming from both their office and their northernness.

10. Ironically, the Yoruba who, by their actions, have by and large been the most nationalistic group in the country, are considered in some circles as the most tribalistic, a stigma attached to their leader, Awolowo. In truth, no leader could ever be as tribalistic as Bello. Saro-Wiwa treats him rather gently, in comparison with his vituperations against others, such as Ojukwu, and, indeed, the Yoruba.

11. *Plain*: 16. Remarkably, Saro-Wiwa writes that Balewa is Prime Minister "at the behest of that great 'Northern" potentate (the last of them?), Sir Ahmadu Bello, the Sardauna of Sokoto, sibling of Uthman Dan Fodio." Yet, he insists that the North-South division is only a myth, or a figment of Bello's imagination. Balewa's regime cannot be fully understood without a primary allusion to Bello's power and the North's interests.

12. In the chapter, "Hostages of Biafra," Saro-Wiwa quotes verbatim a long report written by a fellow Ogoni, a lawyer and his former student, Peter Akere (189-199). It details the atrocities committed by Biafran soldiers and civilians, particularly in refugee camps, against the Ogoni who were forced to flee from their liberated homes into the Biafran hinterland. That hell is contrasted, as it were, with heaven on the Federal side. A remark on this write-up's style: It resembles so much Saro-Wiwa's that one could easily mistake the student for the teacher.

13. On other occasions, too, Awolowo's views on Nigeria's multi- ethnicity are the object of Saro-Wiwa's attention. For example, see *Similia*: 160-161, with quotations from another Awolowo book, *Path to Nigerian Greatness*.

14. One of the low points of Saro-Wiwa's narrative comes when, in an attempt to show the fullness of his "dedication to the cause of Nigeria," he informs us that his wife often told him "how in [his] sleep [he] would swear that Ojukwu would never win." (*Plain*: 118)

15. See, also, *Plain*: 73, 74, 80, 83, 84, 89, 105, 107, 128, 139, 173, 217, 222.

VIII. *SIMILIA*, AN EXAMPLE OF POLITICAL JOURNALISM

"A writer in a country like Nigeria must take a consistent stand on issues." (*Similia*: 129)
"I think this to be the very crux of the problem: the assumption that the mere change of individuals can make a difference in our country." (71)
"Give a good thing to an African and he will spoil it." (23)
"I have not been questioning persons. I have been questioning ideas and actions." (127)

INTRODUCTION: "LIKE CURES LIKE," OR LAUGHTER IN THE FACE OF TRAGEDY

In Nigeria, journalism has always been a thriving profession. Even in this, the eve of the twenty-first century, with the country's collapsing economy and the astronomical cost of newspapers, the Nigerian paradox is, that new publications continue to mushroom, particularly in Lagos, erstwhile capital. There are no reliable statistics on the readership; nonetheless, Lagos does have a popular culture of newspaper *photocopying*: you pay the vendor a fee -about one fifth of the full price- for the right to read several papers and magazines which, naturally, you leave behind after absorbing the contents into your picture-perfect brain. It is a common sight to find such gatherings of avid readers in street-corners and bus-stops on early mornings as they gather important news in preparation for a day of gossips and rumors and sensational stories in filthy offices and on filthier streets. The remarkable thing is, that those masses hardly able to eat one meager meal a day, are still reading; that, in spite of the dictatorship dealing detention and death to those journalists unwilling to take the proverbial brown envelope containing dollars and pound sterling as pay-off for the journalists' conscience and integrity, progressive journalists, and newspapers still exist; that, the existence of such newspapers notwithstanding, Nigeria's reactionary regimes have continued their reckless rule without batting an eye. Which goes to show that, perhaps, in a country ruled by illiterate criminals, newspapers are considered a necessary aberration, a symbol of sham freedom that every democratic dictator can use as an example of his tolerance and civilization. Only, on occasions, an example has to be made of a recalcitrant pen-pusher who, once cajoled and courted, may find himself opening a parcel-bomb instead of a brown envelope stuffed with greenbacks. One such journalist was Dele Giwa.[1]

Saro-Wiwa did not suffer such a fate; at least, not as a direct result of his writing. But, journalism definitely contributed to what has become known as "the final solution." Although not trained as a professional, Saro-Wiwa began writing for newspapers in the mid-60's, following in the long line of intellectuals encouraged by the independent (that is, not government-owned) press to express their opinions on public issues, particularly, the sociopolitical. A prolific writer, Saro-Wiwa already used one column, in *Punch* newspaper, to build a novel, *Prisoners of Jebs*. From another column, "Similia," he put together an article-collection, the difference between the two being that "Jebs" had one story and one setting, while the other was a conglomeration of stories on various problems facing "anomic Nigeria."

In his "Author's Note," Saro-Wiwa informs the reader of the birth of the "Similia" column, first published in the *Sunday Times* in October 1989, upon the invitation of the new Managing Director of the *Times* group of newspapers, Yemi Ogunbiyi, a former lecturer at the University of Ife "who," according to Saro-Wiwa, "like some of us had wandered off into journalism and management." The author expected Ogunbiyi to improve "the intellectual content" of *Times*, a formerly independent newspaper later taken over by government, and thus evolving from a progressive, objective journalism to a status of servitude and puppetry in the hands of retrogressive manipulators of popular destiny.[2] Saro-Wiwa welcomed the invitation, particularly since the Babangida regime, already in power for four years (Babangida was enthroned after the coup of 1985), preached "human rights" which were not practicalized. "All the same, there were definite programmes initiated by the administration which I felt were most important and deserving of support." (9) One such programme was the Directorate of Mass Mobilisation for Self-Reliance, Social Justice and Economic Recovery (Mamser), of which Saro-Wiwa had been appointed Executive Director in 1987. Why Saro-Wiwa ever accepted that post remains a question in the minds of observers of Babangida's corrupt regime. Saro-Wiwa states: "I took the administration at its word, even though I knew that it often said one thing and did another." He continues: "I hope that I would never run foul of the Government or of individuals, since I would only tackle issues." (10) The difficulty and danger inherent in that ideal must have been known to the writer. For, from the beginning, the newspaper editor retained the right to reject Saro-Wiwa's articles. The *Similia* text, containing fifty-seven articles in all, includes those rejected articles, as well as those published in earlier editions of the newspaper but removed from later editions, for the obvious reason that they rubbed some big men the wrong way. The "Similia" column ran from October 1989 to November 1990 when it was unceremoniously axed. It is significant that the last article published was "The Coming War in the Delta," (168) on the agitation and murder of the people in the oil-producing area by soldiers and police. At that point in time, Saro-Wiwa had become more directly critical of the Babangida administration. The closure of his column was therefore expected.

Saro-Wiwa explains his choice of title in his first article, "Similia Similibus Burantor." "Like cures like," the basic formula for homeopathy, indicates that Saro-Wiwa, the ultimate satirist, would propose a ridiculous mimicry of Nigeria's mind-boggling sociopolitical maladies as medicine. Of course, only a naive reader would take the author seriously in an absolute sense, because that announced homeopathic approach itself is being put up to ridicule. As usual, Saro-Wiwa laughs in the face of tragedy, but not just to keep from crying; it is as a sign of defiance before the perpetrators of evil, as well as a symbol of his superior character of integrity amidst the consuming Corruption at the core of a naturally blessed country.

Saro-Wiwa emphasizes Nigerian writers' honesty, and their responsibility to protest against corruption, as the major plank of their work (45). He was not paid for the "Similia" column. He simply wrote and cherished the freedom to write. He explains at length his writing style and habits, and his efforts "to write flawless pieces" (109) in spite of deadlines and, sometimes, the dearth of new ideas. And, as he celebrated the one-and-only-year anniversary of the column, he exudes in the article entitled "A Cannibal Rage": "'Similia' has been busy giving all who read her sleepless nights. Nigeria is a sleeping elephant, molested by flies, maggots and other agents of corruption(...) To wake the big, bad beast from its stupor, a sledgehammer is needed. 'Similia' has had the courage to wield the weapon." (167) The title refers to another journalist's report of a trip to Rivers State where his girlfriend, an indigene, informed him that Saro-Wiwa's Ogoni were cannibals. Saro-Wiwa does not deny the accusation; on the contrary, he uses it to advantage, asserting his right to be enraged, and to threaten with extinction any corrupt elements in the Nigerian entity.

The articles in *Similia* afford the reader an opportunity to assess the author's rage. In order to encourage debate, and to challenge his readers, Saro-Wiwa published responses to his articles. Some of them are attached to *Similia* as appendices. Of course, by the very fact that he has made a selection, the author shows his own bias. Nonetheless, one can say that he is not "an enemy of the people." (127) He is, indeed, a child of "the sleeping giant," that beast described as the victim of corruption but, ironically, as also a collaborator in that very corruption. Saro-Wiwa's involvement in Mamser serves as a poignant example. With regard to his vaunted freedom to write, the manner of his column's exit from the pages of the *Sunday Times* shows the shallowness of any feeling of freedom in the Nigerian setting. Freedom to write, to express an opinion different from those of the self-chosen messiahs, soon becomes a phantom, that is, when the author himself does not disappear with his words.

MAMSER AND OTHER SOCIAL MATTERS

In his "Author's Note," (10) Saro-Wiwa quotes the statement of the organ's objectives as made by Augustus Aikhomu, the military politician who had appointed him as Executive Director in 1987. The list is daunting, to say the least, but, upon close review, its length and language—long-winded, embellished—are symptomatic of the long and winding roads leading to goals laid down by Babangida's administration, thus making them impossible, or unreachable. Briefly, Mamser's goal is, to encourage virtues and patriotism in the people, and to discourage corruption and all forms of vices. Saro-Wiwa is very much aware of Babangida's cunning, but he, Saro-Wiwa is a believer. He revels in his new appointment, in his status as "elder statesman" for having served before in a military government; he was a Rivers State cabinet member (1967-1973).

His article, "Who is mobilising whom for what?" (15) is a response to Chinweizu,[3] another popular columnist who criticized Mamser in *The Vanguard* newspaper. Here, as in some other pieces, Saro-Wiwa becomes a defender, a banner-waving trooper, a role that he is not supposed to play, at least in his announced intentions. Never a candidate for an award in humility, Saro-Wiwa starts out by condemning the other writer's use of English: "The unusual grammatical error was perhaps symptomatic of the faulty thought-process in the [Chinweizu] series." Chinweizu's position is described as cynical, a common attitude during Mamser's first year. Saro-Wiwa's declaration: "It can be said that this cynicism has been laid to rest, at least in part. The Directorate has become part of our national life, tolerated if not entirely understood." (15)

This opinion remains unsubstantiated with any facts of Mamser's achievements. Saro-Wiwa's arguments are largely confusing when not contradictory. For example, regarding Babangida's decision to scrap the already existing program, War Against Indiscipline (WAI), before creating the near duplicate, Mamser, Saro-Wiwa admits that the military President's "argument did not hold water. But it is a tribute to him that he saw the need for Mamser. 'Wai' is a necessary part of Mamser." (16) As for the criticism that the military are not in a position to pontificate a new awareness, Saro-Wiwa claims that the "action of the few could not be representative of the whole. It would appear that for some reason, the military themselves have begun to see the need for a change of lifestyle." He goes on to say that those who criticize the military as leaders of corruption are, indeed, acting in the very spirit of Mamser, to destroy the culture of silence that has allowed the few to cheat and victimize the majority. Saro-Wiwa does not clarify what, besides the spirit of criticism, has ben Mamser's patrimony. If, as he says, "Mamser people" are those fighting for a better nation, he fails to tell us exactly how they would fight besides using words which, in actuality, may even be denied them.

His references to Jesus, and Mohammed (religious leaders), and to Nkrumah, Azikiwe and Awolowo (political leaders) as members of the past phase of our struggle, are strange. "The new phase," he writes, "is to achieve good government and an orderly society." (17) The first two on the list represent foreign spiritual invasion that aided and abetted political colonialism which the three Africans fought to abolish, one daresay, unsuccessfully. For, colonialism, rather than lead to true freedom, has metamorphosed into neo-colonialism, with the only visible change occurring in the skin-color of the masters. Saro-Wiwa himself says that much in his civil war diary and other writings on the Nigerian situation. And when he gladly declares his belief that we are no longer "other people's slaves" (17), he seems to forget that we are now our own people's slaves. His response to Chinweizu, that "good Nigerians are mobilising other

Nigerians for a better, orderly country" (18), is only a statement of opinion, a dream that is yet to be realized.

In Saro-Wiwa's opinion, organized religion seems to be one avenue for realizing the goal of good government and good living. His harsh humor finds a ready object of derision in the innumerable new churches sprouting on the Nigerian landscape. Warehouses, once hidden habitats for essential commodities like rice and cement, are being converted into churches by the day. Saro-Wiwa condemns this "sectarianism and charlatanism," and urges the organized churches to face the challenge and eliminate the quacks. In the article, "A Sober Christmas" (39), he contrasts Christmas in Europe and America, sober, indoor occasion, with the Nigerian celebration full of exuberance and endless excessiveness. His advice is, that Nigerians ought to emulate the Euro-Americans who stay at home, read and reflect. A good advise, one might agree, but hardly relevant or realistic, one must aver. Because Euro-America being of temperate clime, those people are compelled to stay indoors. As for reading, they do so because they can afford to buy books, which are also available. And they have food to eat; so, they are tuned to reading, even though many of them prefer the quick fix of the television image to the time-consuming written text. In Nigeria, not even the intellectuals, fast becoming an endangered species, can afford to read. Almost condemned to the condition of beggardom with which the working and peasant classes are very familiar, intellectuals now view Christmas as a season to savor as respite from the year-long misery.

In the spirit of Mamser, Saro-Wiwa proposed more "style and values" in the lives of Nigerians, in two articles recounting the launching of five of his books by Jerry Gana, Mamser chairman. The latter boasts of individual Nigerians' successes on the world stage, and exhorts others to also pursue excellence. Saro-Wiwa is impressed by Mamser's achievements in its two years' existence. He is also struck by the idea of pursuing excellence. As further examples, he singles out "a certain class of Nigerian women" who dress well, who have thus put some style in their lives. On the male side, he gives the example of a man with one shirt and a pair of pants, who is neater and better dressed than another owning a wardrobe full of clothes. "It is all a matter of style, of taste," he submits. Here is another show of confused thinking: Those well-dressed women no doubt possess over-flowing wardrobes; besides, the man with one shirt and pants soon finds that his clothes are losing threads, fading, falling apart. He will be tempted to go in search of the wealth in which the women are wallowing. Fortunately for him, as some would say, wads of money are waiting for him, if he can just forget his dignity... In a similar vein, Saro-Wiwa claims that the squalor in Nigerian universities is less as a result of lack of funds than of style. He does not explain how style can be used to repair dilapidated buildings, to provide teaching and research tools, to establish and maintain a standard capable of competing with other institutions fundamentally and financially supported by both governments and peoples. The writer refuses to admit that, in Nigeria, education has ceased to be a priority because the government is manned by illiterates.

He laments the absence of a good value system. He believes that traditional values have been diluted or bastardized by Western and Arab values which encourage corruption, and discourage hard work. One would agree with Saro-Wiwa, but not absolutely, particularly when he proposes that the educated ones and those who travel abroad, should create new standards and values. On the contrary, the standards and values already exist in the traditional society from which those educated illiterates and traveling imitators must learn. Cleanliness, accountability, punctuality, just reward for excellence, these are constant aspects of that society being relegated to the footnotes of history by pseudo-civilized leaders.

While he blames Nigerians for generally not valuing intellectual property (59), Saro-Wiwa sees fit to lampoon Tai Solarin, a renowned, iconoclastic educationist whom Soyinka calls the conscience of Nigeria. The article, "Who's Afraid of Tai Solarin," has to be considered as one of the low points of *Similia* (36-38). The writer says that he has never met Solarin, but the reported incident of a Japanese World War II veteran just informed that the war is over, reminds him, Saro-Wiwa, of the schoolteacher recently appointed by Babangida as chairman of The People's Bank. The analogy: a soldier fighting a cause long after there is need for it. Saro-Wiwa makes every effort to dismiss Solarin's achievements as either shallow or mythical. He wonders why Solarin, confessed atheist, has named his school, Mayflower, the epithet of pilgrims, colonialists using the bible to support their extermination of Indians. In response to this, one recalls Saro-Wiwa's own passion for his colonial education at Umuahia.[4] Indeed, he berates Solarin for claiming that it is impossible to prepare students for the terminal school-certificate examination in four years, when Umuahia has already done so with immense success. He ridicules Solarin's stand against the all-importance of the English language as a subject in the examination, and asserts that "Mayflower has not produced a poet, not in English, not in Yoruba." (37) He then compares Solarin to Mahatma Gandhi, both being "confused and misguided." He quotes Chinua Achebe, Nigerian writer, who calls Solarin "an unfeeling, dry-as-dust logic chopper with no capacity at all for respecting human anguish..." (38) As it is, Saro-Wiwa's most convincing statement is the fact that Solarin has been detained so many times that the public's attention is riveted upon him, to Saro-Wiwa's disgust. Achebe for one has done absolutely nothing to show that he himself respects human anguish. At least, Saro-Wiwa admits that Solarin constantly would remove corpses from roads, and that he had the power to make individuals and governments re-assess themselves.

Saro-Wiwa's comment on the People's Bank is further proof of his soft spot for the Babangida regime. The bank is listed among what he calls "improvement programmes." (43) Rather than see the chairmanship as the President's way of putting Solarin to the test, one is tempted to view it as a cunning way of roping in a perceived enemy, of bringing him to the fold of the faithful, of silencing him by tarnishing, or destroying, his reputation, Maradonically! Solarin, like several others of that rare breed blessed with integrity, fell to Babangida's sham call to patriotic service. After his brief mis-service, Solarin saw the light. He regretted his misstep. However, it was not grievous enough to make people forget his great qualities as Nigeria's social conscience. One remembers him, once in a while, on that Saturday of perverted senses, dressed in the ridiculous uniform of Maryam Babangida's money-guzzling "Better Life for Rural Women" program. (128) More regular, and more riveting, is the gaunt figure of the septuagenarian accompanying Soyinka and others on the latter's birthday, on the six-mile "Walk for Justice" in Lagos, on July 30, 1994, to protest the military government's relentless rape of the people (*The Open Sore of a Continent*: 54).

One more article on Mamser, "Okigbo's 'Okparanomics'," lauds the speech of Okigbo, a former Federal government Economic Adviser, at the opening of the Directorate's Conference on Structural Transformation, with Babangida in attendance. Saro-Wiwa combines the contents of the speech with those of another Okigbo lecture, and concludes that the latter has great ability for "extracting the warmth of a basic humanism from cold statistics." Apparently, this comes from Okigbo's manner of supporting Babangida's 1986 dismissal of the public debate on politics and the economy and the recommendation of a socialist system. Or, maybe, Saro-Wiwa is impressed by Okigbo's advocacy of "a structural adjustment programme" (SAP) based upon internal efforts and not upon an IMF-driven set of directives. Saro-Wiwa agrees with Okigbo that the Nigerian currency's exchange rate is being manipulated by foreign exploiters to keep the country in perpetual thrall. The column recommends the economist to Babangida, convinced as he is that his expertise will "knock the IMF out." It is noteworthy that Babangida's regime adopted SAP according to the IMF's order. Perhaps the famous smile flashed by the President on Okigbo, had something to do with that decision; perhaps the same smile, symptom of a contagious disease, "Laughingitis," afflicted the collective brain, making people believe that the economic tragedy was mere comic relief, and that the sinking naira was worth more than the dollar and the pound sterling combined.

BABANGIDANCE, OR THE MILITARY AS POLITICIANS

Saro-Wiwa devotes several articles to Babangida and his administration. In "Babangidance," (18), he writes a song to commemorate the President's Maradonic policy and politics: "A little to the right/ A little to the left/...A bit of that a bit of this." That scenario in Nigeria's history reveals one man's astounding political cunning; an evil genius clad in the cloak of a guardian angel; arguably the best dictator that Nigeria has ever had; inventor *extraordinaire* of everything and anything, including and particularly a Transition Program crafted to terminate many an ambitious political career and to transform Babangida himself into a life-president. People loved that smile of his, revealing that gap between the teeth that made him an all-time charmer. Saro-Wiwa was no exception. Politicians, that very Nigerian specimen of the dogs embedded in human beings, always ready to scamper after bones, they were Babangida's willing and able prostitutes.

Babangidance is supported by Saro-Wiwa for its novelty. We must be willing to try out "new things," without questioning its quality. The proposition is bizarre, coming from a writer and intellectual known for his readiness to protest. The newest of the novelties is Babangida's decision to disband all the thirteen political associations organized through his fiat as the first step towards democratic parties and elections. Reason: corruption, for which "old-breed" politicians have been banned from the process, has again reared its ugly head among "the new breed." Upon the unprecedented dissolution, something even more spectacular was decreed: the formation of two parties by government, with names, manifestoes, operational modalities, infrastructures, and money for their management all in place. Politicians, ever-ready dancers, jumped up and started shaking to the manipulated rhythm of "Babangidance".

Saro-Wiwa sees nothing wrong in the decreed parties. He allots well deserved blame to the corrupt politicians, and praises Babangida for the drastic step. "The imposition of two parties is a novelty." (21) rejects the idea of a North-South arrangement in the two parties' formation, although that would be the assessment from their composition. His objection would surprise no one, since he has been a chronic believer in the majority groups' collaboration in cheating the minorities. He seizes the opportunity to complain about another kind of cheating, that perpetrated by government against the oil-producing areas which have not been paid any money from the Derivation Fund set up to bring justice to those contributing to Nigeria's wealth. Meanwhile, the new party system is a "new opportunity" for politicians. "Babangidance may be hit after all!" Events in the land should have made Saro-Wiwa realize that the hit was not a matter of popularity, but one of harm, that is, the kind of hurt inflicted by a hitman armed with bombs and bullets, to muzzle and maim the people into a state of submission or collusion with the master of deceit. Saro-Wiwa mocks the politicians. He advises them to "know what Babangida wants of you, reads everything, and especially consult an astrologer!" (25) Which is another way of stating that nobody knows what the man wants.

The author commends Babangida for "always seeking answers to problems [and for] not hesitating to try out new things." (33) He only faults him for his slow speed which is not the man's fault, really: it is often the style of the military." Saro-Wiwa also declares that, "in the life of a nation, five years [Babangida's time in office] is nothing." (33) Patience; that, in Saro-Wiwa's opinion, is what Nigerians must cultivate. Yet, "And a New New Year" (41) gives a damaging review of 1989, with "the ghost of Sap pursuing us all," and high prices, no drugs, no money, schools closed, and a bleak future for the children. "The calm," writes Saro-Wiwa, "presages a storm." In the same breath, we are reminded that "the Babangida administration has placed an important number of programmes in place(...) What the government requires is the management which will ensure success. *The responsibility rests fair and square on* the civil service." (43, emphasis mine) Here, we see the author "Babangidancing." The responsibility for success -and failure- is deliberately deflected away from the man that must be held responsible in any right-thinking country, the President. Saro-Wiwa blames the cynicism of critics and makes a patriotic call to people to rally round the government. The same government that abruptly changes the structure of the Civil Service, and then, six months later, arranges a workshop for the high officials "to introduce themselves to the new system." (34) Saro-Wiwa explains the action as a proof of Babangida's dissatisfaction with the hurried reforms and his desire for thoroughness. The same government that throws out people with experience and either replaces them with greenhorns or recycles proven irresponsible hands. Saro-Wiwa advises caution about such appointments, but with humor: candidates should be fast readers, because of the copious reports and recommendations compiled from endless committees, but never implemented. The same government that sets up a protracted debate of the country's future, through a contraption called Political Bureau. Saro-Wiwa blames the refusal to produce a White Paper from the expensive exercise where socialism was soundly recommended, not on Babangida, but upon the Nigerian Army, "probably the most bourgeois (sic) institution in the country, complete with its array [of aides and] hierarchy [and without] patience for such a shibboleth." (52)

Saro-Wiwa himself is no supporter of socialism. Witness his "Comrades No More," a satire on the materialistic maneuvers of Dr. Tunji Otegbeye, "the reddest Nigerian in the sixties," (50) who combines communism with private property and political opportunism. The author faults Nigerian political theorists for being lackeys of their foreign teachers and faithful messengers of their civilized masters. Instead of philosophies and ideologies, which underscore "the backwardness of our society," he proposes "a return to the basics of honour, honesty, competence and hard work." (25)

In supporting "Babangidance," Saro-Wiwa, of course, does not take himself too serious: He uses soccer analogy to identify the Center as important as "the man whose foot is on the ball." He therefore swears not to settle for anything else but the Center, "where the action is (...) Possession is nine parts of the law." Indirectly, he is teasing the opportunists whose life-long vocation is to be where the action is. This sense of humor carries over to other themes, including the much despised "SAP," upon which Saro-Wiwa exchanges ideas during his first visit to a foreign ambassador's residence ("The World Bank and Us"). There, a World Bank official lays out the reason for the program as a consequence of Nigeria's obsession with debts. Saro-Wiwa admits that government's sing-song about "gains of SAP" is nothing but a chimera. (62) Furthermore, he expresses a bitter truth about foreign complicity in Nigeria's woes, hardly hiding his frustration, in one of the most compelling passages of *Similia*: "This may mean that the World Bank and its Euro-American mentors will stop forcing incompetent rulers and brutes upon third and *enth* world societies in the belief that such men will brutalize their peoples and compel them to accept [the World Bank's] bitter pill." (62) Would Babangida be one of such brutish leaders?

Saro-Wiwa warns him not to await "The Judgement of History" before taking cognizance of people's assessment of his administration. "The opinions of today form the grist of history." (64) Claiming to base his utterances on a poll he has conducted, the author says there is a rumor, that Babangida's administration is the most corrupt in Nigerian history. Saro-Wiwa begs to disagree, but avers that the opinion stems from the President's appointment of corrupt people. "My fear is that the errors will receive far more prominence than his successes." (65) Problem: we are never told of any concrete successes, only "novelties."

The aborted April 1990 coup against Babangida is the subject of "The Quality of Mercy." The author again polls the public and reports his findings: people dislike the killing of "fine men" trained at high costs to the state; they recall, with sadness, the earlier execution of other condemned coup-plotters.[5] Saro-Wiwa adds,—for comic relief?—women's thought on the young coup leader's handsomeness and eligibility for marriage. He advises Babangida to act with circumspection. In a footnote, he informs the reader that, before the article appeared, the coup-plotters were killed; the article then came out. Afterwards, a second batch of plotters was also executed. Saro-Wiwa never mentions the innumerable stories on Babangida's thirst for blood and readiness to "waste" anyone perceived as his enemy. While dissuading military men from attempting coups, he does not dissuade Babangida, himself beneficiary of a coup, from trying to hold on eternally to his back-door empowerment. "The Enduring Prosperity of the Future" may surprise critics of military rule;

for, Saro-Wiwa, commenting on the ever-changing Transition Program, claims that the mere handing over to a civilian regime is not an achievement "if the conditions necessary for a successful operation of the succeeding political system have not been achieved." That is the author's way of supporting Babangida's decision to—for the umpteenth time—move back his promised handover to civilians. The military dictator's tiresome pronouncement, "to bequeath a system which will not allow for further military intervention," (145) has become one of the biggest jokes of Nigeria's torture-riddled existence.

The exploits of the President's wife are addressed in the article, "Better Life for All Women." "The women of Nigeria have to be thankful to Maryam Babangida for moving them somewhat forward in the estimation of the men and of society." (94) Maryam, in the author's view, has carved a niche for herself, as national First Lady, and for Military Governors' wives, as state First Ladies. He says that even if many do not like what she is doing, they cannot ignore it. As for him, he does like it, "because I have a lot of my mother in me." He expresses reservations about Mrs. President's lavishly funded program, "Better Life for Rural Women." He believes it should have been named for all women; that the modalities should be different; that a public relations set-up will help gauge the public's mood, and advise the First Lady on what to wear and say, and guard her against over-exposure. The only clear aspect of the article is Saro-Wiwa's support for the program and his admiration for the woman. Everything else is muddled up. Although named for rural women, the program has done nothing for them, besides giving a few the opportunity to travel to the city, to spend a few nights in five-star hotels, and to rub shoulders with eminent women and, of course, men, with the First Ladies smiling eminently to the bank with the public's millions. The program did make life better for the bourgeois women who had a chance to flex their muscles besides the men. "Besides every successful man there is a woman," proclaims Saro-Wiwa. Unfortunately, in the Nigeria example, we are dealing with the success of blood-suckers.

Another article, "Sweet Mother," celebrates woman in a much more authentic fashion. The subject is Winnie Mandela, "who waited at home through those twenty-seven long, dreary years, (...) The woman who led the campaign for her husband's release and for the destruction of the evil system of apartheid." (67) Saro-Wiwa calls her an African monument and our own contribution to "the Great Women of the World;" and he is also convincing enough when he affirms that Winnie is "as good as any man." But, is she "better," as the author claims? Saro-Wiwa emphasizes woman's role as mother and wife. He must be a true gourmand himself, as he devotes time to Winnie's culinary expertise, and how Nelson must have enjoyed the first meal after his release. In essence, it is Winnie's "enduring labour of love" that arrests the author's attention. One must, however, object to this diminished view; for, what makes Winnie—and Nelson—great, goes far beyond their private, conjugal life; it is their role in the extended family of South Africa, and Africa. They are Mother and Father of a Nation.[6]

Saro-Wiwa writes "Nelson's Mantle" to commemorate the great man's release. While admitting that he seems destined to lead South Africa, and Africa, the author foresees problems posed by South Africa's paradoxes and the process of adapting to modernity. The question of inter-ethnic disputes, particularly between the Zulu-based Inkatha Party and Mandela's African National Congress, is used to project a destiny of "turmoil, pain and despair." (92) Saro-Wiwa also uses the Nigerian example as cause for worry; there, he reminds us, paradoxes persist, after a civil war. For the first time, he is categorical in stating "our inability to weld the plethora of ethnic groups in Nigeria into a nation."

His error is in using Nigeria as example for Mantelet. Indeed, it is absurd to compare the two countries. In South Africa, commitment through shared experiences and cultures, is a reality; so also is the people's determination to decide their destiny and to assume their independence, honed by the very pain of apartheid. Nigeria stands at the opposite pole, with conflicting cultures, diverse experiences exacerbated by the colonizer's collusion with certain chosen stooges. No, Mantelet has not had to look to Nigeria; on the contrary, Nigeria would do well to look up to him and his country for a lesson in commitment and accomplishment of nationhood, in spite of all odds. Saro-Wiwa's comment on the outbreak of township violence may be viewed by some as prophetic. But, in fact, that violence has been part of the apartheid experience for many years. His opinion on South Africa's inter-ethnic problems is an indirect way of addressing his favorite subject, Nigeria's majority-minority dichotomy, and the exploitation of the latter by the former.

THE KILLING FIELDS OF MINORITY OIL

The aversion of the *Times*' Managing Director, Ogunbiyi, to the subject of minority oil, is symptomatic of his employer's (Babangida) policy. Saro-Wiwa wrote three articles on the sensitive issue. "The Killing Fields...," submitted in December 1989, was not published because the article's focal point, Lukman, the Oil Minister, had just been hosted by the newspaper. One month later, the Minister was relieved of his post, and the article was published. Saro-Wiwa would be wrong to feel triumphant: Lukman actually gained a promotion, as he was sent to Geneva as OPEC's (the oil-producing executive council) Chairman; just reward, one might say, for his patriotism in implementing government's program of maintaining its vice-grip on oil-wealth. In September 1990, another article, "Developing the Oil-Bearing Areas," was rejected because, in Ogunbiyi's view, the subject had been treated in Saro-Wiwa's earlier articles. It was published by an independent newspaper, *The Guardian*, where Ogunbiyi had wet his feet upon his departure from the ivory-tower. "The Coming War in the Delta" appeared on schedule in November 1990, but only in the early edition. It was pulled from the second edition. That ended Saro-Wiwa's relationship with *Times*. His column was unceremoniously axed.

Unlike other issues discussed in *Similia*, the subject of oil is treated by Saro-Wiwa with overtly increasing aggressiveness, anger and passion. In "The Killing Fields," he contrasts the fluctuating fortunes of Nigerians employed in the oil-sector with the flourishing and fulfilling career of their British counterparts. For example, Robert Reid moved up the ladder, from being Shell-Nigeria Managing Director, to Chairman of Shell-U.K. On the contrary, two prominent Nigerians in the National Nigerian Petroleum Company management, Messrs. Onyia and Aret Adams, were suspended, "not because they have been found incompetent but for purely political reasons." (48) Saro-Wiwa admits that, some individuals, political animals, are the architects of their own misfortune. But, sad to say, both they and those of integrity are "slaughtered in the killing fields of Nigerian politics." The problem is, that the policy of *federal character*, which Saro-Wiwa likes, is not equitably implemented. He refers to the cases of the Ogoni and Isoko, oil-producing minorities that are hardly represented in the Oil Company. He therefore challenges the Minister, Lukman, to do justice.

Saro-Wiwa's analysis is slanted to suit his personal interest. Of course, the victims that he has chosen are from the minority groups. He fails to inform us of the ethnic affiliation of those in charge of oil, including that of the said Minister, a Hausa-Fulani. Besides, he should be well aware that the controversial *federal character* was concocted specifically to level the playing field in favor of the vastly over-matched Hausa-Fulani in matters of expertise in a modern state.

The author's criticism of expatriate power in oil companies, such as Shell, is much more convincing. The federal government's majority shares hardly count. In Ogoni, Shell is dedicated to the ethos of "international capitalism." Profit is the key-word, and the managers are there to promote the interests of the mother company abroad. "Oil is about money. It is money. The oil companies are rich and can hire the best brains in the world." (151) Saro-Wiwa condemns the collaboration between Shell and the Nigerian government. Shell understands officialdom's corrupt nature; hence, it readily forges a partnership of exploitation with this "indigenous colonialism...When the oil companies err, the government looks the other way." The catalog of Shell's ills is sickening. Water from the oil wells is enough to drown the entire community in the area; yet people are reduced to drinking guinea worm-infected water. The only light comes from gas-flaring, which has been the case for some thirty-two years. The company is out to ensure that local people remain poor so that they can be easily exploited.

Saro-Wiwa comments on the President's delegation sent to Rivers State, to assess the progress of the 1.5% Derivation Fund instituted as a result of the 1996 coup attempt. He determines that the inadequate plans constitute a serious indictment of the presidency which, in his opinion, has not shown a desire to bring about justice. He recalls his 1985 article on Derivation, to which Babangida's government paid no mind. More frustrated than ever before, the writer concludes: "The poet's only duty is to warn. Nigeria is fast proving, or has proved, that the gun is mightier than the pen." (148) While plans are underway to flood Ogoni with generators and dig bore-holes, instead of establishing concrete, long-lasting electrification and water-system, a multi-million naira airport was opened in Minna, Babangida's home town. In the same period, a one-kilometer road was opened in Warri, a town in the delta area. Saro-Wiwa's advice to government: place Derivation Fund in Trust for future use; government should carry out development programs in the oil areas; create a competent authority including oil companies, government representatives and citizens, to undertake projects with special funds; create more States. Naturally, his suggestions were not read by those that should.

"The Goose and the Prince" (72) is a satirical commentary on the 1990 visit of Britain's Prince Charles to the Rivers State. The heir to the Queen's throne is welcome by chiefs and princes living in palaces that are, in reality, "thatch homes, tumble down sheds or one room apartments." Saro-Wiwa wonders why the British royalty has this sudden interest in Nigeria, "this debt-ridden, corruption-ridden, wasteful country." The simple answer: profit. With the Babangida regime's decision to privatize Nigerian oil and gas, Britain, the ex-colonizer, is the first collaborator to show. Saro-Wiwa repeats his criticism of Britain already laid out in his war diary, that it did not live up to the treaty to protect Opobo from indigenous colonialism. Today, Shell is having a field day in Rivers, degrading the environment with the collusion of Nigeria's majority groups. Saro-Wiwa sends a message to Prince Charles, to save the delta peoples from deprivation, disaster and doom caused by oil-exploiters. "The goose that lays the golden egg must not die." (75)

More biting satire is displayed in "The Natives Are Friendly!", a fictionalized piece based upon the visit of a government delegation to "the troubled districts." The mission's manager files this report to "Your Honor," from what his men told him. The "trusted aides" were preceded by "top security agents [mandated] to ensure that enemies of progress did not jeopardize the mission's success." (123) The mission: "to pacify the natives and to report back on their environment." Mr. Top Official notices that the natives' eyes are jaundiced, jaundice being the particular disease of the oil area, turning their eyes the color of refined petroleum. The team, blessed with clear eyes, easily finds where the oil is. A trusted aide is detailed to mastermind operations in the President's "imperial interests." At the end of the great mission, the leader is overjoyed that his men "went, they saw, and they returned... The pipelines are humming with expectation." (124) The chiefs received "golden handshakes," and the contractors send "fraternal messages" of continued collaboration.

There is the small problem of "a little man, who is often heard but hardly ever seen, (...) Ken Saro-Wiwa is his name."[7] The little man has been grumbling and whimpering about the Derivation Fund, and how to use it to the benefit of the natives, particularly on education. Mr. Top Official dismisses such native ideas as jaundiced, and quotes the excellent opinion of a non-native, Philip Asiodu, from *On a Darkling Plain*, to the effect that oil-wealth belongs to all and the natives must not be allowed to undermine the nation's stability.

The truth is that Saro-Wiwa's opinion makes more sense than Asiodu's. Since the government is interested in its mission of pacification, which means exploitation, it prefers to listen to patriots like Asiodu. The fear expressed in the fictional report, that the little man "might give the natives ideas of independence," (125) would be borne in mind as the Ogoni struggle garnered strength. The very use of the word, *natives*, underscores the colonialist attitudes and actions of the power that be, in the oil areas. Pity that Saro-Wiwa never got to the bottom of the neo-colonial set-up, to expose the true identity of the colonizers. Meanwhile the natives are restive.

"What Tribe do You Belong To" reveals Saro-Wiwa's deepening frustration in a struggle met by the hard, cold barrel of guns corked by goons. Instead of his confused keep-Nigeria-one crusade of the civil war era, he now states categorically that Nigeria is "a pastiche of tribes" with no hope for that unity for too long used as reason for injustice, corruption and exploitation. He refers to an embarrassing incident at London airport where, because he holds a Nigerian passport, he was thoroughly searched, as if he was a suspected criminal. To eliminate such an experience, he proposes a new passport, on which the holder's tribe would feature. Identified as an "Ogoni-Nigerian, I believe that this will protect me from molestation at immigration check points because I will ensure that other Ogoni-Nigerians behave themselves according to the mores of the tribe." (164)

Saro-Wiwa has done well to publish reactions to this article, including one that carpets his "myopic nationalism with an unimpressive effort to draw public interest, not so much to his ideas but to himself." (198) Of course, the moral qualities that Saro-Wiwa sees in his Ogoni are very common among other ethnicities in Nigeria. His promise to assure Ogoni probity is enough proof that there are factors forcing individuals to deviate from expected or accepted behavior. As Nwabuize rightly asserts, the results of government policies and programs, such as SAP, must be contributory to the disgraceful actions and the subsequent reputation of Nigerians.

Saro-Wiwa becomes increasingly myopic and parochial, as the Ogoni question remains unresolved. Everything now is linked to his tribe's condition as an exploited, marginalized group. "The Language Question" (105) lauds the mother-tongue policy of the Education Minister, Fafunwa, in the hope that it would help preserve the author's minority group against indigenous colonialism symbolized by the *Wazobia* group.[8] Saro-Wiwa calls upon the minister to develop all languages and to not impede the teaching of English as *lingua franca*. Interestingly, nothing is said about logistics, or modalities. Saro-Wiwa is now condemning Fafunwa's predecessor, Aminu—whom he once considered a good Minister,—for seeing Nigeria "through a mirror darkly," as North and South. Before Fafunwa could read and digest Saro-Wiwa's article, he began to hedge. He told Nigerians that he was, indeed, committed to Aminu's program of "nomadic education," that is, the education of the hordes of cattle-rearing Hausa-Fulani moving across the country. Soon enough, "Babs, sorry, Aliyu Fafunwa"[9] was dumped, as suddenly as he had been appointed.

"The National Census" is another example of Saro-Wiwa's obsession with ethnicity. He welcomes the appointment of Shehu Musa, an Ibadan University alumnus, as Director of National Population Commission. The appointment, says the author, "is a credit to the Babangida administration...The administration needs this feather, if only this one, after the severe battering it has taken from Sap, religion, revenue allocation, the Constitution, armed robbery and education." (111) He is certain of Musa's success. However, he complains that, on the trial-census list, ethnic groups and religions are left out. Saro-Wiwa calls these omissions a deliberate attempt to politicize what should be a de-politicized exercise. In the appendix, he publishes the response from Ms. Ogbiyi, the Census Bureau's Public Affairs officer who claims that the omissions are based upon "previous researches," and that Saro-Wiwa should see her for explanations, instead of throwing "a missile on the person of Alhaji Shehu Musa, the Makaman Nupe." (185)

The author's effusion of commendation on Musa and his employers, is truly sad; for, Musa has been one of those constant figures on the Nigerian political scene. He always has a job, everywhere, and failure follows him like a shadow, or second skin. Saro-Wiwa's optimism, as usual, stems from his belief in the superiority of Ibadan and Umuahia alumni, and other friends met in the corridor of power. The Census officer's ego-tripping complements the writer's. In the final analysis, both of them must have been quite satisfied that the census was another exercise in futility; better, another show of incompetence and corruption. Up till now, nobody knows exactly how many people live in Nigeria. What is known for sure is, that the country is "a federation of ethnic groups." (98)

"YORUBAPHOBIA"

After his criticism of the Ibo in *Plain*, Saro-Wiwa uses several articles in *Similia* to examine the Yoruba. In "Yorubaphobia," he says that a Yoruba reader has called him a coward for claiming that the Yoruba, and not the Hausa-Fulani, "the true colonialists," have gained most from the Niger delta petrodollars. According to him, his reaction has been, to sit and laugh at his ignorant detractors. But it is no laughing matter, because it concerns the core of the Nigerian arrangement. It is as essential as, indeed, perhaps more essential than, the Ogoni issue.

Saro-Wiwa insists that "the loss of the Ogoni, Ijaw, Urhobo, (...) and Igbo has been the profit of the Yoruba." (136) He talks of "the preponderant share of political power and therefore resources which the Yoruba have appropriated to themselves," as the reason for his "Yorubaphobia." Yet this phobia is not altogether negative. The author lauds the excellent Yoruba culture and civilization. He gives examples of Yoruba individuals who have excelled in every facet of life. Tongue-in-cheek, he sees them on a "colonizing mission," given the great influence that they continue to have on the country's destiny. And he declares their right to such a mission, because they have had "almost two centuries of Westernization, of Western education." On the negative side, he asks, "Why do the Yoruba live in such filthy environment? Ibadan [is] the vomit of a tuberculosis patient." (137) He ends his article on a high note, expressing his pride to be part of a country which is inhabited by the Yoruba. Given their qualities, he challenges them to "rise to Nigerian leadership, not by what they take away, but by what they give. In this giving inheres true greatness." (138)

We read responses by some Yoruba in Saro-Wiwa's appendix. They include one pretending to commend him for his courage to proclaim himself "a certified tribalist," (192); marveling at his evolution from a gentle soul to a belligerent activist climbing tables to declare his special status as an ex-commissioner, and congratulating him for the extraordinary success of his book, *Plain*. The respondent, Eddie Ojo, sneers at Saro-Wiwa's ignorance for basing his phobia on his Lagos and Ibadan experiences. He also reminds the author that Yorubaland was developed years before oil was found. Besides, no tribe is an exception to tribalism. A second respondent, Sola Oke, Saro-Wiwa's college classmate, envies his Ogoni commitment and wishes he, too, could be so engaged against the exploiters of his people, the Ekiti, who "hardly feel the impact of petrodollars." (189) Waxing socialist, Oke posits that all minorities belong to "the TRUE majority marginalized by the privileged; but we are still better off than the peasants, the poorly paid workers and petty traders." Oke therefore advises Saro-Wiwa that the class question is the real issue in Nigeria, and that the elite, inveterate suckers, must be brought down. A third reader, Tokunbo Olatubosun, admires Saro-Wiwa's "guts, single-mindedness, determination and erudition." (194) In his opinion, the Yoruba are not tribalistic; on the contrary, they have made sacrifices for the unity of Nigeria. Their advancement, which Saro-Wiwa envies, has come in spite of their handicapped situations within the Nigerian context. Olatubosun's advice: "You do not have to wait for the Yorubas to lead Nigeria out of the woods. They have their own problems, too, to contend with. What we need, we have been told, are visionary leaders; and these may come from any part of the country. Why not you, Saro-Wiwa?" (196)

Now, Saro-Wiwa's article and the responses—all by Yoruba readers—prove once again the depth of ethnic divisions in Nigeria. They also show the importance, if not the indispensability, of the Yoruba to the survival of that country. Whether written seriously or satirically, "Yorubaphobia" expresses mixed notions of love and hate, of envy and admiration, a phobia stemming from knowledge of Yoruba socio-cultural superiority. This mixed psychological bag explains the author's confusion in analyzing his subject. The Yoruba, as a group, have been among the least beneficiaries of minority-sourced petro dollars. Saro-Wiwa's braggadocio about his superior knowledge of history is laughable because, if he knew history, he would not allude only to almost two centuries of Westernization. In truth, Yoruba civilization dates back to centuries before then. One only needs to look a the African diaspora—United States, Cuba, Brazil, for example—to realize its continuous impact.

As for his "Awo's Rebuke," the article castigating his critics for their hypocrisy and stupidity, Saro-Wiwa himself deserves to be rebuked for worse crimes, of mean ignorance and repugnant conservatism badly hidden behind a cloak of Awoist progressiveness. It is true that "class and the ethnic question are not mutually exclusive." (159) But, it is absolutely nauseating to list a few Yoruba as "the pampered [elite] minority," without making mention of the plethora of power-and-money-mongering Hausa-Fulani who, with their military kin, have caught the country in a choke-hold of neo-colonialism. Saro-Wiwa's constant reference to Awolowo as his hero is understandable, since the late politician's idea of minority rights has served as rationale of the Ogoni struggle. That self-serving, or selfish, attachment to Awolowo has not, however, opened Saro-Wiwa's eyes to one very significant fact, that Awolowo did not become Nigeria's President, in spite of his exemplar. Why? Because the neo-colonialist hegemony could never imagine a Yoruba—the very individual whose strategies contributed more than anyone else's actions, both in the warfront and the rear, to maintaining Nigeria's unity—ruling the country that they consider their feudal property.

CONCLUSION: "THANK YOU FOR THE LAUGHTER"

It is noteworthy that, in the very last article of *Similia*, Saro-Wiwa finally focusses his satirical magnifying glass upon the sacred cows. "The Hausa-Fulani Union" (176) is full of acrid humor, as well as a very subtle but searing criticism. He comments on the Hausa States of the 19th century where the "rulers operated oppressive laws, imposed uncanonical and excessive taxation, took bribes to pervert justice and forcibly seized the property of their subjects." (177) They also indulged in voluptuous living, blatantly perverted justice, and believed in black magic. The exception to the rule was Uthman dan Fodio, a learned Fulani who embraced Islam.

Regarding the Fulani, Saro-Wiwa quotes from the famous British explorer, Mungo Park: "They evidently consider all the Negro natives as their inferiors; and when talking of different nations, always ranked themselves among the white people." (178) As followers of Mahomet, they adhere rigidly to the teachings of the Koran and force their children to do the same. The latter's character is nurtured to be docile and submissive. Saro-Wiwa, as witty as ever, contrasts rigid, harsh Islam with the more humane, reasonable Christianity. For instance, if the Islamic Sharia law were to be adopted by all of Nigeria, "it would make most present-day Nigerians one-armed. And you can be sure that Nigerians, being Nigerians, would pretend that they lost their first arm in a motor accident and then go on to try to lose the second." (178) The article ends with comments on the presence of Fulani learned men in Hausa kingdoms, serving as the kind of Special Assistants used today by Babangida. They often complained about the rulers' profligacy, Dan Fodio, in particular, preached against "excessive taxation (Sap), official corruption (okokoriko!), wrongful imprisonment (Gani), confiscation of property (oil in Rivers, Bendel, Akwa, Ibom, Imo States) and tyranny (I didn't mention any names)." (179) Saro-Wiwa promises to discuss the result of these preachments in a follow-up article which is, however, not written.

The key-word is *tyranny*. The allusion to the 19th-century Hausa as its perpetrators, and the Fulani as its proscribers is misleading. The perspicacious reader would, nonetheless, easily decipher the message, that the Hausa-Fulani are today's sacred tyrants. Babangida himself must have smiled cynically if he had read the article. His faithful special assistants would have reassured him that Saro-Wiwa was unserious, a disgruntled element, a rabble-rouser. The catch in the whole scenario is, that people did take him seriously, but those ones did not—do not—matter in the configurations of power in the sick society.

"Question Mark Over Nigeria" (129) reviews the evidence of Nigerian history and laments the sheer difficulty of making a nation out of the country. Its survival to date is due to the interest of European capitalism in a single, large market; minority leaders' belief in one Nigeria; prevalence of common sense in times of distress, and Providence, enabling its survival, in spite of pervasive incompetence, corruption, and cruelty. Saro-Wiwa, in this and other later articles of his collection, is very doubtful about the future. He calls for a National Conference, to dialogue, thus echoing the exhortation by other Nigerians. Naturally, Babangida remains deaf to such unpatriotic ideas! And here is where one appreciates Saro-Wiwa's special quality, to make us laugh in the midst of our national disaster. An abnormal reaction, one might say, but, in such circumstances, laughter is one panacea against murder, or suicide. And Nigerians, the kind that would use an arm lost as a result of crime to garner sympathy, would heartily pounce on their sympathy as one new victim of their viciousness. And people would cry for laughing at the criminals' extraordinary inventiveness and persuasiveness. And nobody would have the courage to protest laws that legitimize mangling of the human body and the mutilation of minds, and the massacre of a whole people's psyche, all in the name of unity and peace and patriotism.

An admirer of Saro-Wiwa's work writes: "*Similia* is arguably the most poised, the most distinguished and the most wide-ranging body of such opinions we are likely to have in the country in a long while." (Titi Adepitan: 21) Arguably yes; and arguably no. A sure point of agreement with that assessment would be the constancy of Saro-Wiwa's humor, its sometimes pedestrian and pompous nature notwithstanding. You may disagree with his position, but you cannot help laughing with him, even as he is laughing at you, and at himself. "All in the Family" (141) addresses his forgetfulness, a trait traced back to his mother and projected forward to his son who, as Saro-Wiwa did at an airport, forgot his books and briefcase in the classroom. One can image this short man, looking very preoccupied, searching for his pen which he finally finds in his shirt-pocket. One can image him reading all those love letters from "elegant Nigerian females...called Bola, Dupe, Tola, (all Yoruba) and similar sweetness. They are certainly not Ogoni." (153) They have written in response to his article, "Yorubaphobia," which caused much controversy. Offering a lighter side, these women proclaim their dancing ability with their "shest" (cf. his humorous quote of a popular singer, Sina Peters). These women, "shinamaniacs" all, throw him into "ecstasies of delight" (154) As a firm believer in *dialogue*, —a word Nigerianized into a synonym for *monologue* by officialdom— he advises them to send their letters to Babangida, to ask him to convene a "tribal palaver to discuss the national question." Thus, the comical is subtly used to highlight the serious issues of the Nigerian tragedy. Saro-Wiwa's interest in the female body, in particular, that of the Yoruba woman, must have made not a few mad. His declaration, that many Yoruba women prefer his "virile intervention in their affairs" to their men's contentedness with "a vista of banks," (154) not to forget his reminder about his "tall parts" (159) to a reader making fun of Saro-Wiwa's small stature, cannot be taken too seriously. Yet, each joke reveals the writer's true opinion on each matter. After reading all these articles, one would have liked to keep one's fingers crossed, in a manner similar to that adopted by those women, "Yoruba dames," who followed Saro-Wiwa and sent "a deluge of letters" on the national question to Babangida. They not only kept their fingers crossed, but also their "other personal property." (155)

Unfortunately, Nigeria does not allow one the luxury of waiting. The agents of death are always lurking in the dark, waiting to pounce on their innocent prey. Saro-Wiwa did not have long to wait, to put to test his determination to die with his "bit of timber" stuck in his mouth. "Yes, I know that I am a Mortuary Candidate. But I intend to head for that mortuary with my pipe smoking." (80) To those trying to scare him of the imminence and inevitability of cancer, he is quick to mention his smoking father, nearly ninety and still walking "ramrod straight," and his nearly eighty mother still consulting "the tiny little dark bottle—of snuff." (81) He thanks others for not smoking, happy that, the less the number of smokers, "the greater the share of tobacco." Little did he know when he was savoring the aroma of his smoke, that the medical danger foreseen by friends was nothing compared with the death awaiting him for smoking with words, relentlessly, without giving a quarter. One can only thank him for the laughter, and the smoke.

NOTES TO CHAPTER VIII

1. A superstar of Nigerian journalism, Dele Giwa once worked for Moshood Abiola, winner of Nigeria's annulled 1993 presidential elections and proprietor of *The Concord* newspaper. Giwa later founded a weekly magazine, *Newswatch*, which quickly attained a status similar to that enjoyed on the American shores by *Time* magazine. At the height of his career, Giwa was suddenly blown away by a parcel-bomb (1986). Until today, the case has not been solved, just as other mysterious deaths of "government enemies." Saro-Wiwa alludes to Giwa's murder in the novel, *Pita Dumbrok's Prison*: Pita's death, by a parcel-bomb, remains unresolved, and Pita is a young journalist determined to change society for the better.

2. Readers of *Times* would most likely agree that Yemi Ogunbiyi changed the paper's image by publishing thought-provoking articles and introducing a literary series to which intellectuals were eager to contribute. However, the modalities and logistics of Ogunbiyi's "wandering" into journalism and management left some people wondering about his integrity. He was dismissed as summarily as he had been appointed: The announcement of his demise was heard on radio by friends heading to his palatial home to celebrate with him the New Year.

3. Chinweizu is one of the three authors of a controversial work of criticism, *The West and the Rest of Us*. One of the others is Okechukwu Madubuike, a French major whose doctoral thesis was on the Senegalese novel, with a book appearing

later at Three Continents Press, in the United States. The French major found his niche in Nigerian politics, serving (curiously enough) as Nigeria's Federal Minister of Health in several military administrations.

4. See, "Reviving a Dying School" (21-24). The degradation of the writer's *alma mater* is used as an example of his professor's saying, "Give a good thing to an African and he will spoil it." The article is full of passion due to Saro-Wiwa's sadness at the depreciation. Yet, a close examination reveals a deep confusion and contradiction. Which *African* does the saying castigate? Whose fault is Umuahia's demise? Are Umuahia's Old Boys better, more "honest, efficient, competent, detribalized and meritorious" than others? Who, exactly, is doing the giving? The colonialists interested in exploiting their dear empire? Remarkably, all the alumni listed in the article are *Eastern Nigerians*, a grouping that Saro-Wiwa rejects in *Plain*. And the school's Latin song, In *Unum Luceant* (May they shine in one), can be construed as a form of exclusivism. They are to shine together, distinctly from others, with the Latin language underscoring the classical superiority complex hardly hidden in Saro-Wiwa's book.

5. One of them was Mamman Vatsa, Babangida's classmate and statemate and, reportedly, best friend. Among unconfirmed (and undenied) stories is the report that Babangida feared the threat posed by the more intelligent (and certainly more respected) Vatsa who also knew a potentially damaging secret, that Babangida's origins are in the Yoruba Ogbomosho town, and that his father moved from there to the northern town of Minna which he now calls his one and only home. Coincidentally, there also exists a rumor regarding the origins of the current military dictator, Abacha; that he is from Niger Republic.

6. This fact has since become very clear as the famous couple's marriage unraveled into divorce. The man and the woman's greatness has not been tainted, nonetheless.

7. One of Saro-Wiwa's compelling qualities is his readiness to laugh at himself. In the Appendix, a journalist, Bola Bolawole, relates the incident at the launching of *Plain*, when the author is called upon to deliver his address. Given his shortness, Saro-Wiwa simply disappears behind the lectern. He, however, calls out to the audience: "If you don't see me, don't worry!" (186)

8. *Wazobia* is coined from three words of Nigeria's three major languages: *Wa*, Yoruba; *Zo*, Hausa; *Bia*, Ibo, each meaning, *come*. As a simplistic show of national unity, the anchors on television are required to bid their viewers goodnight in three languages, at the end of each news broadcast. An ironic twist to the language issue has just occurred on the eve of the 21st century: the current Nigerian dictator, Abacha, has decreed that Nigerians must be bilingual, in English and French. Another source of befuddlement for Nigerians, but a boon

for their impoverished neighbors in Benin: the Ministry of Planning has arranged to send French teachers to Nigeria, to share in the latter's oil-wealth.

9. *Similia*: 106. This humorous "slip," well contrived, is a vivid commentary on Fafunwa's character. A highly reputed intellectual and specialist in education known by one and all as Babs Fafunwa, the man metamorphosed into Minister Aliyu Fafunwa, an avowed Moslem, and servant of Hausa-Fulani masters. An official circular was issued to warn everyone to call him by his correct name, or else, heads would roll.

IX. THE OGONI TRAGEDY AND SARO-WIWA'S COMMITMENT

-My worry about the Ogoni has been an article of faith.
(Saro-Wiwa, *A Month and a Day*: 49)
-The flames of Shell are hell
We bask beneath their light
(A popular Ogoni Song, in *Genocide in Nigeria*: 71)
-I do not know what we have done to make God punish us by bringing Shell-BP into our land.
(An Ogoni farmer, in *Genocide*: 76)
-Dance, my people, for we have seen tomorrow and there is an Ogoni star in the sky.[1]

INTRODUCTION: A LOCAL CRISIS, AN INTERNATIONAL AUDIENCE

From all indications, one may say that the last five years of Saro-Wiwa's life (1990-1995) were a culmination of his commitment to the Ogoni cause. The laughter of his other works is very rare in the two books of that period, *Genocide in Nigeria* (1992, henceforth referred to as *Genocide*), and *A Month and a Day* (published posthumously in 1995, and to be cited here as *Month*). Precisely, the author's sense of humor, ever present, is particularly acerbic, marked by a patent and impatient contempt for the arrogant, despicable dictatorship driving his people to the edge of the abyss as it continued to exploit their oil and dehumanize them. In choosing the title of the first text, Saro-Wiwa calls our attention to the United Nation's definition of *Genocide* as "the commission of acts with intent to destroy a national, ethnic, racial or religious group." (*Genocide*: 9) He is fully aware of the impact of his book, full of accusations and condemnations, and he challenges the Nigerian authorities: "I expect the ethnic majority in Nigeria to turn the heat of their well-known vindictiveness on me for writing this book. I defy them to do so." (*Genocide*: 9)

What is particular to *Genocide* and *Month*, is the audience to which they are directed: the international community. Saro-Wiwa explains his decision thus:

"Three recent events have encouraged me to now place the [Ogoni] issue before the world: the end of the Cold War, the increasing attention being paid to the global environment, and the insistence of the European Community that minority rights be respected, albeit in the successor states to the Soviet Union and in Yugoslavia. *What remains to be seen is whether Europe and America will apply in Nigeria the same standards which they have applied in Eastern Europe.*" (*Genocide*: 7, emphasis mine)

This move by Saro-Wiwa is perhaps the most important in regards to his people's continuing struggle in a situation where successive dictatorships consider Ogoni complaints as either minor, mosquito-buzzes to be ignored, or bites to be forestalled by quick, patriotic murders. For their part, the Nigerian populations are too engrossed in their various struggles for survival to appreciate, or empathize with, the Ogoni tragedy. Saro-Wiwa's strategy of exclusivism would, in itself, be a subject of interesting debate among observers. In his defense, one must note that, he did attempt to include other oil-producing ethnic groups in his quest for justice, as we shall see later in this chapter. The appeal to the international community has, at least, drawn attention to the Ogoni plight. It has also made Saro-Wiwa a hero, indeed, a martyr. Nonetheless, considering the West's track record, one must agree with the author, to adopt a wait-and-see attitude about their policy in Nigeria.

Up to date, that policy has been based upon economic selfishness, with only a token interest in humanity. Saro-Wiwa mentions the United States' actions in Nigeria where it buys "stolen property" (oil) from "thieves" (the ethnic majority). Western technology keeps Nigerian oil industry alive. Euro-American shareholders in the multinational oil companies -Shell-BP and Chevron- are beneficiaries of the genocide on Ogoni and the devastation of their land. Saro-Wiwa therefore appeals to Euro-America's sense of moral responsibility. He calls upon the international community to support the drive for Ogoni autonomy within a confederal Nigeria; to prevail upon Shell-BP and Chevron, as well as the Nigerian government that is abetting them, to stop gas-flaring in Ogoni; and to send experts to assist the Ogoni in restoring a semblance of normalcy to their devastated territory.

Genocide would be a very useful text to the foreign reader, because it presents the history of Ogoni nation from the pre-colonial day of isolation; through British colonialism and subjugation, to the present neo-colonialism by what Saro-Wiwa calls the ethnic majority. Saro-Wiwa emphasizes, for all these periods, the half-a-million Ogoni's ferocious desire to preserve their territory, a characteristic that earned them a reputation for cannibalism, and the importance of land: "The land is a god and is worshiped as such." He affirms the sacrosanctity of trees, rivers, and other elements of nature, all of which translates into "a deep awareness of the importance of the environment and the necessity to protect and preserve it." (*Genocide*: 12, 13) He traces the history of Ogoni's love of freedom, subsumed in their courage and rejection of any form of slavery. While the Igbos, for example, were being enslaved, the Ogoni abhorred slavery. They also forbade inter-ethnic marriage, except with the Ibibio. During the colonial subjugation, the Ogoni were, unfortunately, left behind in development. The area stagnated for some twenty years after 1914. It was in 1935, when the new city of Port Harcourt was built with a road linking it to other parts of the region, that real contact with the outside began. Even in those years, the Ogoni, led by the Ogoni Central Union, ruled as part of Opobo Division, were demanding a separate division, created in 1946. The Ogoni State Representative Assembly was formed in 1950 by the much revered Paul Birabi. Saro-Wiwa asserts with pride: "We were very well fed and the Ogoni people lacked for nothing." (*Genocide*: 18) The six kingdoms had a rich soil for agriculture, and rivers full of fishes and other sea food. Ogoni farmers and fishermen flourished, fed their families and, gradually, joined the modernization train. Schools were being built, and Ogoni languages were taught there. A general hospital and dispensaries were constructed. Saro-Wiwa here insists upon his people's enterprising nature, although in earlier texts, such as *Plain*, he has asserted that they were left far behind.

One notes a deliberate attempt by Saro-Wiwa to exaggerate in order to impress his foreign audience, a natural characteristic of any victim pleading his case against the oppressor: propaganda, to prove and underscore innocence, and make the victimizer all the more vicious. Thus, in *Genocide*, the Ogoni are depicted as very willing and able to develop themselves; only the exploiter, Nigeria, is stopping them. Nigeria's intrusion into Ogoni has also begun the process of Ogoni extinction. "While the Ogoni were struggling to pull themselves into the twentieth century, the Nigeria which the British had created and into which the Ogoni had been forced willy-nilly, was planning to drive them to extinction." (*Genocide*: 18) A similar strategy of propaganda may be seen in Saro-Wiwa's later emphasis on the environment. Which is not to claim that he is not genuinely interested in the subject. It is, one would say, an aspect of his activist evolution, that he has placed the matter in the forefront of his people's struggle, knowing full well that it is popular in the international arena. Specifically, as far as oil exploitation is concerned, gas-flaring is a poignant example of environmental degradation, a fact immediately noticed by any visitor to Ogoni. Joshua Hammer, a *Newsweek* bureau chief, writes: "The gas burns incessantly in giant geysers of flames and smoke, and at night the flares that ring the city of Port Harcourt and fishing villages deep within the mangrove swamps cast a hellish glow." (*Harper's Magazine*, June 1996: 58)

A Month and a Day: A Detention Diary, continues and concludes the writer-activist's appeal to the international community. It gives a shocking account of the events leading to, and during, his arrest and imprisonment after the later annulled presidential elections of June 12, 1993. This *diary* is different from the earlier *Plain* in the sense that Saro-Wiwa is no longer a peripheral player in the dance of death described in the civil-war chronicle. He is now at center-stage, the quarry of famished vampires ready to pursue their prey to anywhere. Unlike *Plain*, *A Month* provides ample evidence for whoever wishes to know why Nigeria is being carpeted for human rights' violations, and why, in a country considered Africa's potential leader in almost every facet of life due to its immense human and natural resources, millions are living below the poverty line as easy prey to starvation and the mortal stagnation mandated by messianic murderers posing as patriots. *A Month* also brings together, in a well-crafted narration, all the components of corruption, exploitation, and dehumanization already visited by Saro-Wiwa in other books: Nigerian military pimps, and political prostitutes; Shell-BP and Chevron multinational companies as agents of racist imperialism; the corrupt police well versed in maintaining the law and order of degradation and destruction of human rights and lives; the judiciary as puppets in the hands of powerful pranksters in a land with neither law nor justice; and the Ogoni leadership that, to Saro-Wiwa's dismay, proved to be allies of the enemy of the people. In brief, the story of June 21-July 22 1993, is a prelude to Saro-Wiwa's subsequent arrest, trial, and execution. By reading it, the international community would eschew any notion of understanding the so-called particularity of Nigeria, re-thinking, or second chance, which continues to be the plea by his murderers.

THE NIGERIAN GOVERNMENT AND SHELL-BP: "PARTNERS IN PROGRESS"

Now, of all the details of the Nigerian confusion offered in *Genocide*, the most convincing are those concerning the government policies and practices on oil, "the black gold," and their effects on Saro-Wiwa's people. Due to the roots of ethnicity in the country's fabric, competition for socioeconomic development has been particularly strong in Nigeria. Hence, oil and its sources play a major role in politics and policies. In Saro-Wiwa's view, the three major ethnic groups, Hausa-Fulani, Igbo and Yoruba, have ganged up as "indigenous colonialists" to exploit minority oil-producers, such as the Ogoni. We have already questioned the correctness of that view (for example, see chapter VI), as regards the true identity of the exploiters. What remains irrefutable is the fact of exploitation, by government acting in collusion with the oil companies.

Genocide presents some compelling facts on how Nigeria has been spending the billions accruing from oil, providing the country with some 95% of its income. The 1960 and 1963 Constitutions included a Derivation Policy requiring that 50% of mineral revenue and rents go to each Region where the minerals were found. With the outbreak of the civil war in 1967 and the advent of militarism and unitary government, that policy was deleted from the books. The Head of State, General Gowon, set up a Commission in 1970, to review the policy and make recommendations. The Dina Commission recommended 5% revenue and rent to mineral-producing areas.[2] Government rejected the idea. Gowon decreed that all off-shore oil and its proceeds be confiscated. That, claims Saro-Wiwa, was "the beginning of armed robbery of the Ogoni and other delta minorities." (*Genocide*: 84) The post-Gowon regime led first by Murtala Mohammed and, upon his assassination, by Olusegun Obasanjo, changed the policy to 25% for oil areas. However, the 1979 Constitution ushering in return to civilian rule, gave back 100% control to government. Meanwhile, the Obasanjo regime wrote a Land Use Decree into the Constitution, whereby government owned all the land which it leased to the citizens. Supposedly a nationalist policy, it was, in practice, the legalization of dictatorship over land which every person and group have always cherished as their God-given legacy. The Buhari government that seized power through a coup in 1983, allocated 1 1/2 % of funds to oil areas; however, the money was not paid, but lent to bankrupt states. (88) Finally, the Babangida government, enthroned after the 1985 coup, decided on a 2% Derivation Policy, the money for which was either never paid or, when paid, went into the pockets and personal accounts of the military masters and their faithful civilian servants. A Master of confusion popularly known as Maradona, Babangida created eleven new states and increased the local governments to nearly six hundred. One would disagree with Saro-Wiwa's opinion, that only the states in the oil-bearing areas were viable while those in majority areas were meant to pounce, vampire-like, on the resources of the Ogoni and others. (86) One would, nonetheless, agree that Babangida's ploy was to please his cronies, to give free food to the boys, and to silence his critics by ostensibly giving various groups a chance to develop. In his criticism, Saro-Wiwa, at last, specifies the real beneficiaries of the exploitation of his people: "Whereas the Ogoni are out of school, in *Borno State in the arid north*, there is free education at primary, secondary and tertiary levels." (87, emphasis mine) This opinion does not mean that he is free of the confused idea of an "ethnic majority" working together to the detriment of the people.

Saro-Wiwa's call for an Ogoni State is supported by many facts of their conditions of suffering, exploitation and underdevelopment in a Rivers State for which he himself was a staunch advocate. As he states, Rivers is "a microcosm of Nigeria [where] nothing works." (89) Furthermore, "there is no country. There is only organized brigandage." His most thought-provoking question: "Why is the international community supporting the massive fraud that is the Nigerian nation?" (91) There is nothing original in that statement; what is significant is the fact that its author was once a hard-liner regarding the sacrosanctity of Nigerian solidity. The question put to "the international community," that is, to Euro-America, can only be rhetorical, the author himself having given the answer in his detailed history of colonialism-imperialism and neo-colonialism, the point of convergence of master-exploiter old and new. Another significant point: once Saro-Wiwa decided to deal exclusively with the Ogoni question, he went all out, with all the weapons available to him, and words were a huge part of his arsenal. In addition to points of exaggeration already mentioned, there are other areas where Saro-Wiwa has made of the minorities-the Ogoni, in particular- the only good people in Nigeria. For example, it is not true, as he has claimed (*Genocide*: 26-27), that only the minorities argued for the continued existence of one Nigeria. His explanation of the war as being the result of the Igbo's refusal to accept political restructuring, is simplistic and flawed. He has played hard and long in *Plain* (see chapter VI) on Ojukwu's inveterate lies and "masturbating egotism, intransigence and political illiteracy." (*Genocide*: 27) He actually quotes some fifteen pages from his civil-war diary in the latter text. Still, his position remains unconvincing. One would have expected him, a "thinking" person, to have modified his views, to have made them more realistic and more analytical over the years. Saro-Wiwa also contends that the large number of 30,000 Ogoni deaths during the war, "made no impression whatsoever on Nigerian officials or people. The only conclusion that can be drawn therefore is that the Ogoni live in a nation which is determined to exterminate them and that Ogoni lives mean nothing whatsoever to Nigeria and other Nigerians, and, I dare to add, the murderous country would be pleased to see Ogoni territory rid of all its inhabitants so that its oil resources can fall freely into 'Nigerian' hands." (*Genocide*: 43) Here, Saro-Wiwa confuses the government with the people, the *ruling* victimizers and oppressors with their *ruled* victims and oppressed. In his fervent Ogoni activism, he may have forgotten that there are other victims of the war, not in the least the millions of Igbo led by the egomaniacal Ojukwu to the slaughterhouse. And most interestingly, the author admits the existence and viability of a Nigerian nation as a matter of convenience, to prove the concerted efforts to exterminate his people.

Oil, one must agree, is the cause of the country's curse. If Saro-Wiwa can be criticized for paranoia, the Nigerian vultures are guilty of much worse, from arrogant insensitivity to absolute inhumanism. Witness the claim by officialdom that God put riches into the land and those living on it do not count; in other words, the Ogoni have no right to claim the oil in their area, it is the property of Nigeria. Such fallacy is also mouthed by some so-called progressives, including Kole Omotoso, writer-scholar and Saro-Wiwa's friend, who, in his review of *Plain*, asked: "How true is it to say that the riverine areas 'produce' oil? Are we to assume that the people of the riverine areas produce oil in the same way that the Ondo people produce cocoa or Kano produce cotton?" (*Genocide*: 100) It may interest the reader to know that Omotoso hails from Ondo State, and that the oil-belongs-to-all-of-us lobbyists are fully aware that both cocoa and cotton are almost zero revenue-producing commodities forgotten in the rush for "black gold."

The two books under review prove Shell-BP's role in the Ogoni genocide. As is common in colonial situations, a combination of government's unforgivable ignorance of the oil industry, and the Ogoni's understandable naivete, gave the oil company a free hand to exploit the land. By every reckoning, Shell-BP is a perfect example of international capitalism in its worst character of cruelty, stupidity and racism. From the beginning, when oil was struck in the Niger Delta in the 50's, Shell-BP was able to implement its policy as a partner with government in the progressive devastation of the ecology while pretending to cooperate in developing the areas of operation. With the British colonialists in charge, it was easy; with their Nigerian neocolonialist replacement, it was even easier; for, the oil company only needed to cultivate the culture of corruption with a handful of key players, in order to sidetrack the already lax laws.

In 1970, Ogoni leaders petitioned the military government over Shell-BP's unbridled contravention of civilized rules. The "humble petition" asks for the government's "fatherly attention." It states that the land in the highly populated area is being polluted by Shell-BP; that, agriculture, formerly the people's economic mainstay, has been disrupted as a result of the "connivance between a nation which seems to have allowed Shell-BP, a commercial organization, to enter upon and seize the people's land at will." (*Genocide*: 45) That oil royalties seem to be government's sole interest; that the company pays a meager, one-time one British pound sterling and ten pence fee per acre to farmers on whose land oil is being exploited. Shell-BP is also accused of destroying cash crops. It disregards existing Petroleum Drilling and Production Regulations. Attached to the petition are photographs showing devastated land, and crude-oil overflow that has destroyed mangrove swamps, and rivers and streams with their fishes. The document also contends that, before Shell-BP's coming, the untarred roads were passable; however, the company has broken the roads' resistance with its heavy trucks and equipment. At the human level, Shell-BP hardly employs Ogoni. The same neglect is noticeable in government employment habits. Neither the company nor government gives scholarships for educating Ogoni children. The petition demands that government and Shell-BP make reparations; that the existing Petroleum Regulations, symptomatic of the First Republic's "immoral political thinking" (*Genocide*: 47), be changed to make the oil-producers participants in the laws and beneficiaries of the wealth; that land acquisition should be directly negotiated between the owners and Shell-BP, with government as arbitrator; that one thousand pounds sterling be paid to landowners as rent per acre per annum; that the company should make alternative arrangements for water supply and other life-supporting necessities; that a special rehabilitation program be arranged to settle war-returnee farmers recently deprived of their farms and crops; and that government grant an interview to Ogoni leaders for further discussions.

Shell-BP responded to the military government. Its letter attempts to exonerate it from any wrongdoing and to show that, on the contrary, it has always been the government's "partner in progress." In Shell-BP's view, the Ogoni petition is one of a series, trying, in recent years, "to place development and other responsibilities on this Company which can only be properly undertaken by Government." (50) The Ogoni leaders are accused of lying. Shell-BP would like to highlight its oil-exploitation as the area in which it makes "a very significant contribution to the overall economic development of any country in which it operates." (51) It claims to have meticulously observed agreements made *with the Federal Government* and *the laws* relating to the oil industry in Nigeria. It declares that the Ogoni petition is full of exaggerations and misrepresentations, and a deliberate minimization of the people's benefits, benefits that far outweigh any disadvantages.

In a more comprehensive letter to the Chief Petroleum Engineer of the Federal Ministry of Mines and Power, Shell-BP proudly states that it pays an annual rental fee of four pounds per acre to land-owners, after an initial compensation; that those owners are not the ones complaining; that it is, indeed, a lie that Ogoni Division is the main home of Nigerian oil industry: only 15% of Shell-BP's production comes from the area. Shell-BP, according to the letter, has done its utmost to prevent further oil spillages. River-pollution is not widespread; it is "a temporary, not permanent, condition." (54) It gives a list of roads widened, drained and tarred by the company, the longest being a five-mile stretch, and twenty miles of new roads connecting drilling locations. Shell-BP believes that Ogoni should qualify for employment and scholarships on the same basis as other Nigerian nationals. To show its magnanimity and commitment to the underprivileged, in spite of its belief in a merit system, Shell-BP cites its 1969 scholarship award to an Ogoni boy to study abroad, "even though he had only a West African School Certificate." (56)

Saro-Wiwa, who was then Commissioner for Education in the State government, comments that the Shell-BP letter's signatory may have been another unwilling victim of "a Satanic octopus which demands men's souls in return for cash and security." (56) Although his name is not directly mentioned, it is clear that Saro-Wiwa is one of those accused of lying and trying to mislead the satisfied land-owners. Government did nothing about the Ogoni protest and the Shell-BP response. A few days after the oil company's self-congratulatory document, there was a major blow-out at the Bomu oil field.

"The young people of Dere (Bomu)" responded to the blast with a document to the authorities signed by Sam Bako of Secondary Commercial School, Taabaa. In the oil-polluted land, there is "no food to eat, no water to drink, no homes to live and worst of all, no air to breathe. We now live in what Hobbes may describe as a STATE OF NATURE—a state where peace or security does not exist." (58) It continues: "Shell-BP is the leviathan to whom we have been forced to surrender all our Rights including our very life." (63) A second petition was presented to Shell-BP by The Dere Youths Association. It complains of the company's "Godless economic policy." (64) A third letter, by Dere Students' Union, was sent to the company's Manager and copied to government, seeking meaningful negotiations and compensations for damages. Reaction: "a deafening silence." (70) Meanwhile, the Committee of Ogoni Citizens wrote to the London-based *West Africa* magazine. It did not publish their letter. The magazine, *Africa Impact*, published an article written by Oamen Enaholo, on the oil disaster. That caught the government's attention.

The committee set up by the government, including Saro-Wiwa, wrote a report, establishing that Shell-BP's outdated equipment partially caused the accident, and recommending rehabilitation and resettlement of the area. No action was taken. The company's deviousness and government's disinterest prevailed. Before the report was submitted, some Dere individuals had sued Shell-BP for a two hundred and fifty thousand pounds compensation. The High Court, usually famous for its tardiness, uncharacteristically acted swiftly and made the company pay one hundred and sixty-eight thousand, four hundred and sixty-eight pounds. The judge was soon knighted by the Queen. Until today, the wasteland at the spillage site remains. It is interesting to note that Saro-Wiwa does not take to task the Dere group that was paid off. Such groups, as we shall soon see in the section on the Ogoni leadership, contributed in a significant manner to the author-activist's failure to fulfill his dream of Ogoni triumph over Shell-BP and the military dictatorship.

Saro-Wiwa roundly condemns Shell-BP's sinister attitude in Nigeria, as it flares gas indiscriminately, promotes European culture unashamedly, and kills the Ogoni ecology, while, in Europe, it keeps winning prizes for environmental protection. "In Shell's racist mind, what is good for the whites must not be good for blacks." (82) He exhibits his knack for creative artistry when he describes Shell-BP as the unseen hand manipulating the cruel Nigerian *masquerade* (*Month*: 186) dancing and frightening people. To disrobe the masquerade, Saro-Wiwa reports that he approached its manipulators and, naturally, found that, for them, it is all a matter of money. Their mind set is, that peace and stability are essential for effective imperialism. Saro-Wiwa's use of the masquerade as metaphor, shows the extent of the bastardization of Nigerian ethos and entity. In the normal setting, the masquerade is symbol of ancestry, of the continuity of the culture, with the dead watching over the living to whom they offer their support and from whom they elicit respect and a promise of integrity and dignity. Saro-Wiwa's masquerade is a fluke, an impostor fabricated by the sham leaders and their oil-soaked collaborators.

OGONI LEADERS AS COLLABORATORS

In his account of the events leading to, and during, his 1993 arrest and imprisonment,[3] Saro-Wiwa unmasks those Ogoni leaders, erstwhile associates of his, who have acted in collusion with their people's oppressors and Saro-Wiwa's killers. One of them is Bennet Birabi, son of late Paul Birabi, the most famous Ogoni ever, the man whose name is synonymous with Ogoni nationalism. Saro-Wiwa played a prominent role in the young Birabi's education; Bennet was like a younger brother and a member of the Saro-Wiwa household until his graduation from medical school. Once an activist in the Movement for the Survival of Ogoni People (MOSOP), Birabi later turned pro-establishment. He was a Minister before the 1983 coup. Later, in the Third Republic, he became a Senate Minority Leader. When Saro-Wiwa and others organized the January 4, 1993 march celebrating Ogoni Day, Birabi was conspicuously absent. Yet Saro-Wiwa was not sure of Birabi's collusion with government; for, Birabi accompanied Saro-Wiwa, Leton and Kobani, MOSOP's leaders, to meetings with the Inspector-General of Police and the security chiefs. Birabi did express his opposition to Saro-Wiwa's accepted proposal to boycott the June 12, 1993 presidential election, because it "would not be in HIS political interests." (*Month*: 175) Birabi called together his hometown people on the election day and berated them. Their answer was, that he had not deemed it fit to call them together since his victory at the senatorial election. Birabi never forgot the disgrace, which he blamed upon Saro-Wiwa.

Another turn-coat was Edward Kobani, Vice-President of MOSOP, who was one of the four victims of the May 20, 1994 murders for which Saro-Wiwa and eight comrades were hanged in November 1995. Kobani was a long-time senior friend of Saro-Wiwa's. A known iconoclast, Kobani later became state commissioner and respectable leader. Other Biafran Ogoni, such as Leton, MOSOP's President, were very angry at Saro-Wiwa's efforts in helping Kobani's political progress because, in their opinion, Kobani was dishonorable and untrustworthy. Saro-Wiwa did not pay any mind to that viewpoint. It was later, when he found himself being hounded by government and being betrayed by his compatriots, that he looked back and realized his mistake.

In *Month* (52), he expresses his sad opinion on the prostitute's mentality of the educated Ogoni. To some extent, this makes one wonder about the solidarity constantly proclaimed by Saro-Wiwa. His declaration in *Plain*, and elsewhere, that the ethnic majority has concertedly prevented Ogoni and other minorities from participating in government and from partaking in the booty abounding from petrodollars, would also be brought into doubt. Birabi, Kobani and others (including Saro-Wiwa himself!) have enjoyed various perquisites, such as ministerial posts and directorship in parastatals. The neocolonial masters have never had a problem using minority leaders as handmaids in carrying out their dirty jobs. For example, every electoral commission is invariably headed by a minority stooge, specifically mandated to doctor documents, manipulate the modalities of the exercise, and make sure the government's chosen candidates sail home as winners.

Saro-Wiwa would stand tall as one of the very few to openly and expeditiously identify with the Federal government during the civil war. He also must be commended for maintaining a high level of integrity. While working tirelessly to organize the Ogoni, he was careful not to take public positions of prominence. Even as controversy mounted over the choice of Kobani as Vice-President of MOSOP, Saro-Wiwa stuck by his senior friend. For the presidency, another elder, Dr. Leton, was appointed, although Saro-Wiwa was blamed by two ordinary women for declining the post. (*Month*: 52) Leton, once considered by Saro-Wiwa as "the quintessential Ogoni man," (178) proved to be another opportunist.

Engaged on the Biafran side during the civil war, Leton was ushered back by Saro-Wiwa into the Rivers political fold, and later became a Federal minister. He, however, largely excelled in selfishness. Saro-Wiwa writes: "The generality of the Ogoni were not happy with him, thinking that in all of the positions which he held, he had not been helpful to them." (179) Saro-Wiwa was less bothered by the people's parochial criticism than by Leton's tendency to destroy any Ogoni outfit that he did not lead. That is precisely why Leton was given the post of MOSOP President. Interestingly enough, Leton and others accused Saro-Wiwa of exactly the same shortcoming of power-hunger.

Saro-Wiwa concludes in *Month*, that it is far easier to unite the masses than to associate a handful of graduates with a vision. He complains of the inability of the Ogoni elite to provide leadership. One would assume that the detailed account of events in *Month* are meant to show how Saro-Wiwa tried to provide that leadership. Upon reading the diary, one is impressed by his courage, perception, persuasiveness, and charisma, on one hand; one is struck, on the other, by how easily he aroused his co-elite's anger, envy, and animosity. Could it be that Saro-Wiwa had that superiority complex that turned off others who felt belittled by his bent for absolutism, and his refusal to negotiate positions, to combine the best of his ideas with the best of others'? Perhaps Leton, Birabi, Kobani, and others, were ashamed of being overwhelmed by the brilliant sun in which Saro-Wiwa basked; perhaps they were simply opportunists unable to countenance a man of quality who stood by his principles; perhaps Saro-Wiwa lacked the ability to convince others capable of thinking; or, perhaps there was genuine reason to complain about his stifling complex.

Several actions serve as examples of Saro-Wiwa's commitment to the Ogoni and his co-leaders' complicity with their oppressors. He proposed the celebration of Ogoni Day on January 4, 1993, to mark Ogoni solidarity and commitment to the struggle for autonomy and for reparations from Shell-BP and government. The Rivers State governor, Ada George,[4] opposed the idea and, "as usual, the first persons used were the Ogoni people themselves." (*Month: 142*) George failed to scuttle the celebration which drew 300,000 people in a non-violent march of both contestation and celebration. One of Saro-Wiwa's opponents was an elder, Albert Badey, "a dyed-in-the-wool gerontocrat." (143) Besides, Badey had no faith in the masses. Though very ambitious, he was not successful beyond the state level where he became Secretary to the government in

1970.[5] Badey, having stayed away from the march, gathered together with other reactionaries on January 9, 1993, to express an opinion more conciliatory to government. A communique was issued, reaffirming Ogoni faith in government and reconfirming their commitment to the peaceful pursuit of their grievances. It also expressed an awareness of government's "encouraging actions and hope that "our President... will grant the Ogoni people audience for reasoned presentation of their demand. Consequently, no further demonstration will be held in expectations of the positive reaction of government to their cry." (*Month*: 144) This action was taken without MOSOP's approval, and while Saro-Wiwa and the other leaders were away at Lagos upon the invitation of the Inspector-General of Police. The communique was published in the government-owned newspaper, *Nigerian Tide*. Saro-Wiwa had every reason to believe that the big babies' shameless cry was sponsored by government to deride MOSOP.

With each speech at home and abroad, Saro-Wiwa became a larger target for his enemies inside and outside Ogoni. His successes on the international scene must have left them bewildered and all the more desperate to destroy him. The government's forces were becoming more violent against the people. On April 30, 1993, soldiers visited mayhem and massacre on the villagers of Biara for protesting against Shell-BP's dualized pipeline after a recent oil-spillage. Shell-BP was forced to stop work in the area. A press release by government stooges castigated MOSOP for the soldiers' violence, called upon government to do whatever it wished to establish law and order, while apologizing profusely for the unfortunate incident. "No government will allow a break-down of law and order which will result in a state of anarchy." (159) That advertisement was later cited by Shell-BP as an example of MOSOP's counter-productivity and Saro-Wiwa's lack of support. That was when Babangida signed what was popularly known as *the Saro-Wiwa Decree*, the Treason and Treasonable Felony Decree, 1993, which was later used to condemn him to death in 1995. Fast upon the heels of the promulgated decree came a Shell-BP "Briefing Note," accusing him of seeking political self-determination for the Ogoni—a treasonable felony! In further service as government's mouth-piece, Shell-BP berated Saro-Wiwa for taking the Ogoni case to the Geneva-based Unrepresented Nations and Peoples Organization (UNPO), a non-United Nations' organ and averred that "Nigerian problems should be resolved in Nigeria by agreement between Nigerian people." (165) When Nigeria's Attorney-General, Akpamgbo, was asked whether the Treason decree was specifically crafted to nab Saro-Wiwa, he responded that if the cap fitted, Saro-Wiwa should wear it. Saro-Wiwa traveled abroad to alert the international community of the dangers of the decree. In his absence, Kobani, Leton, and Badey worked feverishly to obtain the people's permission for Shell-BP to resume construction of its pipelines. The people refused.

Saro-Wiwa already thought of boycotting the June 12, 1993 presidential elections in February; only the politicians in MOSOP leadership opposed the idea. When it was later put to vote in the Steering Committee, it passed. Kobani, for example, gave notice that he would rather resign than accept the decision. He and Leton tried to pressurize Saro-Wiwa to help rescind the boycott vote; Saro-Wiwa remained adamant. Both Leton and Kobani informed him of their resignation. Saro-Wiwa went into the community to inform them of the committee's decision. He insisted on a non-violent boycott. In a press conference, he explained the action "in confirmation of the non-violent struggle launched by the Ogoni people on 4 January, 1993 against the planned genocide of the Ogoni by the Nigerian nation-state." (176) He also called for the convening of a sovereign national conference to discuss reforms of the existing system and to redress the balance of power. On election-day, he was at Lagos after having been disallowed to travel to Vienna for the UN World Human Rights Conference. The government radio at Port Harcourt announced that he had urged people to go out and vote. He later learnt that dirty trick was the handiwork of Leton, Kobani and Birabi. The election boycott was the main reason for Saro-Wiwa's June 21 arrest. He was visited in his Owerri cell by family and friends, one of the most memorable being Kobani who reminded him of one of his, Saro-Wiwa's statements, "that the revolution would invariably claim its victims." (199) Little did Kobani know that he himself, Albert Badey, and Samuel Oroge, three signatories to the 1990 Ogoni Bill of Rights, would be among the victims. On May 20, 1994, the three, and Oroge's brother, Theophilus, were murdered.

SARO-WIWA, THE OGONI YOUTH, AND NON-VIOLENCE

Month offers very useful information on Saro-Wiwa's evolution as an activist: the genesis of his commitment; the growth of his personality and power; the organizational skills that helped forge the forceful front that, at his death, caused panic within Nigeria's dictatorship. The diary is essential reading for anyone trying to bring people together as a sociopolitical force. "A lot of energy, patience, and money," (56) those are the three necessary ingredients; the last, he found particularly challenging, since he wished to have financial security with his integrity intact. Till date, it can be said that he did succeed, that he was always able to look anyone in the eyes. Combining business acumen in his grocery store, wholesale trading and landed-property acquisition, with his writing and publishing, as well as the experience in publicity garnered from his television series, Saro-Wiwa built an international reputation unequaled by any other Nigerian activist. He kept learning as he moved along. The lessons from abroad were most useful. The name, MOSOP, was chosen because it reminded people of the Israeli secret service, Mossad. The Soviet Union example opened up to him the vista of the disintegration of a multi-ethnic state. His visits to the United States awakened his awareness of the environment and the politics of the ecosystem.

He saw the usefulness of foreigners, such as the Briton, William Boyd, author of *A Good Man in Africa* and son of a former medical officer at Saro-Wiwa's alma mater, Ibadan University. Boyd advised him to contact Amnesty International and Greenpeace. Interaction with them made him draft the addendum, "An Appeal to the International Community," to the Ogoni Bill of Rights. (*Month*: 89) It also influenced his establishment of the *Ethnic Minority Rights Organization of Africa*. His travels brought him in contact with the English film makers, Glen Ellis and Kay Bishop; the latter made *The Heat of the Moment*, a 1992 documentary on the Ogoni case. The duo helped with other areas of publicity. Saro-Wiwa became involved with other non-governmental organizations, like the *Association of Threatened Peoples of Germany*, the *UN Working Group on Indigenous Populations*, and the aforementioned UNPO, founded by the Dutch, Michael van Walt van der Praag. Saro-Wiwa writes that he was especially impressed that the UNPO "members foreswear violence in their struggle for local autonomy, self-determination or independence." (*Month*: 94)

The philosophy of non-violence *a la Martin Luther King Jr.* and solidarity with Ogoni youth were constant features in Saro-Wiwa's speeches, particularly during the final five years of his life. It appears that Saro-Wiwa was always drawn to youths to whom he acted as a father figure and a leader.[6] His rapport with younger elements must also have been necessitated and facilitated by the conflictual relationship between him and other Ogoni elders. When in 1992, "Babangida's trickery and unpredictability, as he maneuvered and fooled the Nigerian people had lifted the ban on most politicians, [the Ogoni politicians'] commitment to the hard work that was essential in promoting the cause had become questionable." (*Month*: 101) Since MOSOP is not involved in mainstream politics, such individuals as Kobani and Badey could not stay on the sidelines with MOSOP while others were warming up for the race to parliament and, invariably, to the bank. So, Saro-Wiwa found ready support—more reliable, more committed, more easily controllable—among the youths. He was already working with youths, defined as "people who are below the age of forty." (102) The Young professionals that he met during his 1990 American trip encouraged him about the future. (176) Under the auspices of the Ogoni Central Union, he was already organizing seminars to mobilize the youths. He held meetings with the Ogoni Klub of young professionals. Mobilization meant convincing everyone of the nature and necessity of the Ogoni cause "so that everyone knows and believes in that cause and holds it as a religion." (75)

It was not difficult to encourage youths to organize, because of their condition of marginalization. Saro-Wiwa's presence on both the national and international scenes helped, too. After publication of the report on his United Nations trip in 1992, and the film, *Heat of the Moment*, had been shown, a few youths began to attend MOSOP Steering Committee meetings. On his regular tours of the six kingdoms, "there was a large number of youth angry with a society that had cheated them and who were therefore eager to hear us, to learn." (102) Through his influence, youths formed, in 1990, the Committee for Ogoni Autonomy in which his nephew, Barika Idamkue, was the moving spirit. By 1992, Ogoni youths became a constant presence in Saro-Wiwa's public life. He planned the January 1993 march with them. While some elders were being cowardly, the youths were absolutely courageous. They stood by Saro-Wiwa to the bitter end. They served as his bodyguard. On one occasion during the march, they carried him shoulder-high to the rostrum. (125) It would be correct to say that the youths, in their turn, gave him the courage to continue, and that they deserve a large share of the success of the Ogoni struggle.

The State realizes this; hence, the determination to kill any young persons considered pro-Saro-Wiwa. During his 1993 arrest, Saro-Wiwa saw on a police officer's desk a list of youths to be arrested. (21) Since his execution, Ogoni youths have been harassed. A group of them is currently standing trial for treason, the same offense for which Saro-Wiwa lost his life. Now, any analytical review of Saro-Wiwa's life cannot be complete without an understanding of the controversial issue of violence. We have already noted that, in his every pronouncement, he insisted on non-violent protest. We also recall the affirmation of the young Ibani woman who staunchly defends the man's non-violence credo (see chapter 1). He himself writes that, as he went round seeking support for the Ogoni Bill of Rights, "I continued to press the case for non-violent struggle at every available forum." (71) In his keynote address to the Kagote, an elite club, in 1990, he declared: "This is not, I repeat, NOT a call to violent action." (75) And the great march of January 1993 was a peaceful affair: "Almost two-thirds of the Ogoni population had marched peacefully (...) It was a great dance of the anger of the people. Not a stone was thrown and no one was hurt. Some of the youths, out of misguided enthusiasm, did stop travelers going to Port Harcourt to work. But apart from that, there were no incidents whatsoever." (133)

Saro-Wiwa writes of his pride on the outcome of that "liberation day" and the hope that he had started "a movement which might transform Africa." (134) It is not clear whether the emphasis is to be placed on the movement, or the manner of its operation, or, indeed, both. Events subsequent to that day of glory for Saro-Wiwa and the 300,000 marchers, have proved the mistake of thinking that it "signaled the commencement of the non-violent resistance to our denigrators as a people." (13) For, nothing in the narration by Saro-Wiwa shows, beyond his speeches, any plan or strategy to establish and maintain non-violence *in action*. He himself writes about his fear that violence might erupt, for instance, in Port Harcourt after the youths had learnt of his arrest. (30) And there was violence. The youths "made sure that the town of Port Harcourt heard their protest at my arrest." (18)

Saro-Wiwa's choice of non-violence is explained thus by Baton Mitee, an Ogoni activist and brother to Ledum Mitee who was conspicuously acquitted at the Saro-Wiwa trial: "Ken had this idea from the time he was fifteen. He wanted to create a campaign modeled after the American civil-rights movement, with mass protests, sit-ins, boycotts, vigils. He started mobilizing in 1990." (*Harper's Magazine*, June 1996: 61) Saro-Wiwa knew that the Ogoni could not meet the state machine's violence with violence. He therefore placed a premium on the spirit, which no gun can silence. He also said: "I am aware, though, that non-violent struggle occasions more death than armed struggle. And that remains a cause for worry at all times. Whether the Ogoni people will be able to withstand the rigours of the struggle is yet to be seen." (*Month*: 194) The rigors include the barbarity of a government prepared to mow down anyone it deems unfit to live; the absence of legal provisions to affirm and support protester's rights; the silence collusion of an underdeveloped community caught in its own condition of anomy. A comparison of the Nigerian situation with the American, would serve a useful purpose, showing as it does the high risk of the Wiwan engagement.

Martin Luther King, Jr. writes: "Nonviolence is a powerful and just weapon. It is a weapon unique in history, which cuts without wounding and ennobles the man who wields it. It is a sword that heals... Nonviolent direct action proved that it could win victories without losing wars, and so became the triumphant tactic of the Negro Revolution of 1963."[7] The revolution to which the Nobel-winning father of American non-violence is referring, occurred in the right place at the right time. Then-Vice President Lyndon Johnson declared, "Emancipation was a Proclamation but not a fact." (*Why*: 23) Blacks were bent upon arousing America's sleeping conscience. The mood of the nation gave them the courage to go ahead. That courage, one must note, complemented their own courage, born through years of slavery and the unfulfilled dreams of emancipation. Martin Luther King and his followers forced their oppressors to commit their racist crimes openly, certain as they were that their nation would not want to live through such embarrassment before the whole world. On the contrary, Nigeria's oppressors do not care about world opinion. Bold-faced, fanatical vultures, they would dare their critics to do their worst.

Furthermore, King and his brothers and sisters were fighting for integration. Saro-Wiwa and the Ogoni, no. Theirs is a struggle for segregation, or separation. Human rights are, of course, involved; but, the declared ultimate goal is, "to establish a government of Ogoni people by Ogoni for Ogoni people in Ogoni within a confederal Nigeria." (*Month*: 111) Given that goal and Nigeria's particularly inhuman circumstances, one cannot but wonder whether non-violence has a chance to succeed.

Unlike in the United States where King wanted to heal wounds on both sides, to re-humanize both the oppressor and the oppressed, to cure the sick racist and give succor to his victim so that they may both become human again, Nigeria has provided Saro-Wiwa and the Ogoni with the desire to lash out at the enemy, the brute incapable of evolving into a human being.

In spite of any criticism one may have against the United States, one is compelled to accept the fact of its nationhood, with the American Dream swelling each and every heart almost to the point of explosion. That no nation exists in Nigeria is a boring cliche exposed and exploited by all, Saro-Wiwa inclusive. The American nation of the 60's had a president, John F. Kennedy, who was respected by Blacks. King commended his moral commitment. (*Why*: 21) As for Nigeria, Saro-Wiwa writes about its president, Babangida: "I reserved for him that contempt which I normally accord to vermin." (*Month*: 197) In short, the combination of a modern-day disaster called Nigeria, a misleader named Babangida, and his government geared towards the perpetuation of injustice by the most violent means imaginable, can hardly be considered a conducive setting for non-violent struggle.

Saro-Wiwa's use of Ogoni youths as the instruments of his philosophy, is another pertinent subject of debate. In other known cases, such as the King effort, and that of the Mandela-led South Africans, youths have been known to either reject non-violence absolutely, or accept it reluctantly. During the 60's, King was not popular among Black youths, who preferred the direct, militant action of such organizations as the Stokely Carmichael-led SNCC and the Black Moslems. In the annals of "the Negro Revolution," it remains debatable whether King's nonviolence was more effective than Malcolm X's by-all-means-necessary counter violence. The anti-apartheid struggle in South Africa relied heavily on the African National Congress's Youth Wing, basically the armed and dangerous *Spear of the People*. No pretext at peaceful means as the sole, or principal weapon. And, to return to the King example, it is an open secret that, at the time of his assassination, he had lost much of his support within the black masses; and he seemed and sounded disillusioned, ready for martyrdom. Perhaps if he had had a chance to live to continue the struggle to reach the top of the mountain, side by side with his people, King would have changed tactics.

In this critic's humble opinion, Saro-Wiwa could not have imagined that his youthful followers were carrying out to the letter his preaching on non-violence. Knowing full well that the system lived and breathed violence, he must have realized that some form of violence could not be avoided by his own people. His own language in those many speeches quoted in his books, reeks of violence, and necessarily so, in order to conscientize his people, "to fight relentlessly for [their] rights." (*Month*: 132) That notwithstanding, one cannot in any way compare whatever violence existed within Saro-Wiwa's organization, to that, actualized by sophisticated weaponry, in which the government engaged in its oppression of the people.

The behavior of the youths brings to mind one of Saro-Wiwa's stories in *A Forest of Flowers*. "The Bonfire" recounts the life of a village recluse, Nedam who, by dint of hard work, becomes a successful farmer. His co-villagers believe that he is evil, that he is the cause of recent deaths in the community. At the burial ceremony of one of the departed, the youth of the village decide to make Nedam pay. They throw him inside his house and set it on fire. From within "came a horrendous clamour of human screams, a shriek of anguish and terror which rose above the bonfire. As the house burned, the youth of Dukana formed themselves into a ring round it to ensure that their victim did not escape." (*Forest*: 39)

CONCLUSION: PRISON AS A PRELUDE TO DEATH

The narrative of Saro-Wiwa's 1993 imprisonment, for one month and a day, is marked by violence (oppressors) and counter violence (oppressed). From top to bottom, one senses a pervasive atmosphere of tension, like an earthquake preparing for a tremendous eruption. The strange characteristic of the Nigerian example is, that this quake would snuff the life out of the already battered oppressed. For once in his lifetime, here is Saro-Wiwa calling Babangida by an appropriate name, "the monster of Minna." (*Month*: 236) Here he is feeling justified outrage at the magistrate and police chiefs, fellow minority people, "acting for the Hausa bandit, if Hausa he is, called Babangida, who should have been before a firing squad for treason against his country." (220)

The descriptions of the police at their irresponsible best, would be useful reading for any visitor to Nigeria, as a preparation for life among uniformed bandits and robbers of law and order. Arrested in Port Harcourt, Saro-Wiwa is made to write and sign a statement. He is whisked off to Lagos in a van, on a journey lasting hours. At Lagos, he is forced to make another statement; the responsible police officer reminds him: "That was Port Harcourt. You are now in Lagos." (23) The officer expresses uncertainty as to what to do with his famous prisoner. On the following day, Saro-Wiwa is driven back east, to Owerri, where the officer leaves him and two other arrested Ogoni activists with word that he will return in a couple of days. He never does. Some days later, the prisoner is taken to a Port Harcourt court, not to the one at Owerri where Saro-Wiwa's lawyers obtained an order for police to produce him. The magistrate takes only minutes to order him committed to prison custody until her return from a leave lasting two months. In Port Harcourt prison, Saro-Wiwa insists on his human rights. After collapsing he is taken to a hospital and given adequate medical treatment. Efforts are being made at home and abroad to secure his release. Amnesty International declares him and the other two Ogoni prisoners of conscience. The Association of Nigerian Authors sends petitions to the powers that be. As suddenly as he was arrested, he is released on July 22, 1993. Not outright: He is granted bail, for a never clarified offense. The bail-order is not from the court, but from Aikhomu, Vice-President of the confusion called Nigeria. And the bail bond, says the police, has to be signed by Saro-Wiwa's eighty-nine year-old father! Meanwhile, in Owerri, the judge has decided that he has been held illegally all along, and that government must pay him compensation. As he leaves the prison, Saro-Wiwa learns that on July 15, hundreds of Ogoni exiles returning home from the Cameroon were waylaid and murdered.

Saro-Wiwa was arrested for the last time on May 22, 1994. The international community could not secure his release. Saro-Wiwa himself kept in contact with his friends at home and abroad. He kept hoping against hope. He was still alive on the January 4, 1995 anniversary of his cherished Ogoni Day. Like Martin Luther King Jr. who saw the promised land, he told his people about tomorrow, about "an Ogoni star in the sky." Could he be that star? The final real story of his life was his hanging on November 10, 1995.

NOTES TO CHAPTER IX

1. Saro-Wiwa's message to his people from detention, to celebrate the second anniversary of Ogoni Day, Jan. 4, 1995, quoted in *Tell*, Jan. 16, 1995: 21.

2. "The Dina Commission [was] headed by a member of the Yoruba ethnic majority," writes Saro-Wiwa (*Genocide*: 84) This may have been one of the reasons why the writer was obsessed with the Yoruba. See chapter VII: Another reason for the mixture of admiration and envy (love and hate?) would be the advancement of Yoruba civilization. Saro-Wiwa alludes to their long history of contact with the West and "a formidable aristocracy with whom no other Nigerians could compete." (*Genocide*: 19)

Concerning that civilization and culture, note that the British colonialists decided to create the new city of Port Harcourt in the 30's as an alternative port of entry to Lagos, the Yoruba city whose sophisticated culture was feared, as an overwhelming, insurmountable challenge to Britain's objectives of domination.

3. Note that this arrest is prior to the final one culminating in his 1995 execution. Some might wonder why, upon his release in 1993, he did not exhibit more caution. Could he have been lured into a false sense of security by the ever cunning officialdom? We shall return to this question in the concluding chapter.

4. The story of Ada George is another example of some intriguing aspects of Saro-Wiwa's life. A former state government Secretary, George was, before becoming governor, Finance Director in a firm belonging to a Lebanese businessman, Gilbert Chagoury, whom Saro-Wiwa "had known intimately in [his] business days and for whom [he] held a healthy regard. Gilbert knew his onions around Nigeria and Nigerian leaders! And he is a jolly good businessman with a nose for money. Ada George's connection with Gilbert helped him to the position of Governor." (*Month*: 109) Among Chagoury's other friends are the current leader of Nigeria, Abacha. Chagoury was recently reported to have contributed thousands of dollars to the American Democratic party on behalf of the Nigerian government. Did Saro-Wiwa ever benefit from his Chagoury connection?

5. Here is another contradiction in Saro-Wiwa's analysis of the Nigerian situation. Before now, he has made believe that the Ogoni were excluded by the majority from the highest levels of national affairs.

6. This affinity for younger people would, to a certain extent, explain why Saro-Wiwa had a problematic relationship with some of his peers. Either they, as traditionalists, preferred to keep the proverbial distance between the generations, or

he, as an overbearing personality, could not easily relate to those who would stand up to him. For whatever reason, intra-leadership difficulties no doubt contributed to Saro-Wiwa's demise.

7. Martin Luther King, Jr., *Why We Can't Wait*, New York: Penguin, 1964: 26.

Saro-Wiwa pays homage to King; however, he would appear to have forgotten that King was a believer in Mahatma Gandhi whom he, Saro-Wiwa, hardly respected (see *Similia*: 37).

CONCLUSION: *AFRICA KILLS HER SUN*

Your happiness is the happiness of ignorance and your ignorance is it that keeps you in the prison, which is your life. ("Africa Kills Her Sun," in *African Rhapsody*: 297)

The movement cannot die. It is in our blood. (An Ogoni teacher, after Saro-Wiwa's death, in *The Washington Post*, Dec. 10, 1995: A30)

The man dies in all who keep silent in the face of tyranny. (Wole Soyinka, *The Man Died*: 13)

We do not have guns, we do not have bullets. We are only asking the government to give us our rights. (Saro-Wiwa's father, after the writer's death, in *TELL*, Nov. 13, 1995: 15)

If there is a giant of Africa, it is not Nigeria, but Nelson Mandela's South Africa. (*The Economist*, March 25, 1995)

The story of Saro-Wiwa's "judicial murder" -to borrow the now famous words of John Major, Britain's ex-Prime Minister- has become the subject of international analyses. What, to my mind, makes it most interesting is the manner of its actualization, specifically, Saro-Wiwa's growing defiance until the very end, as if he was daring his killers to do their worst. Death is a recurring theme in his works, and this is particularly striking in his final manuscript, *On the Death of Ken Saro-Wiwa*, smuggled out of his cell in his nephew's diaper a month before he was hanged. It was performed as a play by the Contact Theater Company in England in June 1996, and excerpted in *Harper's Magazine* (Sept. 1996: 20-22). The cynicism of the play immediately reminds me of an earlier tale of death, "Africa Kills Her Sun" (in Nadezda Obradovic, *African Rhapsody*: 290-303).

"Africa" is a strange love letter written on the eve of his execution by a convicted armed robber, Bana, to Zole, the love of his youth whom he has not seen in ten years. In this "celebration, a final act of love," the robber declares that he belongs to Zole forever. He asks her "a small favor" and says that the fact that he has unburdened himself to her will make his death on the following day "as pleasant and desirable to [him] as to the thousands of spectators who will witness it." (290) The favor? That, if the newspapers publish a picture of him being shot by the firing squad, Zole cut the portrait and have a sculptor make a stone sculpture of it. He has already instructed his bank to give her money for the project. Although he and his two fellow robbers are likely to be buried in a mass grave, Zole is being asked to make a special grave, all the same, and to place the statue on the gravestone. Bana would also like, for epitaph, the words, *Africa Kills Her Sun*, modification of an African leader's lament on the death of a lieutenant, "Africa kills her sons," words that Bana once read when he was a child. He is elated by his chosen cryptic epitaph; he calls it "a stroke of genius." (302)

In his letter, Bana gives reasons why he committed the crime for which he and his co-robbers have been convicted. His explanation is one more substantiation of the confusion governing the lives of Saro-Wiwa's characters which, as we have affirmed before, is symptomatic of the real societal dilemma rampant in Nigeria. Bana, a former employee in the Merchant Navy, explains his actions with the story of his relationship with a young, beautiful prostitute in St. Pauli in Hamburg. When he asked her why she was in that profession, "she replied that some girls chose to be secretaries in offices, others to be nurses. She had chosen prostitution as a career. Cool. I was struck by her candor. And she set me thinking." (293) When he returned home from that trip, Bana skipped ship and took a situation as a clerk in the Ministry of Defense. There, he came face to face with the open looting of the national treasury by everyone, except himself. He decided to wage a war against the looters; however, he was soon dismissed. He thus had no option but to join the looters, by becoming an armed robber, a bandit. "It was my choice, my answer... Every occupation has its hazards." (294) What, or where, one may ask, is the choice in all this? Bana's attempt to equate his condition to that of the prostitute is nothing more than a cop-out. His justification of armed robbery, based upon his claim that, throughout, he has robbed the rich, is a scam; for, the last action for which he and his friends are convicted, is the botched robbery of a van carrying workers' salaries. His defense of armed robbery as being just as anti-social as the unarmed robbery of millions by government officials, is cynical. He even feels superior to those other thieves. He says he is in good company, "of Presidents of countries, transnational organizations, public servants high and low, men and women. The only difference is that while I'm prepared to pay the price for it all, the others are not." (294) Proof of that preparedness -a question of dignity, one might say!- is the sensational act in the court, where Bana and his mates boisterously and boastfully declare their guilt, and demand that the judge send them summarily to their death. "The death I've chosen is possibly more dramatic, more qualitative, more eloquent than dying in bed of a ruptured liver from overindulgence in alcohol." (293)

In spite of all his braggadocio, Bana does not convince us that he hates life. The very idea of sending a strange love letter to a girl whom he has not seen in ten years, and the very contents of the missive with which he tries to prove to her, and to the public, his human quality, reveal a truly sad and sick soul. Bana is a victim, one of the marginalized majority living with empty stomachs and dehumanized by those murderous, money-munching presidents in whose "good company" he has finally -and so tragically- found himself in his new profession. It is possibly out of frustration consequential to the inability to win the war against looters, that Bana found his niche in armed robbery. In short, he has not made a choice; he has, on the contrary, actualized the behest of those people who told him to join the looters. And his choice of death? That, also, may not be a choice after all: the judge, shocked by the accused's antics, would still have sentenced them to death. By having his statue made, with that mysterious epitaph, Bana would, hopefully, continue to live...

Bana's demeanor reminds us of the characters of Saro-Wiwa's television series. His Americanized language -the flamboyant *cool*, pronounced with the swagger of a Johnny-come-lately- brings to mind another rake, Josco, of *Basi & Co.* Bana is the quintessential Wiwan hero- villain, with the vivacity, the vibrancy, the cockiness, the rebelliousness, the consciousness of being different, all mixed with a certain superiority complex based upon a confusion about qualities which, in essence, would easily be the mask for a deep and depressing inferiority complex. For, how do you define and declare your superiority over others when you yourself are a son of the sullied soil? a product of that space and time mired in the marshlands and swamps of corruption symbolized by robbers armed and unarmed? There is, in Bana, a flaw common to many a Wiwan hero: the belief that, because he "thinks," he is superior to others; that he has the solution to all problems, or that his solution is the best. Bana the bandit would like us to believe that he is a sort of modern-day Robin Hood, robbing the rich to help the poor. He says that, because he himself does not pull the trigger, and does not keep the loot, he is therefore innocent and immune from all culpability. Yet he has money in the bank. He hates life, but he wants to be remembered by posterity. And the society that he blames others for corrupting, he helps to make it even more corrupt. It is also interesting that, as with his other characters, Saro-Wiwa makes Bana pay homage to "education," that is, Western education. The problem: all the education has been used for, is to improve the manner of looting national treasuries. Thus, Bana exudes pride in being in the company of the new African leaders who, unlike their predecessors, have devised modern methods for executing their nefarious activities. Bana's story shows convincingly that good education does not make for integrity or good governance.

The tragedy of this story, is the evolution of a whole people from virtue to vice. Everyone, from top to bottom, is guilty. All are robbers, or collaborators of robbers. The main culprits, however, must be the minority at the top, those individuals whose company is cherished by the likes of Bana! In the past, there were the forbears selling their kinsmen into slavery for beads and mirrors and alcohol. Today's leaders are still selling, for cars and mansions and bloated bank accounts at home and abroad. The police, says Bana, are accomplices in every robbery that happens. In the botched operation for which he and his fellow "bosses" are convicted, the Superintendent failed to do as promised, to keep the patrol unit away from the area. The judge in charge of the case would love to show off his position of power over life and death, since he and his fellow benchwarmers are not interested in justice, but bribery. And, in Africa generally, progress has been made towards the abyss of degradation, as trained robbers are taking over from half-literate politicians.

The people are also condemned by Bana. He foresees the zealous spectators at the shooting exercise holding at the national stadium, there in their thousands as if they were watching a football match. Inured to evil, they would take sadistic pleasure in the execution. Cowards that they are, they will not, they dare not, ask questions in public; if they do, it will be in the secrecy of their homes. "They will salve their conscience with bottles of beer, wash their answers down their gullets and pass question, conscience and answer out as waste into their open sewers choking with concentrated filth and murk. And they will forget." (291)

It is no surprise that Bana is happy to escape the prison of life occupied by those apathetic, coward spectators. For him, death would constitute freedom, a symbolic daylight away from the dungeon of oppression that drove him to armed robbery. But, then, contrary to his perverted philosophy, Bana cannot claim to be an innocent victim. If he can profess to be an honest armed robber, his killers can also claim to be conscientious, committed actors in the national drama of death! When, at dawn, after a sleepless night spent in writing his cryptic letter, his friends, certain that Bana has gone crazy, that he is afraid of death, ask why he never mentioned a girlfriend before, Bana responds that Zole, the girl, was not important in the past, that she is important only now, at the moment of death. He confesses, "I have felt a need to be close to a living being, someone who can relate to others why we did what we did in and out of court." (301) His friends chuckle. The reader can share their laughter, at this man unable to escape the confusion of his life and of his society even when he is so sure that he has found his freedom in death. His letter supposedly speaks for his two friends, Sazan, a dismissed Sergeant who, according to Bana, has enough quality to have made a good General, "in the mold of Idi Amin or Bokassa," two of Africa's most notorious dictators; and Jimba, once a Corporal, who would have made an exceptional Inspector-General of Police, "so versed is he in the ways of the police!" (295) Thus is vice turned into virtue, *a l'africaine*, and a villain calls himself the epitome of the best society can offer. If only both the unarmed and armed robbers of Nigeria, potentially Africa's richest country, could use their talents to amass wealth for the country as a whole. If only the love of self could be transformed into love of community, as African culture traditionally demands. If only the cynicism of the victim were eschewed for the commitment to the conquest of corruption...

Saro-Wiwa, in his life-time, made such valiant efforts, even though, in the final analysis, he himself was not immune to some aspects of the cynicism and confusion exhibited by the likes of Bana. More positively than the latter, Saro-Wiwa would symbolize Africa's son, and sun. Unlike the African president's lieutenant, as corrupt as his superior, the Ogoni leader is deserving of praise for his quest for human rights and justice. Unlike Bana, he has been a shining sun lighting the way for his people caught in the oppressive darkness of Nigeria. The problem, nonetheless, remains in the ambiguity, or dualism, of the symbol. The sun, scorching or soothing; bright and beautiful, it elicits joy and boosts one's energy; burning, it blinds one's vision, and blocks one's brain with its blistering and harsh heat, and saps one's strength. So, the sun can be a boon, or a bane. Given its exceptional quality, it risks causing as much harm as good. Which is where the challenge lies: the true leader would find a way to accomplish the task of letting his light shine upon others, not to blind them, but to show them the way, and to sharpen their vision, and to nurture their strength. In a neocolonial setting such as Nigeria, the task is no doubt very difficult. For, at each turn, an eclipse can occur, and high noon can easily become midnight.

The matter of Saro-Wiwa's final arrest on May 22, 1994, and his hanging on November 10, 1995, will be debated for years to come. Our interest here is not to make a definitive assessment of the process or the outcome; but, simply, to note that, *under normal circumstances*, Saro-Wiwa would not have been killed. Everyone knows, however, that Nigerian circumstances are among the most abnormal in the world. That, to a certain extent, would make one appreciate Saro-Wiwa's courage. Why did he not escape abroad, as have done other activists, such as the Nobel laureate, Soyinka? Incarcerated for two years during the civil war in the sixties, harassed after the 1993 presidential elections for his insistence on the right of the undeclared winner to the presidency, Soyinka read the message of death as the military regime masterminded its perceived opponents' mysterious murders; he fled across the border to the safety of exile. Saro-Wiwa's constant harassment and detentions, as well as the openly displayed program of Ogoni "pacification" by means of murder and mayhem, made him realize that he might be eliminated. He observed that much, specifically when the treason decree of 1993 was promulgated by Babangida. If he had fled, would MOSOP have floundered, or continued to flourish? Alive today, could he have not continued to impact the struggle from abroad? Was his decision to stay a question of courage, or false sense of security?

Saro-Wiwa was held for almost a year without trial. Then, rather than charge him and his eight colleagues to a regular law-court, the military government constituted a special tribunal, including a member of the government. Immediately after the murder of four Ogoni leaders and before any investigation or arrest, the State Administrator had declared that Saro-Wiwa was guilty. There are press reports galore on the proceedings of what Saro-Wiwa called "the kangaroo court" that tried him. As Nigerians say, the tribunal was set up to "work to the answer" of guilt. In the words of Saro-Wiwa's attorney, Gani Fawehinmi, interrogated by security agents on his own role in the case: "You [government] had come to a conclusion before setting up the tribunal... You had a tribunal member or chairman who had obviously been given instructions to deal with

Saro-Wiwa and to abort the MOSOP crusade... Ken refused the bribe of office." (*TELL*, Dec.9, 1996)

The reference is to a reported invitation extended by Abacha, the Head of State, to Saro-Wiwa upon the latter's release from the month-and-a-day imprisonment of June-July, 1993. A presidential jet took the activist to the presidential palace in the capital, Abuja, where his host was waiting. Both activist and actor shared dinner, with the latter distancing himself from his predecessor Babangida's draconian measures and declaring his desire to accede to the Ogoni demands. Saro-Wiwa gladly gave him the Ogoni Bill of Rights, and summarized its main points, including the necessity of political autonomy. Abacha, out of the blues, asked pointedly whether Saro-Wiwa would like to be a minister in the coming, new dispensation. Saro-Wiwa rejected such a thought. End of dinner and discussions. (*TELL*, Nov. 13, 1995: 10-11)

Certain observers of the kangaroo-court proceedings, that is, those not blinded by dollar-bills in brown envelopes, or coerced into complicity for fear of ending up in unmarked graves, are generally in agreement with Fawehinmi's assessment. For example, Joshua Hammer, a foreigner, writes:

"Although the government had preordained his guilt, the question was larger than whether Saro-Wiwa would be executed or merely imprisoned indefinitely. The question was whether one man, dead or alive, had started an indigenous revolt against the tenth-largest, and the most profitable, corporation in the world [Shell-BP], or, in the long view, had failed to prevent that company from poisoning his country." (*Harper's Magazine*, June 1996: 59)

That question may have been wrongly put; for, Saro-Wiwa's struggle was not just against an oil company. Precisely, it was, and is, against Nigeria, and those people trying to transform the place into their private property in the name of patriotism. "Those who cling dishonestly to the frightening failures which characterize today's Nigeria because it works for them are riding the horse of disaster," warns Saro-Wiwa. (*Month*: 149) Riders of the horse of disaster come from within and outside Nigeria. There is Dauda Komo, the State Administrator who personally oversaw the Saro-Wiwa execution and despatched a video-recording to his master, the Head of State. There was the Somalia factional leader, Farah Aidid, who, very supportive of the execution, accused the West of being behind Nigeria's problems. And the Nigerian government, through its various foaming-at-the-mouth agents, has consistently echoed the view that Saro-Wiwa and all other dissidents are sponsored by "European and American imperialists."

Saro-Wiwa's final manuscript, *On the Death of Saro-Wiwa*, is eerily prophetic, or fatalistic. It tells the tale of a certain Saro-Wiwa who dies in the office of the State Investigation and Intelligence Bureau. Over champagne and cheers reverberating all over the filthy room, the boot-clad buffoons plan for disposing of his body. This national task that must be done (one thinks of Nigeria's meaningless civil war and the slogan, *to keep Nigeria one is a task that must be done*) is discussed at length. Since the entire Ogoni territory is now a cemetery filled with the bodies of those obliterated by the gallant troops of *General Jeno Saidu (read: Genocide),* the wise men decide to bury the body there, as symbol of the end of the Ogoni. A military officer wins the contract for the coffin. He hires a carpenter and instructs him to make a coffin five feet long and one foot wide, for Saro-Wiwa's small body. The carpenter, being "innumerate," makes a coffin that is too small. The body, squeezed in, squeaks and screams in protest at the injustice. The officers, all scared, run for dear life. The pallbearers refuse to carry the corpse, as they protest against their unpaid allowance for exterminating the Ogoni. They are paid immediately. The bier is duly carried through the streets of Port Harcourt to show everyone the price to be paid for demanding social justice and redress for environmental degradation. In Ogoni, oil companies and foreign contractors, are waiting for the ceremony, to give the event an international flavor. Shell and Chevron choose the exact spot of burial, so as to be careful not to use a place bearing oil. A tiny, narrow hole is dug. The coffin is buried upright, to save space. Thus, as expressed in his epitaph, "the funny little man" is denied six feet of earth. As the burial procession is about to leave, a message of congratulations flashes across the sky, extolling the Task Force's success and Nigeria's "unanimous election to Permanent Membership of the United Nations Security Council. And Ken Saro-Wiwa laughed in his grave." Just as, in real life, he laughed at the shameless, pot-bellied bullies who tried to cower him into submission by threatening him when he refused to be bribed. Just as he berated the messengers of injustice who claimed that he was a psychiatric wreck. Just as he laughed at the hangmen desperately struggling to work the malfunctioning execution block, final symbol of their country's incompetence and inhumanism.

The fictional victory of Nigeria in the Security Council may not, after all, be a laughing matter. It is all part of the plan of a lawless leadership capable of bidding for anything, not the least being those positions of power coveted by nations with dignity. Events since Saro-Wiwa's death make one wonder whether the international community -precisely, Europe and America- honestly cares about human rights; whether, as it was, it is not now a question of economic exploitation, notwithstanding if Satan himself were the provider/supplier.

South Africa is, of course, Africa's giant, with Nigeria having the dubious honor of contributing in no small measure to that quantum leap. Perhaps it is the ability to push others ahead, mistaken for a capability to better itself, that explains Nigeria's pomposity towards the West. More likely, it is the power of the supplier of "black gold" over the addicted clientele that makes Nigeria strut like a peacock in the face of its hypocritical critics. Nigerian officials have no qualms about lying, and bragging about their iniquities displayed as outstanding qualities. Ikimi, foreign minister, says his country has no human rights problems. His master, Abacha, tells CNN that his regime has no opposition. And, maybe, he is right. A journalist asks rhetorically: "Who dare oppose him? Those who did (or were suspected to harbor the wrong sentiments), like Kudirat Abiola [murdered wife of the detained 1993 presidential election winner], Ken Saro-Wiwa..., are the dead, the detained, the exiled and the fugitives." (Dare Babarinsa, in *TELL*, July 15, 1996: 5) Meanwhile, Chijuka, Defense Information propagandist, boasts: "We can engage America. The American Army is not a well-trained army -they are not rugged soldiers." (Interview in *TheNews*, June 3, 1996:4) Nigeria's rugged soldiers are rampaging through Ogoni and other areas harboring dissenters; they are razing villages to the ground, while ruggedly running away from Bakassi, the oil-rich area being disputed by the Cameroons whose army is well supported by French troops.

And the patriotic government of Nigeria claims that there is conspiracy between extremists and disgruntled elements campaigning against it from within and, particularly, abroad. Saro-Wiwa, they insist, "was sponsored by Europe and America to kill government supporters in oil-producing areas in order to precipitate chaos and ease their access to plundering Nigeria's riches." (*TELL*, Dec. 27, 1995:15) Shell-BP must not be seen as plundering the country's riches, since it is plowing millions from the plunder into the patriotic leaders' pockets. Official paranoia is mixed with the complacency of coxcombs. Never one to take matters lying down, except in the filth of blood money, Nigerian officialdom is able to find friends prepared to oil its propaganda machine, naturally for fat fees. Articles appear everywhere, telling tales of some imagined greatness (for example, John Curry's "Why Nigeria?" in *The American Spectator*, May 1996: 20-24, as well as expensive, twenty-page advertiser's columns in such major publications as *The Wall Street Journal*). African American public and private figures, including the Black Moslem Farrakhan, and the Senator Moseley-Braun, hungry for a share of the black booty, return to the ancestral home, pocket the money and make speeches about some progress, back into slavery! Most ignominiously, precious cash is being spent trying to gain support in the West, the same West condemned for imperialistic designs on Nigerian oil, the same West already doing business as usual while pretending to stand against the dictatorship. Thus continues the confusion.

An advertising supplement in *The Wall Street Journal* (April 21, 1997) covers sixteen pages. On the final page is a "Statement on Advance Fee Fraud Scam" by Central Bank of Nigeria. It alerts "the international business community of the increasing spate of attempts by an *international syndicate of fraudsters* (emphasis mine) to defraud them." It is implied that Nigerians are all clean, that the country's problem is caused by foreign fraudsters. Stupidly enough, the person who crafted the statement forgets that there is, at least, an admission of guilt, that Nigeria is a fertile ground for fraud, which is enough to make honest business people stay away.

Saro-Wiwa's family and friends have run away from their clean country, as Ogoni ethnic cleansing continues. From all indications, however, the cleansing can never be complete as long as some of the people remain alive. The movement is in people's blood, and Saro-Wiwa's work has a great deal to do with that. The resolution of the Ogoni problem can only begin when the government realizes that killing people is not even an option. It can only begin when individuals stop colluding with oppressors and exploiters of the people. Saro-Wiwa hit the nail on the head in his statement to the tribunal that sent him to his death: "The Military do not act alone. They are supported by a gaggle of politicians, lawyers, judges, academics and businessmen, all of them hiding under the claim that they are only doing their duty, men and women too afraid to wash their pants of urine." Tragically, cowardice is the common denominator in neocolonial Nigeria.

Ken Saro-Wiwa's father is an exception to that rule. It is only fitting that the last word of this text belong to that proud, courageous nonagenarian. Interviewed on October 31, 1995, the day his son was sentenced to death, Pa Beeson Wiwa stated:

"We do not have guns, we do not have bullets. We are only asking the government to give us our rights; that is what Ken is struggling for. The oil we have is God-given. There is no regret. Ken has done his best of what God sent him here to do. And that shall be remembered forever. Even the end of Ken will not be the end of the Ogoni struggle. A baby of two years knows about the struggle." (*TELL*, Nov. 13, 1995: 15)

SELECT BIBLIOGRAPHY

A. WORKS BY KEN SARO-WIWA

i. Novels
Sozaboy: A Novel in Rotten English. Port Harcourt: Saros International Publishers, 1985.
Prisoners of Jebs. 1988.
Pita Dumbrok's Prison. 1991.

ii. Short Stories
Adaku and Other Stories. 1969.
A Forest of Flowers. 1986.
"Africa Kills Her Sun." in Obradovic, Nadezda, ed. *African Rhapsody*. New York: Anchor Books, 1994: 290-303.

iii. Poetry
Songs in a Time of War. 1985.

iv. Drama
Basi and Company: Four Television Plays. 1988.
Four Farcical Plays. 1989.
"On the Death of Ken Saro-Wiwa" (excerpts). In *Harper's Magazine*, Sept. 1996: 20-22.
(play performed by Contact Theatre Company, England, June 1996)

v. General
The Ogoni Nationality Today and Tomorrow (pamphlet).
On a Darkling Plain: An Account of the Nigerian Civil War. 1989.
Similia, Essays on Anomic Nigeria. 1991.
Genocide in Nigeria. 1992.
"Ogoni as Metaphor." *TheNews*, Dec. 19, 1994: 7.
A Month and a Day, A Detention Diary. New York: Penguin Books, 1995.

vi. Children's Books
Tambari. Ikeja: Longman, n.d.
Tambari in Dukana. Longman, 1973.
Mr. B. 1987.
Mr. B is Dead. 1991.

B. CRITICAL WORKS ON SARO-WIWA

Achebe, Emeka. "Shell, Not Guilty." *TEMPO*, Feb.9, 1996:2.
Adedayo, Wale. "MOSOP, Others Doubt Shell's Conciliatory Moves." *The Guardian* of Lagos, May 13, 1996: 40.
Adekeye, Muyiwa. "Can You Try This Case?" *TheNews*, March 6, 1995: 20.
The Africa Fund. "Act Today to Stop the Execution of Ken Saro-Wiwa." Nov. 8, 1995.
The Africa Fund. "Saro-Wiwa's Statement to the Court After Receiving the Death Sentence." Nov. 15, 1995.
Ajigbotosho, Dayo. "And the 'Wasting' Goes On." *TELL*, Jan.23, 1995:16.
Ake, Claude. "War and Terror." *TheNews*, Aug. 22, 1994: 9.
Akindoyo, Dele. "Speaking from the 'Grave' - Ken Saro-Wiwa." *June 12 Magazine*, Aug. 17, 1994: 11.
Anon. "After the Hangings." *The Economist* 337, Nov. 18, 1995: 41.
Anon. "Nigeria Faces Criticism After Execution of Writer." *UN Chronicle* 33 (Spring 1996): 80-82.
Anon. "Nigeria: Saro-Wiwa as a Columnist." *West Africa,* Nov.11, 1992.
Babu, A.R.M. "Why Ken Saro-Wiwa Had to Hang." *Jinn Magazine* (Pacific News Service), Nov. 16, 1995.
Bacon, David. "Oil Politics Rule in Nigeria." *Earth Island Journal* 10, 3 (Winter 1995).
Barber, Ben. "Author [Soyinka] Says Nigeria's on Brink." *The Washington Times*, Dec.7, 1994: A17.
Beran, Paul. "Nigeria's Political Progress Essential to Stability of Africa." *Christian Science Monitor*, Oct.24, 1994: 3.
Boyd, William. Introduction to *A Month and a Day* (see also "Death of a Writer," *The New Yorker*, Nov. 27, 1995:51-54).
Bright, Chris. "Eco-justice in Nigeria." *World Watch* 9 (July-August 1996): 9.
Buckley, Stephen. "After 35 Years, Nigerians Still Stumbling Along Road to Democracy." *The Washington Post*, Oct.1, 1995: A1/A28.
Buckley, Stephen. "Nigerian Vows to Quit in 3 Years." *The Washington Post*, Oct.2, 1995: A13.
Buckley, Stephen. "Playwright's Hanging Devastates Followers." *The Washington Post*, Dec.10, 1995: A29.

Buckley, Stephen. "Nigeria's Military Rulers Throttling Independent Press." *The Washington Post*, April 7, 1996: A18.

Cayford, Steven. "Thee Ogoni Uprising: Oil, Human Rights, and A Democratic Alternative." *Africa Today* 43 (April/June 1996): 183-197.

Curry, John. "Why Nigeria?" *The American Spectator*, May 1996: 20-24.

Damu, Jean et al. "Oil Rules Nigeria." *The Black Scholar* 26 (Winter/Spring 1996): 51-54.

Daniels, Anthony. "A Good Man in Africa." *National Review* 47 (July 10, 1995): 51-52.

De Witt, Karen. "Black Group Begins Protest Against Nigeria." *The New York Times*, March 17, 1995: A15.

Ejiogu, E.G. "The Junta's Launderers." *TheNews*, August 22, 1994: 10-13.

Ekwowusi, Sonnie. "The sinister side of an American propagandist." *The Guardian*, Lagos, June 16, 1997: 35.

Ezenwa-Ohaeto. "The Cultural Imperative in Modern Nigerian Drama: A Consolidation in the Plays of Saro-Wiwa, Nwabueze, and Irobi." *Neohelicon: Acta Comparationis Litterarum Universarum* 21, 2 (1994): 207-220.

Fawehinmi, Gani. "The Fire Next Time," interview in *TheNews*, vol.10 no.11, March 23, 1998: 14-21.

Feuser, Willfried. "The Voice from Dukana: Ken Saro-Wiwa." *Matatu* 1, 2 (1987): 49-57.

Fiofori, Ferdinand O. "Saro-Wiwa Satirized Africa's Malaise." *Africa Today* 39, 2 (1989): 24-25.

French, Howard. "Nigeria Accused of a 2-Year War on Ethnic Group." *The New York Times*, March 28, 1995: A12.

French, Howard. "Nigeria Comes on Too Strong." *The New York Times*, Nov.19, 1995: A14.

Gberenen, Joseph. "Come to Ogoniland, Abubakar." *The Guardian*, Aug. 6, 1998: 33.

Gordimer, Nadine. "In Nigeria, the price of oil is blood." *The Guardian*, Lagos, June 2, 1997: 35.

Greenpeace. "October 31 [1995] Press Release" (on Saro-Wiwa's Hanging).

Hammer, Joshua. "Nigeria Crude." *Harper's Magazine*, June 1996: 58-68.

Inyama, N.F. "Ken Saro-Wiwa: Maverick Iconoclast of the Nigerian Literary Scene." *African Literature Today* 20 (1996): 35-49.

Irele, Abiola. "The Fiction of Saro-Wiwa." *The Guardian*, Jan. 17, 1987:

13.
Johnson, Angela. "World Turns Its Back on Saro-Wiwa Again." *The Mail & Guardian*, Johannesburg, Oct.31, 1997.
Knox, Paul. "Saro-Wiwa's Execution Sparks Global Outrage." *The Globe and Mail,* Toronto, Nov.11, 1995: A1, A9.
Lindfors, Bernth. "Ken Saro-Wiwa- in short, a giant." *ALA Bulletin* 20, 2 (Spring 1994): 15-16.
London, Herbert. "The sinister side of a Nigerian 'martyr'." *The Guardian*, Lagos, June 2, 1997: 35.
Mezu, S. Okechukwu, ed. *Ken Saro-Wiwa: the Life and Times*. Randallstown, Maryland: Black Academy Press, 1996.
Naanen, Ben. "Genocide in Nigeria: the Ogoni Tragedy.' *The Journal of Modern African Studies* 32, 3 (Spring 1994): 536-539.
Niboro, Ima. "War Against the Niger Delta." *TELL*, Dec.18, 1995: 15.
Nixon, Rob. "Pipe Dreams: Ken Saro-Wiwa, Environmental Justice, and Micro-Minority Rights." *Black Renaissance Noire*, vol.1 no.1 (Fall 1996): 39-55.
Nnolim, Charles, ed. *Critical Essays on Ken Saro-Wiwa's Sozaboy*. Saros International, 1992.
Nwabueze, Emeka. "Death of a Writer: A Reply to William Boyd." *ALA Bulletin*, no.1, vol.23 (Winter 1997): 11-14.
Nwankwo, Agwuncha Arthur. *Nigerians as Outsiders: Military Dictatorship and Nigeria's Destiny.* Owerri: Fourth Dimension Publishers, 1996.
Obadare, Ebenezer, and Ralph Ugbelu. "Racing To The End." *TEMPO*, Jan. 16, 1994: 4-5.
Obasanjo, Olusegun. "Let's Prevent Another Enthronement of Evil." *TELL*, Feb.14, 1994: 14-17.
Offi, Stepp. "What Manner of Peace?" *TELL*, Aug. 22, 1994: 23.
Offi, Stepp. "Paper Monster of Ogoniland." *TELL*, Jan.30, 1995: 21.
Offi, Stepp. "Pacification in Port Harcourt." *TELL*, Feb.3, 1995: 19.
Offi, Stepp. "Trial and Terror in Port Harcourt." *TELL*, March 13, 1995: 16-17.
Ogbowei, G. Ebinyoo and Ibiere Bell Gam. "*Sozaboy*: Language and a Disoriented World." *English Studies in Africa* 38, 1 (1995): 1-18.
Ojo, Onukaba. *Olusegun Obasanjo*. New York: Africana Legacy Press, 1997.
Osundare, Niyi. "The Longest Day." *ALA Bulletin*, Winter 1997: 7-10.
The Planet. "Hanging of Nigerian Activist Prompts Club Boycott of Shell Oil." Jan./Feb. 1996, vol.3 no.1: 1.

Rapsberry, William. "No Free Ride for Nigeria." *The Washington Post*, March 18, 1995: A17.

Reid, Mark A. *Postnegritude Visual and Literary Culture*. Albany: State University of New York Press, 1997: 33-34.

Roddick, Anita. "Shell Should Wash Its Dirty Hands." *New Statesman* 125 (Nov.8, 1996): 10.

Rose, Lauri. "Thoughts on the Death of Ken Saro-Wiwa." (on Internet, Nov. 12, 1995, as part of ongoing discussions by *Central American Discussion List, Buffalo*, and *Accion Zapatista de Austin*.

Sachs, Aaron. "Dying for Oil." *World Watch* 9 (May-June 1996): 10-21.

Shiner, Cindy. "In Nigeria's Confusion, Military Coup Looks Like Democracy." *The Washington Post*, Dec.4, 1993: A24.

Soyinka, Wole. "Nigeria's Long, Steep, Bloody Slide." *The New York Times*, August 22, 1994: A13.

Soyinka, Wole. *The Open Sore of a Continent*. New York: Oxford University Press, 1996.

Streitfeld, David. "A Laureate's Lament for Nigeria." *The Washington Post*, Dec.7, 1994: C1/C3.

Taribo, Spiff M.K. "The Agonies of the Ogoni." *The Guardian*, March 11, 1994: 17.

TELL Magazine. *Nigeria Held Hostage. Abacha's Years of Terror.* Nov. 20, 1995.

TELL. *Saro-Wiwa. Abacha Takes on the World.* Special edition. Nov. 27, 1995.

TheNews. *He Lives*. Anniversary Special, Nov.18, 1996.

TheNews. *The Prophecy of Ken Saro-Wiwa*. Special Number, Jan.8, 1996.

TheNews ('Outlook' page). "A View on Ogoni," Jan. 6, 1995: 9.

TIME Magazine (cover story). "The Agony of Africa," Sept. 7, 1992: 40-53.

TIME Magazine. "Defiant Hangings." Nov.20, 1995: 25.

Tuyama, N.F. "Ken Saro-Wiwa: Maverick Iconoclast of the Nigerian Literary Scene." *African Literature Today*, 20 (1996): 35-49.

Umunna, Isaac. "Battle for Freedom." *Theweek*, March 6, 1995: 16-17.

Vincent, Theo. "The Rehabilitation of Pita Dumbrok." *The Daily Times* (Lagos), Jan.8, 1992: 7.

Wahab. Gbadamosi. "Contractors in Cassocks." *TheNews*, July 28, 1997: 23-24.

The Washington Post. "Plundering Nigeria," editorial. Oct. 28, 1994: A26.

The Washington Post. "Why Won't Gen. Abacha Just Go?" editorial. Oct. 6, 1995: A24.

Wastberg, Per. *The Writer in Modern Africa.* New York: Africana Publishing Corporation, 1969.
Wheeler, David. "Blood on British Business Hands." *New Statesman and Society* 8 (Nov.17, 1995): 14-15.
Yoruba Autonomy Alert. "On The Future of Nigeria." Vol.1 no.1 (Sept. 1997): 1-3.
Zabus, Chantal. "Mending the Schizo-Text: Pidgin in the Nigerian Novel." *Kunapipi* 14, 1 (1992): 119-127.

C. **FILM** on Saro-Wiwa and the Ogoni struggle: *Delta Force* (A Catma Films production for Channel 4, London, May 1995)

D. **ON THE INTERNET**
i. *Africa Policy Information Center.* "Nigeria: Ogoni Repression Alert," Jan.19, 1998.
"Carrington Statement to Maryland House on Nigeria Sanctions," April 7, 1998.
ii. *Associated Press.* "Nigeria Defends Executions," Nov.11, 1995.
iii. *Electronic Mail and Guardian* (South Africa). "Saro-Wiwa's Brother and Son sue Shell," Nov. 11, 1996.
"This spinelessness about Nigeria," Feb. 18, 1997.
"Wole Soyinka on the rot in Nigeria," March 21, 1997.
""Nigerian chiefs want Abacha to stay," April 15, 1997.
"US policy, four years after Nigeria's 'coup'," June 16, 1997.
"The US leans towards Nigeria," June 18, 1997.
"Ministers feud over Nigeria's oil crisis," June 25, 1997.
"Soyinka on Nigerian 'doublespeak'," July 15, 1997.
"Time for Mandela to get tough with Nigeria," August 1, 1997.
"Abacha's deafening silences," Oct. 2, 1997.
"Nigerian dissidents pressure Commonwealth summit," Oct. 21, 1997.
"World turns its back on Saro-Wiwa," Oct. 31, 1997.
"NIGERIA: Saro-Wiwa's followers remember," Nov. 10, 1997
"NIGERIA: World remembers Saro-Wiwa," Nov. 10, 1997.
"Nigeria has spoken. Mandela must listen," April 27, 1998.
"Recalling hymns of death," October 30, 1998.
iii. *Friends of the Earth.* "Death Sentence for Ken Saro-Wiwa," Nov.1, 1995.
iv. *Pen International.* "Nigeria writer Ken Saro-Wiwa sentenced to death," Oct. 31, 1995.
v. *Reuters News Service.* "Nigerian security forces arrest 20 Ogoni

activists," Jan. 3, 1998.
"Nigerian Ogoni activists say many arrested," Jan. 4, 1998.
"Nigerian authorities say unaware of Ogoni arrests," Jan. 5, 1998.
"Mobil says Nigerian oil slick hits shore," Jan. 19, 1998.
"Minority communities fight back," Jan. 19, 1998.